The meaning of company accounts

The meaning of company accounts

Second Edition

Walter Reid and D R Myddelton

A Gower Press Workbook

First published in Great Britain by Gower Press Limited
Epping, Essex CM16 4BU
1971

Second Edition 1974
© Walter Reid and D R Myddelton
ISBN 0 7161 0158 0

Set in 10/12 point Times Roman and 10/12 point Univers Medium
by St Paul's Press Ltd, Malta
Printed in Great Britain by
A Wheaton & Co., Exeter

Contents

Preface

OBJECTIVES

This book is intended to help those who use company accounts to secure a thorough grasp of what they mean and how they relate to business activities. It is anticipated that managers without formal accounting or financial training will find it useful, and that it will also provide a comprehensive introduction to company accounts for those pursuing formal accounting or management studies programmes.

Considerable care has been taken at each stage to make the book as brief as possible, but it is believed that a superficial approach to company accounts is not enough. Indeed such treatment may be potentially dangerous, since it may lead readers, on the basis of inadequate analysis, to draw wrong conclusions from accounts. Further, it would almost certainly lead to frustration if in dealing with accountants in business, readers were to discover that a wide variety of practical complications existed about whose nature and extent they were unaware. There is thus a need for the book to be comprehensive as well as concise.

"WORKBOOK" DESIGN

The Meaning of Company Accounts brings together a considerable range of both basic and detailed material within a framework which can best be described as a "workbook." This comes somewhere between a standard text book and a programmed text. Like a programmed text it is structured and involves a high degree of participation by the reader, but it is also very flexible, and is designed for use as a reference book as well as for guided reading. Throughout the book the authors have tried to develop ideas in a logical sequence and to present them in a form which makes a strong visual impact. To aid learning further, the text of most sections includes examples which the reader is asked to work through. The need for concise treatment has been a dominant consideration at each stage, but it is recognised that many who use the workbook may experience difficulty with at least some of the topics covered. The opportunity to work through a good selection of examples at such points may be critical to achieving the desired level of understanding, and these have been provided.

Not all readers, of course, will have trouble with the same points, and this poses a problem for the authors. If the workbook is comprehensive on all topics it will be too long for those who have limited time available, while if it is too restricted it will not provide the necessary support in areas of difficulty.

To resolve this dilemma each section of the workbook has been divided into two parts: the text which provides a comprehensive study of the whole subject, but moves quickly from topic to topic; and additional material, in the form of exercises and problems (with solutions), which the reader is free to use as suits him best.

SEQUENCE OF SECTIONS

The sequence of the sections and the choice of material in each should be explained. Broadly the book can be considered in three divisions. The Introduction and sections 1 to 2 cover general accounting issues, the structure of company accounts and some of the formal techniques of financial analysis. It is intended here to define the area which is to be explored in greater depth in the rest of the book and to illustrate the total accounting package before the underlying detail is examined.

Sections 3 to 7 deal with the problems of recording transactions, measuring income and expense, and presenting information in the profit and loss account and balance sheet. An understanding of this material forms a vital foundation on which to base the analysis illustrated in section 8, "Interpreting Company Accounts."

HOW TO USE THE BOOK

In some senses no part of this book can be fully understood without first having considered the other parts—the eight sections form a total structure. For this reason, readers who are not taking part in an organised programme may prefer to read quickly at first and to gain an overall view before tackling difficulties in detail. It is likely that two complete readings will be more rewarding than a single study in depth. Ideas found difficult in the early stages may well become clear on reconsideration after later parts of the book have been covered.

For those with little previous knowledge who wish to acquire a substantial level of competence in analysis, study of the text of each section can usefully be followed by extensive use of the additional material. For those who already have some knowledge of accounting, only certain sections of the latter may be useful. The intention is that each reader should be able to move at his or her own pace throughout, building up strength where weaknesses exist and moving more quickly where further detailed work is not required.

PROBLEMS AND SOLUTIONS

The additional material at the end of each section consists of exercises and problems. The first exercise in sections 1 to 7 contains ten definitions, for which the reader is asked to *write* his answer in the space provided. Suggested definitions are given on the following page. Some readers may find terminology a problem, and a careful tackling of each of the 80 definitions in this book should well repay the trouble.

The remaining exercises and problems have been treated in two ways. First come the more basic problems, for which space is left in the book for the reader to use for his answer, and to which the suggested solution is given on the page immediately following.

Then come rather more difficult problems, solutions to which are given at the *end* of the book. For most of these problems the reader is asked to use his own paper, as it would take up too much space to leave room in the book for all the answers to be written out.

The workbook design clearly places more demands on the reader than a normal text book, but the extra effort required to select the particular material which satisfies each reader's own needs should be adequately rewarded by the rapid development of a real competence to interpret accounting statements. An understanding can be gained which extends significantly beyond the appraisal of results based on a mechanical application of standard analytical techniques. The bibliography at the end of the book will help those who wish to extend further their studies of related and more advanced aspects of accounting theory and practice.

PREFACE TO SECOND EDITION

The major change in the second edition is to combine the two volumes of the first edition (the bound text and loose-leaf problems and solutions) into a single bound volume.

This has required some compression of material, mainly in re-arrangement of layout. Relatively little material in the first edition has been omitted from the second, and there has been a certain amount of expansion in the material relating to topics of current interest, for example accounting for inflation.

Other changes include updating the Marks and Spencer and Imperial Chemical Industries accounts used, revising the pages on taxation, and expanding the number of definition questions and answers.

Walter Reid and D R Myddelton

The Authors

Walter Reid is Professor of Accounting and Financial Control at the London Graduate School of Business Studies. He was formerly Group Financial Controller of Edwards High Vacuum International Limited, and subsequently Senior Lecturer in Accounting at the London Graduate School from 1966 to 1970. Before returning to the School in April 1973 he spent $2\frac{1}{2}$ years as an Associate Consultant with McKinsey and Company Inc. He has written articles on accounting, management education, and professional accounting studies, and has served as a member of the Advisory Board on Education of the Institute of Chartered Accountants in England and Wales. He is a chartered accountant, and is married with two sons.

D R Myddelton is Professor of Finance and Accounting at the Cranfield Institute of Technology. He was formerly Lecturer in Accounting at the London Graduate School of Business Studies. His first book, "The Power To Destroy: a study of the British tax system", was published in 1969, and he has written several articles on taxation and currency debasement. He is a chartered accountant and a graduate of the Harvard Business School.

Acknowledgements

We are grateful to The General Electric Company Limited, Imperial Chemical Industries Limited, and Marks and Spencer Limited for permission to reproduce copies of their annual accounts and extracts from their annual reports to shareholders. We acknowledge the helpful guidance received from these companies, but we remain entirely responsible for the comments and analysis.

We should like to thank the many recent students at the London Business School and the Cranfield School of Management who commented on various drafts of the text. We have also benefitted from the help and encouragement given by colleagues at the London Business School, especially Professor Harold Rose, by A J Merrett and by Hugh Parker of McKinsey and Company Inc.

Walter Reid and D R Myddelton

Introduction
The background
to company accounts

INTERNAL AND EXTERNAL FINANCIAL REPORTS

Managers nowadays have to use a wide variety of financial reports to help them appraise and control business activities. As businesses become larger and more complex, financial reports contain an ever greater proportion of the total information available to senior managers, even though reports of this kind necessarily cover only activities which can be expressed in money terms.

There are two kinds of financial reports: those for use only within a company, and those which have a wider circulation outside as well. The first category comprises management accounts, generally prepared in considerable detail, dealing with the future as well as the past and with particular parts of a business as well as with the enterprise as a whole. The contents and layout of internal reports vary widely between companies, reflecting the different information needs of the managers for whom they are prepared and the different levels of management involved.

The second kind of financial report, which we shall be considering in detail, consists of accounts ("statutory accounts") required by law to be published for use by people outside the business. These published accounts reflect the total financial results of the company to which they relate, and comprise a balance sheet which shows the company's assets and liabilities at the end of its most recently completed accounting period (normally a year), and a profit and loss account which shows the profit or loss made during the period.

Non-financial managers often find it hard to understand published company accounts, whose underlying purpose they may not fully appreciate. The published accounts are prepared in accordance with elaborate conventions which are insufficiently disclosed and much less rigidly defined than managers generally believe.

Accounting conventions are not fixed nor always completely certain: they do not enable a single "correct" profit or loss figure to be determined. They are constantly being developed and adapted to meet the changing demands of business, and at any point in time there may be more than one "accepted" way of treating a particular class of transaction. Principal accounting firms cannot always agree on firm accounting principles.

This lack of certainty may cause confusion and criticism, since alternative "accepted" conventions can produce very different results. Steps are currently being taken by the Institutes of Chartered Accountants in England and Wales, Scotland, and Ireland to develop Statements of Standard Accounting Practice aimed at narrowing the range of acceptable approaches. Rigid rules for profit determination should not be expected, however, since the difficulty of fixing a single correct profit or loss figure reflects the unavoidable subjective element in recording business transactions whose final outcome is often not known at the time the accounts are prepared.

DISCLOSURE

The basic financial statements comprising the statutory accounts of a company are its balance sheet and profit and loss account. The major provisions regulating their content are set out in the Second Schedule of the Companies Act, 1967. Companies whose shares are dealt in ("quoted") on a recognised stock exchange in the UK must also comply with further regulations issued by the Council of the Stock Exchange. In addition, from time to time the major professional accountancy bodies give their members detailed advisory guidance as to the presentation and content of published accounts.

Successive Acts of Parliament, especially the Companies Acts of 1929, 1948 and 1967, have required companies to disclose to the public ever more detailed information about their affairs, despite fears about its potential usefulness to competitors. Until the 1967 Companies Act required it, many companies refused to publish their total sales revenue on the grounds that such disclosure would be damaging to them.

There is a growing feeling, however, that less disclosure should be required from "proprietorship" companies, where a few owners hold all the shares (and may often participate in management as well), than from "stewardship" companies, where widely-spread ownership is almost completely divorced from day-to-day control of the business. A recent Green Paper on Company Law Reform indicates that some changes along these lines may be made in the coming 1974 Companies Bill.

In the case of large companies carrying on several different businesses, unless the entire format of published accounts is altered, practical considerations limit the amount of detail and explanation which can be presented. No doubt more disclosure than is currently given is still desirable, but the real problem lies in the difficulty of representing complex transactions in the form of published accounts.

Although the legal regulations governing company accounts may seem fairly extensive, no attempt is made to prescribe a standard form of account to be used by every company. The reason is clear when considering the total range of business enterprises. Any standard form of account to cover the varied activities of shipping companies, investment trusts, manufacturing companies, merchant banks and retail stores, for example, would have to be either too detailed to be manageable or too vague to be useful.

The main reason today for requiring a minimum level of disclosure is the economic benefit from competition, and the need to encourage capital to flow where it can best be used. Thus accounting disclosure is as important to *potential* shareholders as to existing ones. It should be structured in such a way as not merely to account for historical stewardship of a company's resources, but also to give the capital market as a whole sufficient information about the past to decide whether further capital should be allocated to the same management's control. Of course, the company's intentions for the future, and the market's own evaluation of the future, are also highly relevant in such decisions.

"TRUE AND FAIR VIEW"

Accounts must contain the specific information required by the Companies Acts to be disclosed, and must also show a "true and fair view" of the state of the company's affairs at the balance sheet date and of the profit or loss for the accounting period covered. The phrase "true and fair view" occurs whenever accounts are discussed. What does it mean? Recommendation N18 of the Institute of Chartered Accountants in England and Wales explains:

A true and fair view implies appropriate classification and grouping of the items and therefore the balance sheet needs to show in summary form the amounts of the share capital, reserves and liabilities as on the balance sheet date and the amounts of the assets representing them, together with sufficient information to indicate the general nature of the items. A true and fair view also implies the consistent application of generally accepted principles.

Thus "true and fair" has a technical meaning: appropriate classification of items and the consistent application of generally accepted accounting principles. This illustrates another reason why managers sometimes find accounts confusing: words and phrases in accounts do not always mean the same thing as in everyday use.

Consistency is fundamental in accounting, as in other quantitative fields. Results of one period can sensibly be compared with those of another only if the two sets of figures are prepared on the same basis. Measurement problems, which we shall discuss later in more detail, tend to make financial results for a single year a less reliable guide to a company's performance than accounts prepared on a consistent basis for a number of years. This fact is recognised in the legal prospectus requirements for at least five years' past figures when a company seeks to raise money in the market. The Companies Act, 1948 further requires annual accounts to show figures for the preceding as well as for the current year. Companies must disclose any material changes in accounting treatment, stating how much they have affected the figures.

Incidentally, the legal expression *de minimis non curat lex* applies equally to accounting practice. Accounting, like the law, is not concerned with trivia, and does not require the separate disclosure of figures which are not material.

It has already been noted that "true and fair" is not synonymous with "true worth." Figures shown in the balance sheet for both fixed and current assets are not the amounts expected to be realised if the company were wound up ("liquidated"). They do not disclose the "break-up" value of the company's business but are based on the assumption that the company will continue to trade (the "going-concern" assumption). Except for the recent practice of revaluing interests in land and buildings, fixed assets are generally shown in accounts at historical cost less an allowance for depreciation. Such figures might be very different from current market values. Current assets, including stocks of finished goods and work-in-progress are also shown in the balance sheet at cost, unless net realisable value is estimated to be lower than cost.

The position is essentially unchanged when adjustments are made to reflect the declining purchasing power of money. The supplementary inflation-adjusted figures that companies now show alongside the traditional money amounts do not represent current valuations. They merely express the historical costs in current units of purchasing power (today's rather than yesterday's pounds).

Under section 149 of the Companies Act 1948, responsibility for disclosing a "true and fair view" in accounts rests with a company's directors. Every set of company accounts must be audited, and the auditors must report whether or not in their opinion the accounts do give a "true and fair view." But ultimately it is for the directors to decide on the form and content of a company's accounts, and for the auditors simply to report on those accounts.

CONSERVATISM

The present form of published company balance sheets and profit and loss accounts has developed over the last 120 years. In the early days of the limited liability company it was feared that owners enjoying the protection of limited liability might act with less prudence than those conducting other forms of business enterprise (sole traders and partnerships), who were liable for the business debts up to the entire extent of their private fortunes. As a result, the major emphasis in balance sheets was to satisfy the creditors of a company that it was financially sound. Over the years ownership of the shares in many companies has become largely divorced from control, which is exercised more and more by professional management, and shareholders too have wanted to use published accounts to make sure that their capital was safe and producing an adequate return.

Because it was felt that both creditors and shareholders would regard sharp fluctuations in profits or in asset values as disturbing, directors tended to become very conservative in what they let published accounts reveal. Conservatism is still a feature of accounting practice today. No profit is included in accounts until it is realised, but accounting principles generally require that all known liabilities should be provided for even where the exact amount can-

not yet be determined. The amounts (the "book values") at which assets are shown in balance sheets need not reflect their "true" values, since balance sheets are not intended to show the "net worth" of a business—although published accounts unfortunately sometimes use the phrase "net worth" to refer to the shareholders' interest in a company.

In recent years several factors, including inflation, take-over activity, and legislation, have prompted some companies to make a fuller disclosure in their accounts of the true value of assets, especially properties. Nevertheless, assets are still generally shown at historical cost, less provisions for depreciation when appropriate.

Accounts refer only to aspects of a company's business which can be expressed in money terms. They are thus incomplete statements. Many valuable assets do not appear in company accounts at all, especially management resources. Where intangible assets, such as technical know-how, goodwill, trade marks, and so on, have been built up slowly over time, it is admittedly difficult to value them. But even when large sums have been paid to buy such assets, companies often write the costs off against revenue and leave no trace in the balance sheet. This approach, which stems from the time when creditors looked only to tangible assets for security, can often disguise the true position when intangible assets represent a significant part of the underlying strength of a business.

HISTORICAL COST VERSUS CURRENT VALUE

At first sight it might seem indefensible for accountants to continue to use historical cost figures which can often produce unrealistic results. The heart of the problem, however, lies not so much in showing the present system to be less than ideal (which most accountants would readily accept), but in suggesting a better alternative.

It will be seen later just how difficult it can be to establish what "cost" means in relation to stock and work-in-progress. The determination of a realistic accounting figure is even more difficult in relation to fixed assets, such as land, buildings, plant and machinery, which may have been purchased many years ago and for which, often, no ready market value exists. We shall also see that "profit" is usually not susceptible to precise measurement. The published profit or loss figure is directly affected by accounting methods which can depend heavily on the subjective judgement of a company's directors.

The most obvious alternative to historical cost is to show assets in accounts at their current values. But this raises new questions: what are their current values? Perhaps even more important, who is to say what they are? Those best placed to value a company's assets are its directors, the very people whose stewardship the accounts are intended to assess.

It is technically possible for independent firms of specialists to value tangible fixed assets; but revaluing all business assets every year is not a practical proposition. Even if it were, different firms of valuers would not necessarily arrive at similar figures. Again, the same asset can have different values for different purposes. A building in the centre of a city may be worth much more as an office block than as a hotel. At what value then should it be shown in the accounts of a hotel operating company?

Replacing the historical cost approach with one involving annual valuations would not necessarily produce better results, even if it were practicable. The alternative approach itself raises problems as fundamental as those it seeks to resolve. As a rule accountants use past actual market value (= historical cost) rather than present hypothetical market value because their preference for actual market transactions, as opposed to hypothetical ones, outweighs the undisputed extra usefulness of current as opposed to past values.

The comments expressed in Recommendation N15 (1952) of the Institute of Chartered Accountants in England and Wales are of interest on this point:

The primary purpose of the annual accounts of a business is to present information to the proprietors showing how their funds have been utilised and the profits derived from such use. It has long been accepted in accounting practice that a balance sheet prepared for this purpose is an historical record and not a statement of current worth. Stated briefly its function is to show in monetary terms the capital, reserves and liabilities of a business at the date at which it is prepared and the manner in which the total moneys representing them have been distributed over several types of assets. Similarly a profit and loss account is an historical record. It shows as the profit or loss the difference between the revenue for the period covered by the account and the expenditure chargeable in that period, including charges for the amortisation of capital expenditure. Revenue and expenditure are brought into the account at their recorded monetary amounts. This basis of accounting is frequently described as the historical cost basis . . .

An important feature of the historical cost basis of preparing annual accounts is that it reduces to a minimum the extent to which the accounts can be affected by the personal opinions of those responsible for them. For example, the cost of a fixed asset is known so that in calculating depreciation provisions based on that cost, the only respects in which estimates enter into the matter are in relation to the probable useful life of the asset and its realisable value, if any, at the end of its life. Depreciation provisions computed on this basis are intended, by making charges against revenue over the useful life of an asset, to amortise the capital expenditure incurred in acquiring it. For this purpose estimates of current value or

of replacement cost do not arise. Again, there are limits within which estimates and opinions can properly operate in relation to stock in trade, provided the bases of calculation are sound in principle and used consistently.

Some companies try to resolve the problem by partial revaluations of assets at irregular intervals, and perhaps in the future there will be compulsory regular valuations of major assets. While it is not practical to consider a full revaluation of all assets every year, it may be both practical and relevant every five or ten years to revalue major fixed assets, especially land and buildings. Such valuations, although fairly costly, produce more realistic assets values in the balance sheet and give shareholders a better idea of how much capital is really invested in the business.

The entire problem of asset values is aggravated during periods of rapid or continuous inflation, where the falling value of money makes *all* historical money figures inadequate, in addition to the effect of changing market conditions on particular asset values. The Accounting Standards Steering Committee set up by the major British accounting bodies has recently proposed that companies should publish supplementary statements showing figures adjusted for inflation alongside the historical cost accounts. The proposed adjustments are meant to reflect changes in the purchasing power of money, as indicated, inversely, by the Consumer Price Index. The nature of the adjustments and an example of adjusted accounts are shown in the Appendix to Section 8.

SUMMARY

Already we can form an impression of what published company accounts try to do, and of the general principles on which they are based.

Company accounts are formal financial statements prepared in accordance with accepted conventions. They record only items which can be expressed in money terms, and not all of these. Thus they are at best only incomplete statements.

Accounts record the transactions of a business entity quite apart from the personal affairs of its owners, who are becoming increasingly remote from those making management decisions. As companies grow in size, the need for good financial information becomes ever more important. It is normally assumed in preparing accounts that the business will continue to trade over an unlimited future period (the "going-concern" assumption).

Accounts generally record actual historical market transactions rather than estimated current values. They do not try to reflect the "true worth" of a company. Although accounts have traditionally been prepared on an historical cost basis there is now an increasing desire to allow for the falling value of money over time. A generally conservative approach is a feature of accounting treatment, although here again companies are increasingly inclined to become more realistic.

Accounts are prepared on a consistent basis from year to year, but nearly all accounts contain a significant subjective element, since where incomplete transactions are concerned those responsible for preparing accounts necessarily have to make judgements about the uncertain future.

Section 1
The structure of company accounts

THE BALANCE SHEET AND PROFIT AND LOSS ACCOUNT

In the Introduction we examined the background to published company accounts and the accounting principles and conventions on which they are based. Now let us look at a particular set of accounts to see what information they give and to consider more closely the "classification and grouping of items" which is necessary to present a "true and fair view."

The balance sheet and profit and loss account of General Trading Limited are set out overleaf. In looking at these accounts, consider the following questions:

1 (*a*) What briefly is the purpose of each statement?
  (*b*) Do any items appear in both statements?

2 How does the balance sheet classify items?

3 How does the profit and loss account classify items?

Please study the balance sheet and profit and loss account overleaf and formulate your answers to the questions before reading on.

GENERAL TRADING LIMITED
Balance sheet, 31 March 1973

	£		£	
Share capital		**Fixed Assets**		
100 000 Ordinary shares	100 000	Freehold property	50 000	
		Fixtures and equipment		
Reserves		at cost *less* depreciation	30 000	
Profit and loss account			80 000	
(unappropriated balance)	20 000			
Shareholders' funds	120 000			
Long-term liabilities		**Current Assets**		
Loans	20 000	Stock	40 000	
		Debtors	35 000	
Current liabilities		Cash	15 000	
Corporation tax	7 000			
Creditors	18 000			90 000
Ordinary dividend	5 000			
	30 000			
	£170 000			£170 000

GENERAL TRADING LIMITED
Profit and loss account
for the year ending 31 March 1973

	£
Sales	240 000
Trading profit for the year	17 000
Less: Debenture interest	1 000
Profit before tax	16 000
Corporation tax	7 000
Net profit for the year after tax	9 000
Less: Ordinary Dividend	5 000
Retained out of the year's profit	4 000
Add: Unappropriated balance brought forward	16 000
Unappropriated balance carried forward	£20 000

1(a) What briefly is the purpose of each statement?

The *balance sheet* is a classified summary as at a particular date showing the sources of funds controlled by a business and how it has used these funds.

The *profit and loss account* summarises the revenue and expenses of the business for an accounting period. It shows the tax charged against profit, and the extent to which after-tax profits are paid out as dividends ("distributed") or retained in the business ("ploughed back").

1(b) Do any items appear in both statements?

Yes: three items can be identified.

(*i*) The unappropriated balance on the profit and loss account itself (£20 000) appears in the balance sheet under "Reserves," and represents one of the sources of the business's funds.

(*ii*) Corporation tax (£7000) payable on the profits of the year is shown as an expense in the profit and loss account and also appears as a liability in the balance sheet. In this case the figure is the same, but often the profit and loss account tax charge is included as part of a larger taxation figure in the balance sheet.

(*iii*) Dividends (£5000) are shown in the profit and loss account as an appropriation of profit, and also appear in the balance sheet under "current liabilities," to the extent that they have not yet been paid.

BALANCE SHEET CLASSIFICATION

2 How does the balance sheet classify items?

(a) *A major classification of items in the balance sheet is between:*

   (i) *Sources of funds* (*liabilities*)
      The financial resources which the company controls

   (ii) *Use of funds* (*assets*)
      How the company has used its financial resources

In total, sources of funds always equal uses of funds.
Liabilities always equal assets.

This classification is illustrated opposite (*a*).

(b) *Sources and uses of funds can be long-term or short-term*
Thus the classification of items in the balance sheet reflects a time dimension.

Long-term
The source or use of funds is related to a time span of more than one year from the balance sheet date.

Short-term
The time span involved is less than one year.

This division can be seen in balance sheet (*b*).

(c) *Long-term sources of funds generally subdivide into two parts*
   (i) *Shareholders' funds*
      New capital introduced (share capital)
      Profits retained in the business (reserves)
   (ii) *Loans*
      Lent to the company for fixed periods of time

Thus balance sheet items are classified under five major headings—three major sources of funds and two principal types of use.

These are illustrated opposite (*c*) and described in more detail in the following pages.

(a) GENERAL TRADING LIMITED
Balance sheet

Sources of funds	*Uses of funds*
Share capital and reserves	Fixed assets
Long-term liabilities	Current assets
Current liabilities	

(b) GENERAL TRADING LIMITED
Balance sheet

Sources of funds	*Uses of funds*
Long-term sources	**Long-term uses**
Share capital and reserves	Fixed assets
Long-term liabilities	
Short-term sources	**Short-term uses**
Current liabilities	Current assets

(c) GENERAL TRADING LIMITED
Balance sheet

Sources of funds	*Uses of funds*
1 Share capital and reserves	**4 Fixed assets**
Share capital	Freehold property
Reserves	Fixtures and equipment
2 Long-term liabilities	
Loans	
3 Current liabilities	**5 Current assets**
Tax	Stock
Creditors	Debtors
Dividend	Cash

Sources of funds

1 Share capital and reserves

The share capital is the permanent capital of the business and is generally in the form of ordinary shares (the "equity capital"). It is possible for companies also to issue "preference shares" as part of their share capital, and we shall examine possible forms of capital structure in some detail in section 6. A company cannot reduce its share capital without special permission from the court. (Nor may British companies—unlike American companies—purchase their own shares.)

The reserves representing retained profits (earnings) are legally available to pay dividends to shareholders. In practice, however, dividends are usually paid out of the current year's profits, not out of revenue reserves which are previous years' retained profits.

Although share capital and reserves can be regarded as "liabilities" of a company to its shareholders, no amounts are payable as long as the company continues in business, unless the directors decide to distribute retained profits as dividends.

Note the separate sub-total (£120 000) adding together the issued share capital and reserves. This amount is entitled "shareholders' funds" (sometimes called "owners' equity"), and represents the shareholders' interests in the company.

2 Long-term liabilities

Long-term borrowing (loans, mortgages or debentures) represents semi-permanent capital of the company. It is generally undertaken for fairly long periods, say twenty years, and when repayment becomes due, the item will probably be replaced either by newly issued share capital or by further long-term borrowing.

3 Current liabilities

Current liabilities are due for payment within the near future, and in any event within one year. They include current tax due, trade creditors and the liability to pay the current dividend to shareholders.

Uses of funds

1 Fixed assets

Fixed assets are semi-permanent assets of the business, used to provide goods or services, rather than to be sold in the normal course of business. They include properties, fixtures and equipment. Detailed cost and cumulative depreciation figures have to be shown separately in the notes to the accounts if not on the face of the balance sheet.

2 Current assets

"Current" assets, like "current" liabilities, have an expected time span of not more than one year from the balance sheet date. They are either cash, or in a form which will soon be converted into cash. It is normally expected that stock will be turned into cash at least within twelve months, and that outstanding debts will be collected within that time. The items shown as current assets are usually listed in reverse order of liquidity, the least liquid (stock) being shown first, then debtors, and the most liquid (cash) last.

Summary The balance sheet "classification and grouping of items" is helpful in appraising the current and longer term financial position of the business. Sources and uses of funds are shown separately with assets or liabilities of a like kind being grouped together. At the same time, current assets and current liabilities are separated from longer term items. Later in this section we shall see an alternative way of grouping items which emphasises more strongly the distinction between long-term and short-term funds.

PROFIT AND LOSS ACCOUNT CLASSIFICATION

3 How does the profit and loss account classify items?

The profit and loss account, like the balance sheet, is divided into sections, although in the form of presentation generally used the lines of division are not particularly clear. The total account for a trading company can be divided into three parts:

(a) A trading account

(b) A profit and loss account

(c) An appropriation account

An example of a divided account is set out opposite and the individual sections are there considered in more detail.

(a) The trading account

The trading account deals with sales revenue and the costs of achieving sales. Major deductions from revenue are purchases (or costs of manufacturing goods) and selling and administrative expenses. The final figure in the trading account is the trading profit (or loss) for the period.

What is called "trading profit" in published accounts may differ from what is called "trading profit" in internal management accounts, since the former is calculated *after* deducting selling and administrative expenses, which would probably *not* be considered as trading account items for internal accounting purposes. The difference of treatment stems from the limited amount of disclosure required in published accounts.

(b) The profit and loss account

The profit and loss account begins with the trading profit, to which is added any other income, for example interest and dividends received. Various expenses required by law to be separately disclosed may then be deducted, including depreciation, interest paid, directors' remuneration, and the audit fee. Such items not identified separately in the profit and loss account will have to be disclosed in a note to the accounts.

The balance remaining is the profit before tax, and deducting tax gives the profit for the year after tax. Up to this stage only items relating to the current year are included. Exceptional items relating to the previous periods appear in the statement after the profit "for the year" has been established, and are often referred to as "below the line" items (the line being the "profit for the year" line).

(c) The appropriation account

The appropriation account shows how much of the profit is transferred to special reserves, how much distributed as dividends and how much retained in the account. The accumulated balance unappropriated in previous years is then added to the amount retained from the current year's profit, to give the unappropriated balance to be carried forward to the next period. This is the figure shown in the balance sheet under the heading "profit and loss account" (which is part of the reserves).

A common alternative treatment is to show only the appropriation of the current year's profit. The addition of the amount retained out of the year's profit (£4000 for General Trading Limited) to the accumulated balance from previous years (£16 000) is then shown in a note attached to the accounts. In other words, the part of the appropriation account shown opposite below the dotted line is sometimes omitted.

GENERAL TRADING LIMITED

Trading, profit and loss, and appropriation account for the year ending 31 March, 1973

(a) Trading account

	£
Sales	240 000
Less: Expenses (*not specified in detail in published accounts*)	223 000
Trading profit for the year	£17 000

(b) Profit and loss account

	£
Trading profit for the year	17 000
Less: Debenture interest	1 000
Profit before tax	16 000
Corporation tax	7 000
Net profit for the year after tax	£9 000

(c) Appropriation account

	£
Net profit for the year after tax	9 000
Less: Ordinary dividend	5 000
Retained out of the year's profit	4 000
Add: Unappropriated balance brought forward from last account	16 000
Unappropriated balance carried forward	£20 000

ALTERNATIVE FORMS OF PRESENTING ACCOUNTS

The "net asset" form of balance sheet presentation

When we looked at the structure of the balance sheet we observed a classification under five major headings and a distinction between long-term and short-term items. The headings were:

1 Share capital and reserves
2 Long-term liabilities
3 Current liabilities
4 Fixed assets
5. Current assets

These were arranged in the form shown opposite (the "account" format).

A form of presentation now becoming widely used for published accounts preserves the classification under five major headings, but distinguishes more sharply between long-term and short-term sources of funds. An outline of this form of presentation (the "net asset" format) is shown opposite below.

The new format groups the long-term sources of funds together, and shows the total as "capital employed." *How* the capital is employed (invested in "net assets") is then shown underneath.

Notes on the "net asset" format

1 The same figures appear in both forms of balance sheet, although the balance sheet totals are different.
2 The "net asset" format presents the figures in tabular form (vertically) rather than side by side (horizontally).
3 Current liabilities are no longer grouped with the other liabilities, but instead are *deducted* from the current assets.
4 The net asset total is subdivided under two major headings; fixed assets and net current assets. The idea of net current assets ("working capital") is new. It comprises current assets less current liabilities, and represents the amount of capital permanently tied up in short-term assets whose individual constituent parts are continually turning over.
5 Three new totals are emphasised:
   Capital employed
   Net current assets (working capital)
   Net assets
   It will be seen that capital employed = net assets.

Balance sheet summary
"Account" format

Sources of funds	£	Uses of funds	£
1 Share capital and reserves	120 000	4 Fixed assets	80 000
2 Long-term liabilities	20 000	5 Current assets	90 000
3 Current liabilities	30 000		
	£170 000		£170 000

Balance sheet summary
"Net asset" format

	£	£
1 Share capital and reserves		120 000
2 Long-term liabilities		20 000
Capital employed		£140 000
4 Fixed assets		80 000
5 Current assets	90 000	
3 Less: Current liabilities	30 000	
Net current assets ("working capital")		60 000
Net assets		£140 000

A simplified balance sheet presentation

A second trend in accounting presentation involves removing detailed figures from the face of the statement. The balance sheet of General Trading Limited is set out below both in the traditional "account format" and in the "net asset" format—excluding details—which would be the more usual presentation today.

GENERAL TRADING LIMITED
Balance sheet, 31 March 1973

"Account" format

	£			£
Share capital		**Fixed assets**		
100 000 ordinary shares	100 000	Freehold property		50 000
		Fixtures and equipment		
Reserves		at cost	40 000	
Profit and loss account	20 000	*less* depreciation	10 000	
Shareholders' funds	120 000			30 000
				80 000
Long-term liabilities				
Loans	20 000	**Current assets**		
		Stock	40 000	
		Debtors	35 000	
Current liabilities		Cash	15 000	
Corporation tax	7 000			
Creditors	18 000			90 000
Ordinary dividend	5 000			
	30 000			
	£170 000			£170 000

"Net asset" format
(with details removed and included in notes)

	Notes		£
Shareholders' funds	1		120 000
Loans	2		20 000
Capital employed			£140 000
Fixed assets	3		80 000
Current assets			
Stock	4	40 000	
Debtors		35 000	
Cash		15 000	
		90 000	
Less: Current liabilities	5	30 000	
Net current assets			60 000
Net assets			£140 000

Notes to accounts

Notes 1–5 to the accounts would include the appropriate detail relating to each item.

In summarising complex business transactions in the form of financial statements accountants are faced with many problems. Here we are concerned with the problem of presentation. How much detailed information should accounts give, and in what form?

Obviously it is desirable that published company accounts should meet the needs of the people for whom they are prepared, but this raises an interesting question: for whom *are* company accounts prepared? Creditors? Employees? Directors? Shareholders? Small private shareholders or large institutional investors? Existing or potential investors? The financial press? The government?

In fact, of course, company accounts may serve *all* these groups, so the resulting format is a compromise which may not entirely satisfy any particular group.

While requiring that certain details are disclosed, the law does not usually lay down exactly how such disclosure should be presented—for example, whether in the balance sheet and profit and loss account or in notes to the accounts. Matters of presentation are normally left to each company to decide for itself, and in practice in the absence of multiple forms of statement for a single company accountants are left with the task of presenting company accounts in a form, and with a degree of detail, which will satisfy as well as possible the different needs of the various users.

There has been a trend over recent years to remove from the published accounts much of the technical accounting language and to simplify the figures shown on the face of the balance sheet and profit and loss account. By moving most of the detail into ever more comprehensive notes and statistics attached to the published accounts, company accountants aim to provide statements which laymen can understand while at the same time disclosing separately the detailed figures required by professional financial analysts.

It is important to understand that these "notes" form *part* of the accounts: the balance sheet, profit and loss account *and* notes to the accounts together consitute "the accounts" of a company, on which independent auditors are required to report each year.

The original outline profit and loss account for General Trading Limited on page 12 amalgamated the two parts representing the profit and loss account and the appropriation account. The trading account was omitted, and only the total sales figure given. There is no statutory obligation to disclose the detailed expenses from the trading account (which would, however, normally be shown on copies of the accounts circulated inside the company).

DIRECTORS' REPORT

The Annual Report and Accounts of a public company contain, at the very least, a balance sheet, profit and loss account, notes to the accounts, auditors' report and a directors' report. Certain information, not all of it of an accounting nature, must be shown in the directors' report if not shown elsewhere. In addition, most company chairmen issue a statement to shareholders each year, discussing the company's operations during the year, together with some comments about future prospects. In addition, it is becoming common for companies to publish tables of financial statistics covering a number of years' past results (often ten years).

While the directors' report and chairman's statement, and any other review of operations in the Annual Report, do not strictly speaking form part of "the accounts" of a company, anyone seeking information about the company's financial position should read them carefully as well as analysing the accounts themselves.

SUMMARY

In this section we have considered the structure of company accounts, and defined the purpose of the major financial statements and the principal terms used in them.

We have seen that the major classification and grouping of items in the balance sheet is between sources and uses of funds, and between long-term and short-term sources and uses. We have noted that two alternative forms of presentation are in general use, the "account" format and the increasingly popular "net asset" format which deducts current liabilities from current assets to present a figure for working capital.

We have also studied the three-part structure of the profit and loss account—trading account, profit and loss account, and appropriation account—and noted its more usual abbreviated form.

Now with this basic understanding of the way in which published company accounts present information, we can go on to consider how financial statements can be used to appraise a company's performance and financial status.

PROBLEMS AND SOLUTIONS

You may want to refer to the Preface for guidance on how to make the best use of the problems at the end of each section.

The first few problems in each section are relatively easy, and are immediately followed by the suggested answer overleaf. Later problems are more difficult, and answers to them are given at the back of the book.

1.1 Definitions

In section 1 we have considered the structure and contents of the balance sheet and profit and loss account. We have defined the meaning of the major items which appear in company accounts, and a brief review may be helpful to make sure that your ideas about them are now clear.

Try to define the terms opposite (if you find it helpful, write down your definitions in the space provided), and then check your definitions with those set out overleaf.

(a) Balance sheet

(b) Profit and loss account

(c) Fixed assets

(d) Current liabilities

(e) Shareholders' funds

(f) Current assets

(g) Creditors

(h) Retained earnings

(i) Authorised capital

(j) Ordinary dividends

1.1 Definitions

(a) Balance sheet
A financial statement summarising, as at a particular date, the sources of funds controlled by a business and how those funds have been used.

(b) Profit and loss account
This financial statement summarises the revenue and expenses of a business for an accounting period, and shows the overall profit or loss. It also shows the extent to which the profits are paid out as dividends or retained in the business.

(c) Fixed assets
Resources (both tangible and intangible) with a relatively long economic life, acquired not for re-sale in the normal course of business, but for use in producing other goods and services.

(d) Current liabilities
Liabilities due to be paid within twelve months from the balance sheet date, for example trade creditors, accrued charges, dividends payable, current tax liabilities.

(e) Shareholders' funds
Amounts which ultimately belong to the shareholders; the interests of the owners in a business. They are not "liabilities" in the same sense as are the other sources of funds, since they are payable to shareholders only if the business ceases to exist. They are either in the form of issued share capital, or retained profits, or other reserves. Assets less "external" liabilities = shareholders' funds, which is thus a *residual* amount, depending on the book value attached to assets.

(f) Current assets
Either cash or assets expected to be converted into cash or consumed in the business within twelve months from the balance sheet date (or the normal operating cycle, if longer), for example stocks (both for re-sale and for use), debtors, prepaid expenses, cash.

(g) Creditors
Persons or businesses to whom amounts are due for goods or services purchased on credit (= "trade" creditors). Also includes other amounts payable, for example to the Inland Revenue in respect of tax deducted from employees' wages.

(h) Retained earnings
= Retained profits. The excess of profits over (losses and) dividends paid to shareholders. Can relate either to a particular period, or to the accumulated total over the whole life to date of a business (after deducting any amounts capitalised). (See section 6.)

(i) Authorised (share) capital
The amount of share capital which the company is authorised to issue by its constitution (Memorandum and Articles of Association). The share capital actually issued can never exceed the amount authorised, and is often less. Any excess of authorised over issued share capital represents the amount of "unissued" share capital that a company may issue without having to obtain further approval by the shareholders.

(j) Ordinary dividends
The amount of profits distributed or proposed to be distributed to owners of the ordinary share capital. (The directors of a company propose how much profit to distribute ("pay out") in dividends. If the shareholders do not approve, they may reduce but not increase the dividends.)

1.2 Classification of balance sheet and profit and loss account items

Ability to classify and locate items in financial statements is clearly of great importance. The following exercise is designed to reinforce your work in the section on classification of items. Place a cross for each item shown below in the appropriate balance sheet and/or profit and loss account column. (Some items may appear in more than one column. At least one item is not explicitly disclosed in the accounts.) Then turn over this page to compare your answers with the suggested solutions:

Space for answers

	Balance sheet					Profit and loss account		
	Share capital and reserves	Long-term liabilities	Current liabilities	Fixed assets	Current assets	Trading account	Profit and loss account	Appropriation account
(a) Stock in trade								
(b) Trade creditors								
(c) Leasehold property								
(d) Taxation								
(e) Ordinary share capital								
(f) Cash								
(g) Fixtures and equipment								
(h) Capital reserve								
(i) Ordinary dividend proposed								
(j) Sales								
(k) Retained profits								
(l) Management potential								
(m) Trade investments								
(n) Debtors								
(o) Debenture								

1.2 Classification of balance sheet and profit and loss account items

Solutions

	Balance sheet					Profit and loss account		
	Share capital and reserves	Long-term liabilities	Current liabilities	Fixed assets	Current assets	Trading account	Profit and loss account	Appropriation account
(a) Stock in trade					X			
(b) Trade creditors			X					
(c) Leasehold property				X				
(d) Taxation			X				X	
(e) Ordinary share capital	X							
(f) Cash					X			
(g) Fixtures and equipment				X				
(h) Capital reserve	X							
(i) Ordinary dividend proposed			X					X
(j) Sales						X		
(k) Retained profits	X							X
(l) Management potential								
(m) Trade investments*				X				
(n) Debtors					X			
(o) Debenture		X						

*Trade investments represent significant long-term shareholding in businesses whose activities are closely related to those of the company.

Problems

A number of problems follow involving the construction of company accounts. The problems range in difficulty from the simple to the more complex. A suggested answer to the first problem can be seen overleaf. You are *strongly urged* not to look at it until you have written out your own answer in the space provided. Answers to the later problems are provided separately at the end of the book.

Balance sheets

1.3 The Corner Shop Limited

Compile the balance sheet of The Corner Shop Limited at 30 June 1972 from the following information:

	£
Share capital £1 ordinary shares	10 000
Leasehold shop	8 000
Cash	4 000
Balance on profit and loss account	6 000
Creditors	2 000
Stock	6 000

Space for answer

THE CORNER SHOP LIMITED

Share capital

Fixed asset

Revenue reserve

Current assets

Current liabilities

£ _____

£ _____

Balance sheets

1.3 The Corner Shop Limited

Solution

Notes

1 The heading of the balance sheet shows the name of the company and the balance sheet date.

2 Note the sub-total of the share capital and revenue reserve, which is entitled "shareholders' funds."

2 Current assets—stock comes before cash. The convention is to show current assets in order of liquidity—the least liquid at the top.

THE CORNER SHOP LIMITED
Balance sheet, 30 June 1972

	£		£	
Share capital		**Fixed asset**		
£1 ordinary shares	10 000	Leasehold shop		8 000
Revenue reserve		**Current assets**		
Profit and loss account	6 000	Stock	6 000	
		Cash	4 000	
	———		———	
Shareholders' funds	16 000			
				10 000
Current liabilities				
Creditors	2 000			
	———			———
	£18 000			£18 000

Please use separate sheets of paper for your answers to each of the following problems. Answers to these problems are shown at the end of the book.

Balance sheets

1.4 The Acme Company Limited
The Acme Company Limited prepares accounts to 30 June. From the following information compile the 1972 balance sheet, using the account format.

	£
Cash	2 000
Current tax payable	2 000
Shop fixtures and fittings	3 000
Creditors	3 000
Revenue reserve: profit and loss account	5 000
Share capital: £1 ordinary shares	20 000
Stock	6 000
Freehold shop	15 000
Debtors	4 000

Profit and loss accounts

1.5 General Contractors Limited
Prepare the profit and loss account for General Contractors Limited for the year ending 31 December 1972 from the following information:

	£
Trading profit before depreciation and interest	20 000
Tax on the profit for the year	7 000
Unappropriated balance brought forward	3 000
Proposed dividend	5 000

Amounts of £5000 for depreciation and £1000 for interest paid should be charged in the account. Invoiced sales in the year amounted to £125 000.

1.6 The Marvel Trading Company Limited
The Marvel Trading Company Limited makes up annual accounts to 30 June each year. The company made a trading profit of £100 000 in 1972 after deduction of all charges including depreciation, but before charging interest payable of £8000. Income from investments during the year amounted to £10 000, and the estimated tax charge on the profit for the year was £45 000.

The company proposes to pay a dividend of £40 000 in total in respect of its ordinary shares. The unappropriated balance brought forward on the profit and loss account from the previous year was £8000. You are asked to prepare the company's profit and loss account (including the appropriation account) for the year ended 30 June 1972.

Balance sheets and profit and loss accounts

1.7 The Fine Fare Catering Company Limited

The accounts of The Fine Fare Catering Company Limited for the year ending 31 March 1973 contain the following items. Compile the balance sheet and profit and loss acount.

	£
Sales	15 000
Proposed dividend	1 000
Share capital: £1 ordinary shares	6 000
Fixtures and fittings	1 000
Cash	1 000
Creditors	2 000
Leasehold restaurant	7 000
Stock	2 000
Tax due on profit for the year	1 000
Trading profit after depreciation	3 000

1.8 Andrew Hunt Limited

Andrew Hunt Limited's first accounts, for the nine months ended 30 September 1972 contain the following items. Prepare the balance sheet and profit and loss account.

	£
Cash	2 000
Creditors	3 200
10% Debenture 1987	4 000
Debenture interest paid	300
Debtors	4 700
Depreciation charge for the period	500
Dividend proposed	1 500
Leasehold factory	6 000
Plant and machinery, net (after depreciation for the period)	4 500
Sales	34 000
Share capital, ordinary 50p shares	7 500
Stock	3 300
Tax on profit	2 700
Trading profit before depreciation and interest	6 600

Section 2
Analysing company accounts

ANALYSING COMPANY ACCOUNTS

A company's published accounts, interpreted with due caution, can tell a good deal about its activities and degree of success. Individual items in accounts often indicate the nature of a business: it is not too difficult to distinguish a grocery store from a manufacturing business, a property company from an investment trust. Interest will centre not only in what a company does, but in how well it has been doing it. Examining several years' accounts can provide a fairly detailed picture of a company's policies and pattern of growth (or decline).

Here we shall examine only the commonest of the many techniques available for analysing accounts, concentrating on three main aspects:

1 *Investment*. How do financial results relate to shareholders' funds and to stock market prices?

    Investment measures relate earnings and dividends to shareholders' funds, to each other and to stock market prices, usually on a "per share" basis.

2 *Performance*. How successfully is the business being run?

    Performance appraisal seeks to determine how well a company is using the funds it controls, by relating profit earned to capital employed ("return on investment").

3 *Financial status*. Is the company in a sound financial position?

    Measures of financial status distinguish between solvency and liquidity, between long-term and short-term capacity to meet liabilities.

In each case we are interested not only in the figures for a particular accounting period, but also in the trend over a number of periods. For nearly always the most important question is what indications for the *future* can be gleaned from published accounts which relate to the *past*.

RETURN ON INVESTMENT

The concept of return on investment is fundamental in the world of finance. A person with funds to invest will seek the highest possible return on his money, all else being equal. The qualification is important: all else rarely *is* equal. If an investor happens to want a regular annual stream of income he may prefer a government security with half-yearly interest to an equity investment with irregular (or smaller) dividends, even though, taking capital growth into account, the latter's expected long-run return may be higher.

Again, investment always contains an element of risk, for money is being invested today in the hope of yielding benefits in the uncertain future. Gauging the degree of risk precisely is difficult, but the market tries to quantify it, and adjusts the rate of return available accordingly.

Thus investors content to receive an 8 per cent return from a relatively safe investment in a large well-known industrial company may require a 20 per cent return from an investment in a new mining venture in a politically unstable part of the world. What this means in practice is illustrated opposite.

Investment fixed	Industrial company	Mining venture
Given an available amount to invest of the minimum* return required on the basis of risk involved is:	£2000	£2000
	£160	£400
To give a return on investment of:	$\frac{£160}{£2000} = 8\%$	$\frac{£400}{£2000} = 20\%$

*If the income were *less*, and the amount invested remained the same, then the return on investment obtained would be lower than the minimum required at that level of risk.

Return fixed	Industrial company	Mining venture
Given a desired income of	£240	£240
And a required return on investment for the degree of risk involved of	8%	20%
Then the maximum* amount of investment would be	$£240 \times \frac{100}{8} = £3000$	$£240 \times \frac{100}{20} = £1200$

*If the amount invested were *more*, and the income unchanged, then the return on investment would be *lower* than the minimum requirement.

In short, "return on investment" $= \frac{\text{return}}{\text{investment}}$, though in practice the concept of "return" may include capital growth as well as income.

In applying the return on investment approach, we must first specify which "return" and "investment" figures to use.

Two questions in particular arise. In calculating "return", do we want to use the profit figure before or after tax? In calculating the "investment", are we interested in total capital employed, or only in the funds provided by the ordinary shareholders?

In fact, there are two major measures of return on investment:

1 Return on shareholders' funds, relating profit *after* tax to the funds provided by ordinary shareholders.

2 Return on net assets, relating profit *before* tax to the total capital employed. (This second measure is also called "return on capital employed".)

Return on Shareholders' Funds

This measure deals with the profit "available" for ordinary shareholders, that is profit after tax and after deducting any other amounts *not* attributable to ordinary shareholders (such as preference dividends and minority interests, which we shall discuss in more detail in later sections). The profit available for ordinary shareholders is divided by the funds provided, directly or indirectly, by ordinary shareholders. The two most basic ways for ordinary shareholders to provide funds are by putting up capital in return for shares in the company and by not withdrawing all the profits in dividends, which lets the company grow by retaining profits. (The decision as to dividends is in practice made by the directors of a company.) We shall discuss the detailed accounting consequences of issuing more shares in section 6.

Return on shareholders' funds (also called "return on equity") is probably the most important single measure of all. It takes into account the return on net assets, the company's tax position, and the extent to which capital employed has been supplied other than by the ordinary shareholders (for example by loans).

Return on Net Assets

As we have seen, "net assets" mean the fixed assets of a company plus the working capital (current assets less current liabilities). Because balance sheets balance, this amount is evidently exactly equal to the "capital employed," which includes shareholders' funds and long-term loans. Thus the measure is sometimes also called "return on capital employed."

As we shall see in section 6, the different ways of combining long-term sources of funds between external loans ("debt") and shareholders' funds ("equity") significantly affect the return on *shareholders*' funds. The return on net assets measure ignores the particular methods used to *finance* the business, by concentrating on the profitability (before tax) of the total long-term capital employed, whatever its source.

In our workings we shall use the end-of-year figures as the basis for calculating ratios. Some analysts prefer to use beginning-of-year figures, and there is a good case for using average figures for a period if the information is available. One advantage of our approach is that all the information to be used is available in a single set of accounts.

Let us now turn to the accounts of a specific company, and see what we can learn by analysing them.

The accounts of Precision Locks Limited for the year ending 30 June 1972, are set out below.

Let us analyse the company's accounts and appraise its results, considering in particular:

1 Investment measures

2 Measures of performance

3 Measures of financial status

At each stage in the analysis you will be asked to calculate the appropriate measures first, and then to compare your answers with those set out on the pages which follow. Please examine carefully the profit and loss account and balance sheet set out below and then turn to the following page to begin the analysis.

PRECISION LOCKS LIMITED
Profit and loss account
for the year ended 30 June 1972

		£
Sales		100 000
Cost of sales		70 000
Gross profit		30 000
Selling and administrative expenses	20 000	
Interest payable	1 000	
		21 000
Net profit before tax		9 000
Taxation		3 000
Profit after tax		6 000
Ordinary dividend (10%)		3 000
Retained profit for the year		3 000
Add: Retained profit from previous years		7 000
		£10 000

PRECISION LOCKS LIMITED
Balance sheet at 30 June 1972

		£
Share capital		
30 000 ordinary £1 shares		30 000
Reserves		
Profit and loss account		10 000
Shareholders' funds		40 000
Loan at 10%		10 000
Capital employed		£50 000
Fixed assets		
Factory and machinery at cost		30 000
Less: Accumulated depreciation		10 000
		20 000
Current assets		
Stock	30 000	
Debtors	15 000	
Cash	5 000	
	50 000	
Less: **Current liabilities**	20 000	
Net current assets		30 000
Net assets		£50 000

INVESTMENT MEASURES

Please look at the 1972 accounts of Precision Locks Limited (set out opposite) and calculate the following ratios:

(a) *Return on ordinary shareholders' funds* (*return on equity*)

$$\frac{\text{Profit attributable to ordinary shareholders}}{\text{Ordinary shareholders' funds (owners' equity)}} \quad = \quad \underline{\hspace{2cm}} \quad = \quad \underline{\hspace{1.5cm}} \%$$

$$\text{or} \quad \frac{\text{Profit after loan interest and tax}}{\text{Ordinary share capital and reserves}}$$

(b) *Earnings per share* (EPS)

$$\frac{\text{Earnings attributable to ordinary shareholders}}{\text{Number of ordinary shares in issue}} \quad = \quad \pounds \underline{\hspace{2cm}} \quad = \quad \underline{\hspace{1.5cm}} \text{p.}$$

(c) *Price/earnings ratio* (P/E ratio)

$$\frac{\text{Market price per ordinary share (pence)}}{\text{Earnings per (ordinary) share (pence)}} \quad = \quad \frac{200}{\underline{\hspace{1.5cm}}} \quad = \quad$$

(d) *Dividend yield*

$$\frac{\text{Dividend per share (pence)}}{\text{Market price per share (pence)}} \quad = \quad \underline{\hspace{2cm}} \quad = \quad \underline{\hspace{1.5cm}} \%$$

(e) *Dividend cover*

$$\frac{\text{Earnings per share (pence)}}{\text{Dividends per share (pence)}} \quad = \quad \underline{\hspace{2cm}} \quad = \quad \underline{\hspace{1.5cm}} \text{times}$$

When you have completed the calculations please check your answers against those on the following page.

(a) *Return on ordinary shareholders' funds* (*return on equity*)

$$\frac{\text{Profit after loan interest and tax}}{\text{Ordinary share capital and reserves}} = \frac{£6000}{£30\,000 + £10\,000} = 15\%$$

Notes

1 This important measure relates profit after tax for the year to the ordinary shareholders' funds.
2 Both the amount of the return on investment and the changes in it from year to year are significant items of information.

(b) *Earnings per share*

$$\frac{\text{Earnings attributable to ordinary shareholders}}{\text{Number of ordinary shares in issue}} = \frac{£6\,000}{£30\,000} = 20\text{p}$$

Notes

1 The earnings per share (EPS) figure is widely used, especially in measuring changes from year to year.
2 The earnings (profits) used in the calculation is the same figure as that used in calculating return on equity.
3 The number of shares used in the calculation is the number *issued*, not the number authorised.
4 If any more shares have been issued during the period concerned, a weighted average should be used.

(c) *Price/earnings ratio*

$$\frac{\text{Market price per ordinary share (pence)}}{\text{Earnings per (ordinary) share (pence)}} = \frac{200}{20} = 10$$

Notes

1 "Per share" figures refer to *ordinary* shares unless otherwise stated.
2 This ratio is widely used for quoted shares. Although called the price/earnings (P/E) "ratio," it is expressed simply as a multiple. Precision Locks Limited "has a P/E ratio of 10."
3 The market price of the ordinary shares (a figure which does not appear in the published accounts) takes account of expected *future* profits of a business, whereas the return on investment calculations are based on reported *past* profits.
4 If a company makes a loss, earnings per share in that period is a *negative*

figure. But the shares will still have a positive value in the stock market, so that the price/earnings ratio itself is then negative. And if a company has only just broken even, with earnings per share of, say, only 5p a market price of £4 gives a price/earnings ratio of 80. So caution is needed in interpreting what price/earnings ratios mean.

(d) *Dividend yield*

$$\frac{\text{Dividend per share (pence)}}{\text{Market price per share (pence)}} = \frac{10}{200} = 5\%$$

Notes

1 This measure deals only with the portion of earnings *distributed*.
2 This measure indicates the current income yield provided for an investor in relation to the *present* market value of the shares. This is unlikely to be the same as the amount which he *paid* for his shares (that is the market value at the date of acquisition).

(e) *Dividend cover*

$$\frac{\text{Earnings per share (pence)}}{\text{Dividends per share (pence)}} = \frac{20}{10} = 2 \text{ times}$$

Notes

1 This measure indicates the number of times which the dividend could have been paid from earnings. The higher the cover, the "safer" the dividend.
2 The ratio is sometimes expressed the other way round, as the dividend payout ratio:

$$\frac{\text{Dividends per share}}{\text{Earnings per share}} = \frac{10\text{p}}{20\text{p}} = 50\%$$

Both the dividend yield and the dividend cover affect the price of a company's shares in the market. As a rule investors expect some dividend income each year. However, if a company can show a good record of utilising retained earnings to generate further growth, investors may be prepared to accept a low or even zero yield, and the share price will tend to rise to reflect the rate of internally-financed growth. Shareholders' returns come from dividends *plus* capital gains. Capital gains bear a lower rate of tax than dividends, but are further away in time.

MEASURES OF PERFORMANCE

Using the figures in the accounts on p. 26, please calculate the following ratios:

(*f*) *Return on net assets*

$$\frac{\text{Profit before tax and interest on long-term loans}}{\text{Net assets}} = \text{———} = \quad \%$$

(*g*) *Profit margin*

$$\frac{\text{Profit (before interest and tax)}}{\text{Sales}} = \text{———} = \quad \%$$

(*h*) *Asset turnover*

$$\frac{\text{Sales}}{\text{Net assets}} = \text{———} = \quad \text{times}$$

When you have completed these calculations, please turn to page 30.

(f) *Return on net assets*

$$\frac{\text{Profit before interest and tax}}{\text{Net assets}} = \frac{£10\,000}{£50\,000} = 20\%$$

Notes

1 This measure of performance ignores both tax and the company's method of long-term financing. All the net assets, representing *total* long-term capital employed, are taken rather than just the funds provided by the ordinary shareholders (the "equity" funds).

2 The return on net assets ratio has wider application than the return on ordinary shareholders' funds, and can be used also to measure the performance of divisions within a company.

(g) *Profit margin*

$$\frac{\text{Profit before interest and tax}}{\text{Sales}} = \frac{£10\,000}{£100\,000} = 10\%$$

1 A different "profit margin" often calculated in addition to the above is the "gross profit margin", that is gross profit/sales. The figures needed for this ratio, however, are usually available only when the analyst has access to records within a company.

(h) *Asset turnover*

$$\frac{\text{Sales}}{\text{Net assets}} = \frac{£100\,000}{£50\,000} = 2 \text{ times}$$

1 This ratio is less familiar than the previous one. It represents the number of times that capital "turns over" in a year. Expressing this another way, it represents the number of £s worth of sales generated in a year by each £ of investment.

Return on net assets = Profit margin × Asset turnover
It will be seen, using Precision Locks Limited's figures, that:

Return on net assets	=	Profit margin	×	Asset turnover
$\dfrac{\text{Profit}}{\text{Net assets}}$	=	$\dfrac{\text{Profit}}{\text{Sales}}$	×	$\dfrac{\text{Sales}}{\text{Net assets}}$
20%	=	10%	×	2

This is a significant breakdown of the return on net assets ratio. It is useful not only in appraising a company's past results, but also in providing a framework within which plans to increase the return on investment can be built. It illustrates clearly the need for management to be concerned with the *use of assets* as well as with improving profit margins on sales.

Rates of asset turnover and profit margins vary significantly from industry to industry. A merchandising company will normally expect a high turnover and a relatively low profit margin, while a manufacturing business with a relatively heavy investment in plant and equipment will expect a lower turnover rate and a higher profit margin.

It may be helpful to look in overall terms at what the concept "return on net assets" really means. We can do this by thinking how a company could *increase* its return on net assets. This is shown in the diagram opposite.

It is obvious that the ratio can be increased (in this case an increase is clearly an improvement) either by increasing the profit (the "return") or by reducing the net assets employed, for each £ of sales.

How can the return (that is the profit before tax and before charging interest on capital) be increased? Either by increasing the revenue from sales of goods or services, or by reducing expenses (other than tax on profits, since the ratio refers to *before* tax profits).

In this book we shall not analyse further how sales revenues can be increased or expenses reduced. It is clear that advertising, packaging, product design, market research, etc. may help to increase sales; and that industrial relations, engineering, operations research, purchasing economies, etc. may help to reduce expenses. This indicates what nobody would deny, that while accounting is very important to enable businessmen and others to evaluate business performance (both past *and* future), many other business skills are combined in order to make a profit.

Similarly, reducing net assets employed per £ of sales can be divided between reducing fixed assets and reducing working capital.

Fixed assets per £ of sales can be reduced in various ways, by greater utilisation, by good maintenance enabling replacements to be delayed, by skilful purchasing, perhaps by selling and leasing back. Reducing working capital per £ of sales may mean either reducing current assets—stock, debtors, and cash—or *increasing* current liabilities—creditors, taxation, and bank overdrafts.

Some of the ratios that we shall discuss later focus on particular assets in order to assess whether there may be room for improvement in their use. The essence of a commercial outlook is that one is not merely looking for *technical* efficiency (for example a "better" machine), but for *economic* efficiency (for example a "better" machine that is *worth the extra cost*).

Increasing Return on
Net Assets

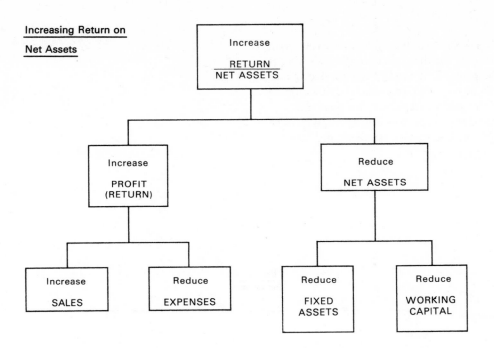

Increase

RETURN
NET ASSETS

Increase

PROFIT
(RETURN)

Reduce

NET ASSETS

Increase

SALES

Reduce

EXPENSES

Reduce

FIXED
ASSETS

Reduce

WORKING
CAPITAL

31

Pyramid of ratios

When internal figures are available it is possible to break down the return on net assets ratio to form a *pyramid of ratios*, as the diagram below shows. This is a simplified pyramid. It would clearly be possible to break the figures down to even finer degrees of analysis should this be required. In particular, it would be useful to analyse the ratios for each of the main categories of a business.

It can also be helpful, using the pyramid structure, to show an analysis over time. This might cover the actual results of, say, three past years and also the planned results for a number of future years.

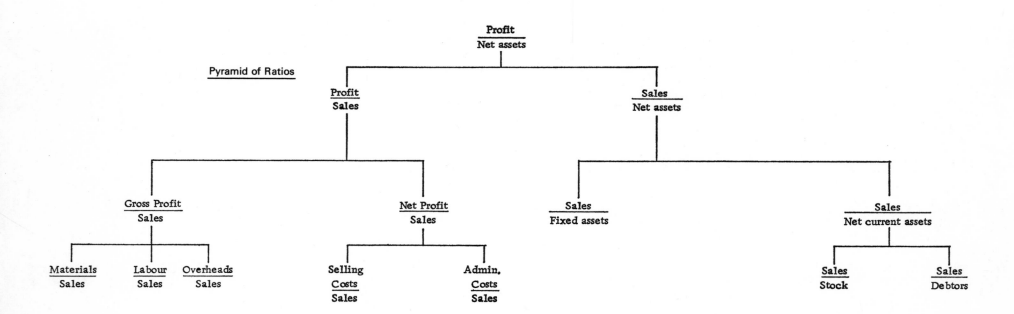

MEASURES OF FINANCIAL STATUS

Measures of financial status measure a company's ability to meet its liabilities.
They can be divided between:
1 *Solvency* ratios, dealing with long-term liabilities
2 *Liquidity* ratios, dealing with short-term liabilities
A further useful ratio not directly related to performance is the tax ratio.

You are asked to calculate the following ratios for Precision Locks Limited, using the figures shown in the 1972 accounts (shown on page 26).

Measures of solvency

(*i*) *Debt ratio*

$$\frac{\text{Long-term loan ("debt")}}{\text{Capital employed}} \qquad = \quad \text{————} \quad = \qquad \%$$

(*j*) *Interest cover*

$$\frac{\text{Earnings before interest and tax ("EBIT")}}{\text{Loan interest}} \qquad = \quad \text{————} \quad = \qquad \text{times}$$

Measures of liquidity

(*k*) *Current ratio*

$$\frac{\text{Current assets}}{\text{Current liabilities}} \qquad = \quad \text{————} \quad = \qquad \text{times}$$

(*l*) *Acid test*

$$\frac{\text{Liquid assets (current assets less stock)}}{\text{Current liabilities}} \qquad = \quad \text{————} \quad = \qquad \text{times}$$

Tax ratio

(*m*) *Tax ratio*

$$\frac{\text{Taxation}}{\text{Profit before tax}} \qquad = \quad \text{————} \quad = \qquad \%$$

Measures of solvency

(i) *Debt ratio*

$$\frac{\text{Long-term loan ("debt")}}{\text{Capital employed}} = \frac{\pounds 10\,000}{\pounds 50\,000} = 20\%$$

Note

1 Debt is 20 per cent of the total capital employed, therefore equity is the other 80 per cent. This relatively low debt ratio gives the lender a fairly high level of safety. The company would have to lose 80 per cent of the book value of its net assets before it became unable to repay the liability represented by the loan. (This 80 per cent is sometimes referred to as the "equity cushion.")

(j) *Interest cover*

$$\frac{\text{Earnings before interest and tax}}{\text{Loan interest}} = \frac{\pounds 10\,000}{\pounds 1\,000} = 10 \text{ times}$$

Note

1 Earnings before interest and tax (EBIT) is related to gross (before-tax) loan interest payable, to show the relative safety of loan *interest* cover in the same way that the debt ratio measures the loan *capital* cover.

These two ratios will be considered later from another aspect in section 6 which deals with capital structure and gearing.

Measures of liquidity

(k) *Current ratio*

$$\frac{\text{Current assets}}{\text{Current liabilities}} = \frac{\pounds 50\,000}{\pounds 20\,000} = 2.5 \text{ times}$$

Note

1 This important ratio indicates to what extent short-term assets are adequate to meet short-term liabilities. Should the ratio show that current liabilities are less than fully covered by current assets, it would indicate a situation deserving attention and perhaps close interest in the acid test ratio below—with the possibility that a rather serious financial position was developing.

(l) *Acid test*

$$\frac{\text{Liquid assets (current assets less stock)}}{\text{Current liabilities}} = \frac{\pounds 20\,000}{\pounds 20\,000} = 1.0 \text{ times}$$

Notes

1 This is the strictest test of liquidity for a company. It excludes the stock figure in calculating the short-term resources available to meet short-term liabilities, on the ground that stock may take several months to turn into cash.

2 Not all current liabilities are necessarily payable within a few months: current taxation, for example, may not be payable for up to twelve months. So it is not unusual for the resulting ratio to be *less* than one; but in that case particular care must be taken in short-term cash planning to ensure that funds are available to meet short-term liabilities as they become due.

Tax ratio

(m) *Tax ratio*

$$\frac{\text{Taxation}}{\text{Profit before tax}} = \frac{\pounds 3000}{\pounds 9000} = 33.3\%$$

Note

1 This ratio is not necessarily equal to the current rate of tax on company profits, for reasons explained in section 5.

SUMMARY OF RATIOS COVERED

We have now examined the most generally used investment measures, measures of performance and measures of financial status, and applied them to the 1972 accounts of Precision Locks Limited. In summary, we have calculated:

Investment measures

(a)	Return on equity	Profit after tax/shareholders' funds
(b)	Earnings per share	Profit after tax/number of shares issued
(c)	Price/earnings ratio	Market price per share/earnings per share
(d)	Dividend yield	Dividend per share/market price per share
(e)	Dividend cover	Earnings per share/dividend per share

Measures of performance

(f)	Return on net assets	Earnings before interest and tax/net assets
(g)	Profit margin	Earnings before interest and tax/sales
(h)	Asset turnover	Sales/net assets

Measures of financial status

Solvency

(i)	Debt ratio	Long-term debt/capital employed
(j)	Interest cover	Earnings before interest and tax/interest

Liquidity

(k)	Current ratio	Current assets/current liabilities
(l)	Acid test	Liquid assets/current liabilities
(m)	Tax ratio	Taxation/profit before tax

STANDARDS FOR ANALYSIS

The calculation of the ratios and other statistics which we have examined in this section forms an essential part of the process of financial analysis but individual figures for a single financial period are not particularly helpful. For the results of analysis to be of use, a comparison has to be made—either with figures for previous periods which would give an indication of trends in the results, or with plans which would show the extent to which desired objectives are being met. Another possibility is to compare the results of one company with those of another or with the results typically achieved by other companies in the same industry.

(a) Last year's results

Assuming that consistent accounting practices have been followed, the results of the previous period should permit a fair comparison (subject to changed conditions). The problem is to assess whether an improvement from last year's performance is still a bad result (or whether a worse result than last year's may still be exceptionally good). The advantage of using past periods' figures is that a comparable trend over a number of years is usually possible, and the figures are available to external analysts.

(b) Internal company budgets

Budgets usually show the performance expected and planned, and actual performance closely corresponding with budget may therefore be thought adequate. The more care spent in preparing budgets, the more they can be relied on as standards, though it may be necessary to allow for changing conditions since the budgets were prepared. A company's own budgets are not normally available to external analysts.

(c) Results of other companies in the industry

Differing accounting practices may make comparisons with other companies difficult, even where sufficiently detailed figures are available. And variations in business policies may also obscure fair comparisons. On the other hand, where these problems are not too serious, inter-company comparisons do at least provide an external standard against which to judge a particular company's results.

(d) Industry averages

Average ratios for groups of companies in the same industry can be useful as a standard, though some of the same difficulties apply as with inter-company comparisons. Since industry averages may be composed of all sizes of companies it may be desirable to break down the averages into separate data for small, medium, and large companies. It may also be desirable to exclude the results of some very poor companies which set far too low a standard.

A more general problem is that the term "industry" is by no means as clear cut as is often imagined. Every business is unique, and although many enterprises have certain features more or less in common with others, there is a perpetual overlapping between so-called "industries" which can make collective statistics somewhat arbitrary. The modern trend towards diversification, for example, can make it hard to decide to which industry a particular company belongs.

PRECISION LOCKS LIMITED
Profit and loss account for the year ending 30 June 1973

1972 £			1973 £
100 000	Sales		120 000
70 000	Cost of sales		80 000
30 000	Gross profit		40 000
20 000	Selling and administrative costs	25 000	
1 000	Interest	1 000	
21 000			26 000
9 000	Net profit before tax		14 000
3 000	Taxation		6 000
6 000	Profit after tax		8 000
3 000	Ordinary dividend 10%		3 000
£3 000	Retained profit		£5 000

Market price per ordinary share	
30 June 1972	£2
30 June 1973	£3

COMPARING ONE YEAR WITH ANOTHER

The profit and loss account and balance sheet of Precision Locks Limited for the year ending 30 June 1973 are set out above. Comparative figures for 1972 which you have already used for analysis in this section are also given. You are asked to calculate various measures relating to investment, performance, and financial status which we have studied and to compare the 1973 results with those for 1972. Space is provided for you to summarise the results of your analysis and to note down the major points which occur to you in looking at the figures. On the next page following that provided for your summary, suggested answers are given. Please work through this analysis carefully, checking at each stage that you are clear which figures should be used and why you are calculating each ratio.

PRECISION LOCKS LIMITED
Balance sheet, 30 June 1973

1972 £			1973 £
	Share capital		
30 000	30 000 ordinary £1 shares		30 000
	Reserves		
10 000	Profit and loss account		15 000
40 000	*Shareholders' funds*		45 000
10 000	**Loan** at 10%		10 000
£50 000	*Capital employed*		£55 000
	Fixed assets		
30 000	Factory and machinery at cost		38 000
10 000	*Less:* Depreciation		17 000
20 000			21 000
	Current assets		
30 000	Stock	35 000	
15 000	Debtors	20 000	
5 000	Cash	4 000	
50 000		59 000	
20 000	*Less:* **Current liabilities**	25 000	
30 000	Net current assets		34 000
£50 000	*Net assets*		£55 000

PRECISION LOCKS LIMITED: ANALYSIS OF RESULTS FOR THE YEAR ENDING 30 JUNE 1973

Investment measures

		1973	1972

(a) *Return on ordinary shareholders' funds* (*return on equity*)

$$\frac{\text{Profit after loan interest and tax}}{\text{Ordinary shareholders' funds}} = \quad \% \qquad = 15\%$$

(b) *Earnings per share*

$$\frac{\text{Earnings attributable to ordinary shareholders}}{\text{Number of ordinary shares in issue}} = \quad \text{p} \qquad = 20\text{p}$$

(c) *Price/earnings ratio*

$$\frac{\text{Market price per share}}{\text{Earnings per share}} = \qquad = 10$$

(d) *Dividend yield*

$$\frac{\text{Dividend per share}}{\text{Market value per share}} = \quad \% \qquad = 5\%$$

(e) *Dividend cover*

$$\frac{\text{Earnings per share}}{\text{Dividends per share}} = \quad \text{times} \qquad = 2 \text{ times}$$

Measures of performance

(f) *Return on net assets*

$$\frac{\text{Profit before loan interest and tax}}{\text{Net assets}} = \quad \% \qquad = 20\%$$

(g) *Profit margin*

$$\frac{\text{Profit}}{\text{Sales}} = \quad \% \qquad = 10\%$$

(h) *Asset turnover*

$$\frac{\text{Sales}}{\text{Net assets}} = \quad \text{times} \qquad = 2 \text{ times}$$

More detailed ratios (see the pyramid of ratios, page 32)

	1973		1972
(n) *Stock turnover*			
$\dfrac{\text{Sales}}{\text{Stock}}$	———— =	times	= 3.3 times
(o) *Debtor turnover*			
$\dfrac{\text{Sales}}{\text{Debtors}}$	———— =	times	= 6.7 times
(p) *Gross profit* (%)			
$\dfrac{\text{Gross profit}}{\text{Sales}}$	———— =	%	= 30%
(q) *Selling and administrative costs/sales* (%)			
$\dfrac{\text{Selling and administrative costs}}{\text{Sales}}$	———— =	%	= 20%

Measures of financial status

Solvency

(i) *Debt/capital employed* (%)			
$\dfrac{\text{Long-term loan}}{\text{Capital employed}}$	———— =	%	= 20.0%
(j) *Interest cover*			
$\dfrac{\text{Earnings before interest and tax}}{\text{Loan interest}}$	———— =	times	= 10.0 times

Liquidity

(k) *Current ratio*			
$\dfrac{\text{Current assets}}{\text{Current liabilities}}$	———— =	times	= 2.5 times
(l) *Acid test*			
$\dfrac{\text{Liquid assets}}{\text{Current liabilities}}$	———— =	times	= 1.0 times
(m) *Tax ratio*			
$\dfrac{\text{Taxation}}{\text{Profit before tax}}$	———— =	%	= 33.3%

SUMMARY OF RESULTS

	1973	1972
Investment		
(*a*) Return on equity (%)		15%
(*b*) Earnings per share		20p
(*c*) Price/earnings ratio		10
(*d*) Dividend yield (%)		5%
(*e*) Dividend cover (times)		2
Performance		
(*f*) Return on net assets (%)		20%
(*g*) Profit margin (%)		10%
(*h*) Asset turnover (times)		2
(*n*) Stock turnover (times)		3.3
(*o*) Debtor turnover (times)		6.7
(*p*) Gross profit (%)		30%
(*q*) Selling, etc. cost/sales (%)		20%
Financial status		
Solvency		
(*i*) Debt/capital employed (%)		20%
(*j*) Interest cover (times)		10
Liquidity		
(*k*) Current ratio (times)		2.5
(*l*) Acid test (times)		1.0
(*m*) Tax ratio (%)		33.3%

You are asked to enter the figures which you have calculated in the "1973" column and then to summarise briefly the major comments which you think should be made in appraising the 1973 performance and financial position as a whole in comparison with the results for the previous year.

When you have completed your appraisal please turn to the next page where a suggested answer is shown.

COMMENTS ON 1973 RESULTS

SUMMARY OF RESULTS

	1973	1972
Investment		
(*a*) Return on equity (%)	17.8%	15%
(*b*) Earnings per share	27p	20p
(*c*) Price/earnings ratio	11.1	10
(*d*) Dividend yield (%)	3.3%	5%
(*e*) Dividend cover (times)	2.7	2
Performance		
(*f*) Return on net assets (%)	27.3%	20%
(*g*) Profit margin (%)	12.5%	10%
(*h*) Asset turnover (times)	2.2	2
(*n*) Stock turnover (times)	3.4	3.3
(*o*) Debtor turnover (times)	6.0	6.7
(*p*) Gross profit (%)	33.3%	30%
(*q*) Selling, etc. costs/sales (%)	20.8%	20%
Financial status		
Solvency		
(*i*) Debt/capital employed (%)	18.2%	20%
(*j*) Interest cover (times)	15	10
Liquidity		
(*k*) Current ratio (times)	2.36	2.5
(*l*) Acid test (times)	0.96	1.0
(*m*) Tax ratio	42.9%	33.3%

Details showing how the above 1973 figures (*a* to *m*) have been calculated are shown opposite. Calculation and notes on the four new ratios (*n* to *q*) are shown on page 42.

COMMENTS ON 1973 RESULTS

1   1973 performance is better than 1972's with return on equity and return on net assets both up.

2   Sales revenue increased by 20 per cent and the profit margin increased from 10.0 to 12.5 per cent, producing a 50 per cent increase in profit before interest.

3   The tax charge in 1973 was twice that in 1972, producing a relatively lower rate of increase in profit after tax (33 per cent) than in profit before interest and tax (50 per cent).

4   The ordinary dividend was maintained, so the dividend cover and retained profits both increased.

5   The price/earnings ratio has moved from 10.0 to 11.1 (which still seems on the low side, considering the rate of return on equity of 17.8 per cent). But general market trends will have affected the share price, as well as Precision Locks Limited's own results. Perhaps the market would appreciate a higher dividend.

6   Stocks again seem rather high relative to sales volume (and even higher relative to cost of goods sold). But in suggesting a "correct" stock level one would need to know more about the nature of the company's business.

7   The average credit period allowed to debtors has increased from 54 to 61 days. Combined with a higher sales volume, this has meant a 33 per cent increase in debtors.

8   As trading activity grows the company will need more funds. With the acid test ratio just below 1.0, the cash position will have to be watched carefully.

PRECISION LOCKS LIMITED: DETAILS OF 1973 RATIOS

Investment	(a) Return on equity:	$\dfrac{\text{Profit after interest and tax}}{\text{Ordinary shareholders' funds}}$	=	$\dfrac{8\,000}{45\,000}$	= 17.8%
	(b) Earnings per share:	$\dfrac{\text{Earnings for ordinary shares}}{\text{Number of shares issued}}$	=	$\dfrac{8\,000}{30\,000}$	= 27p
	(c) Price/earnings ratio:	$\dfrac{\text{Market price per share}}{\text{Earnings per share}}$	=	$\dfrac{300}{27}$	= 11.1
	(d) Dividend yield:	$\dfrac{\text{Dividend per share}}{\text{Market price per share}}$	=	$\dfrac{10}{300}$	= 3.3%
	(e) Dividend cover:	$\dfrac{\text{Earnings per share}}{\text{Dividend per share}}$	=	$\dfrac{27}{10}$	= 2.7 times
Performance	(f) Return on net assets:	$\dfrac{\text{Profit before interest and tax}}{\text{Net assets}}$	=	$\dfrac{15\,000}{55\,000}$	= 27.3%
	(g) Profit margin:	$\dfrac{\text{Profit}}{\text{Sales}}$	=	$\dfrac{15\,000}{120\,000}$	= 12.5%
	(h) Asset turnover:	$\dfrac{\text{Sales}}{\text{Net assets}}$	=	$\dfrac{120\,000}{55\,000}$	= 2.2 times
Financial status	(i) Debt ratio:	$\dfrac{\text{Long-term debt}}{\text{Capital employed}}$	=	$\dfrac{10\,000}{55\,000}$	= 18.2%
	(j) Interest cover:	$\dfrac{\text{Earnings before interest and tax}}{\text{Loan interest}}$	=	$\dfrac{15\,000}{1\,000}$	= 15 times
	(k) Current ratio:	$\dfrac{\text{Current assets}}{\text{Current liabilities}}$	=	$\dfrac{59\,000}{25\,000}$	= 2.36 times
	(l) Acid test:	$\dfrac{\text{Liquid assets}}{\text{Current liabilities}}$	=	$\dfrac{24\,000}{25\,000}$	= 0.96 times
	(m) Tax ratio:	$\dfrac{\text{Taxation}}{\text{Profit before tax}}$	=	$\dfrac{6\,000}{14\,000}$	= 42.9%

Four new performance ratios

			1972	1973
(n) Stock turnover	$\dfrac{\text{Sales}}{\text{Stock}}$		$\dfrac{100\,000}{30\,000} = 3.3$ times	$\dfrac{120\,000}{35\,000} = 3.4$ times

Notes

1 This ratio indicates how quickly goods move through the business. Usually, the quicker the better, though a high turnover may indicate shortages. An increase in the size of stock may reflect additional stocks required for expanding future sales, or alternatively an accumulation of stock as a result of falling sales. In controlling stocks, forecasting future sales plays a vital role.

2 Since closing stock is not necessarily the same as average stock during the year, the above ratio may not reflect the true rate of turnover during the year. Moreover, if there are significant seasonal variations in stock levels, averaging the opening and closing year-end stocks will clearly not produce an "average" stock level *during* the year (for which monthly stock levels would be needed).

3 Ideally stock turnover should be calculated by comparing stock to cost of goods sold. Since the cost of goods sold figure is normally not published, however, the external analyst has to use the sales figure. Although the resulting ratio is less useful than one would like, trends over time may still indicate changes in stock turnover rates.

		1972	1973
(o) Debtor turnover	$\dfrac{\text{Sales}}{\text{Debtors}}$	$\dfrac{100\,000}{15\,000} = 6.7$ times	$\dfrac{120\,000}{20\,000} = 6.0$ times

Notes

1 Where firms sell both for cash and for credit, only credit sales should be used for this ratio. If no split is possible, any calculation based on the assumption that all sales are made on credit may need to be treated with considerable caution.

2 Some analysts prefer to use the reciprocal of the above ratio, and to multiply by 365 to give the number of days' sales represented by debtors.

Thus $20/120 \times 365 = 61$ days.

		1972	1973
(p) Gross profit (%)	$\dfrac{\text{Gross profit}}{\text{Sales}}$	$\dfrac{30\,000}{100\,000} = 30.0\%$	$\dfrac{40\,000}{120\,000} = 33.3\%$
(q) Selling and administrative costs (%)	$\dfrac{\text{Selling and administrative costs}}{\text{Sales}}$	$\dfrac{20\,000}{100\,000} = 20.0\%$	$\dfrac{25\,000}{120\,000} = 20.8\%$

MARKS AND SPENCER LIMITED'S ACCOUNTS

A good example of published financial statements which are relatively simple in form is given by Marks and Spencer Limited's accounts. A copy of the accounts for the year ending 31 March 1972, has been included later in this section. If you feel at this stage that it would be helpful to gain more practice in calculating ratios and analysing company accounts please turn to the statements now, and analyse the results for 1971 and 1972. You will be able to compare the company's performance in each of the two years and the changes in the financial position between 31 March 1971, and 31 March 1972.

FUNDS STATEMENTS

In appraising the Marks and Spencer accounts you may wish to extend your analysis by drawing up a simple sources and uses of funds statement. This form of financial analysis, as its name suggests, seeks to show the major changes during an accounting period in the funds which a company controls and the uses which it has made of them. We shall look in more detail at funds statements in section 8.

A simple form of funds statement for Precision Locks Limited for the year ending 30 June 1973 is set out opposite. The way in which the figures have been derived by comparing the opening and closing balance sheets is also shown. The analysis shows that the company is financing its growth by the use of retained earnings and by extended trade credit. The analysis tends to emphasise the short-term financial pressures which the company is beginning to meet.

PRECISION LOCKS LIMITED
year ending 30 June 1973

Balance sheet changes during the year

	1973 £	1972 £	Difference £
30 000 Ordinary shares	30 000	30 000	—
Reserves: Profit and loss account	15 000	10 000	+5000
Loan	10 000	10 000	—
	£55 000	£50 000	£+5000
Factory and machinery less depreciation	21 000	20 000	+1000
Stock	35 000	30 000	+5000
Debtors	20 000	15 000	+5000
Cash	4 000	5 000	−1000
Less: Creditors	(25 000)	(20 000)	−5000
	£55 000	£50 000	£+5000

Sources and uses of funds statement

Sources of funds £

	£
Retained earnings	5 000
Increase in creditors	5 000
Reduction in cash	1 000
	£11 000

Uses of funds

	£
Increase in fixed assets	1 000
Increase in stock	5 000
Increase in debtors	5 000
	£11 000

THE NEED FOR CAUTION IN ANALYSING ACCOUNTS

So far we have compared one year's results with the previous year's for a particular company. This form of comparison can yield useful results both for external analysts and for managers within a company. It assumes that the two years' figures have been compiled on a consistent basis (you will remember that the idea of consistency is fundamental in preparing accounting statements).

It is a legal requirement to disclose any change in the basis of accounting which might materially impair a consistent presentation, and to adjust the comparative figures as well as the current year's where the accounting treatment has changed. So it may seem reasonable to believe that one can rely on comparisons of one year's accounts with another's. Several assumptions underlying this belief, however, may prove difficult to support.

It might be assumed, for example, that if two periods' accounts show the same totals for particular items such as stock or debtors, the financial meaning of each item must be identical. But this need not be so. The totals appearing in financial statements usually summarise a whole series of transactions or amalgamate separate asset and liability balances, the nature and mixture of which can vary significantly from one period to another. Nor can one assume (as will be seen when we look more closely at the complex problem of income measurement) that accounting measures of performance are exact or that the same transactions would lead inevitably to the same financial result no matter when they occurred or by whom they were measured.

In comparing accounts for periods less than a year, one may need to pay special attention to seasonal factors, which may make direct comparison of one period with another somewhat difficult. And even with annual accounts, the date of the balance sheet may not be typical so that, for example, the liquidity position may seem unusually good if the balance sheet date occurs just after a very heavy selling period when stocks are particularly low.

In comparisons over time within a company, it is often easy to see whether there has been an improvement or not compared with earlier periods; but it can be hard to judge whether those earlier periods' results themselves represent an adequate level of performance. And one must not ignore the possibility that business conditions have changed significantly.

COMPARING THE RESULTS OF DIFFERENT COMPANIES

If problems of this kind arise in comparing the results of one period with another for a single company, even greater caution is needed when the results of different companies are compared. A wide range of accounting conventions is used in presenting accounts and calculating profits, and it would be rash to assume that all items in two separate companies' accounts have been dealt with in the same way. Before any useful comparisons can be made, some at least of the figures may have to be adjusted to bring the accounts on to a common basis. The analyst may lack the necessary detailed figures to make such adjustments, and even if he has enough information, great care is needed if the adjusted comparative figures are not to be misleading.

It is crucially important that people who use accounting figures appreciate what accounts really mean. They need to understand how transactions are recorded and incorporated into accounting statements and to be aware of the various possible ways in which profit can be measured and assets valued. Sections 3 to 7 are designed to give such understanding, and the reader is urged to work through them bearing in mind the implications of the matters discussed in relation to everyday financial statements, both internal and external.

To introduce the issues dealt with in the later sections, and to illustrate how misleading accounting figures can be if used unthinkingly, a comparison is made below between two companies—Brown Limited and Green Limited—which conduct similar businesses. To make the comparison as uncomplicated as possible, and to highlight the results of more detailed analysis, let us start by assuming that the accounts of the two companies to 30 June 1972 looked identical on the surface. We shall then discover that the figures shown on the face of the accounts need not reflect the same underlying reality, and see how opinion significantly affects the reported profit and many of the balance sheet items.

BROWN LIMITED AND GREEN LIMITED
Profit and loss account for the year ending 30 June 1972

	£
Sales	100 000
Cost of sales	60 000
Gross profit	40 000
Selling and administration costs	20 000
Net profit before tax	20 000
Tax	10 000
Profit after tax	£10 000

BROWN LIMITED AND GREEN LIMITED
Balance sheet, 30 June 1972

		£
Share capital		30 000
Reserve: Profit and loss account		20 000
		£50 000
Freehold factory at cost		15 000
Plant and machinery:		
At cost	24 000	
Less: Depreciation	14 000	
		10 000
		25 000
Stock	25 000	
Debtors	18 000	
Cash	2 000	
	45 000	
Less: Creditors	20 000	
		25 000
		£50 000

Analysis
  Results for both companies:

Profit margin $\dfrac{20\ 000}{100\ 000} = 20\%$

Asset turnover $\dfrac{100\ 000}{50\ 000} = 2$

Return on net assets $\dfrac{20\ 000}{50\ 000} = 40\%$

Further information

1 *Cost of sales*

Both companies spent £9000 on developing new products in the year. Brown decided to carry forward as an asset £4000 spent on a particular project, on the ground that it would generate revenue in the following year, in which the £4000 would then be written off. In the current year Brown charges only £5000 in cost of sales. Green writes off all research and development expenditure in the year in which it is incurred, irrespective of which period will benefit.

2 *Freehold factory*

Brown's freehold factory was purchased in 1950 and is estimated (on expert valuation) to have a current market value of £30 000. The current market value of Green's factory, which was purchased in 1970, is about the same as the purchase price.

3 *Depreciation* (that is allowance for wear and tear)

Brown expects plant and machinery to last for 12 years and charges one-twelfth of the cost each year to the cost of sales. Green estimates the life of similar machinery to be 8 years, and writes off an eighth of the cost, charging £1000 a year more depreciation than Brown.

4 *Stock valuation*

Brown's policy is to write down stock which has not moved for 12 months to 50 per cent of cost. At 30 June 1972 stock which had originally cost £4000 is included at £2000. Green writes off the entire cost of stock which has not moved for a year, and has charged £4000 to cost of sales in the year in respect of such stock.

5 *Debtors*

Much of Brown's business is with a few large customers. One of them, Black Limited, is in financial trouble, and it seems unlikely that more than £4000 will be recovered of the £5000 which Black owed Brown at 30 June 1972. Brown has made no provision for the possible loss, believing (perhaps optimistically) that Black Limited will resolve its present troubles and pay the debt in full. Green trades with a large number of smaller customers, and has provided an amount equal to 2 per cent of debts outstanding at the year-end, whereas the average bad debt loss experienced over a number of years has been 1 per cent. The increased level of provision was thought to be necessary because Green felt (perhaps pessimistically) that the coming months might find a number of customers in financial difficulty.

Adjusted statements

Clearly the difference in the facts underlying the disclosed figures makes a comparison of the unadjusted figures fairly meaningless. The two companies are not achieving an equal level of performance, as the original ratio analysis seemed to suggest.

It is possible, in the light of the further information available, to adjust the accounts of the two companies to bring them on to the same basis, but choosing between one basis or another obviously means exercising judgement based on personal preference and subjective estimation of future risk. Who can tell for certain how long an asset will last, whether stock will be sold (and if so at what price) or whether an outstanding debt will be collected? Much depends on the individual balance sheet items which are summarised in the financial statements and the circumstances which surround them.

Adjusted profit and loss accounts for the year ended 30 June 1972

Original	£	BROWN LIMITED Adjusted	£	GREEN LIMITED Adjusted	£
Sales	100 000		100 000		100 000
Cost of sales	60 000	(+4000 Write off R & D +1000 Extra depreciation)	65 000	(−2000 Write off stock over 2 years)	58 000
Gross profit	40 000		35 000		42 000
Selling and administration costs	20 000	(+1000 Bad debt provision)	21 000		20 000
Net profit before tax	20 000		14 000		22 000
Tax (50%)	10 000		7 000		11 000
Profit after tax	£10 000		£7 000		£11 000

Adjusted balance sheets at 30 June 1972

Original	£	BROWN LIMITED Adjusted	£	GREEN LIMITED Adjusted	£
Share capital	30 000		30 000		30 000
Profit and loss account	20 000	(−3000)	17 000	(+1000)	21 000
		Revaluation of factory	15 000		
	£50 000		£62 000		£51 000
Freehold factory at cost	15 000	(+15 000 on revaluation)	30 000		15 000
Plant and machinery after depreciation	10 000	(−1000 extra)	9 000		10 000
	25 000		39 000		25 000
Stock	25 000	(−4000 R & D)	21 000	(+2000 slow-moving)	27 000
Debtors	18 000	(−1000 Provision)	17 000		18 000
Cash	2 000		2 000		2 000
	45 000		40 000		47 000
Less: Creditors	20 000	(−3000 tax)	17 000	(+1000 tax)	21 000
	25 000		23 000		26 000
	£50 000		£62 000		£51 000

BROWN LIMITED AND GREEN LIMITED: adjusted 1972 results

	Original		**BROWN LIMITED** **adjusted**		**GREEN LIMITED** **adjusted**	
Margin on sales	$\dfrac{20\ 000}{100\ 000}$ =	20.0%	$\dfrac{14\ 000}{100\ 000}$ =	14.0%	$\dfrac{22\ 000}{100\ 000}$ =	22.0%
Asset turnover	$\dfrac{100\ 000}{50\ 000}$ =	2.00	$\dfrac{100\ 000}{62\ 000}$ =	1.61	$\dfrac{100\ 000}{51\ 000}$ =	1.96
Return on net assets	$\dfrac{20\ 000}{50\ 000}$ =	40.0%	$\dfrac{14\ 000}{62\ 000}$ =	22.6%	$\dfrac{22\ 000}{51\ 000}$ =	43.1%

The above results show that the adjusted figures, especially Brown's, are very different from the original ones. Brown's margin on sales is reduced by one-third, asset turnover by one-fifth and return on net assets nearly halved. The comparison with Green, whose margin on sales and return on net assets have both slightly improved, shows significant differences now, although the original results based on the published financial statements were identical for the two companies.

This sort of more sophisticated analysis requires a knowledge of the way in which transactions affect the accounts, and involves a number of problems associated with measuring business income. We must look more closely at both these subjects in later sections.

BANK OVERDRAFTS

At this stage it becomes necessary to mention bank overdrafts. They represent negative cash balances, and are shown in balance sheets as current liabilities. Overdrafts are usually arranged "up to" a certain limit, but only the amount actually overdrawn—that is, borrowed, comes onto the accounts or bears interest.

In practice part of the year-end balance overdrawn often amounts to a semi-permanent loan, even though bank overdrafts are nearly always legally repayable on demand. In a recent credit squeeze many companies were surprised and distressed to find that their banks really *did* expect overdrafts to be repaid, or at least substantially reduced, almost on demand.

If any longer-term part of bank overdrafts can be identified it should be shown as a long-term liability, that is as part of capital employed. In calculating the net current assets figure in the balance sheet it is obviously significant whether a bank overdraft is a current liability or not, and depending on how it is treated both the liquidity and the solvency ratios will be affected, as will the return on net assets.

Suppose that in Precision Locks Limited's 1972 balance sheet (summarised opposite) a bank overdraft (assumed to carry 10 per cent interest) accounts for £15 000 of the £20 000 current liabilities. If the overdraft is classed as a long-term instead of as a current liability, the two solvency (long-term) ratios get worse, and the liquidity (short-term) ratios get better.

Some short-term funds employed by a company do not require interest payments, for example liabilities which arise when the company buys on credit. The same is true when sums are set aside to cover liabilities payable at some future date, such as taxation on profits and amounts payable under pension schemes. Generally these are regarded as "spontaneous" sources of funds, as opposed to "negotiated" sources like bank overdrafts. Spontaneous credit in total far exceeds the sum of short-term negotiated credit, but *availability* of bank credit is important to many firms which rarely or never borrow in fact. A business with good credit standing knows that it can borrow if unexpected needs develop, and can therefore undertake larger-scale and riskier operations than would otherwise be possible.

Summarised balance sheet

£15 000 bank overdraft shown as

		Current liability		Long-term liability
		£		£
Shareholder's funds		40 000		40 000
Long-term debt		10 000		25 000
Capital employed		£50 000		£65 000
Fixed assets, net		20 000		20 000
Current assets	50 000		50 000	
Less: Current liabilities	20 000		5 000	
Working capital		30 000		45 000
Net assets		£50 000		£65 000

Summarised profit and loss account

		£		£
Gross profit		30 000		30 000
Selling and administration*	20 000		18 500	
Interest payable on long-term debt	1 000		2 500	
		21 000		21 000
Profit before tax		£9 000		£9 000

*including interest on short-term borrowing

Effect on ratios

Debt ratio	$\dfrac{10\ 000}{50\ 000} = 20.0\%$	$\dfrac{25\ 000}{65\ 000} = 38.5\%$
Interest cover	$\dfrac{10\ 000}{1\ 000} = 10.0$	$\dfrac{11\ 500}{2\ 500} = 4.6$
Current ratio	$\dfrac{50\ 000}{20\ 000} = 2.5$	$\dfrac{50\ 000}{5\ 000} = 10.0$
Acid test	$\dfrac{20\ 000}{20\ 000} = 1.0$	$\dfrac{20\ 000}{5\ 000} = 4.0$
Return on net assets	$\dfrac{10\ 000}{50\ 000} = 20.0\%$	$\dfrac{11\ 500}{65\ 000} = 17.7\%$

SUMMARY

In this section we have considered three major approaches to analysing company accounts:

1 Investment measures

2 Measures of performance

3 Measures of financial status

These approaches help interpret different aspects of a company's affairs. Perhaps at this stage we should emphasise that *each* of these aspects is important. A continuing financial problem for most businesses is to balance liquidity against profitability. If managers of a business were not forced to worry about profitability, they might have a more comfortable time keeping plenty of cash on hand to tide them over any unexpected contingencies. On the other hand, when emphasis is placed only on improving profits there is a danger that the business may run out of liquid assets.

After analysing the 1972 accounts of Precision Locks Limited, we worked through the 1973 accounts, comparing the results of the two years, and preparing a simple funds statement showing the changes in the two year-end balance sheets.

We next discussed some of the reasons why caution is needed in analysing company accounts, and went on to consider the difficulties of comparing the financial results of two different companies. When we looked at apparently identical results for two different companies, we saw that closer investigation disclosed several important differences which were not at first apparent.

Finally we discussed the treatment of bank overdrafts, and saw that it can make a material difference whether they are treated as current liabilities (and hence as a deduction from working capital) or as longer-term liabilities (and hence as part of capital employed). Part of the problem here is the possible distinction between a liability that is *legally* payable "on demand" but which is *really* unlikely to be cleared within twelve months from the balance sheet date.

2.1 Definitions

Write down opposite in the spaces provided your definitions of the ratios set out. Then compare your definitions with those set out overleaf.

(a) Return on net assets

(b) Current ratio

(c) Earnings yield

(d) Acid test

(e) Price/earnings ratio

(f) Dividend yield

(g) Debt ratio

(h) Interest cover

(i) Return on equity

(j) Dividend cover

2.1 Definitions

(a) *Return on net assets*
Earnings before long-term interest and taxes (EBIT) divided by net assets (= capital employed).

(b) *Current ratio*
Current assets divided by current liabilities.

(c) *Earnings yield*
Earnings per share (EPS) divided by market price per share. (Reciprocal of price/earnings ratio.)

(d) *Acid test*
Liquid assets (current assets less stocks) divided by current liabilities.

(e) *Price/earnings ratio*
Market price per ordinary share divided by earnings per share. (Reciprocal of earnings yield.)

(f) *Dividend yield*
Dividend per share divided by market price per share.

(g) *Debt ratio*
Usually defined as long-term liabilities (debt) divided by capital employed (long-term liabilities plus shareholders' funds). Sometimes calculated by dividing long-term liabilities by shareholders' funds.

(h) *Interest cover*
Earnings before interest and taxes (EBIT) divided by interest payable on long-term debt.

(i) *Return on equity*
Profit available for ordinary shareholders divided by ordinary shareholders' funds ("equity interest").

(j) *Dividend cover*
Profits available for ordinary dividends in an accounting period divided by the ordinary dividends declared payable.

2.2 James Smith Limited

The accounts of James Smith Limited are set out below. As a first approach to analysis of the company's 1972 accounts you are asked to calculate the basic ratios set out opposite.

Please write out the description of the relevant items from the accounts, as well as the amounts (as shown in the first ratio, for which an answer has been provided). When you have calculated all the ratios, please check with the suggested answers shown on the following page.

JAMES SMITH LIMITED
Profit and loss account
for the year ended 30 September 1972

		£
Sales		150 000
Trading profit		37 000
Interest	2 000	
Operating expenses	15 000	
		17 000
Profit before tax		20 000
Tax		10 000
Profit after tax		10 000
Dividend		5 000
Retained profit for the year		£5 000

JAMES SMITH LIMITED
Balance sheet, 30 September 1972

	£			£
Share capital and reserves		**Fixed assets**		
Ordinary £1 shares	20 000	Factory and equipment		40 000
Profit and loss account	15 000	**Current assets**		
Shareholders' funds	35 000	Stock	30 000	
		Debtors	20 000	
Long-term liability		Cash	5 000	
8% Debenture 1980	25 000		55 000	
		Less:		
		Current liabilities		
		Taxation	10 000	
		Creditors	20 000	
		Dividend	5 000	
			35 000	
		Net current assets		20 000
Capital employed	£60 000	**Net assets**		£60 000

(a) Return on equity $= \dfrac{\text{Profit after tax}}{\text{Shareholders' funds}} = \dfrac{10\ 000}{35\ 000} = 28.6\%$

(b) Return on net assets $= \underline{} = \underline{} =$

(c) Profit margin $= \underline{} = \underline{} =$

(d) Asset turnover $= \underline{} = \underline{} =$

(e) Debt ratio $= \underline{} = \underline{} =$

(f) Interest cover $= \underline{} = \underline{} =$

(g) Current ratio $= \underline{} = \underline{} =$

(h) Acid test $= \underline{} = \underline{} =$

2.2 James Smith Limited
Solution

(a) Return on equity $= \dfrac{\text{Profit after tax}}{\text{Shareholders' funds}} = \dfrac{10\ 000}{35\ 000} = 28.6\%$

(b) Return on net assets $\dfrac{\text{Profit before interest and taxes}}{\text{Capital employed}} = \dfrac{22\ 000}{60\ 000} = 36.7\%$

(c) Profit margin $= \dfrac{\text{Profit before interest and taxes}}{\text{Sales}} = \dfrac{22\ 000}{150\ 000} = 14.7\%$

(d) Asset turnover $= \dfrac{\text{Sales}}{\text{Net assets}} = \dfrac{150\ 000}{60\ 000} = 2.5 \text{ times}$

(e) Debt ratio $= \dfrac{\text{Long-term debt}}{\text{Capital employed}} = \dfrac{25\ 000}{60\ 000} = 41.7\%$

(f) Interest cover $= \dfrac{\text{Profit before interest and taxes}}{\text{Interest}} = \dfrac{22\ 000}{2\ 000} = 11.0 \text{ times}$

(g) Current ratio $= \dfrac{\text{Current assets}}{\text{Current liabilities}} = \dfrac{55\ 000}{35\ 000} = 1.6 \text{ times}$

(h) Acid test $= \dfrac{\text{Liquid assets}}{\text{Current liabilities}} = \dfrac{25\ 000}{35\ 000} = 0.7 \text{ times}$

2.3 MARKS AND SPENCER LIMITED (see page 57)

MARKS AND SPENCER LIMITED

PROFIT AND LOSS ACCOUNT FOR THE YEAR ENDED 31st MARCH, 1972

1971 (53 weeks)			1972 (52 weeks)	
£	£		£	£
	416,685,000	TURNOVER—Note 1		463,022,000
	50,115,000	PROFIT BEFORE TAXATION—Note 2		53,766,000
	18,900,000	CORPORATION TAX—Note 3		19,350,000
	31,215,000	PROFIT AFTER TAXATION		34,416,000
	—	STAMP DUTY ON INCREASED CAPITAL		136,000
	31,215,000			34,280,000
		GROSS DIVIDENDS		
	105,000	Preference Shares	105,000	
		Ordinary Shares		
7,136,000		9¾% Interim Paid	7,877,000	
15,754,000		21½% Final Proposed	17,369,000	
	22,995,000			25,351,000
	8,220,000	RETAINED PROFIT		8,929,000
	2,393,000	SURPLUS ON DISPOSAL OF ASSETS		203,000
	10,613,000	UNDISTRIBUTED SURPLUS		9,132,000

The notes on page 15 form an integral part of this Profit and Loss Account.

REPORT OF THE AUDITORS TO THE MEMBERS OF MARKS AND SPENCER LIMITED

In our opinion the accounts set out on pages 14 to 18 give a true and fair view of the state of the company's affairs at 31st March, 1972 and of the profit for the year ended on that date and comply with the Companies Acts 1948 and 1967.

LONDON,
18th April, 1972.

DELOITTE & CO.,
Chartered Accountants.

M.C.A.—2—E

NOTES TO THE PROFIT AND LOSS ACCOUNT

1. TURNOVER

Turnover comprises Store Sales, before deduction of refunds amounting to £21,334,000 (last year £18,987,000), and Export Sales.

2. PROFIT BEFORE TAXATION

In arriving at the Profit for the year, charges and income taken into account include the following:—

	1972 £	1971 £
CHARGES		
REPAIRS AND MAINTENANCE of		
Properties	1,982,000	1,858,000
Fixtures and Equipment	785,000	551,000
	2,767,000	2,409,000
DEPRECIATION of		
Properties	1,045,000	999,000
Fixtures and Equipment	3,575,000	3,178,000
	4,620,000	4,177,000
OTHER CHARGES		
Contribution to Employees' Pensions Scheme	636,000	566,000
Contribution to Staff Benevolent Fund	606,000	530,000
Directors' Emoluments	398,000	361,000
Debenture Stock Interest	3,178,000	3,178,000
Auditors' Remuneration	18,000	14,000
INCOME		
DIVIDENDS ON INVESTMENTS		
Quoted	—	241,000
Unquoted	—	16,000
		257,000
BANK AND OTHER INTEREST RECEIVED	1,277,000	1,605,000
	1,277,000	1,862,000

3. CORPORATION TAX

The charge for Corporation Tax at the rate of 40% (last year 40%) on the year's profit has been arrived at after taking into account relief amounting to £2,000,000 (last year £1,400,000) in respect of the excess of Tax Allowances over Depreciation charged.

4. EMOLUMENTS

The number of Directors and employees whose annual salaries are within the following ranges is:—

DIRECTORS Salary Range:—					1972	1971
£30,001–£32,500	..	..	..	..	1	–
£27,501–£30,000	..	..	..	..	2	2
£25,001–£27,500	..	..	..	..	2	1
£22,501–£25,000	..	..	..	..	2	2
£20,001–£22,500	..	..	..	..	–	2
£17,501–£20,000	..	..	..	..	2	2
£15,001–£17,500	..	..	..	..	3	2
£12,501–£15,000	..	..	..	..	8	4
£10,001–£12,500	..	..	..	..	–	7
					20	22

Included in the above are the Chairman's emoluments of £30,200 compared with £28,200 last year.

EMPLOYEES Salary Range:—					1972	1971
£15,001–£17,500	..	..	..	..	2	–
£10,001–£12,500	..	..	..	..	14	5

MARKS AND SPENCER LIMITED

BALANCE SHEET AS AT 31st MARCH, 1972

1971				1972	
£	£			£	£
		FIXED ASSETS			
154,617,000		PROPERTIES—Note 5		167,402,000	
13,932,000		FIXTURES AND EQUIPMENT—Note 6		14,715,000	
	168,549,000				182,117,000
		NET CURRENT ASSETS			
29,642,000		STOCK—at the lower of cost or replacement value		28,397,000	
5,843,000		DEBTORS AND PREPAYMENTS		5,980,000	
7,000,000		TAX RESERVE CERTIFICATES		8,000,000	
23,916,000		CASH AND SHORT TERM DEPOSITS		19,173,000	
66,401,000				61,550,000	
		Less:			
24,548,000		CREDITORS AND ACCRUED CHARGES		21,694,000	
20,587,000		CORPORATION TAX		21,411,000	
15,754,000		PROPOSED FINAL DIVIDEND		17,369,000	
60,889,000				60,474,000	
	5,512,000				1,076,000
	174,061,000	**NET ASSETS**			183,193,000
	45,000,000	DEBENTURE STOCK—Note 7			45,000,000
	1,350,000	PREFERENCE SHARES—Note 8			1,350,000
	127,711,000	ORDINARY SHAREHOLDERS' INTERESTS—Note 9			136,843,000
	174,061,000	**CAPITAL EMPLOYED**			183,193,000

J. EDWARD SIEFF
MARCUS J. SIEFF } *Directors*

F. C. HIRST
J. H. M. SAMUEL } *Joint Secretaries*

The notes form an integral part of this Balance Sheet.

NOTES TO THE BALANCE SHEET

5. PROPERTIES

	1972	1971
	£	£
(a) As valued at 31st March, 1964	87,927,000	88,457,000
Subsequent additions, at cost	85,707,000	71,480,000
	173,634,000	159,937,000
Less: Accumulated depreciation	6,232,000	5,320,000
	167,402,000	154,617,000
(b) Additions in the year, at cost	14,473,000	12,219,000
Disposal of properties in the year	776,000	9,894,000
	13,697,000	2,325,000
(c) Properties after depreciation:—		
Freeholds	119,035,000	110,830,000
Long Leaseholds (over 50 years)	46,664,000	41,931,000
Short Leaseholds (under 50 years)	1,703,000	1,856,000
	167,402,000	154,617,000

6. FIXTURES AND EQUIPMENT

The Fixtures and Equipment are shown at cost, less accumulated depreciation.

	1972	1971
Additions less sales in the year	£4,358,000	£4,738,000

7. FIRST MORTGAGE DEBENTURE STOCK

	1972	1971
	£	£
5½%—1985/1990	5,000,000	5,000,000
6¼%—1989/1994	10,000,000	10,000,000
7¼%—1993/1998	15,000,000	15,000,000
7¾%—1995/2000	15,000,000	15,000,000
	45,000,000	45,000,000

NOTES TO THE BALANCE SHEET (Contd.)

8. PREFERENCE SHARES—Authorised, issued and fully paid	1972 £	1971 £
350,000 10% Cumulative Preference Shares of £1	350,000	350,000
1,000,000 7% Cumulative Preference Shares of £1	1,000,000	1,000,000
	1,350,000	1,350,000

9. ORDINARY SHAREHOLDERS' INTERESTS

ORDINARY SHARES	1972 £	1971 £
The Authorised Ordinary Share Capital amounts to £81,250,000 consisting of 325,000,000 25p. Ordinary Shares of which 323,154,477 are issued and fully paid	80,789,000	53,859,000
RESERVES		
Balance of Surplus on Valuation of Properties	—	22,738,000
Retained Profits	56,054,000	51,114,000
	136,843,000	127,711,000

The Balance of Surplus on Valuation of Properties, together with £4,192,000 from Retained Profits, has been utilised during the year in making a scrip issue to Shareholders.

10. PROPERTY COMMITMENTS

At 31st March, 1972 there were commitments in respect of Properties in the course of development of approximately £22,750,000 (1971 £22,000,000).

Capital expenditure authorised by the Directors, but not yet contracted for, amounted to approximately £21,750,000 (1971 £11,000,000).

11. SUBSIDIARY COMPANIES

The Company's subsidiaries, none of which is trading, are not represented in the Balance Sheet as their figures are insignificant. A schedule of interests in these subsidiaries, as required by the Companies Act 1967, is filed with the Annual Return.

2.3 Marks and Spencer Limited

The accounts of Marks and Spencer Limited for the year ending 31 March 1972 and the notes relating to them are shown on pages 55 to 57.

You are asked to study the accounts and then to:

1 Calculate the ratios set out in the following pages for the two years ending 31 March 1972 and 1971. (The end-of-year share price for the years 1971 and 1972 were 328p and 297p.)

2 Prepare a simple funds statement for the year ending 31 March 1972.

3 Compare the results for 1972 with those for 1971 and comment on any significant changes.

Suggested solutions are given on the pages immediately following the pages left for you to write your answers in.

Analysis of results for the years ending 31 March 1972 and 1971

	1972	1971
Investment measures		
(a) Return on ordinary shareholder's funds (return on equity)		
(b) Earnings per share		
(c) Price/earnings ratio		
(d) Dividend yield		
(e) Dividend cover		
Measures of performance		
(f) Return on net assets		
(g) Profit margin		
(h) Asset turnover		
(i) Stock turnover		
(j) Debtor turnover		

	1972	1971

Measures of financial status

Solvency
(k) Debt ratio

(l) Interest cover

Liquidity
(m) Current ratio

(n) Acid test

(o) Acid test (less tax)

$$\frac{\text{Liquid assets}}{\text{Current Liabilities (ex-cluding corporation tax payable January 1973)}}$$

(p) Tax ratio

MARKS AND SPENCER LIMITED
FUNDS STATEMENT

Balance sheet at 31 March

1972   1971   *Difference*

MARKS AND SPENCER LIMITED
FUNDS STATEMENT: summary
year ending 31 March 1972

MARKS AND SPENCER LIMITED

Analysis of 1972 and 1971 accounts

Summary of ratios	1972	1971	Comments
Investment measures			
(a) Return on equity (%)			
(b) Earnings per share			
(c) Price/earnings ratio			
(d) Dividend yield (%)			
(e) Dividend cover (times)			
Measures of performance			
(f) Return on net assets (%)			
(g) Profit margin (%)			
(h) Asset turnover (times)			
(i) Stock turnover (times)			
(j) Debtor turnover (times)			
Measures of financial status			
(k) Debt/capital employed (%)			
(l) Interest cover (times)			
(m) Current ratio			
(n) Acid test			
(o) Acid test (less tax)			
(p) Tax ratio			

MARKS AND SPENCER LIMITED

Analysis of results for the years ending 31 March 1972 and 1971

Investment measures

	1972	1971

(a) Return on ordinary shareholders' funds (return on equity)

$$\frac{\text{Profit after tax and preference dividend}}{\text{Ordinary shareholders' funds}}$$

1972:
$$\frac{34\ 175}{\frac{34\ 280\ -\ 105}{136\ 843}} = 25.0\%$$

1971:
$$\frac{31\ 110}{\frac{31\ 215\ -\ 105}{127\ 711}} = 24.4\%$$

(b) Earnings per share

$$\frac{\text{Earnings attributable to ordinary shareholders}}{\text{Number of ordinary shares issued}}$$

1972:
$$\frac{34\ 175}{323\ 154} = 10.6\text{p}$$

1971:
$$\frac{31\ 110}{323\ 154^{*}} = 9.6\text{p}$$

*NB: 1 for 2 scrip issue

(c) Price/earnings ratio

$$\frac{\text{Market price per share}}{\text{Earnings per share}}$$

1972:
$$\frac{297}{10.6} = 28.0$$

1971:
$$\frac{328}{9.6} = 34.2$$

(d) Dividend yield

$$\frac{\text{Dividend per share}}{\text{Market price per share}}$$

1972:
$$\frac{7.8^{*}}{297} = 2.6\%$$

1971:
$$\frac{7.1\dagger}{328} = 2.2\%$$

(e) Dividend cover

1972:
$$^{*}31\tfrac{1}{4}\% \times 25\text{p} = 7.8\text{p}$$

1971:
$$\dagger\frac{22\ 995}{323\ 154} = 7.1\text{p}$$

$$\frac{\text{Earnings per share}}{\text{Dividend per share}}$$

1972:
$$\frac{10.6}{7.8} = 1.36\text{ times}$$

1971:
$$\frac{9.6}{7.1} = 1.35\text{ times}$$

Measures of performance

(f) Return on net assets

$$\frac{\text{Profit before loan interest and tax}}{\text{Net assets}}$$

1972:
$$\frac{56\ 944}{\frac{53\ 766\ +\ 3\ 178}{183\ 193}} = 31.1\%$$

1971:
$$\frac{53\ 293}{\frac{50\ 115\ +\ 3\ 178}{174\ 061}} = 30.6\%$$

(g) Profit margin

$$\frac{\text{Profit}}{\text{Sales}}$$

1972:
$$\frac{56\ 944}{\frac{463\ 022\ -\ 21\ 334}{441\ 688}} = 12.9\%$$

1971:
$$\frac{53\ 293}{\frac{416\ 685\ -\ 18\ 987}{397\ 698}} = 13.4\%$$

(h) Asset turnover

$$\frac{\text{Sales}}{\text{Net assets}}$$

1972:
$$\frac{441\ 688}{183\ 193} = 2.41\text{ times}$$

1971:
$$\frac{397\ 698}{174\ 061} = 2.28\text{ times}$$

Measures of performance (contd.)

		1972	1971

(i)   Stock turnover

$$\frac{Sales}{Stock}$$

$$\frac{441\ 688}{28\ 397} = 15.6 \text{ times}$$
$$\frac{397\ 698}{29\ 642} = 13.4 \text{ times}$$

(j)   Debtor turnover

$$\frac{Sales}{Debtors}$$

Not meaningful in this case since (i) "debtors" are combined with prepayments in the balance sheet, and (ii) virtually no retail sales are made on credit.

Measures of financial status

Solvency

(k)   Debt ratio

$$\frac{Debenture\ stock}{Capital\ employed}$$

$$\frac{45\ 000}{183\ 193} = 24.6\%$$
$$\frac{45\ 000}{174\ 061} = 25.9\%$$

(l)   Interest cover

$$\frac{Earnings\ before\ interest\ and\ tax}{Debenture\ stock\ interest}$$

$$\frac{56\ 944}{3\ 178} = 17.9 \text{ times}$$
$$\frac{53\ 293}{3\ 178} = 16.8 \text{ times}$$

Liquidity

(m) Current ratio

$$\frac{Current\ assets}{Current\ liabilities}$$

$$\frac{61\ 550}{60\ 474} = 1.02$$
$$\frac{66\ 401}{60\ 889} = 1.09$$

(n)   Acid test

$$\frac{Liquid\ assets}{Current\ liabilities}$$

$$\frac{33\ 153}{60\ 474} = 0.55$$
$$\frac{36\ 759}{60\ 889} = 0.60$$

(o)   Acid test (less tax)

$$\frac{Liquid\ assets}{Current\ liabilities}$$
(excluding corporation tax payable
1 January 1973)

$$\frac{33\ 153}{39\ 063} = 0.85$$
$$\frac{36\ 759}{40\ 302} = 0.91$$

(p)   Tax ratio

$$\frac{Taxation}{Profit\ before\ tax}$$

$$\frac{19\ 350}{53\ 766} = 36.0\%$$
$$\frac{18\ 900}{50\ 115} = 37.7\%$$

MARKS AND SPENCER LIMITED
FUNDS STATEMENT
Balance sheets at 31 March

	1972 £'000	1971 £'000	Difference £'000
Properties	167 402	154 617	12 785
Fixtures and equipment	14 715	13 932	783
	182 117	168 549	13 568
Stock	28 397	29 642	(1 245)
Debtors and prepayments	5 980	5 843	137
Tax Reserve Certificates	8 000	7 000	1 000
Cash and short-term deposits	19 173	23 916	(4 743)
	243 667	234 950	8 717
Creditors and accrued charges	(21 694)	(24 548)	2 854
Corporation tax	(21 411)	(20 587)	(824)
Proposed final dividend	(17 369)	(15 754)	(1 615)
	(60 474)	(60 889)	415
	183 193	174 061	9 132
Debenture stock	(45 000)	(45 000)	—
Preference shares	(1 350)	(1 350)	—
Ordinary shareholders' interests	(136 843)	(127 711)	(9 132)
	(183 193)	(174 061)	(9 132)

MARKS AND SPENCER LIMITED
FUNDS STATEMENT: summary
Year ending 31 March 1972

	£'000
Sources of funds	
Retained profit	8 929
Surplus on disposal of assets	203
Reduced stock	1 245
Reduced cash	4 743
Increased corporation tax	824
Increased final dividend	1 615
	17 559

Uses of funds	
Increased investment in fixed assets:	
Properties	12 785
Fixtures and equipment	783
Increased debtors and prepayments	137
Increased Tax Reserve Certificates	1 000
Reduced creditors	2 854
	17 559

Alternative presentation

		£'000
Long-term sources of funds		
Internal: Undistributed surplus		9 132
External†:		—
		9 132
Investment in fixed assets		
Properties	12 785	
Fixtures and equipment	783	
		13 568
Reduction in working capital		4 436*

†new issues of shares or debenture stock	
*opening working capital	5 512
Less: closing working capital	1 076
= Reduction in working capital	4 436

Comment:

If new investment in fixed assets again exceeds retained profits by nearly £5 million in 1973, where will the necessary funds come from? Presumably either from increasing creditors, or from an external issue either of ordinary shares or of debenture stock.

    Notice that in 1972 stock actually *fell* by 4 per cent, although sales increased by 11 per cent.

MARKS AND SPENCER LIMITED

Analysis of 1972 and 1971 accounts

Summary of ratios	1972	1971*
Investment measures		
(a) Return on equity (%)	25.0%	24.4%*
(b) Earnings per share	10.6p	9.6p*
(c) Price/earnings ratio	28.0	34.2
(d) Dividend yield (%)	2.6%	2.2%
(e) Dividend cover (times)	1.36	1.35
Measures of performance		
(f) Return on net assets (%)	31.1%	30.6%*
(g) Profit margin (%)	12.9%	13.4%
(h) Asset turnover (times)	2.41	2.28*
(i) Stock turnover (times)	15.6	13.4*
(j) Debtor turnover (times)	n/a	n/a
Measures of financial status		
(k) Debt/capital employed (%)	24.6%	25.9%
(l) Interest cover (times)	17.9	16.8*
(m) Current ratio	1.02	1.09
(n) Acid test	0.55	0.60
(o) Acid test (less tax)	0.85	0.91
(p) Tax ratio	36.0%	37.7%

*NB 1971 = 53 weeks

Comments

1 Because 1971 contained 53 weeks, the improvement in the ratios marked * is rather greater than the numbers show.

2 Despite a drop in profit margins, a higher asset turnover produced a better return on net assets.

3 Stock turnover, already very high, improved significantly.

4 While the debt ratio doesn't look especially low, the high return on net assets results in a high interest cover.

5 The liquidity position may *seem* tight, but with sales being made practically entirely for cash and with stock turnover of 15.6 times, there is really no cause for alarm. Indeed, Marks and Spencer's stock seems to be more "liquid" than many companies' debtors.

6 Although the return on equity has increased to 25.0 per cent, and earnings per share have risen by over 10 per cent, the market price has fallen—probably due mainly to general market conditions. However the price/earnings ratio of 28 is still higher than most other companies, implying that the market expects more growth in earnings per share in future.

7 The main assets—properties—were last valued 8 years ago, apart from subsequent additions which are shown at cost. Presumably a current valuation would produce a substantial increase over the book value. How would a (hypothetical) increase on the amount shown for property of, say, £50 million affect (i) return on net assets, (ii) return on equity, and (iii) debt ratio?

2.4 King Limited and Fisher Limited

Summaries of the 1971 accounts of King Limited and Fisher Limited are shown below. You are asked to calculate, compare, and briefly comment on their liquidity and solvency ratios.

Answers to this and the next problem are shown at the end of the book.

(a) *Debt ratio*

(b) *Interest cover*

Summarised balance sheets at 31 December 1971

	King Limited £		Fisher Limited £	
Shareholders' funds	20 000		40 000	
Long-term debt (10%)	5 000		20 000	
Capital employed	£25 000		£60 000	
Fixed assets	15 000		45 000	
Current assets:				
Stock	15 000		15 000	
Debtors	5 000		15 000	
Cash	5 000		5 000	
	25 000		35 000	
Less: **Current liabilities**	15 000		20 000	
		10 000		15 000
Net assets		£25 000		£60 000
Interest	500		2 000	
Profit before tax	5 000		7 000	

(c) *Current ratio*

(d) *Acid test*

Comment:

2.5 Russell Enterprises Limited

A summary of the results of Russell Enterprises Limited for the last two years is shown below. You are asked to calculate the ratios shown opposite and to comment briefly on each of them.

	1970	1971	1972
(a) Return on net assets			
(b) Profit margin			
(c) Asset turnover			

RUSSELL ENTERPRISES LIMITED

Years ended 31 December

	1970	1971	1972
	£	£	£
Sales	£480 000	£560 000	£690 000
Profit before tax	63 000	70 000	74 000
Tax	23 000	25 000	28 000
Profit after tax	40 000	45 000	46 000
Dividends	30 000	30 000	36 000
Retained profits for year	£10 000	£15 000	£10 000
Share capital (600 000 25p shares)	150 000	150 000	150 000
Reserves	85 000	100 000	110 000
Shareholders' funds	235 000	250 000	260 000
Long-term debt at 10%	65 000	150 000	150 000
Capital employed	£300 000	£400 000	£410 000
Market price per share at 31 December:	100p	150p	125p
Debt interest	£6 500	£15 000	£15 000

(d) Return on equity

(e) Earnings per share

(f) Price/earnings ratio

(g) Dividend per share

(h) Dividend yield

(i) Dividend cover

Section 3
Recording business transactions

BASIC TRANSACTIONS AND COMPANY ACCOUNTS

We are aware that the accounts of a company are summary statements embracing a wide variety of individual transactions and including only items which can be expressed in financial terms. But how do individual transactions become incorporated in the accounts? What is the link between the everyday activities of the business and its published financial statements?

These questions are frequently asked and the answers can easily become lost in detailed discussions of book-keeping entries and accounting adjustments. It is important however that those who use accounting statements should understand how they relate to identifiable business activities. Managers, for example, should be able to foresee how actions which they are planning will be reflected in the company's published financial statements both in the short and longer term.

To secure this understanding and yet avoid the dangers of confusing detail, we must consider separately different aspects of the total process. We must distinguish between:

1 Recording basic transactions.
2 Making adjustments in preparing the final balance sheet and profit and loss account.

Recording basic transactions will be dealt with in this section. The nature of the financial adjustments which are made will form the basis of much of the next four sections. Finally, in section 8, we shall be able to look in detail at published accounts knowing what they represent and how they have been drawn up.

Our task for this section is still ambitious. We are going to consider in the main section the impact of individual transactions on accounting statements and the overall flows of information in recording multiple transactions.

The Appendix to this section deals in more detail with the accounting records and rules—"double-entry book-keeping"—and the stages in preparing published profit and loss accounts and balance sheets. The Appendix is intended to serve the needs of those who require a more detailed examination of how the books of account record business transactions. Readers who want to gain a quick appreciation of how business events affect accounts without going into such detail may well prefer to skim the Appendix, or even omit it altogether.

IMPACT OF INDIVIDUAL TRANSACTIONS ON ACCOUNTS

The changes which take place in the accounting statements of a company when transactions are recorded will most clearly be seen in a simple example. Let us look therefore at a company which is just starting business, and consider the changes made in its accounts to reflect the major transactions undertaken in the first three months of its existence.

These can be grouped into six stages:

1 The issue of ordinary share capital
2 Buying fixed and current assets
3 Selling goods at a profit
4 Buying stock for cash and on credit
5 Selling on credit and paying suppliers
6 Paying operating expenses and incurring a long-term loan

In seeing how the above transactions are reflected in accounts, we shall look at the balance sheet and profit and loss account after each stage. The notes underneath the accounts explain various matters of importance.

STAGE 1 THE ISSUE OF ORDINARY SHARES

On 1 April 1972 a number of investors subscribed £50 000 to incorporate Initial Enterprises Limited (IE Limited), a small trading company. The balance sheet at the moment after incorporation is set out below.

IE LIMITED
Balance sheet, 1 April 1972

Source of funds (liability)		*Use of Funds* (asset)	
Share capital Ordinary shares	£50 000	*Current asset* Cash	£50 000

Notes

1 *The company has a separate legal identity*

The incorporation of IE Limited means that it has been established with a separate legal identity quite distinct from that of its shareholders. Its separate nature and powers are defined in its constitution (its Memorandum and Articles of Association).

Ultimate control of the company's destiny is in the hands of its shareholders but day-to-day control is exercised by the company's directors, of whom by law there must be at least two.

2 *The company views shareholders' capital as a "liability"*

The company, as a separate legal entity, has received £50 000 from its shareholders in return for ordinary shares in the company. There is no intention that the company will repay this "permanent" capital to its shareholders. Nevertheless, there is an *ultimate* liability to repay, and from the company's viewpoint the amount provided by shareholders may be regarded as a liability which will be fully discharged only if the company ceases to exist.

3 *Holding cash is a "use" of funds*

At this early stage in its existence, the company is holding the funds it has received in the form of cash. This is the *use* to which the funds have been put. It is important to note that holding liquid funds (cash) is a use of funds, for it emphasises that resources are always employed *somehow*, that there is no way for a company (or indeed for an individual) to be isolated from the market.

4 *Assets equal liabilities*

The balance sheet balances because the company's assets equal its liabilities—that is, because uses of funds necessarily equal sources of funds.

STAGE 2 BUYING FIXED AND CURRENT ASSETS FOR CASH

During April the company takes steps to set up business:

(a) It buys a small freehold shop for £20 000

(b) It buys stock for £20 000

At the end of April the balance sheet reflects the changes.

```
IE LIMITED
Balance sheet, 30 April 1972

Sources                          Uses
(liabilities)                    (assets)

                        £                                £
Share capital                    Fixed asset
Ordinary shares      50 000      Freehold shop           20 000ᵃ

                                 Current assets
                                 Stock          20 000ᵇ
                                 Cash (50 000

                                     −20 000ᵃ
                                     −20 000ᵇ)  10 000
                                                         30 000
                     _____                            _____
                     £50 000                             £50 000
```

Notes

1 The balance sheet still balances. Assets equal liabilities.

2 No new source of funds has been introduced.

3 The nature of the assets has changed although the overall total has remained the same.

	£	£
Cash	− 40 000	
Freehold shop		+ 20 000
Stock		+ 20 000
	− 40 000	+ 40 000

4 The letters against some balance sheet items refer to the transactions listed at the top of the page.

STAGE 3 SELLING GOODS AT A PROFIT

The company begins to trade, and during May:

(a) It sells stock for £6000 in cash

(b) The stock originally cost £5000

```
IE LIMITED
Balance sheet, 31 May 1972

Sources                          Uses
(liabilities)                    (assets)

                        £                                £
Share capital                    Fixed asset
Ordinary shares      50 000      Freehold shop           20 000

 Profit and loss account         Current assets
Sales              6000ᵃ         Stock
                                 (20 000−5000ᵇ) 15 000
Less: Cost of sales  5000ᵇ
                                 Cash
                     1 000       (10 000+6000ᵃ) 16 000
                                                         31 000
                     _____                            _____
                     £51 000                             £51 000
```

Notes

1 The balance sheet still balances but a significant change has occured. Assets originally costing £5000 have been sold for £6000 giving the company a *profit* of £1000.

(a) The sale

Sales are shown in the profit and loss account as a source of revenue.

The cash received, of course, is added to the cash balance.

(b) The cost of achieving the sale

Physical stock has been reduced, so the balance sheet figure is also reduced.

The *cost* of stock sold is deducted from the sales revenue in the profit and loss account, to show the profit on the transaction. This amount "belongs" to the

71

owners—the ordinary shareholders—though they have no legal right to it unless the company declares a dividend or winds up.

Notice that the accounts record the profit when it is *realised* by an actual market transaction.

2 The impact on the asset and liability accounts can be summarised:

	Liabilities £		Assets £
Profit	+ 1000	Stock	− 5000
		Cash	+ 6000
	+ 1000		+ 1000

STAGE 4 BUYING STOCK FOR CASH AND ON CREDIT

At the beginning of June the company:
(a) Buys stock costing £10 000 for cash
(b) Buys stock costing £5000 on credit

IE LIMITED
Balance sheet, 5 June 1972

	£			£
		Fixed asset		
		Freehold shop		20 000
Share capital		*Current assets*		
Ordinary shares	50 000	Stock (15 000		
Profit and loss account		+ 10 000[a]		
Sales	6000	+ 5000[b])	30 000	
Less: Cost of sales 5000		Cash (16 000		
	1 000	− 10 000[a])	6 000	
Current liability				36 000
Trade creditor	5 000[b]			
	£56 000			£56 000

Notes

1 A further source of funds has become available to the business—that allowed by short term trade credit. The short term nature of the funds is indicated by showing trade creditors as a "current liability."
2 The asset balances change to reflect the movement of cash into stock.
3 The balance sheet still balances and the effect of the transactions can be summarised as follows:

	Liabilities £		Assets £
Trade creditor	+ 5000	Stock	+ 15 000
		Cash	− 10 000
	+ 5000		+ 5 000

4 As in Stage 2, no profit or loss arises on the above transactions. Assets have been acquired which are shown in the balance sheet at cost (cash being reduced by the same amount). A profit or loss arises only when goods or services are *sold* ("realised").

STAGE 5 SELLING ON CREDIT AND PAYING SUPPLIERS

In the remainder of the month, the company completes the following transactions:

		£
(a)	Sells for cash stock which had cost £10 000	12 000
(b)	Sells on credit stock which had cost £5 000	6 000
(c)	Buys stock for cash	10 000
(d)	Buys stock on credit	3 000
(e)	Pays existing creditor	5 000

You may wish, at this stage, to make the necessary adjustments to record the above transactions.

Alter the figures in the balance sheet at 5 June 1972 (shown opposite). Make sure your amended balance sheet balances!

Then compare your solution with that shown overleaf.

IE LIMITED
Balance sheet, 5 June 1972

	£			£
Share capital			*Fixed asset*	
Ordinary shares	50 000		Freehold shop	20 000
Profit and loss account			*Current assets*	
Sales	6000		Stock	30 000
Less: Cost of sales	5000		Cash	6 000
		1 000		36 000
Current liability				
Trade creditor		5 000		
		£56 000		£56 000

73

STAGE 5 SELLING ON CREDIT AND PAYING SUPPLIERS (CONTINUED)

Notes

1 Sales of £6000 on credit rather than for cash involves the introduction of a new item—for debtors. The accounting treatment is similar to that for cash sales:

	Liabilities £	Assets £
(a) Increase sales figure in profit and loss account	+ 6000	
Debtors		+ 6000
(b) Increase cost of figure in profit and loss account	− 5000*	
Reduction in stock balance		− 5000
	+ 1000	+ 1000

*This is an increase in a figure which is being *deducted*.
The net effect of the transaction is to increase profit by £1000 and to increase current assets by £1000 (Debtors £6000 less stock reduction £5000).

2 The payment of a creditor involves a reduction of current liabilities (trade creditor) and current assets (cash) by the same amount (£5000).

3 The entries made in the period can be summarised:

	Liabilities £		Assets £
Profit	+3000	Stock	− 2000
Trade creditor	−2000	Debtors	+ 6000
		Cash	− 3000
	+ 1000		+ 1000

4 Notice that the two stages of a credit purchase amount in the end to the same thing as a cash purchase:

	Liabilities	Assets
Cash purchase		Stock up
		Cash down
Credit purchase		
(a) Purchase	Creditor up	Stock up
(b) Payment	Creditor down	Cash down

IE LIMITED *(working copy)*
Balance sheet, ~~5~~ 30 June 1972

	£		£
Share capital		*Fixed asset*	
Ordinary shares	50 000	Freehold shop	20 000

Profit and loss account			*Current assets*		
Sales +12000ᵃ +6000ᵇ	~~6 000~~ 24 000		Stock −10 000ᵃ −5 000ᵇ +10 000ᶜ +3 000ᵈ	~~30 000~~ 28 000	
Less: Cost of sales +10 000ᵃ +5 000ᵇ	5 000 20 000	4 000 ~~1 000~~	Debtors +6 000ᵇ		6 000
					3 000
			Cash +12 000ᵃ −10 000ᶜ −5 000ᵉ	~~6 000~~	~~36 000~~ 37,000

Current liability		
Trade creditor +3000ᵈ −5000ᵉ	3 000 ~~5 000~~	

| | ~~5~~ £~~56~~ 000 | ~~5~~ £~~56~~ 000 |

IE LIMITED *(final statement)*
Balance sheet, 30 June 1972

	£		£
Share capital		*Fixed asset*	
Ordinary shares	50 000	Freehold shop	20 000
Profit and loss account		*Current assets*	
Sales	24 000	Stock	28 000
		Debtors	6 000
Less: Cost of sales	20 000	Cash	3 000
Current liability	4 000		37 000
Trade creditor	3 000		
	£57 000		£57 000

STAGE 6 PAYING OPERATING EXPENSES AND INCURRING A LONG-TERM LOAN

Before the accounts of the company for the first quarter can be drawn up further transactions have to be incorporated.

(a) The company pays £2 000 operating expenses incurred during the quarter.
(b) In the light of the trading experience gained, it is decided to increase the level of business activity. To achieve this, further capital is required to finance additional stock and debtors. The company therefore borrows £10 000 at 10 per cent a year, issuing debenture stock and using the freehold shop owned by the company as security.

The balance sheet after making these adjustments is illustrated below.

IE LIMITED
Balance sheet, 30 June 1972

	£			£
Share capital		*Fixed asset*		
Ordinary shares	50 000	Freehold shop		20 000
Profit and loss account		*Current assets*		
Sales	24 000	Stock	28 000	
Less: Cost of sales		Debtors	6 000	
	20 000	Cash (3 000		
	4 000	− 2 000[a]		
Less: Operating		+ 10 000[b])		
expenses	2 000[a]		11 000	
Net profit	2 000			45 000
Shareholders' funds	52 000			
10% *Debenture stock*	10 000[b]			
Current liability				
Trade creditor	3 000			
	£65 000			£65 000

Notes

1 Up to now the profit and loss account entries have been incorporated in the balance sheet as an integral part of it. This shows the relationship between the two statements.

2 In practice, as we know, only the final balance of the profit and loss account appears on the face of the balance sheet, the details being shown in a separate profit and loss account. This is illustrated opposite.

3 The profit and loss account balance is added to the share capital to produce a sub-total of "shareholders' funds," as distinct from other liabilities.

IE Limited's final balance sheet, at 30 June 1972 and profit and loss account for the three months ending 30 June 1972 are illustrated below. While we are dealing with the analysis of transactions it is helpful to use the "account" format for the balance sheet since this more closely reflects the way in which entries are made in the accounting records.

I.E. LIMITED
Balance sheet, 30 June 1972

	£			£
Share capital		*Fixed assets*		
Ordinary shares	50 000	Freehold shop		20 000
Profit and loss account	2 000	*Current assets*		
Shareholders' funds	52 000	Stock	28 000	
		Debtors	6 000	
10% *debenture stock*	10 000	Cash	11 000	
				45 000
Current liability				
Trade creditor	3 000			
	£65 000			£65 000

I.E. LIMITED
Profit and loss account for the three months ending 30 June 1972

	£	£
Sales		24 000
Less: Cost of stock sold		20 000
Gross profit		4 000
Less: Operating expenses		
Salaries and wages	1500	
Administration	500	
		2 000
Net profit shown in the balance sheet		£2 000

THE ACCOUNTING RECORDS AND DOUBLE-ENTRY BOOK-KEEPING

In the six stages of Initial Enterprises Limited which we have considered, a variety of business transactions has been expressed in accounting form. The resulting balance sheet shows the assets and liabilities at the end of the period concerned, while the profit and loss account summarises the trading activities during the period.

We have seen how individual transactions are incorporated in the accounts and how the balance between sources and uses of funds is maintained when new funds are introduced, when changes take place in the nature of the assets held, and when the company engages in trading activity.

So far, in looking at the affairs of IE Limited, we have considered a small number of transactions and have made adjustments to record their effect directly on the face of the balance sheet and profit and loss account. This would obviously not be possible when many transactions are involved. They need subsidiary records—the books of account—within which numerous entries can be brought together and summarised.

The basic form of the books of account has developed over time and the ideas incorporated in them can be applied equally to manual or mechanised systems whether based on keyboard machines or computer systems. The major units in the system are:

> The cash book
> The ledger
> The journal

The *cash book* is used to record receipts and payments of cash, and shows the balance of cash remaining, either positive or negative (overdrawn), at any given point in time.

The *ledger* is used to record and analyse all business transactions. It is usually divided into a debtors' ledger and a creditors' ledger (called "personal" ledgers, since they contain the personal accounts of each individual debtor and creditor) and a nominal (or "impersonal") ledger containing all the other accounts, relating to income, expenses, assets and liabilities. Special and confidential accounts and those dealing with long-term assets and liabilities are frequently grouped in a "private ledger" which is a separate part of the nominal ledger.

The *journal* is used to summarise multiple transactions and to explain transfers and adjustments made within the ledger. Sales and purchases on credit occur so frequently in most businesses that they are recorded in subsidiary journals—a "sales day book" and a "purchase day book." The main journal is then used only for special transactions where a primary record or explanation is needed before entries are made in the ledger.

In conjunction, the cash book, ledger, and journal form a system for recording transactions which can deal with all business activities capable of being expressed in financial terms. Using the rules of double-entry book-keeping, the system not only provides the analysis required, but involves a self-checking mechanism. The Appendix to this section discusses in detail how each of these records is used.

On the next page are set out diagrams representing the flow of information in recording business transactions. The diagrams portray:

1 Overall system
2 System in greater detail

INFORMATION FLOWS

1 The overall system

Information flow ⟶

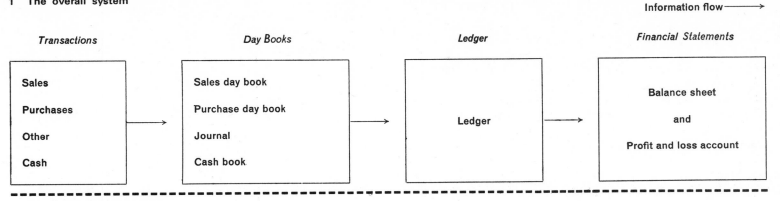

Transactions	Day Books	Ledger	Financial Statements
Sales Purchases Other Cash	Sales day book Purchase day book Journal Cash book	Ledger	Balance sheet and Profit and loss account

----

2 The system in greater detail

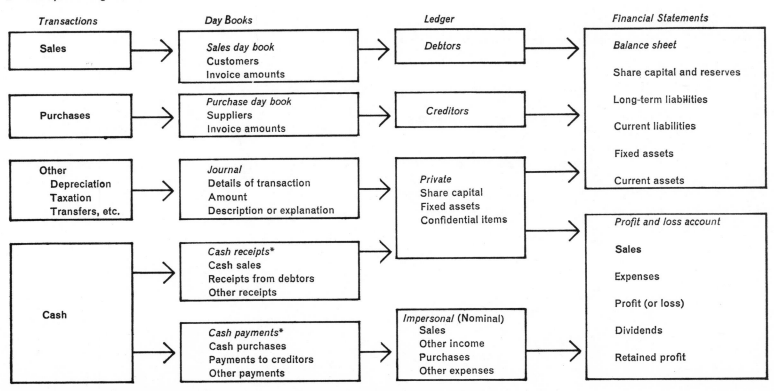

Transactions

- Sales
- Purchases
- Other
  - Depreciation
  - Taxation
  - Transfers, etc.
- Cash

Day Books

- *Sales day book*
  - Customers
  - Invoice amounts
- *Purchase day book*
  - Suppliers
  - Invoice amounts
- *Journal*
  - Details of transaction
  - Amount
  - Description or explanation
- *Cash receipts**
  - Cash sales
  - Receipts from debtors
  - Other receipts
- *Cash payments**
  - Cash purchases
  - Payments to creditors
  - Other payments

Ledger

- *Debtors*
- *Creditors*
- *Private*
  - Share capital
  - Fixed assets
  - Confidential items
- *Impersonal* (Nominal)
  - Sales
  - Other income
  - Purchases
  - Other expenses

Financial Statements

- *Balance sheet*
- Share capital and reserves
- Long-term liabilities
- Current liabilities
- Fixed assets
- Current assets

- *Profit and loss account*
- Sales
- Expenses
- Profit (or loss)
- Dividends
- Retained profit

*The cash book constitutes the ledger account for cash, as well as a book of prime entry.

77

STAGES IN PREPARING PUBLISHED FINANCIAL STATEMENTS

The major sequence of steps in preparing published financial statements is as follows:

1 Record all transactions in the books of account (as described in the Appendix).
2 Total the entries in the cash book and in each ledger account, and calculate the balances.
3 Extract a trial balance (which is a list of all the balances).
4 Make any necessary adjustments (the nature of which is discussed in section 4).
5 Draw up the profit and loss account and balance sheet.

SUMMARY

In this section we first worked through a number of stages showing how individual transactions affect published accounting statements. We then briefly described the accounting records used in practice to handle a large number of transactions, and outlined the overall accounting process with diagrams showing information flows. Finally we have listed above the various stages in preparing financial statements.

We shall now turn in section 4 to the issues involved in measuring profit or loss, and to the financial adjustments which are needed in preparing published accounts.

For readers who want a more specific understanding of how business transactions are recorded in the books of account, the Appendix to this section discusses in more detail the accounting records and rules—"double-entry book-keeping"—and the steps involved in preparing published accounts from the books of account.

Before the Appendix, on the next few pages, are questions covering the material in this section. Immediately following the Appendix are questions covering the material it contains.

Balance sheet changes

3.1 Abacus Book Shop Limited (A)

The balances appearing in the books of the Abacus Book Shop Limited at 1 January 1972 were as follows. You are asked to draw up a balance sheet as at that date:

Balances	£
Cash	2000
Creditors	1000
Debtors	2000
Ordinary share capital	3000
Profit and loss account	4000
Stock	4000

The answer is shown on the next page.

Space for answer

3.1 Abacus Book Shop Limited (A)

Solution

The company's balance sheet at 1 January 1972 is shown opposite.

Notes

1 Did you remember to include the correct headings?
   Share capital
   Revenue reserve
   Current liabilities
   Current assets
2 Did you insert a sub-total to show the total shareholders' funds? (This is not always explicitly named on the face of the balance sheet.)

ABACUS BOOK SHOP LIMITED
Balance sheet, 1 January 1972

	£		£
Share capital		**Current assets**	
Ordinary shares	3000	Stock	4000
		Debtors	2000
		Cash	2000
Revenue reserve			
Profit and loss account	4000		
	7000		
Current liabilities			
Creditors	1000		
	£8000		£8000

3.2 Abacus Book Shop Limited (B)

The balance sheet of the Abacus Book Shop Limited on 1 January 1972 is set out opposite.

During the month of January the company

(a) Received £1000 cash from credit customers

(b) Bought new books for £2000 in cash

(c) Sold books for £3000 in cash which had cost £2000.

You are asked to amend the balance sheet to show the position at 31 January 1972. When you have done so, compare your answer with that shown on the next page.

ABACUS BOOK SHOP LIMITED
Balance sheet, 1 January 1972

	£		£
Share capital		**Current assets**	
Ordinary shares	3000	Stock	4000
Revenue reserve		Debtors	2000
Profit and loss account	4000		
	7000	Cash	2000
Current liabilities			
Creditors	1000		
	£8000		£8000

3.2 Abacus Book Shop Limited (B)

Solution

The amended balance sheet of Abacus Book Shop Limited at 31 January 1972 is shown opposite (top). The final balance sheet is shown opposite (bottom).

Notes

1 Did you remember to alter the date of the balance sheet?

2 It may help to identify each transaction with the appropriate letter of the alphabet.

ABACUS BOOK SHOP LIMITED   *(working copy)*
Balance sheet, 1 January 1972

	£		£
Share capital		**Current assets**	
Ordinary shares	3000	Stock	4000
		$+2,000^b$	
		$-2,000^c$	
Revenue reserve		Debtors	~~2000~~
Profit and loss account	~~5,000~~ ~~4000~~	$-1,000^a$	1,000
$+3,000^c$	~~7000~~		
$-2,000^c$	8,000	Cash	~~2000~~
		$+1,000^a$	4,000
		$-2,000^b$	
		$+3,000^c$	
Current liabilities			
Creditors	1000		
	~~9000~~ ~~£8000~~		~~9000~~ ~~£8000~~

ABACUS BOOK SHOP LIMITED   *(final statement)*
Balance sheet, 31 January 1972

	£		£
Share capital			
Ordinary shares	3000		
Revenue reserve		**Current assets**	
Profit and loss account	5000	Stock	4000
	8000	Debtors	1000
Current liabilities		Cash	4000
Creditors	1000		
	£9000		£9000

Solutions to the following problems are
shown at the end of the book.

3.3 Abacus Book Shop Limited (C)

In February, the Abacus Book Shop Limited was
given the opportunity to buy a long lease on the
shop for £6000. It decided to do so, and to
borrow £3000 on the security of the lease. It also
carried out the following transactions in February.
You are asked to amend the balance sheet shown
opposite to reflect these transactions.

		£
(a)	Receipt of loan at 10 per cent p.a. interest	3000
(b)	Payment for lease	6000
(c)	Sales for cash of books which had cost £2000	3000
(d)	Sales on credit of books which had cost £1500	2000
(e)	Purchases of books for cash	2500
(f)	Purchases of books on credit	2000

ABACUS BOOK SHOP LIMITED
Balance sheet, 31 January 1972

	£		£
Share capital			
Ordinary shares	3000		
Revenue reserve		**Current assets**	
Profit and loss account	5000	Stock	4000
	8000		
Current liabilities		Debtors	1000
Creditors	1000		
		Cash	4000
	£9000		£9000

3.4 Chemical Engineering Company Limited

During August 1972, the Chemical Engineering Company Limited

(a) Bought for cash new plant costing £10 000

(b) Paid creditors £5000

(c) Sold goods on credit for £15 000

(d) The goods sold had cost £18 000

(e) Received £5000 from debtors

You are asked to amend the balance sheet as at 31 July 1972 shown opposite.

Note: The above items are not listed in chronological order: they merely summarise individual transactions at various dates during the period.

CHEMICAL ENGINEERING COMPANY LIMITED
Balance sheet, 31 July 1972

	£		£
Share capital		**Fixed assets**	
Ordinary shares	50 000	Plant at cost	30 000
Revenue reserve		**Current assets**	
Profit and loss account	20 000	Stock	25 000
	70 000	Debtors	15 000
Current liabilities			
Creditors	12 000	Cash	12 000	52 000
	£82 000		£82 000

3.5 Whitewash Laundry Limited

The transactions of the Whitewash Laundry Limited in the quarter ending 31 March 1973 were:

		£
(a)	Total invoiced sales in quarter	60 000
(b)	Cash payments for supplies used in laundry	6000
(c)	Cash received from credit customers	55 000
(d)	Operating costs: wages, fuel, etc.	30 000
(e)	Selling and administrative costs	15 000

The balance sheet at 1 January 1973 is shown opposite. You are asked to compile a profit and loss account for the quarter to 31 March 1973 and the balance sheet at the end of the quarter.

WHITEWASH LAUNDRY LIMITED
Balance sheet, 1 January 1973

	£		£
Share capital		**Fixed asset**	
Ordinary shares	75 000	Laundry and equipment	50 000
Revenue reserve		**Current assets**	
Profit and loss account	15 000	Debtors	30 000
		Cash	10 000
			40 000
	£90 000		£90 000

Profit and loss account

Appendix to Section 3
Double-entry book-keeping

DOUBLE-ENTRY BOOK-KEEPING

In the first part of the main section we considered six early stages in the growth of Initial Enterprises Limited, and in particular how certain individual transactions affected the profit and loss account and balance sheet.

In practice, of course, it would be impossible to adjust a profit and loss account and balance sheet by making alterations on the face of the accounts in respect of every single business event. Instead, to allow for the orderly recording of transactions, entries are made in the "books of account"—the cash book, the ledger and the journal and day books—from which, in total, the figures needed for constructing published financial statements can be extracted.

In this Appendix we are going to consider the books of accounts and double-entry book-keeping procedures in some detail. We shall start by considering how the transactions of Initial Enterprises Limited which we have already looked at once would be recorded in the books of account.

THE CASH BOOK

IE Limited started business on 1 April with £50 000 in cash and by 30 June when we drew up a balance sheet and profit and loss account, this had been reduced to £11 000. Obviously the owners of the company would want to know what happened to the £39 000 difference. A simple cash record might show:

April	Receipt from issue of shares	+50 000
	Bought freehold shop	−20 000
	Bought stock	−20 000
May	Cash sales	+ 6 000
June	Bought stock	−10 000
	Bought stock	−10 000
	Paid creditor	− 5 000
	Cash sales	+12 000
	Proceeds of loan	+10 000
	Salaries and wages paid	− 1 500
	Administrative expenses paid	− 500
	Balance 30 June	+£11 000

But this is not a particularly helpful form of record. It is not easy to distinguish between receipts and payments, and no analysis is given of the transactions undertaken in the period. A better record would be that shown below. This is in the form generally adopted for the cash book and would suit IE Limited's needs very well.

Notes

1 The cash book shows receipts and payments separately.

2 It is a conventional rule that *cash payments are shown on the right and cash receipts are shown on the left*. The rule is fundamental to the double-entry system of book-keeping. There is no particular logic in the choice of sides but the convention is universally established.

One way to remember the "correct" sides for payments and receipts is the cash *payments* are made with the *right* hand and are called Credits—abbreviated to Cr; cash *receipts* are on the opposite side (left) and are called debts—abbreviated to Dr.

3 The cash book is "balanced" at the end of the period to show the cash in hand. Balancing also has the effect of simplifying the totals. Instead of carrying down (c/d) £78 000 for receipts and £67 000 for payments to the next period, only the balance of £11 000 is brought down (b/d). (The expressions "carried forward" (c/f) and "brought forward" (b/f) are used where a new ledger page is concerned.)

4 The column marked "Fo" representing folio or page, refers to a classification/analysis of the cash book entries which is shown in the ledger.

Cash Book

	Receipts	Debits	(Dr)		Payments	Credits	(Cr)
Date	Description	Fo	Amount	Date	Description	Fo	Amount
April	Share capital	1	50 000	April	Freehold shop	10	20 000
May	Sales	50	6 000	,,	Stock	20	20 000
June	Sales	50	12 000	June	Stock	20	10 000
	Loan at 10%	4	10 000		Stock	20	10 000
					Creditor	8	5 000
					Salaries and wages	70	1 500
					Administrative expenses	71	500
							67 000
					Balance	c/d	11 000
			£78 000				£78 000
July	Balance	b/d	11 000				

THE LEDGER

The ledger is generally a bound or loose leaf book (or set of cards or data file) in which a page or specified area constituting a "ledger account" is set aside to record all transactions of a particular kind. Obviously the number of ledger accounts needed will vary according to the complexity of the business and the degree of analysis required by the managers. Careful selection of ledger account headings will make meaningful analysis of the activities of the business much easier. Further, in deciding on the contents of the ledger and the sequence of accounts it is important to remember that the company is required to produce accounts—a balance sheet and profit and loss account—at regular intervals. The ledger accounts will sensibly be designed to assist in this process and the index of a ledger suitable for IE Limited might show ledger account headings as follows:

Ledger Folio

1 Share capital	50 Sales
4 Loan at 10%	60 Cost of sales
8 Creditors	70 Salaries and wages
10 Freehold shop	71 Administrative expenses
20 Stock	
21 Debtors	

It will be seen that these headings reflect the balance sheet and profit and loss account structure. The items cover in turn the liabilities and assets sides of the balance sheet and then the income and expense items of the profit and loss account. Gaps are left in the folio or page number sequence to allow for new accounts to be opened as necessary. For example, folio 2 might be allocated to a capital reserve account should this come into being. Folio 51 might be used for dividends or interest received and so on.

But how, it may be asked, do amounts get into the ledger? How are the cash book and the ledger linked?

"Posting" to the ledger

Entries are "posted" to the ledger or entered in it from the cash book and from the journal. We can see how this is done by looking at the April cash transactions of IE Limited. These were:

Company received for share capital	£50 000
Company purchased	
(a) Freehold shop	£20 000
(b) Stock	£20 000

The cash book and ledger accounts to record these transactions are shown on the next page.

Cash Book,   Folio 1

	Debit				Credit		
Date	Description	Fo	Amount	Date	Description	Fo	Amount
April	Share capital	1	50 000	April	Freehold shop	10	20 000
					Stock	20	20 000
					Balance	c/d	10 000
			£50 000				£50 000
May	Balance	b/d	£10 000				

Ledger

Share Capital   Folio 1

	April Cash	CB1	£50 000

Freehold Shop   Folio 10

April Cash	CB1	£20 000	

Stock   Folio 21

April Cash	CB1	£20 000	

Notes

1 The entry made in the ledger for each cash book item is on the *opposite side* of the central line which separates debit and credit entries. For each cash book credit there is a corresponding ledger debit. For each cash book debit there is a corresponding ledger credit.

2 The cash book balance entered on the credit side of the cash book (balance carried down) is matched by an equal debit entry (balance brought down) on the other side.

3 From the rule that for every credit there must be a corresponding debit it follows that the total of the debit balances must equal the total of the credit balances.

4 The cash book and ledger taken together form a complete self-balancing system. This can be shown by taking out a "trial balance," or listing the balances.

		Debit £	Credit £
Ledger folio	1		50 000
	10	20 000	
	20	20 000	
Cash book	1	10 000	
		£50 000	£50 000

The cash book and ledger

We have now considered a system of records which is capable of recording and analysing cash transactions. Receipts and payments can be separately recorded, totalled and a cash balance calculated at any time. Entries can be "posted" from the cash book to the opposite side of ledger accounts from which useful financial statements can be prepared.

Now we must deal with non cash entries.

In June (in stage 4 of its growth) IE Limited

(a) Bought stock costing £10 000 for cash

(b) Bought stock costing £5000 on credit

The first of these transactions is similar to one which we have already examined and we know that the correct entries in the records are:

		Debit £	Credit £
Cash book	Credit cash		10 000
Ledger	Debit stock account	10 000	

But how do we deal with the purchase on credit? Here we need to use the journal.

THE JOURNAL

The journal or "day book" is used to record transactions, other than normal cash transactions, before they are entered in the ledger. (In a sense the cash book is a cash journal as well as being equivalent to a ledger account.) Unusual cash transactions, such as the raising of share capital, are exceptions to the rule. Because of their exceptional nature they would tend to be entered in the journal where a note would explain the nature of the transaction involved.

To record a purchase on credit a journal entry would be drawn up in the following form and then the items would be posted from the journal to the appropriate ledger accounts.

Date	Description		Fo	Debit	Credit
June	Stock account	Dr	20	5000	
	To creditor *X*		8		5000
	Purchase of stock from *X* on credit.				

Notes

1 The format of the journal differs from that of the cash book and ledger having the debit and credit columns on the right-hand side of the page.
2 It indicates the ledger accounts which have to be debited and credited showing, conventionally, the account to be debited first and that to be credited second. The debits and credits in a journal entry always balance.
3 A journal entry includes a description of the nature of the transactions—here a purchase on credit.

In the ledger the two accounts would appear as follows:

			Stock account					*Folio 20*
May	Cash	CB1	20 000	May	Cost of sales	60	5 000
June	Cash	CB1	10 000	June	Cost of sales	60	10 000
June	Creditor *X*	J/1	5 000				

			Creditors' account			*Folio 8*
			June	Stock	J/1	5 000

The journal entry to record a credit sale would be similar to that for a credit purchase. For example, in stage 5 in the growth of IE Limited:
the company sold for £6000 on credit, stock which had cost £5000.

Date	Description			Debit	Credit
June	Debtor *A*	Dr	21	6000	
	To sales		50		6000
	Sale of stock on credit				
	Cost of sales	Dr	60	5000	
	To stock		20		5000
	Transfer of stock to cost of sales				

It will be clear that transfers from the journal involve two entries in the ledger—a debit and a credit whereas on a posting from the cash book there is only one entry—to the opposite side of the ledger from that on which the cash book entry appears. This is because the ledger and cash book jointly form a total system (the cash book itself constituting, in effect, a "ledger account"), while the journal is only a subordinate record, and not part of the self-balancing system of double-entry accounts.

SUMMARY

By using the journal in conjunction with the cash book and ledger, a system for recording transactions exists which can deal with all business activities capable of being expressed in financial terms. Using the rules of double-entry book-keeping the system not only provides the analysis required but involves a self checking mechanism. If the two sides of the ledger and cash book taken together do not balance when added up, then entries have not been correctly recorded. Either a figure has been wrongly entered or an aspect of a transaction has been omitted.

We have now considered the form and purpose of the cash book, the ledger and the journal.

We have noted some of the basic rules of double-entry book-keeping:

1 Cash payments are shown on the right-hand side of the cash book and are called credits.
2 Cash receipts are shown on the left-hand side of the cash book and are called debits.
3 For every credit there must be a corresponding debit and vice versa.
4 The total of the debit balances must equal the total of the credit balances in the ledger, including the cash book balance.

We can now use the system of book-keeping which we have studied to record the remaining transactions of IE Limited and then we can prepare the company's balance sheet and profit and loss account.

EXTRACTING THE TRIAL BALANCE

As noted already, the major sequence of steps in preparing published accounts is as follows:

1 Record all transactions in the books of account.
2 Total the entries in the cash book and in each ledger account, and calculate the balances.
3 Extract a trial balance (which is a list of all the balances).
4 Make any necessary adjustments.
5 Draw up the profit and loss account and balance sheet.

We can complete these steps using the transactions of IE Limited, which are listed on the next page. The cash book, which we have already studied, is also set out there. On the following pages ledger accounts and journal pages are illustrated, and the transactions representing stages 1–4 in the growth of IE Limited have been entered.

You are now asked to complete the postings to the ledger accounts in respect of stages 5 and 6, preparing further journal entries as appropriate. Then total and balance the accounts and extract a trial balance. Space has been provided for you to do this on page 94. If all the entries made are correct, the trial balance will add up to the same amount on each side. (The solution is included on the pages following the working sheets.)

Note: Take each transaction in turn and make sure that to record it there is a debit entry *and* a credit entry in the ledger or the cash book.

IE Limited

The transactions of this company during the period April to June 1972 were:

Date	Stage		£
		(items posted to ledger)	
April	1	Received on issue of shares	50 000
April	2	Bought freehold shop	20 000
		Bought stock	20 000
May	3	Sold stock, which had cost £5000, for cash	6 000
June	4	Bought stock for cash	10 000
		Bought stock on credit	5 000
		(items to be posted to ledger)	
June	5	Sold stock, which had cost £10 000, for cash	12 000
		Sold stock, which had cost £5000, on credit	6 000
		Bought stock for cash	10 000
		Bought stock on credit	3 000
		Paid existing creditor	5 000
June	6	Paid salaries and wages	1 500
		Paid administrative expenses	500
		Received on loan at 10%	10 000

Cash book   Folio 1

Receipts		Debits	(Dr)	Payments		Credits	(Cr)
Date	Description	Fo	Amount	Date	Description	Fo	Amount
April	Share capital	1	50 000	April	Freehold shop	10	20 000
May	Sales	50	6 000	,,	Stock	20	20 000
June	Sales	50	12 000	June	Stock	20	10 000
,,	Loan at 10%	4	10 000	,,	,,	20	10 000
				,,	Creditor	8	5 000
				,,	Salaries and wages	70	1 500
				,,	Administrative expenses	71	500
							67 000
					Balance	c/d	11 000
			£78 000				£78 000
July	Balance	b/d	£11 000				

Journal   Folio 1

Date				Debit	Credit
May	Cost of sales	Dr	60	5 000	
	To stock		20		5 000
	Transfer on sale of stock				
June	Stock	Dr	20	5 000	
	To creditor X		8		5 000
	Purchase of stock on credit				

Ledger

Date	Detail	Fo	Amount Dr	Date	Detail	Fo	Amount Cr
			Share capital		*Folio 1*		
				April	Cash	1	50 000
			10% Loan		*Folio 4*		
			Creditors		*Folio 8*		
				June	Stock	J/1	5 000
			Freehold shop		*Folio 10*		
April	Cash	1	20 000				
			Stock		*Folio 20*		
April	Cash	1	20 000	May	Cost of sales	J/1	5 000
June	Cash	1	10 000				
,,	Creditors	J/1	5 000				
			Debtors		*Folio 21*		
			Sales		*Folio 50*		
				May	Cash	1	6 000

Ledger

Date	Detail	Fo	Amount Dr	Date	Detail	Fo	Amount Cr
			Cost of sales		*Folio 60*		
May	Stock	J/1	5 000				
			Salaries and wages		*Folio 70*		
			Administrative expenses		*Folio 71*		

IE LIMITED
Trial balance, 30 June 1972

			Debit	Credit
Ledger folio	1	Share capital		
	4	10% loan		
	8	Creditors		
	10	Freehold shop		
	20	Stock		
	21	Debtors		
	50	Sales		
	60	Cost of sales		
	70	Salaries and wages		
	71	Administrative expenses		
Cash book				
			£	£

IE LIMITED—transactions April–June—Solution

Cash book — Folio 1

Receipts	Debits	(Dr)			Payments	Credits	(Cr)	
Date	Description	Fo	Amount		Date	Description	Fo	Amount
April	Share capital	1	50 000		April	Freehold shop	10	20 000
May	Sales	50	6 000		"	Stock	20	20 000
June	Sales	50	12 000		June	Stock	20	10 000
"	Loan at 10%	4	10 000		"	"	20	10 000
					"	Creditor	8	5 000
					"	Salaries and wages	70	1 500
					"	Administrative expenses	71	500
								67 000
						Balance	c/d	11 000
			£78 000					£78 000
July	Balance	b/d	£11 000					

Journal — Folio 1

Date	Description		Fo	Debit	Credit
May	Cost of sales	Dr	60	5 000	
	To stock		20		5 000
	Transfer on sale of stock				
June	Stock	Dr	20	5 000	
	To creditor X		8		5 000
	Purchase of stock on credit				
June	Cost of sales	Dr	60	10 000	
	To stock		20		10 000
	Transfer on sale of stock				
June	Debtor	Dr	21	6 000	
	To sale		50		6 000
	Sale on credit to debtor A				
June	Cost of sales	Dr	60	5 000	
	To stock		20		5 000
	Transfer on sale of stock				
June	Stock	Dr	20	3 000	
	To creditor Y		8		3 000
	Purchase of stock on credit				

Ledger

Date	Description	Fo	Amount Dr	Date	Description	Fo	Amount Cr
	Share capital			Folio 1			
				April	Cash	1	50 000
	10% Loan			Folio 4			
				June	Cash	1	10 000
	Creditors			Folio 8			
June	Cash	1	5 000	June	Stock	J/1	5 000
"	Balance	c/d	3 000	"	"	J/2	3 000
			£8 000				£8 000
				July	Balance	b/d	3 000
	Freehold shop			Folio 10			
April	Cash	1	20 000				
	Stock			Folio 20			
April	Cash	1	20 000	May	Cost of sales	J/1	5 000
June	Cash	1	10 000	June	" " "	J/1	10 000
"	Creditor	J/1	5 000	"	" " "	J/1	5 000
"	Cash	1	10 000		Balance	c/d	28 000
"	Creditor	J/2	3 000				
			£48 000				£48 000
	Balance	b/d	28 000				
	Debtors			Folio 21			
June	Sale	J/1	6 000				
	Sales			Folio 50			
				May	Cash	1	6 000
				June	Cash	1	12 000
				"	Debtor	J/1	6 000
							24 000

Ledger

Date	Description	Fo	Amount Dr	Date	Description	Fo	Amount Cr
	Cost of sales			Folio 60			
May	Stock	J/1	5 000				
June	"	J/1	10 000				
"	"	J/1	5 000				
			20 000				
	Salaries and wages			Folio 70			
June	Cash	1	1 500				
	Administrative expenses			Folio 71			
June	Cash	1	500				

IE LIMITED
Trial balance, 30 June 1972

			Debit £	Credit £
Ledger folio	1	Share capital		50 000
	4	10% loan		10 000
	8	Creditors		3 000
	10	Freehold shop	20 000	
	20	Stock	28 000	
	21	Debtors	6 000	
	50	Sales		24 000
	60	Cost of sales	20 000	
	70	Salaries and wages	1 500	
	71	Administrative expenses	500	
Cash book			11 000	
			£87 000	£87 000

TRIAL BALANCE ADJUSTMENTS

Having summarised the transactions in the books of account and taken out a trial balance little now remains to be done in preparing the published accounts. At this stage are made the financial adjustments which we referred to at the beginning and which we shall deal with in sections 4–7. A summary of the total process is maintained using an "adjusted trial balance." The form of this statement is indicated below. At this stage we have no adjustments to make and the trial balance totals are shown in the profit and loss account and balance sheet columns.

Please note the way in which the profit, calculated as a credit "balance" in the profit and loss account columns, is incorporated as a credit in the balance sheet columns, thus maintaining the double-entry approach. (The profit and loss account credits exceed the debits by £2000. This amount has to be entered in the debit columns to "balance" the profit and loss account: in the ledger account "profit and loss account" this amount would be "carried down" as a debit and "brought down" as a credit.)

The profit and loss account and balance sheet, based on this adjusted trial balance, are set out on the following page. You will see that these are the same as the statements which we prepared when making individual adjustments at the beginning of this section, but this time a method has been used which can be extended to deal with very large numbers of transactions.

IE LIMITED
Trial balance at 30 June 1972

Folio		Trial balance Dr	Trial balance Cr	Adjustments Dr	Adjustments Cr	Profit and loss Dr	Profit and loss Cr	Balance sheet Dr	Balance sheet Cr
1	Share capital		50 000						50 000
4	Loan at 10%		10 000						10 000
8	Creditors		3 000						3 000
10	Freehold shop	20 000						20 000	
20	Stock	28 000						28 000	
21	Debtors	6 000						6 000	
50	Sales		24 000				24 000		
60	Cost of sales	20 000				20 000			
70	Salaries and wages	1 500				1 500			
71	Admin. expenses	500				500			
CB	Cash	11 000						11 000	
						22 000	24 000		
Profit and loss account						2 000			2 000
		£87 000	£87 000			£24 000	£24 000	£65 000	£65 000

IE LIMITED

Balance sheet, 30 June 1972

Share capital	£	Fixed assets	£
Ordinary shares	50 000	Freehold shop	20 000
Profit and loss account	2 000	**Current assets**	
Shareholders' funds	52 000	Stock	28 000	
		Debtors	6 000	
		Cash	11 000	
			45 000
10% Debenture stock	10 000		
Current liability			
Trade creditor	3 000		
	£65 000		**£65 000**

**Profit and loss account
for the three months ending 30 June 1972**

		£
Sales		24 000
Less: Cost of stock sold		20 000
Gross profit		4 000
Less: Operating expenses		
Salaries and wages	1 500	
Administrative expenses	500	
		2 000
Net profit shown in the balance sheet		£2 000

The system of accounts which we have examined provides a basis for recording transactions in small or large companies and can deal with a few or many transactions. If transactions are numerous the basic records are usually divided into parts to deal with recurring transactions of particular kinds. This is especially true in relation to the journal and the ledger.

DETAILS OF THE JOURNAL AND DAY BOOKS

Because transactions involving sales and purchases on credit occur frequently it is, in fact, unusual for these items to be included in the main journal. Separate journals or "day books" are normally used with specially ruled columns in which individual credit sales and purchases transactions are entered. Each item will then be "posted" from the day book to an individual customer's or supplier's account and in *total* only to the ledger accounts for sales or purchases. The main journal or "private journal" is then used only for non-recurring entries where a primary record or explanation is needed before entries are made in the ledger. Specimen day book and journal entries are illustrated in the following pages.

SALES AND PURCHASE DAY BOOKS

Purpose

1 To record details of:
   sales: customers' names, invoice numbers, amounts
   purchases: suppliers' names, goods inwards notes, amounts.

2 To provide a record from which entries can be "posted" to individual customers'/suppliers' accounts in the debtors'/creditors' ledger. (DL/CL).

3 To provide a daily (or weekly or monthly) total credit sales/purchases figure which will be posted to the sales or puchases account in the ledger. (Till rolls would provide the same detail for cash sales.)

Form

1 May be a bound or loose leaf book, perhaps analysed between kinds of goods sold/bought.

2 Now often an add listing attached to a batch of sales/purchase invoices prior to machine analysis and posting.

Sales Day Book

Date	Customer	Invoice No.	DL Fo	Invoice amount £	
1 March	A. Brown	013672	B 12	125	Posted to the *debit* of individual debtors' accounts in the ledger.
1 March	B. Cook	013673	C 8	60	
20 March	Jones & Co.	013674	J 17	420	
				—	
				—	
				—	
					Posted in total to the *credit* of the sales account in the ledger.
Total				£2600	

Purchase Day Book

Date	Supplier	Goods inwards note	CL Fo	Invoice amount £	
1 March	T. Lawson & Co.	732105	L 9	261	Posted to the *credit* of individual creditors' accounts in the ledger.
2 March	E. Thompson Ltd	732106	T 7	481	
3 March	Electrix Ltd	732107	E 11	160	
				—	
				—	
				—	
					Posted in total to the *debit* of the purchases account in the ledger.
Total (for week)				£1900	

99

THE JOURNAL

Purpose

1 To provide a "day book" or book of prime entry for transactions of a special nature such as an issue of shares, recording depreciation, etc.

2 To initiate and explain transfers between accounts if there would otherwise be an insufficient record.

Form

1 Often a bound book.

2 There may be more than one journal:

    (a) a private journal for special transactions in bound form.

    (b) other journals to record transfers in the form of journal vouchers or slips of paper which are used for machine posting and then filed.

Date			Fo	Debit	Credit
				£	£
Jan 17	8% Convertible preference shares	Dr	2	50 000	
	To ordinary shares		1		50 000
	Being conversion of 50 000 8% convertible preference shares of £1 each into 50 000 ordinary shares of £1 each.				
Jan 24	Plant and machinery	Dr	45	1 700	
	To repairs and renewals		85		1 700
	Being transfer of invoice from A & G Maintenance Ltd originally classified as repairs, now capitalised.				
Jan 31	Land and buildings	Dr	40	27 000	
	To capital reserve		4		27 000
	Being revaluation of land and buildings (net book value £83 000) at £110 000.				

Note: Some of the issues involved in the particular entries shown above are dealt with in sections 5 and 6.

DIVISIONS OF THE LEDGER

This too divides on the basis of type of transaction. Where ledger accounts are in frequent use and the transactions involved are repetitive separate parts of the ledger are established. The main divisions usually found are:

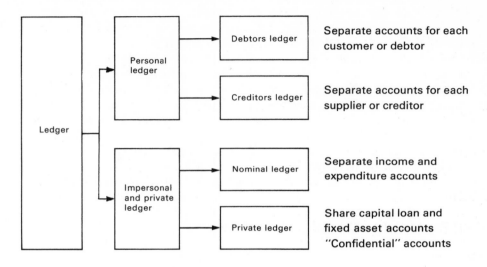

Once split, it becomes possible for work to progress simultaneously on more than one part of the ledger. In a company of any size there will tend to be thousands of entries each month (of a routine nature) in each of the debtors, creditors and nominal ledgers. For this reason they will probably be kept by mechanical or electronic means. Where unusual items occur journal entries will be made in subordinate journals linked with each part of the ledger.

The private ledger includes accounts where transactions occur less frequently—those relating, for example, to share capital, loans, fixed assets—or where the items may be confidential in nature—for example senior managers' and directors' salaries, bonus and pension scheme payments and so on. This part of the ledger will often be kept manually and in it the major accounting adjustments will be recorded.

It is normal for "control" accounts to be kept for each of the debtors, creditors and nominal ledgers in which totals will be accumulated representing all the individual transactions entered in the individual accounts. Thus monthly sales, for example, will be credited in *total* to the sales account in the nominal ledger, and debited in *total* to the debtors ledger control account in the private ledger. This is in addition, of course, to being debited individually to customers' accounts in the debtors ledger. When the totals on the control accounts are brought into the private ledger trial balance together with the cash balance, a self balancing system exists. With this system it is possible to prepare accounts at quite short notice even although there may in fact be many thousands of accounts in the whole system.

INFORMATION FLOWS

We have considered the various parts of a total accounting system and it may be helpful to see the complete process in diagrammatic form. In the final pages of this section a number of diagrams are set out representing:

1 The overall system
2 The system for recording sales
3 The system for recording purchases

The first diagram was shown in the early part of this section to indicate the flows of information in outline. Now the whole system is set out together. You may particularly like to note in looking at the sales and purchases system the way in which the double-entry rules work.

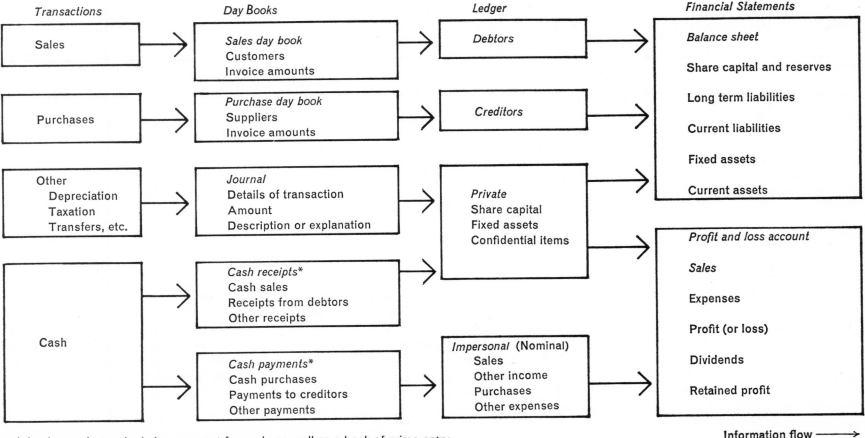

*The cash book constitutes the ledger account for each, as well as a book of prime entry.

Information flow ⟶

2 Recording sales—major information flows

Sales Day Book
(Credit sales)

Brown	—
Cook	—
Jones	—
Total	£2600 (C)

Debtors' Ledger (Control)*

Dr		Cr	
Balance b/f	1200	Cash	2000 B
Sales	2600 C	Balance c/d	1800 F
	£3800		£3800
Balance b/d	1800 F		

Profit and Loss Account

Dr		Cr	
(Expenses)		Sales	4000 D

→ Information flow →

Cash Book

Dr		Cr	
Balance b/f	300	(Payments)	3000
Cash sales	1400 A	Balance c/d	700 E
From debtors	2000 B		
	£3700		£3700
Balance b/d	700 E		

Impersonal Ledger
Sales

Dr		Cr	
P & L a/c	4000 D	Cash	1400 A
		Credit	2600 C
	£4000		£4000

Balance Sheet**

Capital & Liabilities		*Assets*	
(Cr)		(Dr)	
Profit			
		Debtors	1800 F
		Cash	700 E

*Behind the debtors' ledger control will be individual ledger accounts for each debtor, including Brown, Cook, Jones, etc.
Notice the "double-entry" system—each item has both a debit (Dr) and a credit (Cr) entry, identified by letters.

**Notice that balances on the capital and liabilities ledger accounts (Cr) are shown on the *left* of the balance sheet, while asset balances (Dr) are shown on the right. (The "net asset" format avoids a need for "left" and "right.")

3 Recording purchases—major information flows

Purchase Day Book
(credit purchases)

Lawson	—
Thompson	—
Electrix	—
Total	£1900 (C)

Creditors' Ledger (Control)*

Dr		Cr	
Cash	2100 B	Balance b/f	1100
Balance c/d	900 F	Purchases	1900 C
	£3000		£3000
		Balance b/d	900 F

Profit and Loss Account

Dr		Cr	
Purchases	2300 G	(Sales)	4000
Wages	500 H		
Profit c/d	1200 I		
	£4000		£4000
		Profit b/d	1200 I

Information flow →

Cash Book

Dr		Cr	
Balance b/f	300	Cash purchases	400 A
(Receipts)	3400	To creditors	2100 B
		Wages	500 D
		Balance c/d	700 E
	£3700		£3700
Balance b/d	700 E		

Impersonal Ledger
Purchases

Dr		Cr	
Cash	400 A	P & L a/c	2300 G
Credit	1900 C		
	£2300		£2300

Wages

Dr		Cr	
Cash	£500 D	P & L a/c	£500 H

Balance Sheet**

Capital and liabilities (Cr)		Assets (Dr)	
Profit	1200 I		
Creditors	900 F	Cash	700 E
		(Debtors)	1800

*Behind the creditors' ledger control will be individual ledger accounts for each creditor, including Lawson, Thompson, Electrix, etc.

**See note on previous page.

SUMMARY OF THE APPENDIX

In this Appendix we have considered the working of the cash book, the ledger, and the journal (and subsidiary day books), and we have seen how together the cash book and the ledger form a self-balancing entity because each transaction requires a *double* entry in the books—a credit entry and a debit entry. Thus the books (that is, the total of the balances on all the ledger accounts, including cash) should *always* balance.

The cash book may be regarded as the "ledger account for cash": it *is* part of the double entry system. Similarly, the profit and loss account may be regarded as a ledger account to which the various balances on the ledger accounts for sales, purchases, and other expenses are transferred at the end of each accounting period.

The balance sheet, however, is *not* itself a ledger account. It summarises and classifies *all* the balances on the ledger accounts, including the balances on the cash book and on the profit and loss account. Hence the method of presenting the balance sheet is not critical, whether a business prefers the horizontal "account" format or the vertical "net asset" format. Indeed American balance sheets are usually in the "account" format, but with assets on the left and liabilities on the right—the opposite side to those in the British account format.

We have seen how postings are made to the ledger, and how a trial balance is extracted. We have considered—in outline form only at this stage—how any necessary adjustments to the trial balance would be made, and how the figures required for the final profit and loss account and balance sheet are extracted from the trial balance schedule.

We have also discussed certain practical extensions of the basic double-entry idea. One of the most useful in practice is the "control account" system, whereby *all* the balances on the debtors' ledger are reflected in a single "debtors' control account" (and the same with the creditors' ledger).

It is not the intention of this book to provide a comprehensive survey of the mechanics of book-keeping, merely to outline the main concepts. These apply equally whether manual or machine accounting systems are employed. Those readers who want to consolidate their understanding of the basic procedures may want now to turn to the problems (and worked solutions) which will give some practice in working through book-keeping exercises.

Review—double-entry book-keeping

We can summarise the rules of double-entry book-keeping as follows:

1 Cash payments are made with the *right hand* and are called *credits*.
2 Cash receipts are made with the *left hand* and are called *debits*.
3 For each *credit* there must be a corresponding *debit* and vice versa.
4 The total of the debit balances in the ledger accounts must equal the total of the credit balances (including the cash book as a ledger account). A number of subsidiary rules can be derived from the major rules which are useful in recording transactions.
5 Following from the fact that cash payments are on the *right hand* side and *credits* then assets and expenses (which are the other side of the cash payments) appear in the ledger on the *left hand* side and are *debits*. Assets and expenses are debits whether they arise from cash transactions or from transactions on credit.
6 Following from the fact that cash receipts are on the *left hand* side and are *debits* then liabilities and revenue appear in the ledger on the *right hand* side and are credits. Liabilities and revenue are credits whether they arise from cash transactions or from transactions on credit—for example, credit sales.

Finally:

7 Transactions which *reduce assets and expenses* (which are debits) in the ledger must be credits—for example, sale of asset or refund of expenses.
8 Transactions which *reduce liabilities and revenue* (which are credits) in the ledger must be debits—for example, payments to creditors and payments for expenses.

3.6 Definitions

Write down opposite your definitions of the terms shown. Then compare your answers with the definitions overleaf.

(a) A credit entry

(b) The cash book

(c) A journal entry

(d) Ledger posting

(e) The "balance" on a ledger account

(f) A trial balance

(g) Debtors' control account

(h) Double-entry book-keeping

(i) Debit

(j) Write-off

3.6 Definitions

(a) A credit entry is an entry on the right-hand side of the ledger account or cash book (a debit entry being one on the left-hand side). It may increase a credit balance on a liability or income account, or *decrease* a debit balance on an asset or expense account. In accounting "credit" carries no favourable connotation.

(b) *The cash book* is the accounting "book" (or other record) in which are entered (either individually or in summary) all cash receipts and payments. The cash book represents the "ledger account for cash" as well as being a day book from which a ledger account entry is made.

(c) *A journal entry* sets out the debit and credit entries to be made in the ledger in respect of a business transaction, and describes the nature of the transaction. A journal entry always "balances", with debits equalling credits in total.

(d) *Ledger posting* is the process of making entries in the ledger from either the journal (or other day books) or the cash book.

(e) *The "balance" on a ledger account* is the difference between the total of the credit entries and the total of the debit entries. Where the former are greater, there is a "credit balance". Balances are periodically "carried down" to simplify the ledger account and to facilitate regular accounting.

(f) *A trial balance* is a list of all the balances on ledger accounts (including the cash book balance). It forms the basis for preparing published accounts. Since there ought to be a debit for every credit, the debit balances should always equal the credit balances in total.

(g) *Debtors' control account* is a ledger account in which are entered (in total) all items posted to the accounts of individual debtors. The balance on the control account equals the total of the individual balances.

(h) *Double-entry book-keeping* (which Goethe called "one of the finest inventions of the human mind"!) is a system of accounting for business transactions which recognises the dual aspect—sources of funds necessarily equals uses of funds. Thus there is a debit entry for every credit entry in the books.

(i) *Debit* may mean "a debit entry", which is the opposite of a credit entry. A debit entry is an entry on the left-hand side of a ledger account. It carries no unfavourable connotation. Alternatively "debit" may mean "make a debit entry".

(j) *Write-off* means charging an amount as an expense. "A write-off" means an amount so treated.

3.7 Identifying debit and credit balances

Indicate for each of the following whether it would appear as a debit or credit balance *in the ledger*.

	£
Cash held on deposit	1 000
Payment of telephone expenses	200
Share capital	50 000
Debtors	5 000
Cash received on sale of fixed assets	2 000
Stock held for resale	8 000
Received from debtors	1 000
Creditors	7 000
Purchase of motor car	1 500
Share premium account	10 000
Paid to suppliers (creditors)	3 000
Repayment of loan	1 000

When you have entered the amounts in the correct columns compare your answers with those shown on the next page.

Note: There are *other* items in the ledger. The above don't "balance".

Dr £	Cr £

3.7 The items shown below would appear
in the ledger **as follows:**

	£			Dr £	Cr £
Cash held on deposit	1 000	(Asset	Cash previously received)	1000	
Payment of telephone expenses	200	(Expenses	Opposite of cash payment)	200	
Share capital	50 000	(Liability	Opposite of cash receipt)		50 000
Debtors	5 000	(Asset	Opposite to sale which is a credit)	5000	
Cash received on sale of fixed assets	2 000	(Reduction of asset	Opposite to cash receipt)		2 000
Stock held for resale	8 000	(Asset	Opposite to cash payment or creditor)	8000	
Received from debtors	1 000	(Reduction in asset	Opposite to cash receipt)		1 000
Creditors	7 000	(Liabilities	Opposite to expenses or assets)		7 000
Purchase of motor car	1 500	(Asset	Opposite to cash payment)	1500	
Share premium account	10 000	(Liability	Opposite to cash receipt)		10 000
Paid to suppliers (creditors)	3 000	(Reduction in liability	Opposite to cash payment)	3000	
Repayment of loan	1 000	(Reduction in liability	Opposite to cash payment)	1000	

Double-entry book-keeping exercises

3.8 Midmarsh Golf Club

The book-keeper of the Midmarsh Golf Club has been trying for some time to draw up the accounts of the Club for the year ending 31 March 1972. He has taken out a trial balance (from his ledger accounts and cash book) but it does not balance! You are asked to examine his work and to alter the entries to make the two sides balance.

	Book-keeper's Trial Balance		Correct Trial Balance	
	Dr £	*Cr* £	*Dr* £	*Cr* £
Subscription income		3000		
Cash in hand	200			
Bar stock		950		
Sports equipment for resale	450			
Subscriptions due, not received		100		
Electricity bills paid	250			
Staff wages paid		2300		
Profit on annual dance		400		
Creditors	300			
Fixtures and fittings	1400			
Profit on bar sales	500			
Accumulated surplus: 1 April 1971	2500			
Repair bills paid		450		
Cleaning expenses	600			
	£6200	£7200	£	£

When you have completed your entries and arrived at a trial balance which balances, please compare your answer with that shown on the next page.

MIDMARSH GOLF CLUB:
Trial balance, 31 March 1972

	Correct Trial Balance	
	Dr	*Cr*
	£	£
Subscription income		3000
Cash in hand	200	
Bar stock	950	
Sports equipment for resale	450	
Subscriptions due, not received	100	
Electricity bills paid	250	
Staff wages paid	2300	
Profit on annual dance		400
Creditors		300
Fixtures and fittings	1400	
Profit on bar sales		500
Accumulated surplus: 1 April 1971		2500
Repair bills paid	450	
Cleaning expenses	600	
	£6700	£6700

Please turn over

3.9 Abacus Book Shop Limited (D)

The cash book and journal are illustrated on this page, and the ledger on the next. The balance at 1 January, as shown in the balance sheet opposite, has been incorporated in the books. The transactions for January, which were previously entered directly onto the balance sheet, are shown below and you are now asked to:

(a) Enter the transactions in the books of accounts

(b) Extract a trial balance

(c) Prepare a profit and loss account and balance sheet

When you have completed your answer please turn to the solution shown on the following pages.

Transactions during January:

(a) Received £1000 cash from credit customers

(b) Bought books for stock for £2000 cash

(c) Sold books for £3000 cash which had cost £2000

ABACUS BOOK SHOP LIMITED
Balance sheet, 1 January 1972

	£		£
Share capital		**Current assets**	
Ordinary shares	3000	Stock	4000
		Debtors	2000
Revenue reserve		Cash	2000
Profit and loss account	4000		
	7000		
Current liabilities			
Creditors	1000		
	£8000		£8000

Journal

Date	Description	Fo	Dr	Cr

Cash Book

Date	Description	Fo	Amount	Date	Description	Fo	Amount
Jan	Balance		2000				

Ledger

Share capital
	Jan Balance	3000

Revenue reserve
	Jan Balance	4000

Creditors
	Jan Balance	1000

Stock
Jan Balance	4000	

Debtors
Jan Balance	2000	

Sales

Cost of sales

When you have posted all the entries to the ledger accounts, extract a trial balance and then prepare a profit and loss account and balance sheet. The solution is shown on the next two pages.

ABACUS BOOK SHOP LIMITED
Trial balance, 31 January 1972

	Dr £	Cr £	Profit and loss account Dr £	Profit and loss account Cr £	Balance Sheet Dr £	Balance Sheet Cr £
Share capital						
Revenue reserve						
Creditors						
Stock						
Debtors						
Sales						
Cost of sales						
Cash book						

Balance sheet

Profit and Loss Account

113

3.9 Abacus Book Shop Limited (D)

Solution

Transactions during January:

(a)   Received £1000 cash from credit customers

(b)   Bought new books for £2000 cash

(c)   Sold books for £3000 cash which had cost £2000

Journal

Date	Description		Fo	Dr	Cr
(c)[1]	Cash	Dr		3000	
	To Sales				3000
	Sale of books				
(c)	Cost of sales	Dr		2000	
	To stock				2000
	Stock transferred to cost of sales				

[1]This entry can be omitted.

ABACUS BOOK SHOP LIMITED
Balance sheet, 1 January 1972

	£		£
Share capital		**Current assets**	
Ordinary shares	3000	Stock	4000
		Debtors	2000
Revenue reserve		Cash	2000
Profit and loss account	4000		
	7000		
Current liabilities			
Creditors	1000		
	£8000		£8000

Cash Book

Date	Description	Fo	Amount	Date	Description	Fo	Amount
Jan	Balance		2000	(b)	Stock		2000
(a)	Debtors		1000		Balance	c/d	4000
	Sales		3000				
			£6000				£6000
	Balance	b/d	4000				

Ledger

Share capital

		Balance	3000

Revenue reserve

		Balance	4000

Creditors

		Balance	1000

Stock

	Balance	4000	(c) Cost of Sales	2000
(b)	Cash	2000	Balance c/d	4000
		£6000		£6000
	Balance b/d	4000		

Debtors

	Balance	2000	(a) Cash	1000
			Balance c/d	1000
		£2000		£2000
	Balance b/d	1000		

Sales

		(c) Cash	3000

Cost of sales

(c)	Stock	2000	

Note: The balance sheet is the same as that shown on page 115. The profit and loss account derived from ledger account balances was not shown separately on page 115.

ABACUS BOOK SHOP LIMITED
Trial balance

	Dr	Cr	Profit and loss account Dr	Profit and loss account Cr	Balance sheet Dr	Balance sheet Cr
Share capital		3 000				3000
Revenue reserve		4 000				4000
Creditors		1 000				1000
Stock	4 000				4000	
Debtors	1 000				1000	
Sales		3 000		3000		
Cost of sales	2 000		2000			
Cash book	4 000				4000	
Profit			1000			1000
	£11 000	11 000	3000	3000	9000	9000

Balance sheet, 31 January 1972

	£		£
Share capital		**Current assets**	
Ordinary shares	3000	Stock	4000
		Debtors	1000
Revenue reserve		Cash	4000
Profit and loss account	5000		
	8000		
Current liabilities			
Creditors	1000		
	£9000		£9000

Profit and loss account
for month ending 31 January 1972

	£
Sales	3000
Cost of sales	2000
	1000
Balance b/f	4000
Balance c/f	£5000

115

3.10   A. Green Limited

The balance sheet of A. Green Limited (vegetable wholesalers) at 31 March 1973 is shown opposite.

In the three month period to 30 June the following transactions took place:

		£
(a)	Purchases of vegetables on credit	16 000
(b)	Sales for cash of vegetables which had cost £12 000	15 000
(c)	Sales on credit of vegetables which had cost £4000	5 000
(d)	Operating expenses paid in cash—wages, vans etc.	2 000
(e)	Cash payments to suppliers	14 000
(f)	Cash receipts from debtors	3 000

You are asked to:

(a) Open up cash book and ledger accounts and enter the opening balances (shown in the 31 March balance sheet).

(b) Record the transactions shown above and balance the accounts, as necessary.

(c) Extract a trial balance.

(d) Prepare a profit and loss account for the quarter ending 30 June 1973 and a balance sheet as at that date.

The suggested solution to this problem is shown at the end of the book.

A. GREEN LIMITED
Balance sheet, 31 March 1973

	£		£
Share capital		**Fixed assets**	
Ordinary shares	3000	Vans	4000
Revenue reserve		**Current assets**	
Profit and loss account	2000	Debtors	1000
	5000	Cash	3000
			4000
Current liability			
Creditors	3000		
	£8000		£8000

3.11 Precision Engineering Limited

The balance sheet and profit and loss account of Precision Engineering Limited, for the half year ending 30 June 1972 is set out on the right-hand side. During the second half of 1972 the following transactions took place:

		£	Cost of goods sold £
(a)	Sales for cash	35 000	25 000
(b)	Sales on credit	15 000	11 000
(c)	Purchases of goods for cash	25 000	
(d)	Purchases of goods on credit	8 000	
	Cash payments in addition to cash purchases		
(e)	Expenses	10 000	
(f)	Payments to creditors	9 000	
	Cash receipts in addition to cash sales		
(g)	Receipts from debtors	13 000	

You are asked to open up a cash book and ledger accounts incorporating the balances at 30 June 1972. You are then asked to:

(a) Record the transactions in the books of account for the second half of 1972 and balance the accounts as necessary.

(b) Extract a trial balance.

(c) Prepare a profit and loss account for the year ending 31 December 1972 and a balance sheet as at that date. (Leave the tax provision at £1000.)

The suggested solution to this problem is shown at the end of the book.

Please use separate paper to prepare your own cash book, ledger, trial balance, profit and loss account, and balance sheet.

PRECISION ENGINEERING LIMITED
Balance sheet, 30 June 1972

	£			£
Share capital		**Fixed assets**		
Ordinary shares	30 000	Factory and machinery		25 000
Revenue reserve		**Current assets**		
Profit and loss account	15 000	Stock	20 000	
	45 000	Debtors	6 000	
Current liabilities		Cash	4 000	
Creditors	10 000			30 000
	£55 000			£55 000

Profit and loss account
for half year to 30 June 1972

		£
Sales		40 000
Cost of sales		30 000
	Gross profit	10 000
Expenses		7 000
	Profit before tax	3 000
Tax		1 000
	Profit after tax	2 000
Balance brought forward 1-1-1972		13 000
Balance carried forward 30-6-1972		£15 000

Section 4
Measuring profit or loss

PROFIT DETERMINATION AND THE ACCOUNTING PROCESS

So far we have not been concerned with the problems of measuring profit. We have simply accepted that revenue (sales in the case of a trading company) less expenses equals profit (or loss when expenses exceed revenue). This uncomplicated approach is adequate as far as it goes, but it assumes that revenue and expenses can be measured precisely. In many cases, however, measurement is difficult, and elaborate accounting rules have been developed to deal with more complex situations.

Even using these rules, the profit reported for a given period is often much less certain than is generally understood because questions arise in which subjective judgements are involved. The reason for this is apparent when the impact of the accounting process on a typical business is considered. Businesses are normally ongoing concerns, and the measurement of profit involves "freezing" them at regular intervals (say annually) for long enough to measure all the constituent parts. The diagram below illustrates this.

Measuring transactions which are incomplete at the chosen accounting date presents particular problems, whose nature may become clearer by looking at two simple examples. In the first example, the transactions fall within one accounting period; in the second, incomplete transactions are involved.

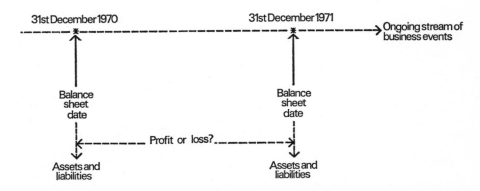

Profit determination: all items within one accounting period

A. Green runs a wholesale greengrocery business.

In the year to 31 December 1972 his transactions were:

	£
Sales for cash	100 000
Purchases of goods	80 000
Cash paid for operating expenses	10 000

There is no opening or closing stock.

The revenue and expense figures are known amounts which clearly relate to 1972, and the net profit before tax is £10 000.

	£
Sales	100 000
Cost of sales	80 000
Gross profit	20 000
Operating expenses	10 000
Net profit before tax	£10 000

Profit determination: incomplete transactions

Now suppose that *in addition* to the facts in the previous example:

1 Mr Green had sold a further £5000 on credit to Mr *X* who had paid £4000 of the amount due. The balance of £1000 remains outstanding and Mr *X* is in financial difficulties. It seems unlikely that he will be able to pay the full amount.

2 Mr Green had goods left in stock at 31 December 1972 which had cost £2000. Half the goods were highly perishable and would become worthless if not sold on the following day. The other half would keep for up to a week.

Under these conditions, what is Mr Green's profit for 1972? Here a range of possible figures exists. Two are shown below:

Alternative A		£	Alternative B		£
Sales		105 000	Sales		105 000
Purchases	80 000		*Less:* Bad debt		1 000
Less: Stock	2000				104 000
		78 000	Purchases		80 000
Gross profit		27 000	Gross profit		24 000
Operating expenses		10 000	Operating expenses		10 000
Net profit		£17 000	Net profit		£14 000

The difference between the two profit figures illustrates clearly the different views taken about the outstanding debt of £1000 and the remaining stock which had cost £2000. Alternative *A* assumes that the whole £1000 will be collected and that the entire remaining stock will be sold. Alternative *B* takes a pessimistic view about the outcome of both transactions. Notice that both alternatives make assumptions about *uncertain future events*.

Obviously if the debt is collected and the stock is sold, then under alternative *B* an extra profit of £3000 will be made *in 1973*. On the other hand, if the debt proves to be bad and the stock is not sold, then under alternative *A* profits in 1973 will be *reduced* as these amounts are written off. Judgements made under such conditions thus affect the profits of *two* periods, not just one. The "true" 1972 profit lies between £14 000 and £17 000 and depends on the view taken about the value of the asset represented by the stock and the debtor at the year-end.

Profit measurement as a valuation process

Our conception of profit can be extended by defining it not only as "revenue less expenses" but also as "the change in book value of net assets" during an accounting period.

The example below shows a profit in 1971 of £7000, a figure which is both "sales less expenses" and also "closing net assets (capital employed) less opening net assets (capital employed)."

In calculating profit as the difference between the closing and opening capital employed figures, it is assumed that adjustments are made to eliminate any capital transactions in the period. Thus if £10 000 new capital had been introduced in the year, the difference in net assets would increase to £17 000 of which only £7000 is profit. It would also be necessary to add back any dividends paid and to make any other appropriate adjustments.

The valuation process may be simple or difficult depending on the nature of the assets involved. If, for example, the net current assets figure shown in the accounts is a cash balance there will be no problem, but if it comprises stock or debtors, judgements will have to be made concerning their value at the balance sheet date. The position is still more complex with fixed assets as we shall see in section 5.

Defining profit in these two interrelated ways may make it easier to understand why the methods of valuation used in determining balance sheet figures are just as relevant in calculating profit or loss as determining the level of income or expenses to be reported. They are two aspects of the same process dealing with incomplete transactions. Variations in balance sheet figures are reflected in those for profit, and vice versa.

Profit and loss account for the year ending 31 March 1971

1970 £		1971 £
100 000	Sales	120 000
80 000	Cost of sales	90 000
20 000	Gross profit	30 000
10 000	Operating expenses	15 000
10 000	Profit before tax	15 000
5 000	Taxation	8 000
£5 000	Profit after tax	£7 000

Balance sheet at 31 March 1971

1970 £		1971 £
30 000	Share capital	30 000
15 000	Profit and loss account	22 000
£45 000	*Capital employed*	£52 000
20 000	Fixed assets	25 000
25 000	Net current assets	27 000
£45 000	*Net assets*	£52 000

Profit = £7 000

{
  Sales £120 000   *Less*   Expenses (£90 000 + £15 000 + £8 000)

  Closing capital employed £52 000   *Less*   Opening capital employed £45 000
}

Our interest, in looking at the measurement of profit, lies not so much in dealing with the theoretical problems of accounting but with securing a clear idea of what the figures actually disclosed in company accounts mean, how they have been calculated, and within what range of possible profit (or loss) figures the disclosed result falls. We shall see that the degree of accuracy of published results will vary according to the nature of the business whose performance is being measured. The larger the number of incomplete transactions involved, the longer the time span between the beginning and end of the transactions being measured, and the greater their significance in relation to the total business during the period, the greater will be the range of possible profit figures.

We shall consider the problems of measuring profit and loss under two main headings: (*a*) net current assets, and (*b*) fixed assets. The fixed asset adjustments will be dealt with in the next section when we consider cost and valuation of fixed assets, depreciation provisions and the impact of inflation.

In this section we shall look at problems mainly involving net current assets, in the following order:

1 Accrual accounting
2 Measuring sales revenue
3 Valuing stock: (*a*) in a trading company (*b*) in a manufacturing company
4 Measuring expenses
5 Measuring profits on long-term contracts
6 Non-recurring items and prior years' adjustments

ACCRUAL ACCOUNTING

We have seen that the accounting process seeks to "freeze" the business as at the date to which accounts are to be made up, but in the normal course of events many transactions will be in progress at this date, and adjustments will be required in calculating the profit or loss. Indeed, much of the difficulty in accounting stems from the arbitrary "chopping up" of a business's whole life into accounting periods.

In accrual accounting, income and expense are recognised when they accrue due, not when they are actually received or paid. It is of fundamental importance to distinguish between cash receipts and "income," between cash expenditure and "expense."

In analysing the accounts of a small property company for the year ending 31 December 1970, for example, one might find the income and expense adjustments as set out on the following pages. These illustrate the difference between amounts received and paid in a period on the one hand and the reported accounting income and expenses on the other.

Receipts and income

The following transactions are shown below:

(a) Annual rent of £1000 received in advance in July 1969, half of which relates to 1970.

(b) Annual rent of £500 received in advance in January 1970, all of which relates to 1970.

(c) Annual rent of £800 received in advance in April 1970, one quarter of which relates to 1971.

(d) Half-yearly rent of £600 received in arrear in March 1971, half of which relates to 1970.

Note that in accounts prepared on an accrual basis, income is allocated to the period to which it *relates* as opposed to that in which it is *received* (cash basis).

Thus "rent income" for 1970 is £1900, although only £1300 cash was actually *received* in 1970.

Similar considerations apply in dealing with expenditure and expense, as shown on the next page.

(A) $\frac{1}{2}$ × £1000 in advance = £500 liability at 31 December 1969
(C) $\frac{1}{4}$ × £800 in advance = £200 liability at 31 December 1970
(D) $\frac{1}{2}$ × £600 due (receivable) = £300 asset at 31 December 1970

(A)	£500 received in 1969 relating to 1970	(a) $\frac{1}{2}$ × £1000 =	£500
	£1300 cash received in 1970	(b)	£500
(C)	(£200) received in 1970 relating to 1971	(c) $\frac{3}{4}$ × £800 =	£600
(D)	£300 relating to 1970 received in 1971	(d) $\frac{1}{2}$ × £600 =	£300
	£1900 = Rent "income" in 1970 =		£1900

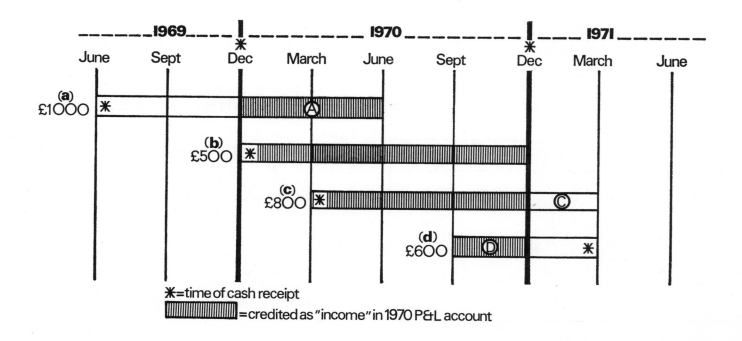

✳ = time of cash receipt

▮▮▮▮▮ = credited as "income" in 1970 P&L account

Expenditure and expense

The following transactions are shown below:

(a) Annual rent of £800 paid in advance in October 1969, three quarters of which relates to 1970.

(b) Half-yearly rent of £600 paid in advance in October 1970, half of which relates to 1971.

(c) Annual rent of £500 paid in arrear in December 1970, all of which relates to 1970.

(d) Annual rent of £400 paid in arrear in June 1971, half of which relates to 1970.

Note that in an accrual accounting system rent payable is charged in the period to which it relates, not in the period in which cash is paid.

Thus rent "expense" in 1970 is £1600, although only £1100 was actually *paid* in the period.

On the next page are shown the entries in the books of account to record the items of rents receivable and rents payable which we have been considering.

(A) $\frac{3}{4}$ × £800 in advance = £600 asset at 31 December 1969
(B) $\frac{1}{2}$ × £600 in advance = £300 asset at 31 December 1970
(D) $\frac{1}{2}$ × £400 due (payable) = £200 liability at 31 December 1970

(A)	£600	paid in 1969 relating to 1970	(a)	$\frac{3}{4}$ × £800 =	£600
	£1100	cash paid in 1970	(b)	$\frac{1}{2}$ × £600 =	£300
(B)	(£300)	paid in 1970 relating to 1971	(c)		£500
(D)	£200	paid in 1971 relating to 1970	(d)	$\frac{1}{2}$ × £400 =	£200
	£1600	= Rent "expense" in 1970 =			£1600

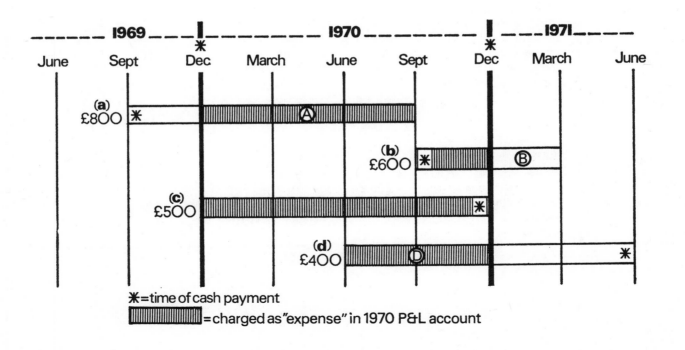

✳ = time of cash payment

▓▓▓▓▓ = charged as "expense" in 1970 P&L account

RECEIPTS AND INCOME

Cash Book

1970	£		£
Jan (b) Rent	500		
Apr (c) Rent	800		
	1300		

Ledger Account

Rents Receivable

1970	£	1970	£
Dec Profit and loss account:		Jan Balance b/d:	
"Income" in 1970	1900	Rent received in advance	500 (a)
Dec Balance c/d:		Jan Cash	500 (b)
Rent received in advance	200 (c)	Apr Cash	800 (c)
		Dec Balance c/d:	
		Rent receivable accrued	
		due	300 (d)
	£2100		£2100
1971		1971	
Jan Balance b/d:		Jan Balance b/d:	
Rent receivable accrued due 300 (d)		Rent received in advance	200 (c)
(Shown in the balance sheet as a debtor)		(Shown in the balance sheet as a creditor)	

EXPENDITURE AND EXPENSE

Cash Book

	£	1970	£
		Oct (b) Rent	600
		Dec (c) Rent	500
			1100

Ledger Account

Rents Payable

1970	£	1970	£
Jan Balance b/d:		Dec profit and loss account:	
Rent paid in advance	600 (a)	"Expense" in 1970	1600
Oct Cash	600 (b)	Dec Balance c/d:	
Dec Cash	500 (c)	Rent paid in advance	300 (b)
Dec Balance c/d:			
Rent payable accrued due	200 (d)		
	£1900		£1900
1971		1971	
Jan Balance b/d:		Jan Balance b/d:	
Rent paid in advance	300 (b)	Rent payable, accrued due	200 (d)
(Shown in the balance sheet as a debtor—"prepayment")		(Shown in the balance sheet as a creditor—"accrued charge")	

Rentwell Limited

Rentwell Limited's book-keeper had drawn up the profit and loss account and balance sheet shown opposite (tax is ignored to simplify the example).

An examination by the company's auditor revealed that adjustments were required to cover:

(a) Annual rent received of £4000 for one property, relating to the year ending in September, had all been included in the accounts to 30 June.

(b) No adjustment had been made in the accounts for rent payable by Rentwell on Blackacre. This property was held on a long lease at £2000 per annum, with rent payable six-monthly in arrears on 31 March and 30 September.

(c) Rates of £400 per annum on another property had been paid for a year in advance on 1 April. No allowance had been made for the amount paid in advance at 30 June.

(d) Repair work for which Rentwell was liable was being carried out at 30 June on one of the company's properties. The work, which cost £200, was not finished until 31 July, and was estimated to be half finished at 30 June.

You are asked to amend the profit and loss account and balance sheet opposite to show the correct figures for the year ending 30 June 1970. Strike out any figures which need changing and insert the correct ones. The answer is shown overleaf.

RENTWELL LIMITED

Profit and loss account for the year ending 30 June 1970

		£
Rents receivable		60 000
Less: Rents payable	40 000	
Rates	5 000	
Other expenses	4 000	
		49 000
Net profit		£11 000

Balance sheet at 30 June 1970

		£
Ordinary shares		30 000
Profit and loss account		20 000
		£50 000
Leasehold properties		45 000
Debtors and prepayments	5 000	
Cash	1 000	
	6 000	
Less: Creditors and accrued charges	1 000	
		5 000
		£50 000

Final Solution
RENTWELL LIMITED

Profit and loss account for the year to 30 June 1970

		£
Rents receivable		59 000
Less: Rents payable	40 500	
Rates	4 700	
Other expenses	4 100	
	49 300	
Net profit		£9 700

Balance sheet at 30 June 1970

		£
Share capital		
Ordinary shares		30 000
Reserves		
Profit and loss account		18 700
		£48 700
Fixed assets		
Leasehold properties		45 000
Current assets: Debtors and prepayments	5 300	
Cash	1 000	
	6 300	
Less: Current liabilities		
Creditors and accrued charges	1 600	
Amounts received in advance	1 000	
	2 600	
		3 700
		£48 700

Working paper
RENTWELL LIMITED

Profit and loss account for the year ending 30 June 1970

Rents receivable − 1000 ª   59 000 / 60 000 £

Less: Rents payable + 500 ᵇ   40500 → 40 000

Rates − 300 ᶜ   4700 → 5 000

Other expenses + 100 ᵈ   4100 → 5 000

49 300 / 49 000

Net profit   £11 000 / 9 700

Balance sheet at 30 June 1970

Ordinary shares   30 000

Profit and loss account   18,700 → 20 000

48700 → £50 000

Leasehold properties   45 000

Debtors and prepayments + 300 ᶜ   5300 / 5 000

Cash   1 000

+ 500 ᵇ + 100 ᵈ   6300 → 6 000

Less: Creditors and accrued charges   1600 → 1 000   3700 / 5 000

Amount received in advance + 1000 ª   1 000

2600   £50 000 / 48 700

This case illustrates how the adjustments affect both the profit and loss account and the balance sheet. Obviously the changes would not normally be made on the face of the accounts. It is for adjustments of this kind that the "adjustments" column which we saw in the trial balance in the Appendix to section 3 would be used. The adjustments would then be incorporated in the books of account when the "final" accounts had been completed.

The entries would appear on the trial balance schedule as follows:

	Trial balance Dr	Trial balance Cr	Adjustments Dr	Adjustments Cr	Profit and loss Dr	Profit and loss Cr	Balance sheet Dr	Balance sheet Cr
	£	£	£	£	£	£	£	£
Share capital		30 000						30 000
Profit and loss, balance b/f		9 000[1]						9 000[1]
Leasehold properties	45 000						45 000	
Debtors and prepayments	5 000		300[c]				5 300	
Cash	1 000						1 000	
Creditors		1 000		500[b] 100[d]				1 600
Received in advance				1 000[a]				1 000
Rents receivable		60 000	1 000[a]			59 000		
Rents payable	40 000		500[b]		40 500			
Rates	5 000			300[c]	4 700			
Other expenses	4 000		100[d]		4 100			
					49 300			
Profit for the year[2]					9 700[2]			9 700[2]
	100 000	100 000	1 900[3]	1 900[3]	59 000	59 000	51 300	51 300

[1] This is the opening balance. The items which make up the net profit for the year are shown individually.

[2] The profit for the year, £9700, is added to the balance brought forward on the profit and loss account, £9000, to give the figure carried forward on the balance sheet, £18 700.

[3] Notice that the adjustments "balance," since they follow the double-entry principle.

Accrual accounting: a summary

We have seen that receipts must be distinguished from income, and expenditure from expense. Income and expense are "recognised" when they accrue due, not when they are actually received or paid. Amounts paid or received in advance or in arrear are the subject of adjustments in preparing accounts and give rise to debtor or creditor balances in the balance sheet.

The basis for many adjustments is *time,* amounts being included in the *period* to which they relate. There is often little difficulty in making apportionments of income and expense on a time basis.

Another basis used for making adjustments, which we shall consider later in this section, is to charge expense in the accounting period in which the related revenue is recognised. Thus expenditure may be carried forward from the period in which it is actually incurred so that it can be "matched" in a later period against the revenue which it has generated. Here there are much greater difficulties, for the "asset" represented by this kind of "deferred revenue expenditure" may sometimes be of dubious value. How can anyone tell, for example, whether a major film costing £2 million is ever going to recover its cost? Yet a judgement has to be made for accounting purposes, which will affect the results of more than one accounting period.

It follows from what has been said that merely because a company has made a *profit* does not imply that it has a corresponding amount of *cash* on hand. The profit may result from *credit* sales for which cash has not yet been received; and even if sales revenue has been received in cash the cash may already have been spent (for example on advertising future products, or on investment in fixed assets).

It is also worth emphasising that not all expenses *can* be directly matched against specific revenue. Against which sales, for instance, should the audit fee be matched? Or what about the cost of a flight to Brazil in an (unsuccessful) attempt to win a large sales order?

Summary of accrual accounting adjustments

Seven different kinds of expenditure/expense (or receipt/income) mix can be distinguished, as shown below, of which five relate in some way to this year:

	EXPENDITURE	"EXPENSE"		
1	Last year	Last year	=	Last year
2	Last year	This year	=	Asset start of year
3	This year	Last year	=	Liability start of year
4	This year	This year	=	This year
5	This year	Next year	=	Asset end of year
6	Next year	This year	=	Liability end of year
7	Next year	Next year	=	Next year

	RECEIPTS	"INCOME"		
1	Last year	Last year	=	Last year
2	Last year	This year	=	Liability start of year
3	This year	Last year	=	Asset start of year
4	This year	This year	=	This year
5	This year	Next year	=	Liability end of year
6	Next year	This year	=	Asset end of year
7	Next year	Next year	=	Next year

MEASURING SALES REVENUE

As we have seen, the sales ("turnover") figure in accounts plays an important role not only in determining the profit shown but also in various aspects of interpretation, the key "profit margin" and "asset turnover" ratios being based on the sales total.

The sales total generally represents cash receipts from cash sales plus a figure for credit sales—that is the value of goods and services invoiced to customers in the period. A sale takes place when title or ownership passes to the purchaser, which is usually at the time of delivery. This is taken in accounts to be the moment of "realisation," and accrual accounting does *not* wait until cash has been received from the customers before "recognising" credit sales as revenue. This can give rise to problems of bad debts if customers do not pay.

Where goods are delivered "on approval" or "on sale or return," ownership does not pass, and such transactions cannot properly be recognised as sales. The goods delivered must be included as stock (at cost) in the accounts of the "selling" company, and no profit can be shown. Where customers are allowed by a company to return goods which they have purchased, any returns should be deducted from the sales total in the company's accounts, and the goods returned to stock at cost—thus eliminating the profit on those goods.

Complications can arise with hire purchase transactions, where care must be taken to ensure that profit is brought into account over the life of the extended sale and not in total at the time the transaction is entered into. With instalment sales, however, where title to the goods passes at the time of the transaction, revenue on the sale is normally credited straight away, except any revenue relating to finance charges on outstanding instalments, which are spread over the contract period.

In respect of sales between divisions of a company, no profit can be taken until the goods are sold to an outside customer. Any "profit" from such transactions shown in the books of account must be eliminated when preparing the company's accounts. This subject is discussed in more detail in considering group accounts in section 7.

It is customary for the sales figure to be shown net of trade discount, though the effect of this treatment is not always appreciated. If substantial discounts are given at varying rates or on different proportions of sales from year to year, the net sales figure shown in the accounts will not necessarily reflect changes in the level of activity over time. Thus a company which appears to be selling less compared with a previous period may actually be selling the same, or an even greater, volume of goods, but giving away more in discounts. Unless the potential effects of changes in the sales figures caused by discount are appreciated wrong conclusions can easily be drawn from ratio analysis using the sales figures. Trade discount is a special instance of the general formula:

$$\text{Sales revenue} = \text{price} \times \text{volume}$$

A common cause of difficulty in a multi-product company in interpreting sales revenue figures and their effect on profit is a change in "sales mix." If a higher proportion of a high-profit item is sold in one period than in the previous period, it is quite possible for profit to increase even though total sales have fallen. The reverse is also true, which has obvious implications in any reward system based on sales levels.

VALUING STOCK IN A TRADING COMPANY

The "cost of sales" figure in the accounts of a trading company includes those expenses which are necessary "to bring the goods into a saleable condition." This covers the cost of purchasing the goods (buying materials and making the goods in a manufacturing company) and the related expenses of transport inwards, purchasing, warehousing and stockholding.

The heading "operating expenses" includes those expenses needed to sell the goods and to run and finance the business. Such expenses include advertising, packing, transport outwards, commissions, sales and administrative staff salaries, rent, rates, electricity, interest payable, audit fees and so on.

Where a trading company sells identifiable separate items of stock, such as cars or furniture, the cost of sales figure is merely the cost of the individual items which have been sold. Any items left in stock can readily be valued at their cost, and (subject to adjustments) this amount will appear as an asset in the balance sheet setting out the position at the end of the accounting period.

Where the goods sold are too numerous or too small for individual records to be kept showing the cost of each item (as, for example, in a grocery store), the cost of sales has to be calculated *indirectly*.

Obviously the cost of sales in any period equals the total goods made available in the period less any goods left at the end. The goods made available are the opening stock and the purchases during the period. Thus *cost of sales* equals:

Opening stock	x
Add: Purchases	x
=Total available	x
Less: Closing stock	x
=*Cost of sales*	x

Cost of sales therefore equals purchases less the increase in stock during the period—or *plus* the *decrease* in stock. Opening stock and purchases are shown in the books of account, but it is more difficult to obtain a closing stock figure, for which a physical stock check may be needed. This involves:

1 Physically locating and counting each item of stock
2 Valuing each item (normally at the lower of cost or net realisable value)

Possible errors in stock figures

Physical stock checking is often tedious and time-consuming (and may even involve temporary restrictions on trading). As a result, many businesses take a physical stock check only once a year, probably at a time when stocks are at a seasonal low. An alternative to checking all items in stock at a single date is to keep "perpetual" stock records, which are checked physically against actual stock regularly throughout the year, though not altogether at one time. These records can be used to supply "closing stock" figures at the end of any accounting period. Clearly the "cost of sales" figure is heavily dependent on the opening and closing stock valuations, which are subject to various possible errors. There may be an accidental omission or double count of physical stock items during the stock check, or errors in pricing individual items on the stock sheets, in calculating stock value, or in adding and summarising stock sheet totals. These errors can occur in either the opening or closing stock figures. Audit checks will typically lay heavy emphasis on verifying the stock balances.

Example

The accountant of Self Service Stores Limited is preparing the annual accounts to 31 March 1970, and wishes to calculate the cost of sales figure. He knows the opening stock figure, based on a stock check carried out on 31 March 1969, was £80 000. The purchases figure for the year, shown in the books of account, was £450 000. From stock sheets prepared on 31 March 1970, he calculates that the closing stock at that date was £65 000. What was the cost of sales? Show your calculation in the space below, and then compare your answer with that shown on the next page.

SELF SERVICE STORES LIMITED
Cost of sales
Year to 31 March 1970

£

131

Self Service Stores Limited calculated cost of sales figures is £465 000, as shown below. This is intended to represent the cost of goods actually sold, but the figure is calculated in such a way that the total will also include the cost of stock losses, thefts and wastages, since these too will result in a lower closing stock figure. If individual items of stock are large or of high value it may be possible to control them separately. Otherwise the calculated cost of sales figure based on a stock check will have to be compared with some standard in order to discover any significant stock losses.

SELF SERVICE STORES LIMITED
Cost of sales
Year to 31 March 1970

	£
Opening stock 31 March 1969	80 000
Purchases	450 000
	530 000
Less: Closing stock 31 March 1970	65 000
Cost of sales	£465 000

Where the pricing policy of the company is to add a fixed percentage mark-up on to the purchased cost of goods a standard can be calculated without too much difficulty and used to measure the accuracy of the cost of sales figure based on the stock check.

Example: Assuming that Self Service Stores Limited add $33\frac{1}{3}$ per cent on to cost, and that sales in the year to 31 March 1970 were £600 000:

Cost of sales, based on stock check	= £465 000
Cost of sales "should be" $\frac{3}{4}$ × £600 000	= £450 000
Unexplained stock loss	= £ 15 000

On the basis of this variance steps can be taken to find explanations for the difference. It looks as if Self Service Stores may have a shoplifting problem!

Since few companies maintain a standard level of mark-up on all goods, however, it is often not easy to arrive at a standard with much degree of accuracy. In most cases the best standard available will be to use an estimated cost of sales percentage based on past experience. If there is a difference, however, there is still a problem, since it may not be entirely clear whether it is the standard or the stock check figure which is wrong. Nevertheless, such a check can give an indication of substantial errors or losses.

Obsolescent and slow-moving stock

The accounting rule is that for balance sheet purposes stock should be shown "at the *lower* of cost or net realisable value." The question which then arises is: "Under what conditions should the book value of stock be written down to less than cost or written off altogether?"

Where stock items are damaged or missing an adjustment is clearly needed to eliminate the lost investment from the accounts by making a charge against current profits. This will have the effect of *increasing* cost of sales (thus reducing profit) and *reducing* the amount of the asset in the balance sheet.

Where, however, the stock exists in good condition, but is moving slowly or becoming out of date, how much, if anything, should be written off? Here is a very difficult area of decision, involving a judgement about the likely market demand for the stock in future periods.

Example

Bargain Motors Limited started business on 1 January 1969, buying and selling cars and accessories. During 1970 the company bought stock for £60 000. During the year it sold for £65 000 items which had cost £40 000. Operating expenses were £20 000. The preliminary profit and loss account and balance sheet showing a profit of £5000 and net assets of £35 000 (ignoring tax) are set out below in the left-hand column.

The balance sheet stock figure was calculated as follows:

Stock items purchased, at cost	£60 000
Less: Items sold, at cost	£40 000
Calculated closing stock, at cost	£20 000

A detailed investigation of the items left in stock revealed that:

1 The stock included a number of rapidly obsolescing items relating to discontinued models which had cost £5000, but which could now be sold for only about 20 per cent of cost.

2 Cars which had cost £4000 had been damaged and were now thought to be worth only £2000.

Revised accounts for 1970 are set out below in the right-hand column, incorporating the stock adjustments, which affect both the profit and loss account and the balance sheet figures.

BARGAIN MOTORS LIMITED

Profit and loss account for 1970

	Preliminary £'000	Revised £'000
Sales	65	65
Cost of sales	40	46
Gross profit	25	19
Operating expenses	20	20
Net profit (loss)	£ 5	£(1)

Balance sheet at 31 December 1970

	Preliminary £'000	Revised £'000
Share capital	20	20
Profit and loss account	15	9
Capital employed	£35	£29
Stock	20	14
Other net assets	15	15
Net assets	£35	£29

Methods of stock valuation

So far we have assumed that there are no problems in attaching a "cost" to each stock item, but this may not always be the case. Companies generally keep price records (or copy invoices) showing the invoice price of each item purchased. The values shown on the most recent invoice will normally be used. But what happens when the stock level on hand at the end of a period exceeds the quantity of items purchased on the most recent invoice? What happens when the price of an item fluctuates or continually increases, as frequently happens in periods of rapid inflation? To deal with these issues a company policy must be established which will affect both the stock figure and the profit or loss shown in a particular accounting period.

Example

The Glass Bottle Company Limited buys and sells a standard glass bottle. In the year to 30 September 1972 sales were £30 000. The stock and purchases accounts showed the following figures:

	Units	Unit cost £	Total £
1 October 1971 Opening stock	2000	3	6 000
1 January 1972 Purchases	2000	5	10 000
1 September 1972 Purchases	1000	7	7 000
	5000		£23 000

The stock at 30 September amounted to 2000 bottles. What was the cost of sales in the year, and what is the stock value at 30 September 1972?

Several answers are possible to the Glass Bottle Company Limited stock problem. The two most likely are:

(*a*) "First In First Out" basis (FIFO)

(*b*) The "average cost" basis

These are illustrated opposite.

(a) "First In First Out" basis (FIFO)

This assumes that stock is sold by clearing the oldest items first. On this basis the cost of sales of the 3000 bottles sold (5000 in opening stock or purchases less 2000 closing stock) would be:

2000 at £3	£6 000
1000 at £5	5 000
Cost of sales	£11 000

Stock value (2000 bottles):

1000 at £7	£7 000
1000 at £5	5 000
Stock value	£12 000

(b) The "average cost" basis

This assumes that a new average cost is calculated each time a purchase is made, and that charges to cost of sales and to stock are based on the calculated averages. (Let us assume that the stock level on each replenishment was 1000 units.)

	Stock	Units	Average cost £	£	Cost of sales £
1 Oct 71	Stock	2000	3.00	6 000	
	Issues	1000	3.00	3 000	3 000
		1000	3.00	3 000	
1 Jan 72	Purchases	2000	5.00	10 000	
		3000	4.33	13 000	
	Issues	2000	4.33	8 670	8 670
		1000	4.33	4 330	
1 Sept 72		1000	7.00	7 000	
30 Sept 72		2000	5.67	£11 330	£11 670

The results reported in the profit and loss account and balance sheet will vary depending on the method of stock valuation used. Applying the two bases above, the figures for the Glass Bottle Company Limited would be:

	FIFO	Average cost
Sales	£30 000	£30 000
Cost of sales	11 000	11 670
Gross profit	£19 000	£18 330
Closing stock	£12 000	£11 330

In such a case there is no single "right" answer. Different methods of stock valuation give different results.

VALUING STOCK IN A MANUFACTURING COMPANY

We have seen that problems arise in valuing stock in a trading company because of changes in purchase prices during a year, but at least in such a case purchase invoices can be used to determine the cost of an item at certain points in time. But what is the cost of an item which a company manufactures itself?

The total scope of this question is beyond the limits of this book, and involves consideration of cost systems related to different methods of manufacture—unit costing, batch costing, process costing and so on. All that we can attempt here is a general consideration of one major system—batch costing—which is widely used in industry. From this we can indicate the kind of problems which will arise under any costing system.

In accounting presentation for a manufacturing company it is usual to show a separate manufacturing account which is distinct from the trading and profit and loss account. An example of such an account is set out below.

METAL MANUFACTURING LIMITED
Manufacturing account for the year ending 31 March 1971

	£
Direct material	20 000
Direct labour	50 000
Factory indirect expenses	75 000
	145 000
Add: Opening work-in-progress	15 000
	160 000
Less: Closing work-in-progress	20 000
*Cost of finished goods**	£140 000

*transferred to trading account.

A number of items in the manufacturing account are new to us.

Direct material and direct labour

These are items of expenditure which can be directly identified with individual batches of products. A separate cost record will accumulate the relevant labour and material costs for each batch, and will show the total material and labour cost for each completed batch. It will usually be possible to compare this actual cost with a predetermined standard and to investigate any significant variance from standard. Unit costs can be calculated by dividing batch costs by the number of items produced.

Factory indirect expenses

Factory "indirect" or "overhead" expenses will include the costs of supervision, depreciation and maintenance of machinery, factory rent, light and heat and so on. It is often difficult to allocate these costs to individual batches, and in a factory using sophisticated manufacturing processes the indirect expenses may be significantly higher than the direct expenses. Depreciation of fixed assets is dealt with in section 5.

Work-in-progress

"Work-in-progress" refers to stock in an incomplete state at the end of a financial period. Valuation of this work, and of finished manufactured stock, presents new problems. (Raw materials stock can be valued in the same way as a trading company's stock.)

Manufacturing accounts show the *total* direct and indirect costs incurred in making the items which are transferred as finished stock into the cost of sales. If all items were sold in the year of manufacture there would be no problem, for all the manufacturing costs incurred in a year would be charged in that year's profit and loss account. But usually at the end of each accounting period there are left varying quantities of stock in various stages of completion, which it becomes necessary to value. The aim then is to charge manufacturing costs in the period which will take credit for the related sale.

Valuing manufactured stock

Clearly the cost of a finished product is the total direct and indirect costs incurred in making it. From the cost records it is generally possible to determine the direct costs (material and labour), but how much of the total indirect costs relate to a particular product? This is a difficult question. Who can say how the works manager's time (and salary) or the factory rent should be apportioned over all the products made in a period?

Example

Timber Box Limited makes wooden boxes and owns a small factory and some machinery. It employs a works manager and other staff, some of whom are engaged directly in making boxes, while others are concerned with purchases, stores, maintenance, cleaning and so on. On 31 December 1970, the following balances appeared in the books:

Sales	£140 000
Direct material	60 000
Direct labour	15 000
Indirect manufacturing expenses ("overheads")	45 000
Selling and administrative expenses	25 000

At the end of the year the company had finished boxes in stock for which the direct costs were: material £7000, labour £2000.

At what figure should stock be shown? What profit or loss did the company make in the year? More than one answer is possible.

The conventional accounting approach would try to relate the indirect expenses of the business to the goods produced. The problem, of course, is how to do this. Two methods are illustrated on the next page.

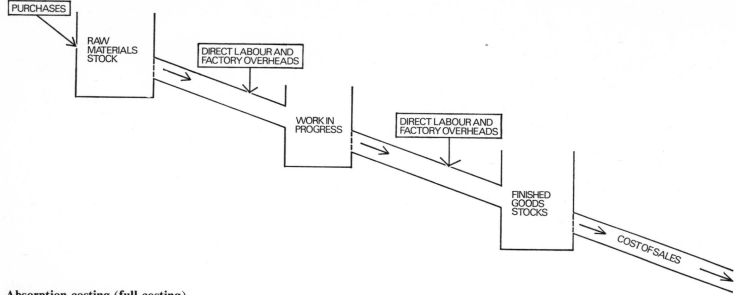

Absorption costing (full costing)

One frequently used method is to add factory overheads as a percentage on to direct labour costs. The overhead rate of Timber Box Limited would be 300 per cent.

$$\frac{\text{Overheads}}{\text{Direct labour}} = \frac{£45\,000}{£15\,000} = 300\%$$

On this basis, stock would be valued as follows:

Direct material	£7 000
Direct labour	2 000
Overheads (300% × direct labour)	6 000
Stock value	£15 000

Accounts prepared on the alternative bases are set out on the next page.

Perhaps a better distinction than between "direct" and "indirect" expenses is between "fixed" and "variable" expenses. For it is possible that "fixed" expenses—that is expenses that do not vary with the volume produced—may be "direct," in the sense that they can be directly identified with a particular product. The marginal costing approach considers what extra costs will be incurred (or saved) by making one more (or one less) product unit.

Marginal costing

Economists often favour a marginal costing approach, which makes no attempt to allocate indirect costs to products. It is argued that the indirect costs (overheads) represent the necessary provision of a capacity to produce, and that since such costs are "period costs," incurred on a time basis (as opposed to "product costs"), they should be entirely written off in the period in which they are incurred.

On this basis, the stock value will be simply the direct costs incurred:

Direct material	£7000
Direct labour	2000
Stock value	£9000

Accounts on the alternative bases

	Absorption (full) costing		Marginal costing	
	£	£	£	£
Sales		140 000		140 000
Direct material	60 000		60 000	
Direct labour	15 000		15 000	
Factory overheads	45 000		45 000	
	120 000		120 000	
Less: Closing stock	15 000		9 000	
		105 000		111 000
Gross profit		35 000		29 000
Selling and administrative expenses		25 000		25 000
Net profit before tax		£10 000		£ 4 000
Stock shown in the balance sheet:		£15 000		£ 9 000

Only two methods of valuing stock (and thus cost of sales) have been shown, which have led to very different results. In the first method all indirect manufacturing costs were taken into account (absorption costing), and in the second all were ignored (marginal costing). In a more sophisticated business the ratio of indirect to direct costs might be even higher (giving an overhead loading on direct labour of perhaps 500 per cent or more), and the difference in profit resulting from the two methods could be even greater. It is true that the amount gained or lost in one period is reflected in the accounts for the next, but a particular period's results could be significantly affected, especially where stock levels fluctuate.

In practice some figure between the two extremes would normally be arrived at. Some indirect costs may be so closely related to making the product that they should clearly be included in valuing stock, for the same reason that direct costs are included. For example, costs associated with individual machines can be apportioned on the basis of reasonable use to give machine-hour cost rates, which can be used to establish a standard overhead cost for each product. This can then be related to the standard material and labour cost. At the same time, the stock valuation may exclude other costs which are too remote to associate with individual products—for example the works manager's salary, drawing office costs, and so on.

Evidently two managements with different methods could arrive at very different stock valuations and thus profit or loss figures. The requirement for a consistent basis of valuation from year to year helps ensure standard practices within a single company, but comparisons between companies can be extremely hazardous in the absence of very detailed information about methods of valuing stock.

MEASURING EXPENSES

Having dealt with cost of sales, let us now consider briefly two other categories of expense that can cause problems of allocation between accounting periods.

(a) Research and development expenditure
(b) Selling expenses
(c) Bad debts

(a) Research and development expenditure

To an increasing extent companies are investing large sums of money in basic and applied research and in developing new products. Allocating this kind of expenditure to the "correct" accounting period can raise problems. When roughly the same amount is spent each year, writing off relatively small expenditure in the year in which it is incurred is a reasonable solution. But what if major investments in product development arise at irregular intervals? The company's profit pattern would be seriously affected if expenses were recorded in one period and related revenue in later periods. In such cases some adjustment is needed.

Although the dividing line may not always be very clear, classifying total research and development expenditure between basic research, applied product research, product development and advanced engineering can be useful. Expenditure within each category can then be treated separately.

It is customary to regard basic research as a time-based charge (since it cannot easily be related to subsequent revenue), and to write off the expenditure in the period in which it is incurred. The same approach may be taken with applied product research, but large sums (in relation to particular products) may, at least partly, be carried forward to a later period in which revenue will be generated. Similar considerations apply to product development and advanced engineering, but with an increasing tendency, as the expenditure becomes more specifically associated with individual products, for sums to be "capitalised" and carried forward to later periods in which they will be written off against related revenue. Here the "matching" concept operates against the convention of "conservatism". Obviously decisions about this kind of expenditure have a direct impact on profit, affecting more than one accounting period.

(b) Selling expenses

The treatment of most selling expenses is straightforward, with the amount incurred in a year being charged as an expense in that year. One obvious example is salesmen's commission, which can be directly related to particular items of revenue. As selling becomes more sophisticated, however, certain categories of selling and marketing expenditure raise similar problems to research and development expenditure.

Consider a company which launches a major product approximately every third year, when it updates the previous model. Let us assume that the company's year ends on 31 December and that it spends £1 million between September and December 1970, on television and other advertising for a product launch which is to take place in February 1971. In which period should the £1 million be charged?

This kind of expenditure is not incurred every year, and if the general rule is followed of charging costs in the year in which they are incurred, the results of both 1970 and 1971 will be distorted. But how much should be carried forward? This is a question to which a wide range of answers is possible, and illustrates once again how subjective considerations enter into the process by which the annual profit or loss is determined.

(c) Bad debts

A critical area which may require that a company make significant charges against profits relates to outstanding debts. Sales revenue is normally "recognised" in accounts when an invoice is sent; but sometimes the question arises whether a particular customer will pay the amount he owes. If a debt is undoubtedly "bad" —that is irrecoverable—there is no alternative to a complete write off against profit in the period in which the status of the debt is discovered (which may be a later period than that in which the sale was made).

But what happens when payment has been delayed, or the debtor's financial position has deteriorated? Management may reckon there is a "good chance" of getting paid eventually, but once again the opinion of those preparing the accounts can significantly affect the level of reported profits. (This was noticeable in the accounts of several companies to which Rolls Royce Limited owed large amounts.) The amount of any provision for bad debts will vary according to whether an optimistic or a pessimistic view is taken about necessarily uncertain future events. This in turn may well be influenced by the current level of profits. Any provision for bad debts in a period will be charged against profit and deducted from the total debtors figure in the balance sheet, only the net figure normally being shown.

MEASURING PROFITS ON LONG-TERM CONTRACTS

It was pointed out at the beginning of this section that the larger the number of incomplete transactions involved, the longer the time span between the beginning and end of transactions being measured, and the greater their significance in relation to the total business during the period, the greater will be the range of possible profit figures. The force of this statement will now be obvious.

We have seen that when a transaction stretches over two periods decisions have to be made as to the period in which revenue should be taken or expenses charged. The problems are increased when more than two accounting periods are involved, as illustrated by the following example of a construction company engaged on a long-term contract.

Example

Alpha Construction Limited enters into an agreement to build a small office block for Omega Property Limited for £300 000. Alpha estimates that the project will cost £210 000 and that construction will take three years. At the end of the first year the job is one third finished, and costs incurred, at £70 000, are on target.

What profit has Alpha made in the first year?

A number of answers are possible:

1 No profit, since the job is incomplete. (This will mean that the entire potential profit of £90 000 will be taken in year 3.)
2 £30 000, since one third of the work has been performed.
3 £90 000, since the agreement was signed in year 1.
4 Some figure between £0 and £90 000, because various judgements can be made about events which might arise between the end of year 1 and the completion of the project. The total cost may exceed £210 000, completing construction may take more than another two years, etc.

What is Alpha's profit? How can the expected total profit be allocated over the three periods? It is fairly obvious that not all the profit was made the day the contract was signed, and equally that such profit as is made will not accrue on the final day when the last work is completed. Some basis has to be found for allocating the total anticipated profit over the three accounting periods.

The example illustrates the extent to which judgement must necessarily enter into the process of determining accounting profits when incomplete transactions are involved. Accounting rules exist which narrow the range within which profit can be said to fall. Depending on the nature of the business whose results are being measured the range may be narrow, as in the case of Rentwell Limited or wide, as in the case of Alpha Construction Limited. In neither case is the profit an "exact" amount.

Because of the uncertainty inevitably involved in a further two years of construction it is likely that the doctrine of conservatism will operate in Alpha's case, and that all else being equal the profit taken in year 1 will be a small rather than a large amount. However, what if Alpha is showing a loss on its other transactions? What if the contract involves a different kind of work from that normally carried out. How will these factors affect the decision?

In dealing with a situation such as Alpha's, the scope open to the directors to show varying levels of profit cannot be denied. The company's auditors can ensure that a consistent basis is adopted from year to year, but the directors are in the best position to make the necessary judgements, and unless their conclusions are clearly unreasonable the auditors can hardly disagree with them. However, it should be obvious to the analyst that profit measurement under these conditions is difficult and that accounting measures indicate a *range* within which profit falls but do not define an exact figure. Where the element of uncertainty is great, judgements play a crucial role.

NON-RECURRING ITEMS AND PRIOR YEARS' ADJUSTMENTS

Some companies include only regular "normal" items in the profit and loss account, and transfer directly to the reserves non-recurring items or material adjustments to prior years' figures. Such items then never appear at all in the profit and loss account. Obviously a reported profit which includes a significant non-recurring item is not likely to provide a reliable guide to next year's profit. This approach aims to provide a reported profit figure which can be regarded as "maintainable" profit.

On the other hand, many accountants argue that the purpose of the profit and loss account is to report *last* year's profit, not to provide a reliable guide to a level of future "maintainable" profit (or loss). In addition, economists would argue that, by their nature, profits are not "maintainable," though accounting profit may be so to the extent that it represents interest on equity capital (which an economist would want to deduct in arriving at "pure" profit or loss). Best modern practice is to include *all* revenue items in the profit and loss account, with those reckoned to be non-recurring or related to prior years being shown "below the line."

From the analyst's point of view, the important thing is to recognise that different accounting treatments in this area do occur and can be significant, and to be on the alert to make any necessary adjustments. The base figure for normal analysis would be the "profit for the year," and "below the line" items would simply be excluded.

Where prior years' figures have been incorrectly reported, the analyst may want to "carry back" the adjustments into their appropriate periods (if he has enough information), to show a more accurate trend over time. Two of the commonest items in accounts relating to prior years are profits and losses on the disposal of fixed assets (which arise because the "correct" depreciation cannot usually be estimated in advance), and tax adjustments (which arise because the rate of corporation tax is announced retrospectively, after the end of the year). These subjects are discussed in section 5.

SUMMARY

In this section we have seen that receipts must be distinguished from income, and expenditure from expense. Income and expense are "recognised" when they accrue due, not when they are actually received or paid.

The basis for many adjustments is *time*, amounts being included in the *period* to which they relate. Another basis, using the *matching* concept, is to charge expense in the same accounting period as that in which related revenue is recognised. This may lead to certain research, development and promotional expenditure being carried forward as an asset on the balance sheet, notwithstanding its more or less intangible nature.

Particularly important in determining the "cost of sales" is calculating a stock value. Major problems here include obsolescence, the method of valuation—for instance, FIFO, average cost, and others—and, in a manufacturing company, the treatment of factory overheads. Different accounting treatments in any of these areas can lead to major differences in reported profit.

Indeed, throughout this section we have emphasised that the process of determining profit and loss usually contains a considerable element of individual judgement. It would therefore be quite wrong to suppose that most reported profit or loss figures are in any sense uniquely "correct".

4.1 Definitions

Write down opposite your definitions of the terms shown. Then compare your answers with the definitions overleaf.

(a) Matching

(b) An accrued charge

(c) Turnover

(d) Sales mix

(e) FIFO

(f) Work-in-progress

(g) Marginal costing

(h) Bad debts

(i) "Below the line" items

(j) Overheads

4.1 Definitions

(a) *Matching* is the process of charging expenses in the same accounting period as that in which related revenue is recognised.

(b) An *accrued charge* is an expense (often relating to a period of time, for example rent due) which has become legally payable as at a particular date, but which has not yet been invoiced or paid.

(c) *Turnover* is a synonym for sales (or sales revenue). It includes both cash and credit sales, but does *not* include the sale of fixed assets.

(d) *Sales mix* describes, in a multi-product company, the particular combination in a given accounting period of the sales revenue of all the company's different products. The mix can change while total sales revenue remains constant.

(e) *FIFO* is a method of valuing stock (First In First Out) which assumes for accounting purposes that goods are sold or issued in the same order as that in which they were purchased or received. This method of valuation may be used even if it is not physically true.

(f) *Work-in-progress* (WIP) is a category of stock in a manufacturing company, representing products on which the manufacturing process has begun (otherwise they would be raw materials) but not yet been completed (otherwise they would be finished goods) as at the balance sheet date. It is reduced by any advances or progress payments received from the purchaser in the course of manufacture, and can thus conceivably be *negative* (if progress payments on account of the final selling price exceed costs incurred and allocated to work-in-progress).

(g) *Marginal costing* is a method of allocating costs to products which takes into account only variable costs directly associated with a product—ignoring indirect (overhead) costs. It is to be contrasted with "absorption" (full) costing.

(h) *Bad debts* are amounts owing to a business (debts) which are valueless, either because the debtor *cannot* pay—for example, through bankruptcy—or because he *will* not—for instance, through some dispute over quality.

(i) *"Below the line" items* come below the "profit for the year after tax" line in the profit and loss account. They represent either extraordinary non-recurring items or items relating to prior years.

(j) *Overheads* are indirect costs which cannot easily be identified with particular products. For accounting purposes (for example valuing stock) they are often allocated to products on some more or less arbitrary basis, such as a percentage of direct labour costs.

4.2 Mercury Travel Limited

Mercury Travel Limited started business as a travel agency on 1 November 1970. The company's first accounting year ended on 31 October 1971, by which time £3800 had been paid in cash in respect of telephone expenses.

This was made up as follows:

Rent
2 months to 31 December 1970	£ 80
3 months to 31 March 1971	£120
3 months to 30 June 1971	£120
3 months to 30 September 1971	£120

Calls
2 months to 31 December 1970	£ 640
3 months to 31 March 1971	£1520
3 months to 30 June 1971	£1200
Total cash paid	£3800

At 31 October 1971, there was an unpaid account for £1600 in respect of calls for the 3 months to 30 September 1971 (£1480) and rent for the 3 months to 31 December 1971 (£120). Calls for the month of October 1971, were estimated to amount to £540.

Calculate how much should be charged as telephone expense for the year ending 31 October 1971, and show the ledger account for the year.

The answer is shown on the next page.

4.2 Mercury Travel Limited

Solution

In addition to the £3800 cash paid, the following amounts should also be included in telephone expense for the year ended 31 October 1971:

Rent	October 1971	£ 40
Calls	3 months to 30 September 1971	£1480
	October 1971	£ 540
"Accrued charges" at 31 October 1971:		£2060

Thus total telephone expense for the year ending 31 October 1971 is £5,860.

Ledger account

Telephone expense

Year 1970/71	£	Year 1970/71	£
Cash	3800	Profit and loss account	5860
Accrued charges c/d	2060		
	£5860		£5860
		Year 1971/72	
		Accrued charges b/d	2060

Notice how the £2060 accrued charges are brought down as a credit in year 1971/72. The effect will be to *reduce* the expense in 1971/72 (the year in which the amounts concerned will actually be *paid*). What would happen if some or all of the £2060 accrued charges were *not* paid in the year 1971/72? Answer: presumably these amounts would be paid in a later year, and should therefore again be carried forward as accrued charges at the end of the year 1971/72 *in addition* to any extra telephone expenses incurred (but not paid) in the year.

4.3 Urban Properties Limited

The accounts of Urban Properties Limited for the year ending 30 June 1971, are shown opposite.

The following items are to be taken into account:

(a) No adjustment has been made in respect of rates for the year to 31 March 1972 paid in advance, amounting to £1600 a year.

(b) Rent receivable of £300 for the June quarter has not been included.

(c) Rent received for the half year to 30 September 1971 (£800) has all been included in the accounts to 30 June 1971.

(d) There is a dispute about the rent payable on one property. No rent has been paid since £600 was paid in advance in October 1970, in respect of the quarter to December 1970. It is estimated that as from the end of 1970 only half the level of rent previously payable will ultimately be due.

Please amend the balance sheet and profit and loss account shown opposite to incorporate any necessary adjustments in respect of the above items.

The answer is shown on the next page.

URBAN PROPERTIES LIMITED
Profit and loss account
Year ending 30 June 1971

		£
Rent receivable		28 600
Other income		2 500
		31 100
Rent payable	6400	
Rates payable	4100	
Other expenses	3100	
		13 600
Profit before tax		17 500
Tax (at 40%)		7 000
Profit after tax		£10 500

Balance sheet, 30 June 1971

	£			£
Share capital	50 000	**Fixed assets:**		
Reserves	21 400	Properties, net		66 000
	71 400	**Current assets**		
		Debtors	600	
Current liabilities		Cash	12 700	
Creditors	900			13 300
Tax	7000			
	7 900			
	£79 300			£79 300

4.3 Urban Properties Limited

Solution

Note

You may not have adjusted the tax charge and the corresponding tax liability. In the absence of definite instructions it is not wrong to leave the tax figures as they were, but in fact the kind of adjustment being made in this problem *would* also affect tax.

URBAN PROPERTIES LIMITED
Profit and loss account
Year ending 30 June 1971

		£
Rent receivable $+300^b$ -400^c		~~18,500~~ ~~28 600~~
Other income		2,500 ~~2 500~~
		31,000 ~~31 100~~
Rent payable $+600^d$	7,000 ~~6 400~~	
Rates payable -1200^a	2,900 ~~4 100~~	
Other expenses	3,100 ~~3 100~~	
	13,000 ~~13 600~~	
Profit before tax		18,000 ~~17 500~~
Tax (at 40%) $+40\% \times £500$ increased Profit before tax		7,200 ~~7 000~~
Profit after tax		10,800 ~~£10 500~~

Balance sheet, 30 June 1971

	£		£
Share capital	50 000	**Fixed assets**	
Reserves $+300$	21,400	Properties, net	66 000
See P & L A/c	71,400	**Current assets**	
		Debtors $+300^b$ 900 ~~600~~	
Current liabilities		Cash 12 700	~~13 300~~
Creditors $\{+400^c$ 900 ~~1,900~~			
Tax $\{+600^d$ ~~7 000~~ 7,200	9,100 ~~7 900~~	Prepayments $+1,200^a$ 1,200	14,800
$+200$	~~79 300~~ 80,800		£~~79 300~~ 80,800

4.4 Wheeler Limited: Adjusting trial balance and preparing final accounts.

The trial balance of Wheeler Limited extracted from the books at the end of the year ended 31 March 1971 is shown below.

The following items have not been taken into account:

(a) An audit fee (administrative expenses) of £500 is to be provided for.

(b) Loan interest is payable half-yearly at 30 June and 31 December. The last payment was on 31 December 1970.

(c) Finished goods stock in the books at £1200 is obsolete, and is to be written off as cost of goods sold in the current year.

(d) Tax of £12 500 is to be provided for.

(e) An ordinary dividend of 40 per cent is proposed.

1. You are asked to make the necessary adjustments in the adjustments column of the trial balance schedule, and extend the figures into the profit and loss account and balance sheet columns. Each pair of columns should balance.

2. From the trial balance schedule as adjusted, please now prepare in final form the profit and loss account and balance sheet of Wheeler Limited for the year ended 31 March 1971.

Answers to this problem and to later ones in this section are given at the end of the book.

	Trial balance Dr £	Trial balance Cr £	Adjustments Dr £	Adjustments Cr £	Profit and loss Dr £	Profit and loss Cr £	Balance sheet Dr £	Balance sheet Cr £
Cash book	20 100							
Ordinary share capital		20 000						
Profit and loss account b/f		28 300						
12% Loan		30 000						
Fixed assets: cost	94 200							
Fixed assets: accumulated depreciation		34 700						
Sales ledger control	18 300							
Stock	14 100							
Purchase ledger control		3 900						
Accrued charges								
Tax liability								
Dividend payable								
Sales		144 200						
Cost of goods sold	81 800							
Selling and administrative expenses	29 900							
Loan interest	2 700							
Tax expense								
Ordinary dividend								
Profit for year retained								
	£261 100	£261 100						

4.5 Canning and Sons Limited: writing-down stock

The 1970 accounts of Canning and Sons Limited, sellers of toys, are shown opposite as they were prepared for audit.

The auditor raised only one significant point, concerning the valuation of stock. The company normally sold most of its toys in the final 3 months of the year, and a large consignment of expensive electric cars had been imported from Switzerland in good time for Christmas. Unfortunately one of the manufacturing safety checks had been omitted, and it had been impossible to make the cars safe for sale until the week before Christmas.

As a result, most of the stock was still unsold at the year end—the cost of cars still in stock being £4000—and there was a major doubt whether such a large quantity could be sold before next Christmas. There was also doubt whether even then it would be possible to sell them at anything like this year's price, since competition from Japan was expected to reduce prices all round.

Although the company's directors were most reluctant, they felt they had no choice but to accept the auditor's insistence that the stock be written down to 50 per cent of cost. The only other adjustment to be made to the accounts set out opposite was to reduce tax by 40 per cent of the stock write-down.

Amend the accounts to allow for the write-down.

CANNING AND SONS LIMITED
Balance sheet, 31 December 1970

Shareholders' funds		£			£
Share capital		40 000	Fixed assets, net		33 000
Profit and loss account		24 300	Current assets:		
		64 300	Stock	21 300	
			Debtors	25 400	
Current liabilities:			Cash	2 600	
Creditors	13 200				49 300
Tax	4 800	18 000			
		£82 300			£82 300

Profit and loss account for 1970

		£
Sales		112 700
Cost of sales: Opening stock	14 600	
Purchases	93 800	
	108 400	
Less: Closing stock	21 300	
		87 100
Gross profit		25 600
Selling and administrative expenses		11 300
Profit before tax		14 300
Tax		4 800
Profit after tax		£ 9 500

Please use separate sheets of paper for your answers to the following problems. When you have completed them, you will find suggested answers at the end of the book.

4.6 Anderson Tiles Limited:
Stock valuation FIFO

At 1 April 1970, Anderson Tiles had 3000 cases of a particular kind of tile in stock. They were shown as costing £4 per case.

In the year to 31 March 1971, three batches of cases were purchased. In June 4000 cases at £4.25 per case, in October 2000 cases at £4.75 per case, and in December 3000 cases at £5 per case.

Anderson Tiles used the FIFO method of stock valuation. On that basis calculate the closing stock valuation at 31 March 1971, when there were 6000 cases in stock.

Then compute the cost of sales for the year in respect of this particular kind of tile. Verify your cost of sales figure by identifying the volume of tiles and related costs per case assumed to be sold.

4.7 Berwick Paper Limited:
Stock valuation: Average cost

Berwick Paper Limited replenished its stock of a certain type of paper at the end of each quarter. For the year 1970, opening stock was 1200 cwt, and the quantities purchased were 1800 cwt in March, 2400 cwt in June, 1200 cwt in September, and 1800 cwt in December. The cost per hundredweight attributable to the opening stock was £21.0. Purchase prices per cwt were respectively £18.0, £15.0, £25.0 and £20.0.

The quantities issued each quarter were:

March quarter	900 cwt
June	1700 cwt
September	1400 cwt
December	1900 cwt

Thus closing stock amounted to 2500 cwt (opening stock 1200 cwt plus purchases 7200 cwt less issues in year 5900 cwt).

Assuming that purchases are made at the end of each quarter, and that the average cost method of valuing stock and issues is used, calculate the closing stock at the end of December 1970 and the cost of paper issued during the year.

4.8 Newport Machines Limited:
Absorption and marginal costing

In the year ending 30 June 1971, Newport Machines incurred the following factory costs:

Direct material	£450 000
Direct labour	£300 000
Overheads	£540 000

At 30 June stock was on hand on which had been incurred £30 000 direct material costs and £20 000 direct labour costs. This meant that, if marginal costing were adopted, the stock would be valued at £50 000 for accounting purposes.

Calculate the overhead percentage on direct labour, and value the stock on the absorption cost basis.

4.9 Wingate Hardware Limited: Cost of sales

In preparing the accounts of Wingate Hardware Limited for the year ended 31 August 1970, the chief accountant had to decide at what figure the closing stock should be stated.

From the company's books he knew that opening stock (at 1 September 1969) had amounted—after some adjustments—to £17 400; and that purchases during the year totalled £52 700.

The total of the stock sheets summarising the physical stock check taken on 31 August 1970, was £21 600, but two items required special consideration.

A small quantity of kitchen utensils remained in stock which had been purchased more than two years earlier. They had been damaged slightly in a fire soon after purchase, and although their cost was £800 they had been written down at 31 August 1969, to £200. It had been decided that they were now valueless and should be completely written off.

More important, a major consignment of dustbins which it had been expected could be sold to a local council had turned out to be of an obsolete design. They had cost £1600, but it was thought they were now worth no more than £900. They had been purchased early in 1970.

Calculate the cost of sales for the year.

4.10 Tiptop Office Supplies: Bad debts

Tiptop Office Supplies sold to many small customers who, in total, owed £42 600 at 30 September 1970. This did not include £1700 bad debts which had been written off during the year. (The journal entry was:

Dr Bad debt expense
   Cr Debtors ledger control.)

Tiptop's practice was to provide 4 per cent of outstanding debtors at the year-end as an expense in respect of anticipated bad debts. (The journal entry was:

Dr Bad debt expense
   Cr Provision for bad debts.)

Because credit policy in 1970 had been somewhat laxer than in previous years, however (in an attempt to boost sales volume), Tiptop decided to provide 5 per cent in respect of debtors at 30 September 1970.

The provision for bad debts account had a balance brought forward at 1 October 1969, of £1000—representing 4 per cent on £25 000 (which had been the total debtors outstanding at the end of the previous year).

What is the amount of the provision for bad debts to be carried forward at 30 September 1970, and how much is the 1970 charge for bad debts?

Write up ledger accounts for "provision for bad debts" and "bad debts expense" for 1970.

Section 5
Fixed assets and depreciation

CAPITAL EXPENDITURE, FIXED ASSETS AND DEPRECIATION
We have seen that an accrual accounting system distinguishes between expenditure and expense. So far, we have only been dealing with expenditure associated with the day-to-day running of the business, and our concern has been to allocate this kind of "revenue" expenditure between two successive accounting periods. Now we must look at "capital" expenditure. This is expenditure laid out in the purchase or production of "fixed assets" which have a life stretching over a number of accounting periods and which are held by a business to provide goods or services and not for resale.

Typical fixed assets are land and buildings, machinery and equipment, office furniture and so on. For such items intentions rather than physical characteristics determine whether a particular asset represents capital or revenue expenditure and whether it should appear in the balance sheet as a fixed or current asset. Cars, for example, which are fixed assets for most companies, are current assets (stock) for British Leyland, although some cars will be fixed assets even for that company.

As fixed assets are used to provide goods or services their value to the company declines, and this fact is recognised by making a provision for "depreciation" each year. This involves charging as an expense in the profit and loss account part of the cost of the fixed asset, and reducing its book value in the balance sheet by the same amount. The purpose of providing for depreciation is to spread the cost of the fixed asset over its expected life, so that its entire cost has been written off by the time it ceases to be of use. During its life a fixed asset's net book value (cost less accumulated depreciation to date) in the balance sheet will decline as its historical cost is gradually written off. As a general rule, the net book value in any particular balance sheet is intended to represent, *not* the asset's market value, but merely the unallocated residue of its historical cost. Providing for depreciation is a process, not of valuation, but of allocation—spreading out the cost of a fixed asset over its effective life.

The operation of depreciation can be illustrated simply in looking at an example involving a short lease.

Example

On 1 January 1970 Electrical Appliances Limited purchased a three-year lease of a shop for £6000. The accounts to 31 December 1970 would include the following entries in relation to the lease:

Profit and loss account
For the year ending 31 December 1970

Operating expenses
Depreciation on lease   £2000

Balance sheet 31 December 1970
Lease at cost   £6000
Less: Depreciation   £2000

Net book value   £4000

At the end of the following year the accounts would show:

Profit and loss account
For the year ending 31 December 1971

Operating expenses
Depreciation on lease   £2000

Balance sheet, 31 December 1971
Lease at cost   £6000
Less: Accumulated depreciation   £4000
Net book value   £2000

Finally, at the end of the third year, when the lease expires, it will be fully written off. This means that both cost and accumulated depreciation will be £6000, and the original outlay will have been charged as depreciation to the profit and loss account over the life of the lease.

The example of the lease is quite straightforward but, as we shall see, questions of some complexity often arise in determining both the cost and depreciation figures to be shown in the accounts, and decisions made on these issues can significantly affect reported profit and asset figures over a number of years.

We shall consider the issues involved under a number of headings:

1 Determining the cost of fixed assets
2 Calculating depreciation: estimating useful life and residual value
3 Methods of depreciation
4 Effect of varying depreciation charges on reported results
5 Profit or loss on the sale of fixed assets

DETERMINING THE COST OF FIXED ASSETS

In most cases, determining the cost of fixed assets is not difficult. Capital expenditure normally relates to items which have been purchased, and the amount "capitalised" will be the invoice cost. Greater problems can arise, however, where a company manufactures fixed assets for its own use. The amount capitalised in such cases is often restricted to the direct outlay for labour and materials (ignoring overhead costs); but where this treatment is inadequate difficult decisions may be needed as to the amount of associated overheads to be capitalised in addition to the direct costs.

The *total* costs of acquiring fixed assets and preparing them for use are normally capitalised. Thus, legal costs incurred in acquiring a lease would be capitalised along with the purchase consideration, as would transport and installation costs associated with the acquisition of an item of plant or equipment.

On occasions the amounts to be included as "fixed assets" can be a matter of opinion. Problems might arise, for example, where substantial repairs are carried out to a building or machine. If the repairs merely restore the asset to its former condition they are revenue expenses chargeable in the year in which they are incurred. To the extent however that they create an improvement over the asset's original condition and the amount involved is material, they should strictly be capitalised. An improvement may consist of increasing the asset's capacity, lengthening its productive life or improving the quality of its output. Obviously the choice of treatment will affect the reported profits for a number of accounting periods.

Expenditure on projects which are expected to benefit future periods can provide even greater scope for the exercise of opinion. For example, it may be very difficult to decide how much of the costs incurred to develop or launch a new product should be carried forward as an asset on the balance sheet and how much should be charged as an expense against current profits. Where it is capitalised, this kind of "deferred revenue expenditure" is often shown with current assets on the balance sheet (maybe as part of the stock figure), even if it is being written off, like a fixed asset, over a number of years.

CALCULATING DEPRECIATION: ESTIMATING USEFUL LIFE AND RESIDUAL VALUE

We have already seen that provision must be made for depreciation when a company uses fixed assets to earn profits. It is obvious that unless the depreciation charge is adequate the profits reported for a period will be overstated, and the net book values shown for fixed assets in the balance sheet will be too high. There may also be a danger that the company will unwittingly distribute capital as dividends in the mistaken belief that it is income.

Let us now look at a slightly more complicated example, the case of Furniture Removals Limited.

Example

Furniture Removals Limited was set up on 1 January 1970, purchased a van for £3000 and started to trade. During the year cash receipts amounted to £5000 and running costs for wages, petrol and so on were £3000.

The preliminary accounts for the year before making any provision for depreciation are shown below. Obviously these do not reflect the true picture. Profits are overstated in the absence of a charge for using the van, and the van is shown in the balance sheet at a figure which makes no allowance for deterioration through use.

FURNITURE REMOVALS LIMITED
Preliminary accounts
Balance sheet, 31 December 1970

	£		£
Capital	3000	Van	3000
Profit	2000	Cash	2000
	£5000		£5000

Profit and loss account for 1970

	£
Revenue	5000
Costs	3000
Net profit	£2000

The question is: *how much* should be provided for depreciation?

An annual charge must be calculated so that the van is written down to zero or some other residual value at the end of its useful life. Two questions must be answered:

1 For how many years will the van be used by the company?
2 What will it be worth at the end of that time?

These questions may be difficult to answer; in any event they clearly involve subjective estimates by the company's management. The likely useful life of an asset may be limited, according to the nature of the asset, by:

(*a*) The passing of time
(*b*) Physical wear and tear
(*c*) Technical obsolescence

Let us assume that in this case it is expected:

1 That the van will be used for five years, and
2 That it will be worth £500 at the end of that period

On this basis, the net cost of the van to the company will be £3000 − £500 = £2500. This is the total amount which must be provided for depreciation over the five years.

The next question is: how much of this £2500 should be charged in the first year, how much in the second, and so on? As we shall see, this question too can give rise to a number of answers, but let us assume for the moment that it is decided to make an *equal* charge in each year, that is $\frac{£2500}{5} = £500$.

The accounts incorporating this charge are shown below.

FURNITURE REMOVALS LIMITED
Final accounts
Balance sheet, 31 December 1970

	£		£
Capital	3000	Van at cost	3000
Profit	1500	*Less:* Depreciation	500
			2500
		Cash	2000
	£4500		£4500

Profit and loss account for 1970

		£
Revenue		5000
Operating costs	3000	
Depreciation	500	
		3500
Profit		£1500

Distribution of profit

Let us now make a further assumption—that the directors decide to distribute all the available profits as dividends. The balance sheet below shows the position after paying the dividends.

FURNITURE REMOVALS LIMITED

Balance sheet after payment of dividend

	£		£
Capital	3000	Van at cost	3000
		Less: Depreciation	500
			2500
		Cash	500
	£3000		£3000

It can be seen that the effect of charging depreciation is to reduce the amount of profits available for dividends. The cash thus withheld can be used to replace the expired asset at the end of its life. In the absence of an adequate depreciation charge, too little will be retained and the company will effectively be distributing part of its capital in the guise of dividends.

It will be clear that at the end of year 5, when the asset has been written down to £500, the cash retained will be £2500. If the van then realises the predicted amount of £500 on disposal, the company will once again have its original capital (£3000) in money terms. Of course, in periods of inflation this may not be enough to purchase a similar van. The company may have lost part of its capital measured in terms of purchasing power.

Alternative asset lives and residual values

We were able to complete the accounts of Furniture Removals Limited for 1970 by making particular assumptions about the expected life and residual value of the van which had cost £3000.

Let us now consider what difference it would have made to the reported results had the directors taken a different view of the uncertain future. What would have been the effect of estimating a four-year useful life with a residual value of £600?

The calculation of the depreciation charge, the net profit (assuming constant profits before depreciation), and the balance sheet net book value figures for each year of the anticipated life of the asset are set out below (left) on the basis of the original assumptions.

You are asked to calculate and enter (below right) the equivalent figures based on the assumption of a four-year life and £600 residual value (continuing to assume that an equal charge should be made in each year).

When you have completed your calculations, please look at the next page.

Assumption 1

Cost		£3000
Estimated asset life		5 years
Estimated residual value		£500

Annual depreciation: $\dfrac{3000 - 500}{5} = £500$

	Depreciation charge	Net profit	Net book value
	£	£	£
Year 1	500	1500	2500[1]
Year 2	500	1500	2000
Year 3	500	1500	1500
Year 4	500	1500	1000
Year 5	500	1500	500

Assumption 2

Cost		£3000
Estimated asset life		4 years
Estimated residual value		£600

Annual depreciation:

	Depreciation charge	Net profit	Net book value
	£	£	£
Year 1			
Year 2			
Year 3			
Year 4			
Year 5			

[1]Net book value = Cost less accumulated depreciation (end of year).

Furniture Removals Limited

The figures based on the alternative assumptions concerning asset lives and residual values are set out opposite (top). You will note that both the profit and loss account and balance sheet figures are affected by the alternative assumptions—even though the *same* asset and the *same* business is involved!

Disposal of the van for £700 at the end of year 4

Had the van in fact been sold at the end of year 4 for £700, the entries opposite (centre) would have appeared in the profit and loss account in year 4 under each assumption.

Notice that the total net amount charged in each case is £2300 (that is cost £3000—proceeds £700).

Assumption 1

Cost £3000
5-year life
£500 residual value
Annual depreciation: $\dfrac{3000 - 500}{5} = £500$

	Depreciation charge	Net profit	Net book value
	£	£	£
Year 1	500	1500	2500
Year 2	500	1500	2000
Year 3	500	1500	1500
Year 4	500	1500	1000
Year 5	500	1500	500

Year 4		£
Profit		2000
Less : Depreciation	500	
Loss on sale (*a*)	300	
		800
		£1200

(*a*) NBV £1000 less proceeds £700.

Assumption 1: 4 × £500 = £2000
+ loss on sale £ 300

Assumption 2

Cost £3000
4-year life
£600 residual value
Annual depreciation: $\dfrac{3000 - 600}{4} = £600$

	Depreciation charge	Net profit	Net book value
	£	£	£
Year 1	600	1400	2400
Year 2	600	1400	1800
Year 3	600	1400	1200
Year 4	600	1400	600
Year 5			

Year 4		£
Profit		2000
Less: Depreciation	600	
Profit on sale (*b*)	(100)	
		500
		£1500

(*b*) Proceeds £700 less NBV £600.

Assumption 2: 4 × £600 = £2400
− profit on sale £(100)

METHODS OF DEPRECIATION

We have seen that estimates of likely lives and residual values of fixed assets can significantly affect reported results. Even more significant may be the choice of depreciation *method*. So far we have assumed that the company would wish to charge an equal amount of depreciation each year, but this is only one approach from a range of possible methods.

The two most common methods of providing for depreciation are:

(*a*) Straight line—this is the one we have used so far
(*b*) Declining balance

(*a*) The Straight Line Method

The straight line method of depreciation which we have considered so far is the simplest of all. It involves writing off an equal charge each year based on the asset's estimated net cost and its estimated life.

This was the method used by Furniture Removals Limited:

$$\frac{£3000 - £500}{5} = £500 \text{ a year depreciation}$$

Its effect is represented graphically opposite, showing the "straight line" declining net book value.

Depreciation calculated on the straight line basis can always be expressed as a constant percentage of original cost. In the Furniture Removals case it was:

$$\frac{£500}{£3000} = 16 \cdot 7\% \; (= 1/6\text{th})$$

Where no account is taken of a possible residual value at the end of the asset's life, the percentage is a simple fraction based on the number of years the asset is expected to last. For example:

$$\frac{£3000}{5} = £600 \text{ a year} = 20\% \text{ of cost } (= 1/5\text{th})$$

The Straight Line Method

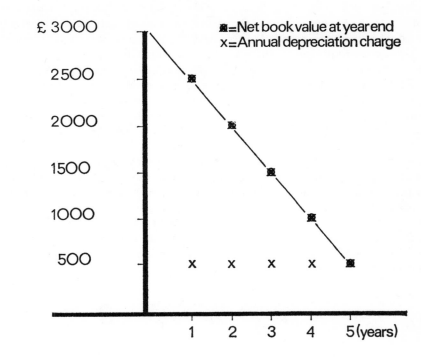

■=Net book value at year end
x=Annual depreciation charge

	Depreciation charge		Accumulated depreciation	Net book value
		£	£	£
Year 1	1/6 × £3000 = 500		500	2500
Year 2	1/6 × £3000 = 500		1000	2000
Year 3	1/6 × £3000 = 500		1500	1500
Year 4	1/6 × £3000 = 500		2000	1000
Year 5	1/6 × £3000 = 500		2500	500

(b) The Declining Balance Method

The declining balance method of ("accelerated") depreciation charges larger amounts in earlier years than in later years. The annual charge is calculated by applying to the net book value of the asset at the start of each accounting period a constant percentage intended to reduce the book value of the asset to (approximately) its residual value at the end of its estimated useful life.

Had Furniture Removals Limited used this method, the required rate to reduce the book value of the van to its expected residual value of £500 at the end of year 5 would have been 30 per cent. This can be calculated using the formula $r = [1 - (R/c)^{1/n}] \times 100$ where r = rate of depreciation per period, c = original cost, R = residual value, n = number of periods of useful life. The depreciation is represented graphically opposite.

Obviously this method will never reduce an asset to zero book value, since one always takes away only 30 per cent of what is left. However, the balance will become very small in relation to cost and can then be written off entirely in a single year.

Notice that a higher percentage rate is needed to write an asset off in a given time than under the straight line method. Notice too how quickly the asset's net book value falls, and how much the depreciation charge itself has declined after the first year or two.

The Declining Balance Method

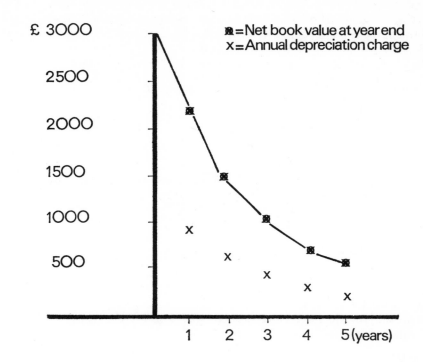

■ = Net book value at year end
x = Annual depreciation charge

	Depreciation charge		Accumulated depreciation	Net book value
		£	£	£
Year 1	30% × £3000 =	900	900	2100
Year 2	30% × £2100 =	630	1530	1470·
Year 3	30% × £1470 =	441	1971	1029
Year 4	30% × £1029 =	309	2280	720
Year 5	30% × £ 720 =	216	2496	504

Had Furniture Removals Limited used the declining balance method of depreciation, profits in earlier years would have been reduced and those in later years would have been higher, as shown below.

Some companies might argue that accelerated depreciation reduces the risk of heavier charges in later years should it prove that insufficient allowance has been made for obsolescence in estimating the asset's useful life. It is also true that the net book value of assets in the balance sheet often more closely approximates to their declining market value when accelerated rather than straight line depreciation is used. On the other hand, it may be argued that this is quite irrelevant if there is no intention of selling a fixed asset before the end of its originally estimated life.

Whichever method is preferred, and for whatever reasons, the figures below show that there can be significant differences between the two methods, both in the net profit figures and in the asset net book values year by year.

Straight line and declining balance methods compared

Profit before depreciation = £2000

	Straight line method			Declining balance method		
	Depreciation charge	Net profit	Net book value	Depreciation charge	Net profit	Net book value
	£	£	£	£	£	£
Year 1	500	1500	2500	900	1100	2100
Year 2	500	1500	2000	630	1370	1470
Year 3	500	1500	1500	441	1559	1029
Year 4	500	1500	1000	309	1691	720
Year 5	500	1500	500	216	1784	504

In appropriate cases other methods of depreciation can be used.

(c) Machine-Hour Method

Under this method, the depreciation charge for a period is based on the number of hours the machine is used in the period.

Example

A company purchased a special processing machine for £1000. The technical director estimated that the machine could be used for 10 000 hours before it would be worn out. If the company uses the machine for 2000 hours in the first year and for 3500 hours in the second, the charges for depreciation will be respectively £200 and £350, assuming there will be no residual value.

The machine-hour method bases the depreciation charge on usage, not on a time basis. Its accuracy depends on how well the machine's total working life, in hours of usage, is estimated; and on the residual value.

(d) The annuity method

The methods which we have looked at so far take no account of the fact that money retained in the business in providing for depreciation will be earning a return. To obtain an even *net* charge each year, after deducting such return from the depreciation charged, the annuity method uses the formula: C/S_{ni}, where:

C = Cost of the asset
n = Estimated asset life in years
S_{ni} = The sum to which an annual instalment of 1 will accumulate over n years at an interest rate of i per year.

This method gives rise to an even *net* charge each year (the *gross* depreciation charged still equalling the asset's total net cost), but involves more complicated calculations than the other methods. It is not suitable where additions are made to original cost during an asset's life. The annuity method is claimed to have significant advantages in measuring return on investment, for it does not (as other methods do) tend to show an *increasing* return on investment over an asset's life.

EFFECT OF VARYING DEPRECIATION CHARGES ON REPORTED RESULTS

Enough has been said about the different possible methods of depreciation to show that in trying to compare the results of two companies great care is needed to ensure that like is being compared with like. The force of this warning can be appreciated by working through an example where considerable differences arise in the figures.

Let us take the case where the possibility of technical obsolescence will have a significant influence in making judgements concerning the likely effective life of an asset. While engineers can often forecast physical wear and tear fairly accurately, the effects of technical (that is market) obsolescence are much harder to foresee. In calculating depreciation we are concerned with an asset's *economically* useful life, not solely with its physical life in working order.

Example

Let us assume that two companies, Green Limited and Brown Limited, are in the same type of business and that they are both regularly making profits before depreciation of £20 000 a year. (Ignore tax to simplify the example.) Let us further assume that they both acquire identical machines for use in production at a cost of £10 000 each.

Green's technical director believes that the machine could soon be replaced by a more sophisticated machine. He proposes that the company should write it off over three years, allow for residual value of only £1250, and use accelerated depreciation in case the life is even shorter than expected.

The technical director of Brown Limited, acting quite independently, regards the machine as being of such a standard design that it will continue in effective use for at least five years after which time it should be possible to sell it for £2500. The company accepts his estimates and uses straight line depreciation as usual.

You are asked to show the results of implementing these technical judgements in the accounts of Green Limited and Brown Limited. (Space is provided for your answers opposite.)

GREEN LIMITED

Cost of machine: £10 000

Estimated life: 3 years

Residual value: £1250

Method of depreciation: Declining balance

(Percentage to reduce asset to £1250 in 3 years = 50 per cent)

	Profit before depreciation	Annual depreciation	Net profit	Accumulated depreciation	Net book value
	£	£	£	£	£
Year 1	20 000				
Year 2	20 000				
Year 3	20 000				

BROWN LIMITED

Cost of machine: £10 000

Estimated life: 5 years

Residual value: £2500

Method of depreciation: Straight line

	Profit before depreciation	Annual depreciation	Net profit	Accumulated depreciation	Net book value
	£	£	£	£	£
Year 1	20 000				
Year 2	20 000				
Year 3	20 000				
Year 4	20 000				
Year 5	20 000				

Please now compare your answers with those shown on the next page.

GREEN LIMITED

Depreciation 50 per cent declining balance

	Profit before depreciation	Annual depreciation	Net profit	Accumulated depreciation	Net book value
	£	£	£	£	£
Year 1	20 000	5000	15 000	5000	5000
Year 2	20 000	2500	17 500	7500	2500
Year 3	20 000	1250	18 750	8750	1250

BROWN LIMITED

Depreciation 15 per cent straight line

	Profit before depreciation	Annual depreciation	Net profit	Accumulated depreciation	Net book value
	£	£	£	£	£
Year 1	20 000	1500	18 500	1500	8500
Year 2	20 000	1500	18 500	3000	7000
Year 3	20 000	1500	18 500	4500	5500
Year 4	20 000	1500	18 500	6000	4000
Year 5	20 000	1500	18 500	7500	2500

Comments

This example illustrates the impact of opinion on reported results, for the widely different figures shown for the two companies represent the same physical facts.

When the depreciation methods and rates were chosen there was no way to tell which would produce the more "correct" answer.

If Green's anticipation of swift obsolescence proved true, then Brown would have shown profit figures which were too high in years 1 to 3, and would be left with an asset balance to be written off against profits which it may no longer be able to generate.

If Brown's judgement proved to be correct, then both the profits and asset book values shown in Green's accounts in years 1 to 3 are understated.

In the absence of detailed knowledge it would be very easy for an analyst, using the reported financial figures only, to draw quite wrong conclusions about the performance and status of the two companies.

	Net Profit		Net Book Value	
	Green	Brown	Green	Brown
	£	£	£	£
Year 1	15 000	18 500	5000	8500
Year 2	17 500	18 500	2500	7000
Year 3	18 750	18 500	1250	5500
Year 4		18 500		4000
Year 5		18 500		2500

PROFIT OR LOSS ON THE SALE OF FIXED ASSETS

We have seen that depreciation charges are based on estimates of the useful life and residual value of fixed assets. We have also seen that these estimates are often inaccurate and can cause distortions in the trend of reported results. Since balance sheets do not purport to show current market values, differences between the figures at which fixed assets are included in accounts and their true worth can go undetected for years. When the assets are sold, however, adjustments are required in the financial records to reconcile the "written down" and "market" figures.

Insignificant differences—small profits or losses on disposal—are usually absorbed in the depreciation figure, and are thus hidden from the external analyst. Substantial profits or losses on disposal, however, require separate disclosure in the year of sale, either as a "below the line" item in the profit and loss account* or as a change in reserves. The latter case may call for careful reading of the notes to the accounts to determine the nature of the adjustment, especially as movements in reserves are not always as fully explained as one might wish.

A profit or loss on the sale of fixed assets normally represents an adjustment to previous years' depreciation charges. Significant profits (or losses) on disposal appearing regularly in a company's accounts may indicate a definite tendency to overprovide (or underprovide) for depreciation.

Where the amount received on disposal exceeds the original cost of a fixed asset, a *capital* profit has been made (in addition to recovering any depreciation charged), which must be added to capital reserves, as explained in more detail in section 6.

Undisclosed results of wrongly estimated depreciation

Where fixed assets are kept in use after the end of their estimated useful life the results of poor original estimates will often not be specifically disclosed in the accounts although they will affect the profit figure.

*As in Marks and Spencer Limited's accounts.

Example

A machine costing £1000 was estimated to have a three-year life and a residual value of £400. Using straight line depreciation the accounts would show:

	Profit and Loss Account Depreciation charge	Balance Sheet Net book value
	£	£
Year 1	200	800
Year 2	200	600
Year 3	200	400

Assuming that the machine were used for a further year and then sold for £300 at the beginning of year 5 the accounts for years 4 and 5 would show:

Year 4	200	200
Year 5 Profit on sale	100*	

*£300 proceeds less £200 net book value.

In year 4, while the asset was still in use, the error in calculating the annual depreciation was not disclosed. The "profit on sale of fixed asset" figure arose only when the asset was sold.

Had the asset been retained for a total of eight years and then scrapped at zero value, the error in the depreciation charge would never have been shown explicitly. But the actual depreciation and profit patterns would have diverged from a "correct" position as follows:

	Depreciation actually charged	"Correct" depreciation	Error in profit reported	
			Understated	Overstated
	£	£	£	£
Year 1	200	125	75	
Year 2	200	125	75	
Year 3	200	125	75	
Year 4	200	125	75	
Year 5	200	125	75	
Year 6	—	125		125
Year 7	—	125		125
Year 8	—	125		125
Total	£1000	£1000	£375	£375

BOOK-KEEPING ENTRIES FOR FIXED ASSETS

It is usual for fixed asset and depreciation figures to be recorded in separate ledger accounts in the books, in order that separate totals can easily be determined for cost and accumulated depreciation figures (required by statute to be disclosed separately in the published accounts).

The following entries would appear in the books of Furniture Removals Limited in the first three years of the life of the van costing £3000, using the five-year life and £500 residual value.

Notes

1 The "van" and "accumulated depreciation: van" accounts will remain open in the books during the life of the van, *even if* the van lasted longer than five years and was completely written off.

2 The "depreciation charge" account is "closed off" each year to the profit and loss account, and would be used to bring together the depreciation charges relating to all fixed assets.

3 At 31 December 1970, the amounts marked (*a*) and (*b*) would appear in the balance sheet; at 31 December 1971, (*a*) and (*d*); and at 31 December 1972, (*a*) and (*f*).

4 For the year 1970, the amount marked (*c*) would appear as a charge in the profit and loss account; for 1971, (*e*); and for 1972, (*g*).

Ledger Accounts

Van — Fo 40 (£)

Date	Particulars	Fo	£
1-1-70	Cash	CB	3000 (*a*)

Accumulated depreciation: van — Fo 41 (£)

Date	Particulars	Fo	£	Date	Particulars	Fo	£
31-12-71	Balance	c/d	1000	31-12-70	Depreciation charge	80	500 (*b*)
				31-12-71	Depreciation charge	80	500
			1000				1000
31-12-72	Balance	c/d	1500	1- 1-72	Balance	b/d	1000 (*d*)
				31-12-72	Depreciation charge	80	500
			1500				1500
				1- 1-73	Balance	b/d	1500 (*f*)

Depreciation charge — Fo 80

Date	Particulars	Fo	£	Date	Particulars	Fo	£
31-12-70	Accumulated depreciation	41	500 (*c*)	31-12-70	Profit and loss account	150	500
31-12-71	Accumulated depreciation	41	500 (*e*)	31-12-71	Profit and loss account	150	500
31-12-72	Accumulated depreciation	41	500 (*g*)	31-12-72	Profit and loss account	150	500

Book entries to record profit or loss on disposal of fixed assets

The usual way of recording disposals is to open up a separate "disposals" account, in which all entries relating to a particular fixed asset disposal can be brought together. The entries which would appear in the books of Furniture Removals Limited had the van in fact been sold for £700 at the end of year 4 (when the net book value was £1000) are shown below. It would be customary to record the disposal and loss in a series of journal entries, which are shown opposite.

Journal Entries

	Fo 18	Fo	Dr £	Cr £
31-12-73	Disposal of fixed assets	99	3000	
	To Van	40		3000
31-12-73	Accumulated depreciation: van	41	2000	
	To Disposal of fixed assets	99		2000
31-12-73	Cash	CB	700	
	To Disposal of fixed assets	99		700
31-12-73	Profit and loss account	150	300	
	To Disposal of fixed assets	99		300
	Being entries to record loss of £300 on disposal of van for £700 cash			

Ledger Accounts

			£				£
				Van	*Fo 40*		
1-1-70	Cash	CB	3000	31-12-73	Disposal of fixed assets	J 18	3000
				Accumulated depreciation: van	*Fo 41*		
				1- 1-73	Balance	b/d	1500
31-12-73	Disposal of fixed assets	J 18	2000	31-12-73	Depreciation charge	80	500
			2000				2000
				Depreciation charge	*Fo 80*		
31-12-73	Accumulated depreciation	41	500	31-12-73	Profit and loss account	150	500
				Disposal of fixed assets	*Fo 99*		
31-12-73	Van (cost)	J 18	3000	31-12-73	Accumulated depreciation	J 18	2000
				31-12-73	Cash	J 18	700
				31-12-73	Profit and loss account: loss on sale	J 18	300
			3000				3000

SUMMARY

Fixed assets are used to provide goods or services over a period of years, not to be sold in the ordinary course of business. Intentions, not physical characteristics, determine whether a particular asset is fixed or current.

Over the whole life of a fixed asset, depreciation = cost less residual value. Once the cost of a fixed asset has been determined there are three main problems in calculating depreciation:

1 Estimating a fixed asset's useful life—which may be limited by the passing of time, wear and tear or technical obsolescence.
2 Estimating residual value—which, in practice, is often ignored.
3 Choosing a depreciation method—the two main methods being straight line and declining balance.

Straight line depreciation writes off a constant percentage of cost each year, while the declining balance method writes off a constant percentage of the (declining) net book value at the beginning of each year.

Different depreciation methods write off the same total amount, but allocate it differently between accounting periods. The differences affect both reported profit (or loss) and total capital employed. Depreciation does not result from a process of valuing the fixed asset each year, but from a process of allocation of cost.

On the sale of a fixed asset, unless proceeds of sale are more than original cost, any profit or loss on sale represents an adjustment of previous years' depreciation charges.

It would not be appropriate to leave the subject of fixed assets without some mention of three further important topics:

1 The effect of inflation on accounts
2 The effect of leasing fixed assets
3 The treatment of fixed assets and depreciation for tax purposes

These subjects, which we now discuss briefly in turn, may be omitted on a first reading of this book, or by those readers who feel no need for more than a basic understanding of fixed assets and depreciation.

DEPRECIATION AND CURRENCY DEBASEMENT: THE EFFECTS OF INFLATION

Balance sheets generally show assets "at cost" (unless market value is *lower* than cost). But many companies periodically revalue upwards their fixed assets (especially land and buildings) for balance sheet purposes. The increase of the valuation over original cost is debited (added) to the fixed asset account, and credited to capital reserves. Except for land (which is not usually depreciated) this increases the amount of depreciation to be written off as an expense in future periods. Over the rest of the asset's life, the *whole* of the (newly increased) net book value will be written off as depreciation, thus gradually cancelling out the original credit to reserves by reducing retained profits below what they would otherwise have been.

As explained earlier, "cost" = "past actual market value," and "market value" = "present hypothetical market value." Pressure for upvaluation becomes strongest when current market values are much higher than past costs. This can always occur with particular assets for a variety of reasons, but it happens *generally* and to *all* non-monetary assets when the value of money has been falling fast. In the United Kingdom the value of money has been falling at an average rate of more than 4 per cent a year since 1935. The result is that the purchasing power of £1 in 1973 is less than one-fifth as much as the purchasing power of £1 in 1935. (See Table opposite.)

Some accountants advocate adjusting *all* items in accounts to allow for currency debasement (inflation), by means of a general index of the purchasing power of money. For this purpose, despite various statistical problems, the reciprocal of the monthly Retail Price Index is probably as suitable as any other index. Currency debasement adjustments do *not* strictly constitute a departure from historical cost accounting. In effect they treat a different year's money as if it were a "foreign" currency, and convert it into current money terms at the appropriate "exchange rate."

The Retail Price Index shows that the value of money fell by 60 per cent between 1947 and 1970. So to buy as much as £100 bought in 1947 one needed £250 in 1970. Thus $_{47}£100 = _{70}£250$. Conventional accounts assume that the value of money is stable—that is, that $_{47}£100 = _{70}£100$. In calculating profit and loss they aim to maintain *money* capital, not *purchasing power* capital. Those who advocate currency debasement adjustments to conventional accounts think it is more useful to reckon in terms of purchasing power capital when the value of money is falling fast.

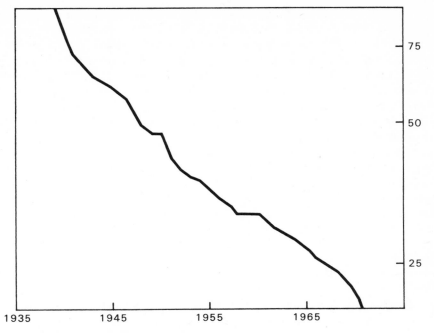

PURCHASING POWER OF THE POUND

RETAIL PRICE INDEX*

1935	30	1948	60	1960	94
1936	30	1949	62	1961	98
1937	31	1950	63	1962	102
1938	31	1951	69	1963	104
1939	33	1952	75	1964	107
1940	38	1953	78	1965	112
1941	42	1954	79	1966	117
1943	47	1955	83	1967	119
1944	48	1956	87	1968	125
1945	49	1957	90	1969	132
1946	52	1958	93	1970	140
1947	56	1959	93	1971	153
				1972	164

*January 1962 = 100. Retail Price Index annual averages from 1948, linked for earlier years to London and Cambridge Consumers' Expenditure Average Value Index.

In respect of a fixed asset costing £5000 in 1947, expected to last for 25 years, and depreciated on the straight line basis, the conventional depreciation charge in 1970 will be £5000 × 1/25 = £200. *Adjusted* 1970 accounts would convert the original money cost ($_{47}$£5000) at the appropriate "exchange rate" ($_{47}$£100 = $_{70}$£250) to produce an "adjusted cost" of $_{70}$£12 500. Straight line depreciation is then calculated as usual: £12 500 × 1/25 = £500. Adjusted 1970 depreciation is thus £500 (= $_{70}$£500) instead of the conventional £200 (= $_{47}$£200), thus producing lower profits in adjusted than in conventional (unadjusted) accounts.

In adjusted accounts the net book value of fixed assets is increased too, since the *cost* of fixed assets is always increased more than the accumulated depreciation. Thus in *both* respects the return on net assets ratio is worsened. The increase from original money cost ($_{47}$£5000) to adjusted cost ($_{70}$£12 500) is balanced by a similar increase in shareholders' funds. This reflects the increased money amount representing the *same* purchasing power capital. It is *not* a "profit," any more than one makes a "profit" of $140 when converting £100 into $240.

Because of the long life of many fixed assets, adjustments to accounts to allow for currency debasement tend to be most dramatic in respect of depreciation adjustments. But to be consistent adjustments are necessary also in respect of stock, monetary assets (debtors and cash), and monetary liabilities (both current and long-term). From the point of view of a company's shareholders there is a real loss involved in a company holding monetary assets when the value of money is falling, and a real gain in a company having monetary liabilities. Adjusted accounts include such gains and losses in the profit and loss account, while conventional (unadjusted) accounts do not.

It is widely recognised as a practical matter that adjustments *are* necessary where the rate of inflation is sufficiently high, but most businessmen assume that an annual inflation rate of 4 or 5 per cent is not sufficiently high to require adjustment. This assumption must be open to question when the cumulative effect is considered. The matter has recently become more urgent as the British rate of inflation over the past few years has accelerated well above 5 per cent a year.

The Institute of Chartered Accountants in England and Wales last made a formal recommendation on the subject in 1952 (N 15: Accounting in relation to changes in the purchasing power of money), to the effect that "unless and until a practicable and generally acceptable alternative is available" conventional accounting practices should continue to be used.

The matter is currently being investigated, and an Exposure Draft (No. 8) has been issued by the Accounting Standards Steering Committee proposing that from 1974 companies should publish supplementary statements in their Annual Reports adjusting conventional accounts, by means of a general index of the purchasing power of money, in order to allow for the effects of inflation.

The Exposure Draft is not yet a formal Statement of Standard Accounting Practice, and it may (like earlier Exposure Drafts) be altered or even withdrawn. But it does now seem likely that some formal adjustments to allow for inflation will be required for company accounts in the near future, and for those readers who are interested an Appendix is included at the end of section 8 to illustrate in some detail the adjustments that are currently envisaged by Exposure Draft 8.

Depreciation and replacement

Depreciation charges do not purport to provide funds with which to "replace fixed assets." By reducing the amount of profit available for distribution as dividends, however, depreciation charges do at least force companies to maintain their capital employed, subject to "losses" in purchasing power due to inflation.

A company formed to last only as long as its depreciable assets (that is one which intended not to replace them) would still have to charge depreciation in its accounts to calculate its profit or loss. If the company's entire life were a single accounting period, the fixed assets' total net cost would have to be charged as an expense in that period. Thus the "going-concern" assumption is not necessary to justify depreciation. Depreciation simply *allocates* the expense of fixed assets between accounting periods where fixed assets last longer than a single period.

A limited company can reduce its capital only with formal permission from the court—though the law requires maintenance only of *money* capital, which in practice permits companies (wittingly or not) to reduce "real" (purchasing power) capital over time. A *division* of a company, on the other hand, commonly transfers to its parent company all funds available, receiving further funds for investment (*inter alia* for replacing fixed assets) only if sufficiently profitable projects can be found. Total capital employed in a particular division can thus be reduced quite fast, by withdrawing the funds represented by depreciation and simply not investing any more.

LEASING FIXED ASSETS

Leasing assets is a way of enjoying the *use* of assets without actually owning them. In business it is usual to distinguish between "operating" leases and "financial" leases (see Table opposite).

In the simplest lease, the only accounting entry will be to charge the lease payments as an expense in the profit and loss account. No asset will be shown in the balance sheet.

Where a capital amount ("premium") has been paid for a lease (as is often the case with leasehold properties), the balance sheet will show that amount as an asset, and the profit and loss account will be charged with *two* amounts— the annual lease payments and a depreciation charge in respect of the asset (usually on the straight line basis over the period of the lease).

The conventional accounting treatment outlined above makes no distinction between the "operating" lease and the "financial" lease. The asset being leased is shown as an asset in the lessee's balance sheet only if a premium has been paid.

Some accountants argue that "financial" leases should be capitalised (i.e. an amount should be shown as a capital asset on the balance sheet) even where no capital amount has been paid as a premium. They contend that where a business has incurred a non-cancellable commitment to pay lease rentals for practically the entire expected economic life of an asset, the effect is virtually the same as if the asset had been purchased outright. It is argued that much of the annual rental charge is then effectively equivalent to an instalment of the purchase price of the asset (the balance of the rental charge each year representing "interest" on the unpaid "instalments" of the purchase price), and that in such circumstances leasing is really only an alternative method of financing the purchase of the asset.

	"Operating" lease	*"Financial" lease*
Period	May be very short	Usually at least half the asset's economic life
Payments	May be very small	Usually total more than the cash purchase price
Commitment	Cancellable	Non-cancellable
Repairs	Done by lessor	Responsibility of lessee

The proposal is that the capitalised amount of the lease should be shown as an asset, and that the total unpaid "instalments" be shown as a long-term liability on the balance sheet. Then each rental payment would have to be split between interest (charged to the profit and loss account as an expense) and capital instalment (deducted from the "liability" account). In addition to the "interest" part of the rental payment, the profit and loss account will also be charged each year with an amount representing depreciation of the capital asset.

Assuming that under this scheme depreciation and interest together would not normally differ very much from the present rental charge, the net effect on the profit and loss account might be relatively small (though the interest cover would be reduced). More important, in most cases, would be the effect on the balance sheet of adding a fixed asset and a long-term liability if leases were capitalised. Such a change would particularly affect the return on net assets (which would be reduced), and the debt ratio (which would be increased).

An illustration of the sort of effect that capitalising leases could have on accounts is shown opposite, using hypothetical amounts.

Those who oppose the capitalisation of leases argue that there is a distinction between a liability in respect of services already rendered and a commitment in respect of services to be rendered in future. (For example, they ask, should "liabilities" in respect of employment contracts be capitalised?) They also point out possible important differences between unrestricted ownership of an asset, and a more limited right to its services under special conditions.

Fuller disclosure of the different nature of various assets and liabilities can probably meet both these objections. There are also undoubted difficulties in choosing an interest rate to determine how much of an annual rental charge represents interest and how much represents an instalment of the "purchase price". But consistent use even of a somewhat arbitrary approximation might be adequate for accounting purposes, once a departure is accepted from reporting what actually happened in favour of reporting what is thought to be its equivalent.

	Conventional accounts £'000	Capitalising leases £'000
Balance sheet		
Property leased	—	40
Other fixed assets	100	100
Net working capital	60	60
	160	200
Long-term debt	50	90
Shareholders' funds	110	110
	160	200
Profit and loss account		
Depreciation	10	14
Interest payable	5	9
Lease rental	8	—

DEPRECIATION FOR TAX PURPOSES

A company cannot affect its tax liability by its depreciation policy because statutory rules determine the depreciation allowed for tax (called "capital allowances" or "writing-down allowances").

The simplest company tax calculation begins with reported "book" profits for a period, adds back depreciation charged (to eliminate it from the expenses), deducts instead the statutory capital allowances, and so reaches the amount of taxable profit. Multiplying taxable profit by the tax rate gives the amount of corporation tax payable in respect of the period's profit, as shown below.

Simple tax computation

Straight line "book" depreciation	£2 000
Reported profit before tax	£6 000
Statutory capital allowances	£5 000
Tax rate assumed, 50%	
	£
Book profit before tax	6 000
Add back: Book depreciation	2 000
	8 000
Less: Tax capital allowances	5 000
Taxable profit	£3 000

Tax payable = 50% × £3 000 = £1 500

Deferred tax reserves ("tax equalisation" accounts)

Annual tax capital allowances are normally 25% of the declining balance, but many companies use the straight line method of depreciation in their accounts. Thus tax depreciation may be higher than book depreciation in the early years of a fixed asset's life; and the tax payable will then be less than book profits multiplied by the tax rate. The discrepancy is especially high where as much as 100% of cost is allowed as a tax deduction in the first year of an asset's life.

Some companies (like Company A below) regard the difference as a tax liability *deferred* by the accelerated tax depreciation, and credit it to a deferred tax reserve account ("tax equalisation"). The deferred tax reserve in respect of a particular fixed asset will be cleared by the end of its life, but if a company increases its total level of investment the total deferred tax reserve account will tend to grow larger.

Some companies ignore possible deferred tax. Like Company B below, they simply charge the actual tax payable as an expense in their accounts. This leads to a "low" tax charge (25% in the example shown below) when compared with the pre-tax profit shown in the accounts. Notice that reported profit after tax (the basis for earnings per share and other financial ratios) is affected.

In both cases the *actual* tax liability is £1500

	Company A	Company B
Published accounts		
Profit before tax	£6 000	£6 000
Less: Corporation tax	3 000	1 500
Profit after tax	£3,000	£4 500
Deferred tax reserve	£1 500	—
Tax capital allowances	£5 000	
Book depreciation	2 000	
Excess	£3 000	
Excess £3000 × tax rate 50% =	£1 500	

THE NEW TAX SYSTEM

The system of corporation tax introduced in April 1965 was changed as from April 1973. Under the old system, companies paid a 40 per cent rate of *corporation tax* but also had to pay the Inland Revenue *income tax* deducted from dividends distributed to shareholders. Under the new system, companies pay corporation tax at 50 per cent but do *not* have to pay over income tax deducted from dividends paid as well.

One other change deserves mention. The old system had a "standard rate" income tax of 38.75 per cent *minus* Earned Income Relief of 2/9ths (up to £4,005) on "earned" income (wages, salaries, etc.). The new system has a "basic rate" income tax of 30 per cent *plus* an additional tax of 15 per cent on "unearned" income (interest, dividends, etc.) above £2000 a year gross. Since 7/9ths of 38.75 per cent = 30.14 per cent, the change makes little difference to people with only earned income below £4,005.

The table below illustrates how the old and new systems work for a company earning profit before tax of £1000 and paying out gross dividends to shareholders amounting to £450. The new system is called the "imputation" system because part of the £500 corporation tax liability is "imputed" to the shareholders (*as if* it were income tax deducted at source). The company pays £135 advance corporation tax (ACT) to the Inland Revenue at the time the net dividend is paid to shareholders; and the balance of corporation tax due (£365) is payable nine months after the year end (or later for companies formed before 1965). The shareholders are then treated as having received gross dividends of £450, of which the basic rate 30 per cent income tax (£135) is deemed to have been "deducted at source". But the "income tax" so imputed is merely an *advance* payment of corporation tax from the company's point of view.

Old system 1965–1973	£
Profit before tax	1000
Corporation tax (40%)	400
Profit after tax	600
Gross dividend	450
Retained profits	£ 150
Shareholders	
Net dividend	276
Income tax at standard rate (38.75%)	174
Gross dividend	£ 450

New system from 1973	£
Profit before tax	1000
Corporation tax (say 50%)	500
Profit after tax	500
Net dividend	315
Retained profits	£ 185
Shareholders	
Net dividend	315
Imputation credit (30%)	135
Gross dividend	£ 450

INVESTMENT MEASURES UNDER THE NEW TAX SYSTEM

The new tax system affects some of the investment measures outlined in section 2. In this second edition we have retained the basic explanation of ratios described in the first edition, since company accounts for 1973 will cover the "transitional" period between the old and the new systems. When the new system is in full force, however, from 1974 onwards, some investment measures based on after-tax earnings will have to be calculated in a different way.

Under the old system, the profit after corporation tax was available for payment of gross dividends, and constituted the basis for calculating the "after-tax" investment measures. The corporation tax payable was not affected by the level of dividends paid. Under the new system, the total corporation tax payable by a company may vary depending on the level of dividends paid. This poses a difficulty for the investment analyst. Which of the following three earnings figures should be used?

Nil basis—earnings after corporation tax, on the assumption that *no* dividends are paid.

Net basis—earnings after corporation tax, after charging any foreign tax not able to be offset against UK corporation tax, and after charging any ACT which may not be deductible from UK corporation tax in the foreseeable future (unrelieved ACT will arise for companies which pay little or no UK corporation tax, when they pay dividends).

Maximum distributable ("full") basis—the "grossed up" equivalent of earnings on the "net" basis, assuming that the company distributes as dividends *all* the available earnings for the period. (The "net" dividends paid are "grossed up" by multiplying by 100/70, using the basic income tax rate of 30 per cent. The difference between the gross and net dividends is the amount of ACT paid by the company at the time that the dividends are paid.)

The "Net" approach treats any unrelieved foreign tax or unrelieved ACT as a charge against profit, leaving a smaller amount of "earnings", whereas the "Nil" approach treats any unrelieved ACT as related to *dividends* rather than to profits, and hence gives an "earnings" figure unaffected by any change in the level of dividends paid. In practice, for most companies earnings on the net basis will be the same as the nil basis. Where there is a difference, most financial services are calculating the earnings on the net basis.

Of the five investment measures described in section 2, under the new tax system three measures will use the net basis of calculating earnings—*return on equity*, *earnings per share*, and *price/earnings ratio*. *Dividend yield* will, as before, use gross dividend paid (that is, the net dividend paid grossed up by multiplying by 100/70). The final measure, *dividend cover*, will relate the grossed up actual dividend paid to the grossed up earnings on the "maximum distributable" basis.

Examples of the various investment measures on both on old and the new tax systems are shown on the next page.

CALCULATING INVESTMENT MEASURES BEFORE AND AFTER THE "IMPUTATION" TAX SYSTEM

Old tax system

		£
Profit before tax		1000
Corporation tax		400
Earnings	(1)	600
Gross dividend	(5)	450
Retained profit	(3)	£ 150

Shareholders

Net dividend	(2)	276
Tax at standard rate (38.75%)	(4)	174
Gross dividend	(5)	450

Investment measures

Ordinary shares of 25 p	(6)	20 000
Share price	(7)	60 p
Earnings per share (1) ÷ (6)	(8)	3.0p
Price/earnings multiple (7) ÷ (8)	(9)	20.0
Dividend per share (gross) (5) ÷ (6)	(10)	2.25 p
Dividend yield (gross) (10) ÷ (7)	(11)	3.75 %
Earnings yield (8) ÷ (7)	(12)	5.0%
Dividend cover (1) ÷ (5) or (8) ÷ (10)	(13)	1.33

[1] UK Corporation tax at estimated rate of 50%.

New "imputation" tax system

		All UK tax	Unrelieved ACT or foreign tax
		£	£
Profit before tax		1000	1000
Corporation tax, say		500[1]	540[2]
Earnings	(1)	500	460
Net dividend	(2)	315	315
Retained profit	(3)	185	145

Shareholders

Net dividend	(2)	315	315
Imputation tax credit (ACT) (30%)	(4)	135	135
Gross dividend	(5)	450	450
Maximum distribution (Earnings × 100/70)	(5a)	714	657

Investment measures

		"Net" basis	
Ordinary shares of 25 p	(6)	20 000	20 000
Share price	(7)	60 p	60 p
Earnings per share (1) ÷ (6)	(8)	2.50 p	2.30 p
Price/earnings multiple (7) ÷ (8)	(9)	24.0	26.0
Dividend per share (gross) (5) ÷ (6)	(10)	2.25 p	2.25 p
Dividend yield (gross) (10) ÷ (7)	(11)	3.75%	3.75%
		"Maximum" basis	
Earnings per share (5a) ÷ (6)	(8a)	3.57p	3.29p
Earnings yield (8a) ÷ (7)	(12)	5.95%	5.48%
Dividend cover (5a) ÷ (5) or (8a) ÷ (10)	(13)	1.59	1.46

[2] Corporation tax, unrelieved ACT, and foreign tax in excess of 50%.

5.1 Definitions

Write down opposite your definitions of the terms shown. Then compare your answers with the definitions overleaf.

(*a*) A fixed asset

(*b*) Depreciation

(*c*) Net book value

(*d*) Residual value

(*e*) The straight line method

(*f*) The declining balance method

(*g*) Accelerated depreciation

(*h*) A tax equalisation account

(*i*) Amortisation

(*j*) Capital commitments

177

5.1 Definitions

(a) A *fixed asset* is a resource (either tangible or intangible) with a relatively long economic life acquired not for resale in the ordinary course of business but for use in producing other goods and services.

(b) *Depreciation* (of fixed assets) is the process of allocating part of the cost of fixed assets as expense to a particular accounting period. Accumulated depreciation is the total amount so provided to date for assets still held by the company; it must be shown separately in the balance sheet or in the notes to the accounts.

(c) *Net book value* (NBV) is the difference between the cost of a fixed asset (or, in some cases, the amount of its valuation) and the accumulated depreciation in respect of that asset. It does *not* represent market value.

(d) *Residual value* is the amount for which a fixed asset can be sold at the end of its useful life. The expected residual value is taken into account in calculating depreciation during the asset's life (often it is treated as zero).

(e) *The straight line method* of depreciation charges an equal amount of depreciation in each year of an asset's life, by writing off a constant percentage of the asset's original cost.

(f) *The declining balance method* of depreciation writes off a constant percentage of the declining net book value of a fixed asset shown at the start of each accounting period. The percentage rate used tends to be higher than for the straight line method.

(g) *Accelerated depreciation* is any depreciation method which charges higher amounts in the early years of an asset's life than in the later years. Declining balance is one such method.

(h) *A tax equalisation account* represents tax on the difference between the accelerated depreciation allowed for tax purposes and the straight line depreciation charged by most companies in their accounts. It is treated as a long-term liability, and is sometimes called "deferred taxation."

(i) *Amortisation* is the name often given to depreciation of intangible fixed assets.

(j) *Capital commitments* are significant amounts of capital expenditure which a company is contractually bound to pay in the future.

5.2 Jonas Limited (A): Straight line depreciation

Jonas Limited buys a fixed asset for £8400, expects it to last for six years, and proposes to write off depreciation on the straight line basis.

Calculate the depreciation charge each year and the book value at the end of each year.

5.3 Jonas Limited (B): Different lives

Jonas Limited buys a fixed asset for £8400, expects it to last for six years, and proposes to write off depreciation on the straight line basis.

(a) What happens if the asset is sold for £2000 after only four years?

(b) What happens if the asset lasts for eight years?

5.4 Jonas Limited (C): Changes in net cost

Jonas Limited buys a fixed asset for £8400, expects it to last for six years, and proposes to write off depreciation on the straight line basis.

(a) What difference would it make if Jonas Limited wanted to allow in its depreciation charges for expected salvage proceeds of £600 at the end of year 6?

(b) How would you take into account an improvement to the asset, costing £1200 at the start of year four, which was not expected to affect the asset's life?

Space for answer

		£
	Cost	8400
Year 1	Depreciation	
	Book value, end of year	_____
Year 2	Depreciation	
	Book value, end of year	_____
Year 3	Depreciation	
	Book value, end of year	_____
Year 4	Depreciation	
	Book value, end of year	_____
Year 5	Depreciation	
	Book value, end of year	_____
Year 6	Depreciation	
	Book value, end of year	_____

Space for answer

(a)

(b)

Space for answer

(a)

(b)

Answers to these three questions are shown overleaf.

5.2 Jonas Limited (A) *Solution*

		£
	Cost	8400
Year 1	Depreciation	1400
	Book value, end of year	7000
Year 2	Depreciation	1400
	Book value, end of year	5600
Year 3	Depreciation	1400
	Book value, end of year	4200
Year 4	Depreciation	1400
	Book value, end of year	2800
Year 5	Depreciation	1400
	Book value, end of year	1400
Year 6	Depreciation	1400
	Book value, end of year	—

5.3 Jonas Limited (B) *Solution*

(*a*) At the end of the fourth year, the £800 difference between the net book value (£2800) and the sale proceeds (£2000) will have to be written off as a loss on sale.

Thus over the 4-year life of the asset the total amount written off will be:

Depreciation: 4 × £1400 =	£5600
Loss on sale (year 4)	800
	£6400

Notice that this is equal to the original cost (£8400) less the sale proceeds (£2000).

(*b*) No depreciation will be charged in years 7 and 8, since the asset has already been completely written off by the end of year 6. Any sales proceeds at the end of year 8 will be treated as a profit on sale.

In the balance sheet at the end of years 6 and 7 the asset will appear as follows:

Fixed asset, at cost	£8400
Less: Accumulated depreciation	8400
Net book value	—

5.4 Jonas Limited (C) *Solution*

(*a*) The annual depreciation charge would be reduced by

$$\frac{£600}{6} = \text{by £100 to £1300.}$$

$$\left(\frac{£8400 - £600}{6} = \frac{£7800}{6}\right).$$

The net book value at the end of year 6—the asset's expected life—would then be £600—the asset's expected residual value.

(*b*) The cost of the improvement, £1200, would have to be written off over the remaining 3 years of the asset's life, that is an extra £400 a year in years 4, 5 and 6.

Since this is an "improvement" it would have to be "capitalised"—that is added to the cost of the fixed asset in the books—rather than written off as an expense in year 4.

Answers to the following problems are given at the end of the book.

5.5 Lawson Limited (A): Profit or loss on disposal

Lawson Limited paid £7200 for a fixed asset which is expected to last for six years. It is to be written off on the straight line basis, assuming ultimate salvage proceeds of £600.

Calculate the depreciation charged each year, and the profit or loss on disposal, if the asset is actually sold for:

(a)   £3500 at the end of year 4.

(b)   £1400 at the end of year 5.

(c)   How would the asset be shown in the balance sheet at the end of year 3?

5.6 Lawson Limited (B): Journal entries

Lawson Limited paid £7200 for a fixed asset which is expected to last for six years. It is to be written off on the straight line basis, assuming ultimate salvage proceeds of £600.

The asset is actually sold for £3500 at the end of year 4.

Prepare the necessary journal entries for each year in connection with the fixed asset.

5.7 Lawson Limited (C): Ledger accounts

Using your journal entries in Lawson Limited (B), prepare ledger accounts (including one for cash) recording the transactions.

Please close off accounts to profit and loss where appropriate.

5.8 James Hillier Limited (A): Declining balance

James Hillier Limited buys a fixed asset for £8000, and expects salvage proceeds of £750 at the end of its anticipated four-year life. The asset is to be written off by the declining balance method, using a 50 per cent rate.

Calculate the depreciation charge and the net book value each year. What profit or loss is expected on disposal?

5.9 James Hillier Limited (B): Treatment of disposals

James Hillier Limited buys a fixed asset for £8000, and expects salvage proceeds of £750 at the end of its anticipated four-year life. The asset is to be written off by the declining balance method, using a 50 per cent rate.

The asset actually lasts for six years, at the end of which time it is sold for £600.

(a) Starting with the net book value at the end of year 4, complete the depreciation schedule.

(b) Set out the journal entries relating to the fixed asset in year 6.

5.10 Gilbert Limited and Sullivan Limited: Differing depreciation policies

Gilbert Limited and Sullivan Limited are identical companies except for their depreciation policies.

In respect of a fixed asset costing £7200, Gilbert estimates a life of ten years, a salvage value of £1200, and proposes to use the straight line method of depreciation.

Sullivan estimates a life of six years, no salvage value, and proposes to use one third as the annual proportion of the declining net book value to be written off each year.

The asset becomes technically obsolete at the end of year 4, and has to be scrapped with salvage proceeds of only £200.

Calculate for each of the two companies the depreciation charge each year, the net book value at the end of each year and the profit or loss on disposal.

5.11 Hobson Limited: Statutory tax allowances

Hobson Limited acquires plant costing £20 000.

For tax purposes writing-down allowances are as follows:

60 per cent of cost in year 1
25 per cent of declining written down value in each subsequent year.

Set out the tax writing-down allowances and written down values for each of the plant's six years of useful life.

What happens if the asset is sold for £2000 at the beginning of year 7?

5.12 Adam Limited and Bede Limited (A): Deferred tax

Adam Limited and Bede Limited are identical companies, except that Adam ignores "deferred" tax, while Bede sets up a deferred tax reserve (tax equalisation) account. Each company makes an annual profit, before depreciation and tax, of £28 000.

At the beginning of year 1 each company buys a machine costing £40 000, to be written off on the straight line basis in the books, over five years. For tax purposes the rates of writing-down allowance (= "tax depreciation") are 60 per cent of cost in year 1, and 25 per cent of the declining balance in each subsequent year.

Show for each company for years 1 to 5:

(a) Tax writing-down allowances

(b) Actual liability to tax

Assume that the tax rate is 40 per cent throughout, that the machine lasts for five years and is then scrapped for zero proceeds, and that there is no other depreciation to take into account.

5.13 Adam Limited and Bede Limited (B)

Given the same facts as in the (A) problem, show for each company for years 1 to 5:

(a) Reported profit before tax, reported tax charge and reported profit after tax

(b) Deferred tax reserve account

Section 6
Capital structure and gearing

TYPES OF LONG-TERM CAPITAL

Having considered some of the problems of measuring profit and loss and of reporting figures for fixed and current assets, now let us look at how companies finance their activities.

In our approach to analysing accounts we have defined "capital employed" as those amounts which a company can use for more than twelve months. We have deducted *current* liabilities from the current assets, to give a net figure for "working capital."

In analysing "capital employed," the major distinction is between "equity" (ordinary share capital and reserves) and "debt" (long-term loans and medium-term liabilities). Preference share capital (which is usually relatively unimportant) falls between the two. The proportions of equity and debt capital vary from company to company and for a particular company over time. The "cost of capital" will vary according to the particular mix chosen: one of the most important aspects of financial management is to secure the best possible mix.

Major differences between equity and debt capital relate to risk and profit. From the holders' point of view, ordinary shares are riskier than debt capital, but their potential profit—both in terms of dividends and increased market value—may be much higher. From a company's point of view the reverse is true: debt capital is cheaper than equity, but riskier because of the fixed nature of the commitments.

In this section we shall look more closely at the items which constitute "capital employed":

1 Ordinary share capital and reserves ("equity")
2 Preference share capital
3 Long-term loans ("debt")
4 Medium-term liabilities

ORDINARY SHARE CAPITAL AND RESERVES ("EQUITY")

Ordinary shares are shares in the ownership of a company, and give ultimate rights of control over its affairs. Issued ordinary share capital and reserves together constitute a company's "equity capital," which is the same thing as ordinary shareholders' funds.

Let us look first at ordinary share capital, and then at reserves.

Ordinary share capital

The breakdown of the ordinary shareholders' funds in Finance and General Limited is set out opposite.

The number of shares which a company is authorised to issue is indicated in its constitution (memorandum of association) which also specifies the nominal amount of each share, for example, ordinary shares of £1 each or A ordinary shares of 10p each.

Once issued, ordinary shares represent permanent capital, not normally redeemed during a company's existence. If an individual shareholder wants to recover his capital investment while the company continues in business, he must sell his shares to someone else. The price the seller can get for his shares (the market value) varies continually as market conditions vary. Quoted companies' ordinary shares are owned by the public and traded on a stock exchange (not necessarily London). Unquoted companies' shares are privately owned: they are often held closely by members of one or two families, and can be bought or sold much less freely than quoted shares.

Ordinary shareholders may get no dividend income on their shares, but given favourable trading conditions the level of dividends which can be paid may be very high indeed. Dividends are payable only out of profits, and there is no guarantee that a company will make a profit. Even if it does, there is no legal commitment to declare any ordinary dividends. The company's directors may choose to retain all the profits within the company ("plough back" the profits). Clearly the dividend policy adopted may affect the share price.

In a winding-up—that is, when the legal existence of the company is brought to an end—ordinary shareholders will get, not the nominal ("par") amount of their shares, but whatever is left over after short-term and long-term creditors and preference shareholders have been repaid in full. The residual amount left per ordinary share has no upper limit. In a successful company it would normally be much more than the nominal amount, but it may be less, and in the case of an unsuccessful company it could even be nothing. While the ordinary shareholder's potential profit is unlimited, his maximum liability is always limited to the nominal amount per share (hence the name "limited company"). This contrasts with the position of a partner in a partnership, where personal liability for the debts of the partnership is *unlimited*.

FINANCE AND GENERAL LIMITED
Ordinary shareholders' funds

	£'000
Share capital	
Authorised: £5 million	
Issued 4 000 000 ordinary £1 shares	4 000
Reserves	
Share premium account	2 000
Revaluation of fixed assets	1 000
Profit and loss account	3 000
	6 000
Ordinary share capital and reserves	£10 000

Capital reserves

Capital reserves are generally not available for distribution as dividends, while revenue reserves can be used to pay dividends in any period in which earnings are not sufficient to cover the desired level of dividend payment. The 1967 Companies Act ended the statutory requirement to refer explicitly to "capital" and "revenue" reserves, though various categories of reserve have to be distinguished.

Capital reserves typically arise either on issuing ordinary shares at a premium (which we shall examine more closely later) or on revaluing or selling fixed assets.

Surplus on revaluation of fixed assets

When fixed assets are revalued, any surplus over book value is incorporated in the accounts by showing the fixed assets at the new higher figure and including the surplus as a capital reserve. (If a revaluation shows the assets to be worth *less* than the amount at which they are shown in the accounts, the asset figure is reduced by the amount of the shortfall, and an equal amount *deducted* from reserves.)

A revaluation giving rise to a surplus is illustrated opposite. The directors of Land Holdings Limited had the company's leasehold property revalued as at 31 December 1970. The accounts show the position before and after the revaluation, which indicated that the current value of the leasehold property was £150 000.

Clearly the changes in equity and net assets will significantly affect return on investment calculations. Where depreciable fixed assets are revalued future depreciation charges in the profit and loss account will also be affected.

A capital reserve can arise when a fixed asset is sold for more than its cost. If Land Holdings Limited sold its property at the current value of £150 000, the capital reserve entries would be similar to those on a revaluation. The £50 000 profit on sale would be credited (after deducting any tax due) to a capital reserve.

LAND HOLDINGS LIMITED
Balance sheet, 31 December 1970

Before revaluation	£
Ordinary share capital	60 000
Revenue reserve	20 000
Equity	80 000
Loans	40 000
Capital employed	£120 000
Leasehold land and building at cost	100 000
Net current assets	20 000
Net assets	£120 000

After revaluation	£
Ordinary share capital	60 000
Capital reserve	50 000
Revenue reserve	20 000
Equity	130 000
Loans	40 000
Capital employed	£170 000
Leasehold land and building at valuation, 31-12-70	150 000
Net current assets	20 000
Net assets	£170 000

Revenue reserves

These are amounts available for the payment of ordinary dividends but retained in the business as a matter of policy. You will recall that "dividend cover" is the measure of how much earnings exceed dividends in any period. A typical dividend cover is about one and a half times. Dividends are declared either as money amounts per share or (more usually) as a percentage of the nominal amount. This latter practice can lead to misunderstandings, since the basis used in calculating the dividend percentage (the nominal issued ordinary share capital) is only part of the total ordinary shareholders' funds.

Star Trading Limited earns 20 per cent after tax on its owners' equity each year, and the board's dividend policy is to pay out 50 per cent of earnings. The accounts set out opposite, at the top, reflect an early stage in the company's development, while those at the bottom reflect the current position. The revenue reserve has been built up out of retained profits.

The dividend percentage has increased from 12½ to 50 per cent on nominal capital, but the company has earned a constant 20 per cent on owners' equity throughout.

The use of the limited nominal capital base for the calculation accounts for the rise in the percentage figure, and might mislead those who do not understand how the figures are calculated to suppose that the company is making "excessive" profits which it is passing on to its shareholders.

To avoid this possibility, and to show a more realistic share capital total, many companies choose to "capitalise" their reserves from time to time by converting them into ordinary shares which are then issued as "bonus shares" to shareholders. This we can now consider in looking at the various ways in which the ordinary share capital can be increased.

STAR TRADING LIMITED

Early accounts	£
Ordinary share capital	200 000
Revenue reserves	50 000
Equity	£250 000
Earnings = 20% × £250 000 =	£50 000
Dividends = Half annual earnings =	£25 000
= 12½% × nominal share capital	

Current accounts	£
Ordinary share capital	200 000
Revenue reserves	800 000
Equity	£1 000 000
Earnings = 20% × £1 000 000 =	£200 000
Dividends = Half annual earnings =	£100 000
= 50% × nominal share capital	

EQUITY ISSUES

The ordinary share capital of a company can be increased in a number of ways:

1 Issues for cash (or other assets) 2 Bonus issues 3 Rights issues

Issues for cash (or other assets)

You will recollect (from section 3) that when Initial Enterprises started business with a capital of £50 000 the balance sheet immediately after the issue showed ordinary shares of £50 000 on one side and cash of an equivalent amount on the other. Had the company been formed to take over the assets of an existing business which were worth £50 000, individual asset accounts would have appeared in place of cash.

But what happens when an established business requires new equity capital?

The accounts of Astral Creations Limited (AC Limited) are set out below. AC Limited is a quoted company whose £1 shares are currently standing in the market at 300p. The directors decide to issue a further 50 000 shares at 300p (£3) each. The balance sheet showing the position after the issue is set out below. There are no long-term liabilities.

The proceeds of the issue—£150 000—represent:

£50 000 for 50 000 shares with a nominal value of £1 each
£100 000 premium on the issue of £1 shares at £3 each
(that is, 50 000 shares × £2 per share premium).

AC LIMITED
Balance sheet, 30 June 1971

Before new share issue	£
Ordinary share capital	100 000
Revenue reserve	150 000
Equity	£250 000
Net assets	£250 000

After new share issue	£
Ordinary share capital	150 000
Share premium	100 000
Revenue reserve	150 000
Equity	£400 000
Net assets	£400 000

Bonus issues

A "bonus" issue (or "scrip" issue) involves capitalising reserves to issue existing shareholders "bonus" shares for which no cash price has to be paid. Let us re-examine Star Trading Limited's balance sheet. The company is currently paying dividends of £100 000 (50 per cent) from earnings of £200 000. Assuming that the market would be satisfied with a 5 per cent dividend yield, the £1 shares will be standing in the market at £10 each. This price would be "heavy" for the London market, with some consequential narrowing of the group of investors who would be attracted to buying the shares. (A "normal" price per share in London would not exceed £5, whereas on Wall Street the normal price is much higher—between $20 and $100.)

To reduce the share price and the size of the dividend percentage without in any way impairing the company's financial status, the board of the Star Trading company could issue bonus shares by converting some of the reserves into paid-up ordinary issued share capital. It could, for example, issue two bonus shares to each ordinary shareholder for each share already held. The balance sheet would then appear as set out below.

STAR TRADING LIMITED

Before bonus issue	£
Ordinary share capital 200 000 shares of £1	200 000
Revenue reserves	800 000
Equity	£1 000 000
Dividend £100 000 = 50% × £200 000	

After bonus issue	£
Ordinary share capital 600 000 shares of £1	600 000
Revenue reserves	400 000
Equity	£1 000 000
Dividend £100 000 = 16.7% × £600 000	

After this 2 for 1 bonus issue:

The share price would fall from £10 to 333p.
The dividend percentage* would fall from 50 to 16.7 per cent.

(*Calculated on *nominal* capital.)

Notice that *total* equity is unchanged after a bonus issue, but a larger proportion is "nominal" issued ordinary share capital after the "capitalisation" of reserves.

Share splits

Share splits are intended to reduce the market price per share, like bonus issues, but they do *not* involve capitalising reserves. If Star Trading Limited felt that the share price was still too high, at 333p after the 2 for 1 bonus issue, there might be a share split dividing each 100p (£1) share into four 25p shares. The nominal capital would remain unchanged at £600 000 but the number of shares in issue would increase. (Since 600 000 shares at 100p each = £600 000 = 2 400 000 shares at 25p.) The share price would be expected to fall from 333p to 83p, but the nominal rate of dividend (16.7 per cent) would remain unchanged.

STAR TRADING LIMITED

After share split	£
Ordinary share capital 2 400 000 shares of 25p	600 000
Revenue reserves	400 000
Equity	£1 000 000
Dividend £100 000 = 16.7% × £600 000	

Notice that a "2 for 1" bonus issue means "two new shares *in addition to* every one old share," whereas a "4 for 1" share split means "four new shares *instead of* every one old share."

In comparative statistics covering a number of years, adjustments are made to earnings per share and dividends per share to convert figures prior to a bonus issue or share split on to the same basis as the later figures.

Rights issues

As we have seen, share splits do not affect nominal capital in total, and bonus issues raise no additional cash from shareholders but merely convert reserves into issued capital. Rights issues, on the other hand, *do* raise more cash for a company.

Let us imagine that Star Trading Limited, having issued bonus shares and split its £1 shares into 25p units, now wishes to raise more capital. It could go to the open market, where its 25p shares are now standing at 83p, and seek new funds. An alternative approach is to make a "rights issue" to existing shareholders.

If the company wished to raise £200 000, it could offer 400 000 new 25p ordinary shares to existing shareholders for 50p cash per share, on the basis of a 1 for 6 rights issue. A holder of 600 25p shares would then have the right to subscribe for 100 new 25p shares at 50p each, involving a cash payment of £50. If he did not wish to invest more cash, he could sell his rights in the market. The buyer of the rights would then subscribe the necessary 50p per share and obtain the new shares. Assuming that the share price was static throughout the issue, the shareholder would receive 33p (83p − 50p) per six shares held for his rights. If the shareholder failed either to sell his rights or to take them up himself, the company would normally sell the rights in the market on his behalf.

Because shareholders can always sell their rights, in theory it makes no difference to them at what price a rights issue is made: the result can always be regarded as a new issue at the current market price combined with a bonus issue whose terms depend on the terms of the rights issue.

The balance sheet of Star Trading Limited before and after the 1 for 6 rights issue is set out below. Notice the treatment of the premium on the issue of the new 25p shares at 50p each.

STAR TRADING LIMITED

Before rights issue	£
Ordinary share capital	
2 400 000 ordinary shares of 25p each	600 000
Revenue reserve	400 000
Capital employed	£1 000 000

After rights issue	£
Ordinary share capital	
2 800 000 ordinary shares of 25p each	700 000
Share premium	100 000
Revenue reserve	400 000
Capital employed	£1 200 000

Having considered that part of the capital of a company represented by ordinary shares and reserves ("equity"), we must now look at the remaining types of permanent and long-term capital: preference share capital and long-term loans ("debt").

PREFERENCE SHARE CAPITAL

As we noted at the beginning of this section, in character preference shares fall between ordinary shares and debt. They form part of the share capital of a company, but have limited rights to participate in profits. Generally they are entitled only to a fixed percentage dividend, but unlike lenders, who can take legal action to enforce payment of interest, preference shareholders receive dividends only if these are declared by the directors. However, their dividend rights are normally "cumulative," so that if a dividend is "passed"—that is, not paid—in any particular period, preference shareholders have a first call on subsequent profits. This means that no dividends can be paid to ordinary shareholders until all dividends due to preference shareholders have been paid, both those currently due and any arrears. As a result, in normal circumstances preference dividends are paid with the same regularity as loan interest.

On a liquidation, preference shareholders again have preferential rights over ordinary shareholders, in the same way that creditors have over both preference and ordinary shareholders. They will receive any arrears of dividends and the nominal value of their shares before any amounts are paid to the ordinary shareholders. However, again their rights of participation are limited. No matter how large the surplus on realisation of all the assets, the preference shareholders will normally receive back only the nominal value of their shares.

Preference shares may seem to provide companies with a very attractive means of financing, since they combine the limited capital obligation of debt with the dividend flexibility of ordinary shares. However, as we have seen, in normal circumstances the payment of preference dividends in any particular period is not really a matter of discretion if any ordinary dividends are to be paid.

In addition, preference dividends are regarded for tax purposes as distributions of after-tax profits (like ordinary dividends) while debt interest is regarded as an *expense* to be deducted before calculating taxable profits. This tends to make financing by preference shares expensive, especially when tax rates are high. For Finance and General Limited (whose accounts are shown opposite) the before-tax cost of £2.5 million 10 per cent debentures is £250 000 a year, while the annual cost of £2.5 million 10 per cent preference shares is £250 000 *after* tax, which is equivalent to £417 000 *before* tax assuming a tax rate of 40 per cent (£250 000 × 100/60).

Because preference capital is so expensive many companies are paying it back and substituting debt capital in its place.

The "in between" nature of preference capital can give rise to problems in financial analysis. Should preference shares be treated as equity or as debt capital? Later in this section we shall be dealing with the concept of "gearing," and considering the consequences of different mixes of debt and equity in the capital structure. Preference shares are often treated as equivalent to debt, but circumstances could arise—for example where a severe cash squeeze exists—in which the unique characteristics of preference shares would need to be taken into account separately.

FINANCE AND GENERAL LIMITED

Balance sheet, 31 December 1970

	£'000
Ordinary shares	4 000
Share premium	2 000
Reserves	4 000
Equity	10 000
10% Preference shares	2 500
10% Debentures 1985	2 500
Capital employed	£15 000
Net assets	£15 000

Profit and loss account, 1970

		£'000
Operating profit		4 000
Interest on 10% Debentures		250
Profit before tax		3 750
Tax at (say) 40%		1 500
Profit after tax		2 250
Dividends:		
10% Preference	250	
Ordinary, 30%	1 200	
		1 450
Retained profit		£800

LONG-TERM LOANS ("DEBT")

A company issuing debt capital—that is, borrowing—must repay the sum borrowed at the promised time, and pay interest on the debt outstanding in the meantime. Failure to do either entitles the lender to take legal action to recover the amount due, and in the event of a company going into liquidation all debts must be paid in full before any amounts can be paid to preference or ordinary shareholders.

Companies may raise long-term debt from merchant banks, the Industrial and Commercial Finance Corporation Limited (ICFC), insurance companies or other institutions, and (for large companies only) from the stock exchange. For smaller companies, individual shareholders may sometimes be prepared to advance long-term debt capital on suitable terms. In certain cases government loans may be available for companies unable to borrow commercially.

In its simplest form a loan is merely a contractual relationship between the lender and the borrower with terms covering the payment of interest and repayment of capital. Such a loan would be "unsecured," the lender being treated, in the event of liquidation, on the same basis as a trade creditor. Often lenders will seek greater protection, and their rights will be "secured" by a charge or mortgage on all or some of the assets of the company. In the event of a liquidation, this will entitle the lender to recover his debt in full before trade and other "unsecured" creditors receive any proceeds from the charged assets.

The terms of a long-term loan can vary considerably, but will usually be for a period of between ten and twenty years. The rate of interest will depend on prevailing conditions in the money market and on the financial status of the borrower. The greater the risk the lender perceives, the higher the interest rate he will require for a loan.

Converting convertible debt

A special category of debt capital exists which can be converted on prearranged terms into ordinary shares at the holder's option. When convertible debt has been converted it is indistinguishable from ordinary equity capital. Its special interest, for both the company and the holder, lies in the period prior to conversion. As long as it retains its character as debt it combines the safety of debt with the profit potential, represented by conversion rights, of equity.

In practice, companies issuing convertible debt *want* it to be converted: they intend in effect to borrow for a year or two against the proceeds of a later equity issue. If not converted during the option period, convertible debt becomes simply debt capital when the conversion rights lapse.

Where conversion of convertible debt would add a significant number of ordinary shares to those already issued, earnings per share may fall significantly in future years simply as a result of conversion. This effect is known as "equity dilution." It has become general practice to calculate "per share" earnings figures on *two* bases:

1 Actual ordinary shares now in issue.
2 Potential total ordinary shares in issue if all existing conversion rights are exercised.

A similar situation may arise where companies give employees rights ("options") to acquire shares in future at less than the then market price, though the amount of dilution involved is usually small. The effect of converting convertible debt is illustrated below.

HIGHWAYS LIMITED
Balance sheet, 31 March 1972

	Now	After conversion
Share capital and reserves	£	£
60 000 £1 ordinary shares	60 000	80 000†
Share premium	—	30 000
Revenue reserves	30 000	30 000
Equity	90 000	140 000
Long term liabilities		
8% Convertible loan stock*	50 000	—
Capital employed	£140 000	£140 000

Profit and loss account	£	£
EBIT	25 000	25 000
Interest payable	4 000	—
Profit before tax	21 000	25 000
Tax (say 40%)	8 400	10 000
Profit after tax	£12 600	£15 000
Shares in issue	60 000	80 000†
Earnings per share	21p	18.75p

*Convertible at £2.50 per share until 31 December 1974.

$$†\frac{£50\ 000}{£2.50} = 20\ 000 \text{ new ordinary shares of £1.}$$

MEDIUM-TERM LIABILITIES (MORE THAN TWELVE MONTHS)

The main amounts under this heading in accounts generally relate to items such as: provisions for pensions or other deferred payments, future tax liabilities, or medium-term loans.

Provisions are amounts set aside to provide for known liabilities the amount of which cannot be determined with substantial accuracy. A typical example is the provision made in some companies' accounts for unfunded future pension payments. Such amounts may be available for use by a company for fairly long periods, and are included in the "capital employed" figure.

The provision for future tax stems from the delay (which can vary from nine months to over two years) between profits being earned and the related corporation tax liability becoming payable. Where the tax liability (which can be relatively large) is not payable until more than twelve months after the balance sheet date, it may be treated as a medium-term, not a current liability.

Medium-term loans may appear separately in accounts, but sometimes items which are really medium-term loans may be included with current liabilities. For example although in theory bank overdrafts are repayable on demand, it is not unusual for companies to go through financing cycles in which overdrafts play a bridging role between the dates at which the company raises permanent capital (either equity or long-term debt). The result may be that over a period of perhaps three or four years the overdraft will increase each year before it is eliminated as the company raises fresh equity or long-term debt capital and repays the amount due to the bank. The cycle can then start again. Clearly during the interim period the company is enjoying the use of medium-term capital provided in the form of an overdraft. If possible, such a medium-term element in a bank overdraft should be identified and treated as capital employed rather than as a current liability.

A similar position (which may be even more difficult for an outside analyst to identify) can arise in the dealings between subsidiaries and their holding company where amounts which are shown as current assets and liabilities may include elements of semi-permanent internal group lending. The problem applies to the separate accounts of the holding company and its subsidiaries, not to the *consolidated* group accounts in which the inter-company balances will cancel out (see section 7).

The balance sheet set out opposite (at top) represents the unadjusted accounts of Union Holdings Limited. The company made a profit before tax and long-term interest of £15 000, which indicates a return on net assets of 25 per cent. Included in the current liabilities are a bank overdraft of £25 000 (the opening overdraft was also £25 000), and an amount due to a subsidiary of £30 000 (half of which had been outstanding for more than 12 months).

Clearly the holding company has been partly financed by the bank—the average loan being some £25 000 (at an interest rate of 12 per cent)—and by its subsidiary (interest-free) to the extent of at least £15 000. The adjusted balance sheet is set out below (at bottom). Revised profits before interest and tax of £18 000 (£15 000 + £3000) related to the revised capital employed (=net assets) figure of £100 000, give an adjusted return (before tax) of 18 per cent.

UNION HOLDINGS LIMITED
Balance sheet

Before adjustment

		£'000
Shareholders' funds		50
Loans at 10%		10
Capital employed		£60
Fixed assets, net		40
Current assets	80	
Less: Current liabilities	60	
		20
Net assets		£60

After adjustment

		£'000
Shareholders' funds		50
Loans at 10%		10
Other loans:		
Bank	25	
Subsidiary	15	
		40
Capital employed		£100
Fixed assets, net		40
Current assets	80	
Less: Current liabilities	20	
		60
Net assets		£100

Finally in this section let us consider two aspects of company borrowing:

1 Measuring debt burden
2 Gearing

MEASURING DEBT BURDEN

Two ratios are commonly used to measure the amount of debt in the capital structure of a company:

1 Debt ratio (related to capital)
2 Interest cover (related to income)

These are the two solvency ratios discussed earlier in section 2.

Debt ratio

The balance sheet of United Engines Limited is shown below. The total debt capital (treating preference shares as debt) is £50 000, and the debt ratio can be expressed in two ways:

$$1 \quad \frac{\text{Debt}}{\text{Capital employed}} = \frac{£\,50\,000}{£200\,000} = 25\%$$

$$2 \quad \frac{\text{Debt}}{\text{Equity}} = \frac{£\,50\,000}{£150\,000} = 33\tfrac{1}{3}\%$$

Unfortunately both these ratios are called the "debt ratio" (the former being more common), so that care is needed to avoid confusion.

UNITED ENGINES LIMITED
Balance sheet, 30 June 1970

	£'000
Ordinary share capital	60
Reserves	90
Ordinary shareholders' funds	150
5% Preference share capital	20
10% Loan	30
Capital employed	£200
Fixed assets, net	130
Net current assets	70
Net assets	£200

Interest cover

United Engines Limited's outflows to cover fixed commitments are:

Loan interest	10% × £30 000 = £3000
Preference dividends	5% × £20 000 = £1000

As we have already seen, however, this comparison is misleading. The loan interest is paid from profits before tax, while the preference dividend is paid from profits *after* tax, as the profit and loss account below makes clear.

UNITED ENGINES LIMITED
Profit and loss account, Year ended 30 June 1970

		£
Operating profit		23 000
Less: Loan interest		3 000
Profit before tax		20 000
Tax at 40% (say)		8 000
Profit after tax		12 000
Less: Dividends		
Preference 5%	1000	
Ordinary 12$\tfrac{1}{2}$%	7500	
		8 500
Retained profits		£3 500

To obtain a comparative statement the preference dividend has to be converted into terms of the cost before tax, when the figures become:

	Pre-tax cost	*Capital*	*Percentage*
Loan interest	£3000	£30 000	10.0
Preference dividends	£1667*	£20 000	8.3
	£4667		

$$*£1667 = £1000 \times \frac{100}{60}$$

Using the above figures, the interest cover can be calculated:

$$1 \quad \text{Interest cover} = \frac{£23\,000}{£3\,000} = 7.67 \text{ times}$$

$$2 \quad \text{Cover for interest and preference dividend} = \frac{£23\,000}{£4\,667} = 4.93 \text{ times}$$

GEARING

The total capital employed by a company can be split between debt (including preference shares in this category) and equity. The proportion of each type of capital is a matter for decision by a particular company's board of directors.

The larger the proportion of debt in a company's capital structure, the more highly "geared" the company. The higher the gearing, the greater the risk for the owners of equity, but the greater their prospect of profit if all goes well.

In the example shown below, the highly geared company Beta (debt ratio 50 per cent) has a significantly higher return on equity in year 1 than Alpha (debt ratio 10 per cent). In year 2, however, when earnings before interest and tax (EBITs) are low, there is very little left for Beta's ordinary shareholders, after payment of loan interest, while Alpha's—with lower gearing—still get a 3.3 per cent return.

The diagram below illustrates how gearing works. When the return on capital employed exceeds 10 per cent (the rate of interest payable on debt in this case), Beta's return on equity is higher than Alpha's; but the reverse is true when the return on capital employed is less than 10 per cent.

The effect of gearing is to make return on equity change more sharply than return on capital employed; and, of course, this works in both directions, that is, when profits are falling as well as when they are increasing.

As the debt ratio increases, at least beyond a certain level, new capital becomes more expensive as the risk grows, both for lenders of debt capital and for subscribers of equity capital. In estimating whether a debt ratio is "too high," the nature of the business is of fundamental importance. The more stable the nature of a particular industry, the higher the debt ratio can safely be.

In addition to this kind of "financial" gearing, most companions have some degree of "operational" gearing. If most expenses vary directly with sales, operational gearing is low, while a relatively large amount of fixed expenses implies high operational gearing. In assessing the overall riskiness of the ordinary shareholders' position one needs to take both sorts of gearing into account, that is both "financial risk" and "business risk".

	Low gearing Alpha Limited £	High gearing Beta Limited £
Equity	90 000	50 000
Debt at 10%	10 000	50 000
Capital employed	£100 000	£100 000
Debt ratio:	10%	50%
Year 1, Return on capital employed: 20.0%	£	£
EBIT	20 000	20 000
Loan interest	1 000	5 000
Profit before tax	19 000	15 000
Tax at 40% (say)	7 600	6 000
Profit after tax	£11 400	£9 000
Return on equity:	12.7%	18.0%
Interest cover:	20.0	4.0
Year 2, Return on capital employed: 6.0%	£	£
EBIT	6000	6000
Loan interest	1000	5000
Profit before tax	5000	1000
Tax at 40% (say)	2000	400
Profit after tax	£3000	£600
Return on equity:	3.3%	1.2%
Interest cover:	6.0	1.2

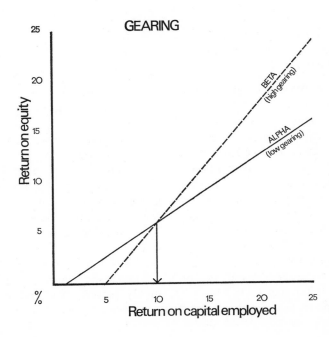

GEARING

SUMMARY

The major categories of "capital employed" are:

> Ordinary share capital and reserves ("equity")
> Preference share capital
> Long-term loans ("debt")
> Medium-term liabilities

In analysing capital employed, the major distinction is between equity and debt. From a company's point of view debt is cheaper than equity, but riskier. Major differences are shown in the table opposite.

Capital reserves (which are not available for distribution as dividends) typically arise either on issuing ordinary shares at a premium or on revaluing fixed assets.

Revenue reserves (which *are* available for distribution as dividends) typically arise through "retained profits" (that is, the excess of profits after tax over ordinary dividends paid). But some companies still transfer directly to revenue reserves non-recurring items or material adjustments to previous years' figures, though it is now more common to treat such items as "below-the-line" items in the profit and loss account.

The ordinary share capital of a company can be increased in a number of ways:

1 (*a*) Issues for cash
  (*b*) Issues for other assets
2   Bonus issues ("scrip" issues)
3   Right issues

Bonus issues involve capitalising reserves, which merely transfers amounts out of reserves and into issued share capital, *without* causing any increase in total equity. Rights issues *do* increase total equity.

Preference share capital carries rights to a fixed dividend payable before any ordinary dividend, and to a fixed money amount on redemption or liquidation. Its characteristics are on the whole closer to those of debt capital than to equity, though in exceptional circumstances the absence of a binding legal commitment to pay a preference dividend can be valuable to a company in trouble. Preference dividends are paid out of after-tax profits, unlike debt interest which can be charged before tax. Thus preference capital tends to be expensive compared with debt.

The two main ways of measuring a company's debt burden are the debt ratio (capital) and the interest cover (income). The larger the proportion of debt in a company's capital structure, the more "highly geared" it is said to be. The higher the gearing, the greater the risk for ordinary shareholders, but the greater their prospect of profit if all goes well.

Differences between Equity and Debt

	Equity	Debt
Capital		
Amount	Residual	Fixed
Period	Permanent	Limited
Income		
Amount	Variable	Fixed
Period	Variable	Regular
Commitment	Discretionary	Legal liability
Cost	After-tax	Before-tax

6.1 Definitions

Write down opposite your definition of the terms shown. Then compare your answers with the definitions overleaf.

(a) Capital employed

(b) Equity

(c) Capital reserves

(d) Ordinary shareholders' funds

(e) A dividend of 15 per cent

(f) Share premium

(g) A bonus issue

(h) Preference share capital

(i) A highly geared company

(j) A rights issue

6.1 Definitions

(a) *Capital employed* is long-term capital. It consists of equity capital (ordinary share capital and reserves) plus long-term debt, and also includes items of semi-permanent capital such as deferred tax. Looked at from the asset side, capital employed equals total assets minus current liabilities.

(b) *Equity* is the ordinary (issued) share capital plus reserves.

(c) *Capital reserves* are permanent reserves not available for distribution as ordinary dividends to shareholders. They typically arise either from share premiums or from revaluations of fixed assets.

(d) *Ordinary shareholders' funds* is a synonym for "equity."

(e) *A dividend of 15 per cent* is a dividend expressed as a percentage (15%) of *nominal* issued ordinary share capital (*not* as a percentage of ordinary shareholders' funds).

(f) *Share premium* is the excess of the actual proceeds of an issue of shares over their nominal ("par") value. It is treated in accounts as a capital reserve, not available for distribution as dividends.

(g) *A bonus issue* is the issue of ordinary shares to existing shareholders at no cost, that is, the company does not receive any consideration. It results from the capitalisation of reserves, that is, the process of converting reserves into issued ordinary share capital.

(h) *Preference share capital* is permanent capital carrying preferential rights over ordinary share capital, both as to dividends and as to capital repayment in a winding-up. It resembles debt capital in entitling holders only to a *fixed* amount of dividends and to a *fixed* money amount in a winding-up, but it differs from debt in that payments of dividends on preference capital, unlike debt interest, are not legally obligatory. Preference dividends are usually "cumulative," which means that if they are passed in a particular period, they have to be made up later before any ordinary dividend may be paid.

(i) *A highly geared company* is one with a high proportion of debt capital compared to total capital employed (debt capital plus equity capital). This is *financial* gearing. Operating ("business") gearing means a high proportion of fixed expenses (that is, not varying with sales) compared to total expenses.

(j) *A rights issue* is an issue of ordinary shares to existing shareholders at a price somewhat less than the current market price. "Rights" to take up such shares are available to shareholders in proportion to the number of shares they already hold, and can be sold by any shareholder who does not want to invest more capital by taking up the rights.

6.2 Highsight Properties Limited (A): Revaluation

The balance sheet of Highsight Properties Limited at 31 July 1971 is shown opposite. It does not include a professional valuation of land and buildings at £500 000 as at 31 July 1971.

Please incorporate the revaluation in the accounts by amending the balance sheet where necessary.

The answer is shown on the next page.

HIGHSIGHT PROPERTIES LIMITED
Balance sheet, 31 July 1971

	£'000		£'000
Share capital and reserves		**Fixed assets**	
200 000 ordinary shares	200	Land and buildings, at cost less accumulated depreciation	340
Profit and loss account	25		
	225	**Net current assets**	35
Long-term loans	150		
	£375		£375

6.2 Highsight Properties Limited (A)

Solution

Notes

1 Did you remember to change the description "at cost less accumulated depreciation" in the balance sheet to "at valuation"? (The *date* of the valuation should be given in a note to the accounts.)

2 Notice that the debt ratio, which was 40 per cent, has fallen to 28 per cent as a result of the revaluation.

HIGHSIGHT PROPERTIES LIMITED
Balance sheet, 31 July 1971

	£'000		£'000
Share capital and reserves		**Fixed assets**	
200 000 ordinary shares	200	Land and buildings, at	
Capital reserve	160	valuation	500
Profit and loss account	25		
	385	**Net current assets**	35
Long-term loans	150		
	£535		£535

6.3 Highsight Properties Limited (B): Bonus issue

Following the revaluation of land and buildings at 31 July 1971, Highsight Properties Limited balance sheet is as shown opposite.

The capital reserve arising on the revaluation is largely to be recognised as permanent capital by making a bonus issue of 3 for 4 as at 31 July 1971.

Please amend the balance sheet opposite to show how it will look after the bonus issue.

The answer is shown on the next page.

HIGHSIGHT PROPERTIES LIMITED
Balance sheet, 31 July 1971

	£'000		£'000
Share capital and reserves		**Fixed assets**	
200 000 ordinary shares	200	Land and buildings, at	
Capital reserve	160	valuation	500
Profit and loss account	25		
	385	**Net current assets**	35
Long-term loans	150		
	£535		£535

6.3 Highsight Properties Limited (B)

Solution

Notes

1 The 3 for 4 bonus issue involves the issue of 150 000 £1 shares in respect of the 200 000 ordinary shares already in issue.

2 Did you remember to change the *number* of shares issued, as well as the money amount?

3 Notice that the bonus issue does not affect the £385 000 total of ordinary shareholders' funds.

HIGHSIGHT PROPERTIES LIMITED
Balance sheet, 31 July 1971

	£'000		£'000
Share capital and reserves		**Fixed assets**	
350 000 ordinary shares	350	Land and buildings, at	
Capital reserve	10	valuation	500
Profit and loss account	25		
	385	**Net current assets**	35
Long-term loans	150		
	£535		£535

6.4 Edwards Limited, Thomas Limited and Charles Limited: Ordinary share issues

Edwards Limited, Thomas Limited and Charles Limited each have an issued ordinary share capital of £120 000 in £1 shares, an accumulated balance of £70 000 on profit and loss account, and no other reserves. The authorised ordinary share capital in each case is £200 000.

The companies make the following issues relating to ordinary share capital:

Edwards Limited issues 20 000 new shares at £1.50 each.

Thomas Limited makes a 1 for 3 bonus issue.

Charles Limited makes a 1 for 4 rights issue at £2.

Answers for Edwards Limited are already entered opposite. Please show for Thomas Limited and Charles Limited:

(a) The appropriate journal entries in each case.

(b) The amounts of share capital and reserves after the various issues.

Answers are shown overleaf.

Space for answers

	Dr	Cr
(a) Journal entries	£'000	£'000
Edwards Limited		
Cash	30	
Ordinary share capital		20
Share premium		10
Thomas Limited		
Charles Limited		

(b) Shareholders' funds

	Edwards £'000	Thomas £'000	Charles £'000
Share capital			
£1 ordinary shares	140		
Reserves			
Share premium account	10		
Profit and loss account	70	____	____
Shareholders' funds	£220		

Notes

1 Modern practice is to show only a single figure for reserves on the face of the balance sheet; and many companies now show only a single total for shareholders' funds. In such cases the supporting details are shown in the notes to the accounts.

2 It may be helpful in analysing this kind of problem to start by concentrating on the *total* shareholders' funds. How much has *total* capital been increased by a particular issue? When that question has been resolved, the changes in the ordinary share capital and share premium account can then be considered.

6.4 Edwards Limited, Thomas Limited and Charles Limited
Solution

	Dr £'000	Cr £'000
(a) Journal entries		
Edwards Limited		
Cash	30	
Ordinary share capital		20
Share premium		10
Thomas Limited		
Profit and loss account	40	
Ordinary share capital		40
Charles Limited		
Cash	60	
Ordinary share capital		30
Share premium		30

(b) Shareholders' funds	*Edwards* £'000	*Thomas* £'000	*Charles* £'000
Share capital			
£1 ordinary shares	140	160	150
Reserves			
Share premium account	10	—	30
Profit and loss account	70	30	70
Shareholders' funds	£220	£190	£250

Answers to the following problems are shown at the end of the book.

6.5 Kent Traders Limited: Rights issue

The balance sheet of Kent Traders Limited at 30 April 1970 is shown opposite.

You are asked to amend the balance sheet to give effect to a 1 for 4 rights issue on that date at 200p a share.

KENT TRADERS LIMITED
Balance sheet, 30 April 1970

	£		£
100 000 ordinary 50p shares	50 000	Fixed assets, at cost	93 000
		Less: Accumulated depreciation	18 000
Profit and loss account	26 000		75 000
	76 000	Current assets	
		Cash	7 000
Long-term loans	27 000	Stock	26 000
		Debtors	19 000
			52 000
		Less:	
		Current tax	11 000
		Creditors	13 000
			24 000
			28 000
	£103 000		£103 000

6.6 Antrobus Lathes Limited: Convertible debt

The 10 per cent convertible loan stock of Antrobus Lathes Limited was all converted in 1971 into ordinary £1 share capital on the basis of 40 ordinary £1 shares for every £100 of 10 per cent loan stock.

You are asked to amend the summarised 1970 accounts shown opposite to give effect to the conversion of the 10 per cent loan stock, assuming no other changes to the 1970 figures.

Space for answer

ANTROBUS LATHES LIMITED

1970 Balance sheet

	Actual	*With loan converted*
	£'000	£'000
Ordinary £1 shares	240	
Reserves	110	
Shareholders' funds	350	
10% Convertible loan stock	150	
8% Loan stock	100	
Capital employed	£600	
Debt ratio	$\frac{250}{600} = 42\%$	

1970 Profit and loss account

EBIT		143
Interest: 10% Loan	15	
8% Loan	8	
		23
Profit before tax		120
Tax (assume 40%)		48
Profit after tax		£ 72
Earnings per share	$\frac{72}{240} = £0.30$	

6.7 Western Enterprises Limited (A): Share issues

The balance sheet of Western Enterprises Limited at 1 January 1970, is summarised opposite.

The following events connected with long-term capital occurred during the year to 31 December 1970:

(a) March 1970. 5000 ordinary £1 shares were issued to employees at £3 each.

(b) June 1970. Land and buildings were re-valued at £150 000.

(c) September 1970. There was a 2 for 1 bonus issue.

(d) December 1970. Profit for ordinary share-holders (that is profit after tax and after preference dividends) for the year 1970 was £38 000.

A 12 per cent cash dividend is proposed, plus a 1 for 15 bonus issue.

Amend the balance sheet opposite to record the above events. Assume that retained profit is reflected in increased working capital. Identify your amendments by the letters *(a), (b), (c)* and *(d)*.

WESTERN ENTERPRISES LIMITED
Balance sheet, 1 January 1970

	£'000
Fixed assets:	
Land and buildings, at cost	70
Plant, net book value	170
	240
Working capital	80
Net assets	£320
70 000 ordinary £1 shares	70
Share premium account	35
Profit and loss account	95
Shareholders' funds	200
20 000 8% £1 Preference shares	20
10% Loan stock	100
Capital employed	£320

6.8 Western Enterprises limited (B): Share issues

The balance sheet of Western Enterprises Limited at 1 January 1971, is summarised opposite.

The following events connected with long-term capital occurred during the year to 31 December 1971:

(a) *March 1971*. A rights issue of ordinary shares was fully subscribed. The terms were 1 for 4 at 116·67p each.

(b) *June 1971*. An offer to convert each 8 per cent preference share into £1 of 10 per cent loan stock was accepted by 50 per cent in number and 75 per cent in value of preference shareholders.

(c) *September 1971*. There was a 5 for 1 share split.

(d) *December 1971*. Profit for ordinary in 1971 was £48 000. A 15 per cent cash dividend is proposed, plus a 1 for 10 bonus issue.

Amend the balance sheet opposite to record the above events, using the letters (a), (b), (c) and (d) to identify your amendments. Assume that retained profit is reflected in increased working capital.

WESTERN ENTERPRISES LIMITED
Balance sheet, 1 January 1971

	£'000
Fixed assets:	
Land and buildings, at valuation	150
Plant, net book value	170
	320
Working capital	106
Net assets	£426
240 000 Ordinary £1 shares	240
Profit and loss account	66
Shareholders' funds	306
20 000 8% £1 Preference shares	20
10% Loan stock	100
Capital employed	£426

6.9 Debt ratios

The balance sheets of three companies in the same industry are shown below.

Please calculate and compare their debt/capital employed ratios and interest cover.

	A	B	C
	£'000	£'000	£'000
Ordinary share capital	30	60	100
Reserves	50	80	200
6% Preference share capital	—	—	50
Long-term 10% loans	20	40	150
Current liabilities	60	70	250
	£160	£250	£750
Fixed assets, net	90	160	400
Current assets	70	90	350
	£160	£250	£750
Profit before tax	30	40	100
Tax (40%)	12	16	40
Profit after tax	18	24	60

Space for answer

6.10 Sadler Limited (A): Income cover for interest

Sadler Limited has 200 000 £1 ordinary shares in issue, 60 000 5 per cent cumulative preference shares of £1 each, and £80 000 10 per cent debentures, repayable in 1974. Reserves amount to £60 000.

For the year ending 31 December 1970, the company reported a profit before tax of £40 000. Tax is to be provided for at 40 per cent. An ordinary dividend of 8 per cent is proposed for the year.

Calculate:

(a) The interest cover.

(b) The cover for interest and preference dividend.

(c) The dividend cover.

6.11 Sadler Limited (B): Capital cover

At 31 December 1970, Sadler Limited's profit and loss account balance is £60 000. There are no other reserves. Other accounts are the same as in the (A) problem.

Calculate:

(a) The debt ratio.

(b) The amount per share the preference shareholders would receive if the company were liquidated at 31 December 1970, and the net assets—that is, total assets less current liabilities—realised £125 000.

(c) The amount per share that ordinary shareholders would receive if the net assets realised £190 000.

6.12 Bell Limited, Book Limited and Candle Limited: Gearing

The net assets of Bell, Book and Candle are identical, but they have different capital structures, as shown below:

	Bell £'000	Book £'000	Candle £'000
Ordinary £1 shares	15	30	40
Reserves	25	50	60
Equity	40	80	100
10% Loans	60	20	—
Capital employed	£100	£100	£100

Please calculate the following for each company, assuming EBIT (Earnings Before Interest and Tax) (*a*) of £18 000 in 1970, and (*b*) of £5000 in 1971.

Tax of 40 per cent should be assumed. You may assume that all 1970 profits after tax are distributed as dividends.

To be calculated:
(i) Return on net assets (= on capital employed)
(ii) Return on equity
(iii) Interest cover
(iv) Earnings per share

Space for answer

	Bell Limited	Book Limited	Candle Limited

(*a*) *1970*
EBIT
Interest
Profit before tax
Tax
Profit after tax
(i) Return on net assets
(ii) Return on equity
(iii) Interest cover
(iv) Earnings per share

(*b*) *1971*
EBIT
Interest
Profit before tax
Tax
Profit after tax
(i) Return on net assets
(ii) Return on equity
(iii) Interest cover
(iv) Earnings per share

Section 7
Consolidated accounts

CONSOLIDATED ACCOUNTS

We have been concerned in our study so far with the accounts of independent limited liability companies. We have seen that the published accounts of such companies must conform to the provisions of the Companies Acts 1948 and 1967. These Acts also require that where one company (a "holding company" or "parent company") controls other companies ("subsidiaries") the holding company must present consolidated accounts (group accounts) dealing with "the state of affairs and profit and loss of the company and the subsidiaries." "Control" in this context means either a majority shareholding (over 50 per cent) in each subsidiary or control of the composition of the board of each subsidiary. (Where substantial voting rights attach to certain classes of share, a holding company may gain "control" by owning a relatively small proportion of the total share capital.)

The typical accounting package of a holding company with subsidiaries comprises:

1 The balance sheet of the holding company
2 A consolidated balance sheet
3 A consolidated profit and loss account

Under the 1948 Act, however, a holding company need not present consolidated accounts, if:

1 It is impracticable or of no real value.
2 The result would be misleading or harmful to the business.
3 The business of the holding company and that of a subsidiary are so different that they cannot reasonably be treated as a single undertaking.

Abbreviated consolidated accounts of ICI for 1970 (which we shall examine in greater detail in section 8) are set out on the next page. These show a number of accounting headings which we have not encountered before (marked *) and it is with these that we shall be concerned in this section.

COMPANY BALANCE SHEET
31 December 1970

Assets employed		£m
Fixed assets		685
Goodwill	(a)	39*
Interests in subsidiaries	(b)	313*
Interests in associated companies		55
Net current assets		146
		£1238

Financed by	£m
Capital and reserves	845
Investment grants and deferred taxation	140
Loans	253
	£1238

Notes

(a) Except for that arising on the acquisition of British Nylon Spinners in 1964, all goodwill has been charged against reserves.

(b)	£m
Shares at cost less amounts written off	167
Scrip issues capitalised	14
	181
Amount owed by subsidiaries	175
	356
Less: Amounts owed to subsidiaries	43
	£313

(c) Minorities: part of the capital employed by the Group is provided by outside shareholders in subsidiary companies.

(d) By parent company	12*
By subsidiaries	12*
	£24

GROUP BALANCE SHEET
31 December 1970

Assets employed		£m
Fixed assets		1077
Goodwill	(a)	39*
Interests in subsidiaries not consolidated		62*
Interests in associated companies		112
Net current assets		368
		£1658

Financed by		£m
Capital and reserves		
Applicable to parent company		941*
Applicable to minorities	(c)	117*
		1058
Investment grants and deferred taxation		158
Loans		442
		£1658

GROUP PROFIT AND LOSS ACCOUNT
for the year ending 31 December 1970

		£m
Sales		1462
Trading profit		161
Investment income		18
		169
Less: Interest payable		35
Profit before tax		134
Taxation (net)		35
Profit after taxation		99
Applicable to minorities		10*
Applicable to parent company		89
Dividends paid and proposed		65
Retained in the business	(d)	£24

From the abbreviated ICI statements the general nature of the consolidation process will be clear. In the holding company's balance sheet the investment in subsidiaries (including loans to them) appears as a separate item. In the consolidated (group) balance sheet (*a*) the assets and liabilities of all group companies are brought together, (*b*) inter-company balances cancel out, (*c*) the excess of the purchase price over the parent company's share of ordinary share capital and reserves of subsidiaries *at the date of acquisition* is shown as goodwill, and (*d*) any outside (minority) shareholders' interests in the net assets of the group are shown separately. In the consolidated profit and loss account the earnings of all the group companies are added together, the minority interests in the profit after tax are deducted, and the dividends paid or proposed are then shown. The extent to which retained profits are held in the accounts of the holding company or in those of the subsidiaries is indicated in the notes.

It is desirable for all companies in a group to use the same accounting policies unless there are very good reasons against it.

It will be helpful now to look a little more closely at how consolidated accounts are prepared and the special items which arise only in consolidated accounts. In this section we shall look at:

1 Basic consolidation procedures
2 Goodwill arising on consolidation
3 Consolidation reserves (or negative goodwill)
4 Pre-acquisition profits
5 Minority interests
6 Inter-company transactions
7 Non-consolidated subsidiaries and associated companies

We shall then consider briefly some accounting problems of:

8 International groups
9 Mergers

BASIC CONSOLIDATION PROCEDURES

A simple example of consolidation procedures is shown by the accounts set out opposite (top) of *H* Limited (a holding company) and *S* Limited (its wholly-owned subsidiary). The accounts represent the position immediately following the acquisition of *S* by *H* for a purchase consideration exactly equal to the net assets of *S* (= £40 000).

A small "inter-company loan" has been made immediately after the acquisition.

The consolidated balance sheet is shown opposite (bottom).

Notes

1 On consolidation *H*'s balance sheet is expanded to incorporate the individual assets and liabilities of the subsidiary in place of the item "investment in subsidiary."

2 Inter-company balances cancel out.

In fact it would be unusual for the purchase price exactly to equal the net assets of *S*. If the purchase price, based on some projection of *S*'s earning power, *exceeds* the net assets of *S* an item "goodwill on consolidation" will arise when group accounts are prepared. If the purchase price is *less* than the net assets of *S* (perhaps because *S* was making losses), then a consolidation reserve (or negative goodwill) item arises.

We shall deal with these in turn.

H Limited

		£'000
Share capital		100
Revenue reserve		20
		£120
Fixed assets		50
Investment in subsidiary	40	
Loan to subsidiary	10	
		50
Net current assets		20
		£120

S Limited

		£'000
Share capital		£40
Fixed assets		30
Current assets	20	
Less: Loan from *H*	10	
		10
		£40

H Limited and its subsidiary
Consolidated balance sheet

	£'000
Share capital (of *H*)	100
Revenue reserve (of *H*)	20
	£120
Fixed assets (50 + 30)	80
Net current assets (20 + 20)	40
	£120

GOODWILL ARISING ON CONSOLIDATION

Let us consider a more complex situation. The separate balance sheets of H Limited (holding company) and S Limited (its wholly-owned subsidiary) as at 31 December 1971 are set out below (top). The accounts represent the position immediately after the acquisition of S by H for £15 000. The consolidated balance sheet of H Limited and its subsidiary is set out below (bottom).

H LIMITED AND S LIMITED
Balance sheets, 31 December 1971

Separate balance sheets

	£'000			£'000	
	H	S		H	S
Share capital	50	6	Fixed assets	50	7
Revenue reserves	20	3	Investment in S	15	—
Shareholders' funds	70	9	Net current assets	30	6
Long-term debt	25	4			
Capital employed	£95	£13	*Net assets*	£95	£13

Consolidated balance sheet

	£'000		£'000
Share capital (of H)	50	Fixed assets (50 + 7)	57
Revenue reserves (of H)	20	Goodwill (see note 2)	6
Shareholders' funds	70	Net current assets (30 + 6)	36
Long-term debt (25 + 4)	29		
Capital employed	£99	*Net assets*	£99

Notes

1 In preparing the consolidated balance sheet the general approach is to add together the amounts shown in the separate balance sheets. However, the amounts shown in the boxes, representing the equity acquired and the amount paid for it, are eliminated and brought together into a "goodwill on consolidation" account. The balance of £6000 on this account consists of the excess of the purchase consideration (£15 000) over S's shareholders' funds (£9000).

2 Goodwill on consolidation is a technical accounting term which appears only to the extent to which payment has been made for it: it implies the existence of *cost*, but its absence does not imply the non-existence of value.

Implications of goodwill

One way to avoid or reduce the "goodwill" item on consolidation would be to revalue S's assets upwards. The revaluation would increase S's equity and thus reduce or eliminate the amount by which it falls short of the purchase price of £15 000. If, say, £6000 were added to the book value of S's fixed assets (and the same amount to capital reserves, forming part of S's equity), then in the consolidation total fixed assets would amount to £50 000 (H) + £13 000 (S) = £63 000, leaving no need for the item "goodwill £6000."

Notice that if S's fixed assets *were* upvalued by £6000, the depreciation charges in future years would necessarily be increased (and profits reduced) as the new, higher book value of S's fixed assets was written off over their estimated remaining life. For this reason it is quite usual for the asset values to be left unchanged. A figure for goodwill will then be retained in the balance sheet in subsequent years. The justification for this treatment is that the price H paid for S related to the *whole* business of S, not merely the fixed assets; and that as long as S continues in business there is no need to write off the goodwill.

An alternative treatment involves writing goodwill off against reserves, by deducting the goodwill figure from the accumulated reserves in the consolidated balance sheet and showing a net figure on the face of the accounts.

Alternative consolidated assets

With goodwill		*Revaluing S's fixed assets*	
	£'000		
Fixed assets (H50 + S7)	57	Fixed assets (H50 + S13)	63
Goodwill	6		
Net current assets	36	Net current assets	36
	£99		£99

Alternative depreciation charges[1]

With goodwill[2]		*Revaluing S's fixed assets*	
	£'000		£'000
H's fixed assets	5 000	H's fixed assets	5 000
S's fixed assets	700	S's fixed assets	1 300
Total depreciation	£5 700[1]	Total depreciation	£6 300

[1]Assuming that all fixed assets have 10 years' life remaining and are depreciated on the straight line basis.

[2]The goodwill of £6000 *might* be amortised (charged as an expense) either over 10 years, or over a longer period.

CONSOLIDATION RESERVE: "NEGATIVE" GOODWILL

Goodwill arose because H paid more than £9000 (S's equity) for S. The same kind of problem would arise if H had paid *less* than £9000 for 100 per cent of S's equity, except that then the difference would have to be shown on the liabilities side of the consolidation balance sheet. In fact it would be shown as a capital reserve—consolidation reserve—which in such a case can be thought of as a kind of negative goodwill.

Suppose that H had paid only £5000 for S's shares. Then the separate and consolidated balance sheets would be as shown opposite.

Notice that *if* it were correct to upvalue S's fixed assets by £6000 (or amortise goodwill over 10 or more years), then it ought logically to be correct to *write back*—that is, to *credit* profit and loss account with—one-tenth of any capital reserve arising if H paid less than £9000 for S. But this is not often done in practice.

H LIMITED AND S LIMITED
Balance sheets, 31 December 1971
(Assuming H paid only £5000 for S)

Separate

	£'000 H	£'000 S		£'000 H	£'000 S
Share capital	50	6	Fixed assets	50	7
Reserves	20	3	Investment in S	5	—
Equity	70	9	Net current assets	40[1]	6
Long-term debt	25	4			
Capital employed	£95	£13	*Net assets*	£95	£13

[1]H's cash balance assumed £10 000 higher than before, since H has paid £10 000 less than before for S.

Consolidated balance sheet

	£'000		£'000
Share capital	50	Fixed assets	57
Capital reserve	4[2]	Net current assets	46
Other reserves	20		
Equity	74		
Long-term debt	29		
Capital employed	£103	*Net assets*	£103

[2]£9000 (S's equity) less £5000 (what H paid for S).

PRE-ACQUISITION PROFITS

At 31 December 1971, when H acquired S, S had revenue reserves representing distributable profits of £3000. H had revenue reserves of £20 000. However, on consolidation (see p. 212) the total shown for revenue reserves is only £20 000. What has happened to the other £3000? The answer is that from H's point of view S's reserve is "pre-acquisition profits" (PAP). On consolidation the £3000 has been "capitalised" by H and is not available to the group for distribution as dividends. If S were to distribute its reserve as dividends to H, which it could, H could not in turn distribute this amount to its shareholders. Instead the dividend would have to be used to write down the investment in S—to £12 000. This transaction would not affect goodwill which would remain at £6000—that is, £12 000 less £6000 share capital.

As a general rule S would not distribute its pre-acquisition profits but would retain them as part of its permanent capital. On consolidation in each subsequent year the reserves of S would be divided into the non-distributable pre-acquisition portion and the distributable post-acquisition portion which is, of course, available to the group for distribution as dividends.

The adjustment to eliminate pre-acquisition profits is shown opposite where the consolidation of the accounts of H and S one year later is shown. In 1972 H has retained profits of £10 000 and S has retained profits of £5000, and these amounts are reflected in higher fixed assets and net current assets.

H LIMITED AND S LIMITED
Balance sheets, 31 December 1972

Separate

	£'000			£'000	
	H	S		H	S
Share capital	50	6	Fixed assets	55	8
Revenue reserves	30	8*	Investment in S	15	—
Shareholders' funds	80	14	Net current assets	35	10
Long-term debt	25	4			
Capital employed	£105	£18	*Net assets*	£105	£18

Consolidated balance sheet

	£'000		£'000
Share capital	50	Fixed assets	63
Revenue reserves		Goodwill (as before)	6
(30 + 8 − PAP 3)	35		
Shareholders' funds	85	Net current assets	45
Long-term debt	29		
Capital employed	£114	*Net assets*	£114

*PAP 3 + 1972 Retained profit 5

MINORITY INTERESTS

So far we have been considering consolidation where the holding company owns 100 per cent of the subsidiary. But now suppose that H acquired only $66\frac{2}{3}$ per cent of its subsidiary S. From H's point of view, the $33\frac{1}{3}$ per cent of the shares in S held by outside shareholders represent minority interests in a subsidiary.

When consolidating S's accounts with its own, H might include only $66\frac{2}{3}$ per cent of each of S's assets and liabilities. But the H group wants to show the total assets it *controls*, and in practice H will consolidate 100 per cent of S's assets and liabilities but show as a liability—"minority interests in subsidiaries" —the amount of S's net assets which it does not own.

The same procedure applies to consolidated profit and loss accounts, 100 per cent of subsidiaries' profits and losses being included, and a separate deduction being made where necessary to represent the share attributable to minority interests.

Of course, if all subsidiaries are 100 per cent owned ("wholly-owned") there will be *no* minority interests.

H LIMITED AND S LIMITED
Balance sheets, 31 December 1971
(Immediately following the acquisition by H of a $66\frac{2}{3}$ per cent interest in S for £10 000.)

Separate

	£'000 H	£'000 S		£'000 H	£'000 S
Share capital	50	6	Fixed assets	50	7
Reserves	20	3	Investment in S		
Equity	70	9	(66⅔% of S's shares)	10	—
Long-term debt	25	4	Net current assets	35	6
Capital employed	£95	£13	*Net assets*	£95	£13

Consolidated balance sheet

	£'000		£'000
Share capital	50	Fixed assets	57
Reserves	20	Goodwill	4[2]
Equity	70	Net current assets	41
Minority interests	3[1]		
Long-term debt	29		
Capital employed	£102	*Net assets*	£102

[1] $33\frac{1}{3}$% $\times$ S's equity £9000 = £3000.

[2] Excess of H's investment in S (£10 000) over H's £6000 share of S's equity ($66\frac{2}{3}$% $\times$ £9000 = £6000 = £9000 − £3000 minority interests).

INTER-COMPANY TRANSACTIONS

In practice, certain adjustments ignored up to now would be needed on consolidation to eliminate two kinds of inter-company transactions:

(a) Inter-company balances
(b) Unrealised inter-company profits

(a) Inter-company balances

Eliminating inter-company balances on consolidation (that is, amounts owing to and by companies in a group) is relatively easy. For example, suppose that *A* owns *B* and *C*, and details of current assets and current liabilities at the balance sheet date are as shown below.

It is easy to see that £92 000 is owed within the group (23 + 48 + 21); and that this amount must be eliminated from total current assets and current liabilities leaving only *external* current assets and current liabilities respectively of £583 000 and £324 000. Exactly the same kind of procedure applies to long-term inter-company loans and advances.

Separate balance sheets (Extracts)

Current liabilities	£'000 A	B	C	Current assets	£'000 A	B	C
Creditors:				Stock	186	64	48
A	*	—	23	Cash	31	12	17
B	48	*	—	Debtors:			
C	—	21	*	A	*	48	—
Others	174	87	63	B	—	*	21
	£222	108	86	C	23	—	*
				Others	140	44	41
					£380	168	127

Consolidated balance sheet (Extracts)

Current liabilities	£'000	Current assets	£'000
Creditors (174 + 87 + 63)	324	Stock	298
		Cash	60
		Debtors (140 + 44 + 41)	225
	£324		£583

(b) Unrealised inter-company profits

As a single entity for accounting purposes, a group of companies earns no revenue until sales are made to the outside world. This is the realisation principle applied to a group.

Inter-company—that is, intra-group—purchases and sales must therefore be eliminated from consolidated accounts, together with any related profit which has been included in the accounts of individual subsidiaries, providing that they are "unrealised" from the group's point of view. Otherwise the total group figures would overstate the volume of group sales, the level of group profits and of group stocks, and artificial intra-group transactions could easily be arranged to manipulate the figures.

The eliminations are made on work-sheets quite outside and apart from the books of account. They do not affect the permanent accounting records of the individual companies.

Suppose *S*, a subsidiary, has sold to *H*, its holding company, for £48 000 goods which cost *S* £30 000. The three possibilities arising from this transaction are considered below.

The key question is not whether there are inter-company profits, but whether those profits have, at the date of the balance sheet, been *realised* by the group as a whole by means of sales to outside customers. Only *unrealised* profits have to be eliminated from the group accounts.

Wholly realised by group
If *H* has sold all the goods costing £48 000 to outside customers for £60 000, *H* will show a profit of £12 000, *S* will show a profit of £18 000, and the group profit is £30 000—that is, the £60 000 sales proceeds from outside customers less the £30 000 cost from outside suppliers to *S*. No adjustment is needed on consolidation, because the group's profits (*H* £12 000 + *S* £18 000) have all been realised externally.

Wholly unrealised by group
If *H* has sold none of the goods purchased from *S*, they will be shown in *H*'s stock as costing £48 000. But for the purpose of group accounts that stock must be shown as costing £30 000—that is, the cost to *S* on a purchase from outside suppliers. Group profits must be reduced by £18 000 to eliminate, for the time being, *S*'s profit on the sale to *H*. This profit has not yet been realised by the group. (Notice how double-entry is preserved in these adjustments: reduce *H*'s stock value by £18 000 and reduce *S*'s profit by £18 000.)

Partly realised by group
If *H* has sold, say, two-thirds of the goods, and one-third is still in stock, then only £6000 (one-third of £18 000) needs to be subtracted from group stock and from group profit.

NON-CONSOLIDATED SUBSIDIARIES

Where a holding company (*H*), does *not* consolidate the accounts of a particular subsidiary (*S*), for one of the reasons mentioned earlier (see p. 209), there are two alternative accounting treatments: the "cost" method and the "equity" method.

The "cost" method. H shows the investment in *S* at cost in the balance sheet, and credits any *dividends* received from *S* as income in the profit and loss account. Any profits of *S* not paid out in dividends (or any losses) are simply ignored.

The "equity" method. H includes in the profit and loss account *H*'s entire share of *S*'s profit *or loss. H*'s investment in *S* on the balance sheet is shown at cost *plus H*'s share of *S*'s *retained* earnings—that is, profits less dividends—*since acquisition*. The dividends paid by *S* to *H* will, of course, increase *H*'s cash balance.

The Institute of Chartered Accountants in England and Wales has recently recommended that companies use the "equity" method even for investments in associated companies, where they both (*a*) hold 20 per cent or more of the shares and (*b*) take some share in the management of the company.

One reason for using the "equity" method—especially in the case of *subsidiaries* that are not consolidated—is that the holding company *controls* the dividend policy of the subsidiary. If the "cost" method were used, the holding company would be able to affect its own reported profits by changing the subsidiary's dividend regardless of underlying profits.

H buys 100 per cent of *S* at 31 December 1971 for £40 000 cash. In the year to 31 December 1972 *H* makes a profit of £19 000. *S* makes a profit of £7 000 and pays a dividend of £2 000. *S* is treated by *H* as a non-consolidated subsidiary.

Balance sheets at 31 December 1971	£'000	
	H	*S*
Investment in *S*	40	—
Other assets	140	24
Net assets	£180	£24

H LIMITED
Profit and loss account, 1972

	£'000	
	"Cost" method	"Equity" method
Profit of *H*	19	19
Dividend from *S*	2	—
Share of *S*'s profit	—	7
Total profit	£21	£26

H LIMITED
Balance sheet at 31 December 1972

	£'000	
Investment in *S*	40	45[2]
Other assets	161[1]	161[1]
Net assets	£201	£206

[1] 140 + 19 + 2   [2] 40 + 5 (*S* retained profit)

We now turn briefly to two subjects connected with consolidated accounts: international groups and mergers.

INTERNATIONAL GROUPS

The accounts of foreign subsidiaries may cause some particular problems in connection with foreign currencies.

Non-consolidation and the use of the "cost" method solves these problems easily, by ignoring them. But, despite the difficulties, consolidation of the accounts of foreign subsidiaries will generally give a fairer view of a group's overall position.

When subsidiaries operate in foreign currencies, for consolidation purposes their accounts have to be converted into the holding company's monetary unit. "Real" assets—in particular, fixed assets—are converted at the exchange rate at the date of *purchase*, while monetary assets and liabilities are converted at the official end-of-year exchange rate. In modern conditions, with restrictions imposed by governments on the free convertibility of nearly all currencies, using end-of-year "official" exchange rates for converting monetary assets is more or less hypothetical. The amounts involved are often not material, related to the size of the group as a whole, but the difficulty illustrates again that accounts are only approximations.

A special problem connected with converting foreign currencies arises when one currency is *devalued* in terms of another. A devaluation officially happens at a particular moment of time, but it really relates to a period of time, often several years. While the profit or loss which arises on devaluation is treated as a "special" or "non-recurring" item in accounts, such items may actually be a normal part of the trading results of an international group, even though any particular devaluation seems at the time to be a "special" event.

For example, it may be possible to borrow Eurocurrency—say deutsch-marks—at an apparently low rate of interest. Thus the interest charge in the profit and loss account will be low. But the loss on devaluation when (if) the pound is devalued against the deutschmark, which will presumably be treated as an "extraordinary" non-recurring loss, really represents an addition to the interest charge.

If a foreign subsidiary (F) is prevented by government exchange controls from remitting dividends to its holding company (H), the latter may be unwilling to take credit for its share of F's earnings. One of the difficulties is that government regulations change. Suppose that F's accounts had been consolidated in the past in the usual way, and that H had taken credit in the profit and loss account for its whole share of F's profits. What happens if a sudden crisis in F's country leads to the imposition of remittance restrictions which "freeze" F's retained earnings (for which H has already taken credit)?

Depending on the amounts involved, and on how long the restrictions were thought likely to last, it might be best to continue consolidation as before and ignore the new restrictions. An alternative procedure would be to consolidate as before but mention the remittance restrictions in a note to the accounts. A third possibility would be to change back from consolidation to the "cost" method. F's frozen retained earnings since acquisition would then have to be deducted from reserves.

MERGERS

So far we have been dealing with the situation where one company H "acquires" another company S. In some circumstances, however, business combinations may be treated as "mergers" (which Americans call a "pooling of interests") rather than as "acquisitions."

With an "acquisition," either the previous shareholders in one company are bought out for cash or else (if there is an exchange of shares) there is such a disparity in size between the combining companies that one party to the deal is clearly dominant.

In contrast, in a "merger" the shareholders in both companies become the owners of a single company owning the combined assets *and* there is no gross disparity in size between the surviving equity interests in the combined undertaking. (The English Institute has recently suggested that 3 to 1 is the largest acceptable disparity in size of equity interests which would permit merger treatment.)

In an "acquisition," as we saw earlier, when one company (H) buys the shares of another company (S)—whether for cash or for shares in H—"goodwill" appears in H's consolidated accounts to represent the excess of the purchase price over the net book value of the assets acquired. Such goodwill may be (a) written off against reserves; (b) amortised by charges against profits over a period; or (c) left on the balance sheet indefinitely as an intangible asset.

Such a variety of alternative accounting treatments can clearly lead to the same transaction having widely different reported results. For example, amortising ICI's £39 million goodwill against profit over 10 years would reduce after-tax profits by nearly £4 million a year. Writing it off directly against reserves would immediately reduce capital employed by £39 million. (This was done in 1971.)

In the example we studied, S's retained profits at the date of acquisition become "pre-acquisition profits" in H's consolidated accounts: such profits are regarded as capital reserves and are not available for distribution as dividends by H. (Any distribution by S after the acquisition would be regarded as reducing the cost to H.)

In a "merger," however, the constituent companies' assets and liabilities are simply combined at their former book values. No goodwill therefore arises.

If the new combined company's issued capital is more than the total of the constituent companies' issued capitals, the excess is deducted from reserves. If less, the difference is shown as a capital reserve.

In a merger, the combined retained profits of the constituent companies *remain* available for distribution as dividends. The constituent companies' profits for the entire period in which the merger occurred are reported as profits of the combined company (and the profits of former periods may also be restated on a combined basis).

Acquisition and Merger Accounting

A Limited acquires all B Limited's 4000 £1 shares for 25 000 £1 shares in A Limited, worth £50 000.

Before acquisition	£'000	
	A	B
Issued share capital	65	4
Reserves	35	6
Net assets	£100	£10
Profit after tax	£10	£2
		(in following year)

After acquisition (1 year later)	£'000	
	"Acquisition"	"Merger"
Issued share capital	90A	90A
Share premium	25B	—
Other reserves	31C	20D
Capital employed	£146	£110
Goodwill	36E	—
Other net assets	110	110
Net assets	£146	£110
Profit after tax	12	12
Less: Goodwill amortised	4	—
Net profit after tax	£8	£12

Notes

A £65 000 + £25 000 = £90 000.

B 25 000 £1 shares issued at £2 each produces a premium of £1 per share = £25 000.

C £35 000 A's reserves less £4000 goodwill written off.

D £35 000 A's reserves plus £6000 B's reserves (= £41 000) less the excess of A's nominal capital issued (£25 000) over B's nominal capital acquired (£4000) (= £21 000). £41 000 − £21 000 = £20 000.

E £40 000 (= £50 000 *value* of A's shares issued, less £10 000 book value of B's assets acquired), less £4000 goodwill written off (one-tenth of £40 000 goodwill).

1 Return on equity:

Acquisition: $\dfrac{8}{146} = 5.4\%$

Merger: $\dfrac{12}{110} = 10.9\%$

2 Former owners of B end up with 25/90 (28 per cent) of the equity of the new combined business. The disparity is less than 3 to 1 (which would be 75 per cent to 25 per cent) and merger accounting would be used.

SUMMARY

In this section we have dealt with the major adjustments necessary to "consolidate" the accounts of a holding company and those of its subsidiaries into "group accounts." On consolidation inter-company balances cancel out and *unrealised* profits on inter-company transactions are eliminated. "Goodwill on consolidation" arises in group accounts when the purchase price that a holding company pays for its investment in a subsidiary exceeds the net book value of the subsidiary's assets less liabilities.

We have seen that when a subsidiary is not "wholly-owned" by a holding company there are "minority interests" in that subsidiary from the group's point of view. These must be shown separately as a source of capital on the group balance sheet, and an appropriate part of the group's profit after tax must be deducted in the group profit and loss account, as being applicable to minority interests.

If a particular subsidiary's accounts for some good reason are *not* consolidated into group accounts, either the "cost" method or (increasingly) the "equity" method of accounting for the holding company's investment can be used. Finally, we briefly discussed some problems of an international group's foreign subsidiaries whose accounts are expressed in foreign currencies, and dealt with the differences between "merger" and "acquisition" accounting treatment.

Now we move on to our final section, dealing with a detailed analysis and interpretation of ICI's 1970 group accounts.

7.1 Definitions

Write down opposite your definitions of the terms shown. Then compare your answers with the definitions overleaf.

(a) Minority interests

(b) Goodwill

(c) Pre-acquisition profits

(d) Subsidiary company

(e) Investment in subsidiary

(f) Non-consolidated subsidiaries

(g) The "cost" method

(h) The "equity" method

(i) An associated company

(j) A trade investment

7.1 Definitions

(a) *Minority interests* are the equity interests of shareholders other than the holding company in the assets (and profits or losses) of subsidiaries that are not wholly owned by the holding company.

(b) *Goodwill* is the excess of the purchase price paid by a holding company for its investment in a subsidiary over the net book value of the subsidiary's assets less liabilities at the time of acquisition. In accounting, it represents cost not value, and is considered as an "intangible" asset.

(c) *Pre-acquisition profits* are the retained profits of a subsidiary company at the date at which it became a subsidiary.

(d) *Subsidiary company* is a company which is controlled by another (the "holding company") which either owns (directly or indirectly) more than 50 per cent of its equity capital or controls the composition of its board of directors.

(e) *Investment in subsidiary* is the total amount invested in a subsidiary by a holding company, including the cost of ordinary shares and loans or advances to the subsidiary (and *less* loans or advances *by* the subsidiary).

(f) *Non-consolidated subsidiaries* are subsidiaries whose accounts are *not* consolidated with those of the holding company. A number of reasons may justify non-consolidation (see p. 209).

(g) *The "cost" method* of treating non-consolidated subsidiaries has the investment shown at cost, and the group profit and loss account is credited only with dividends, when they are received.

(h) *The "equity" method* is an alternative method of accounting for non-consolidated subsidiaries. The investment is shown in the balance sheet at cost plus the holding company's share of the subsidiaries' retained profits *since* acquisition. The group profit and loss account includes the holding company's full share of the subsidiaries' profits or losses as they arise (that is its share of dividends plus its share of retained profits).

(i) *An associated company* is a company in which another company *both* owns at least 20 per cent of the ordinary share capital (but not enough—more than 50 per cent—to make it a subsidiary), *and* participates in management.

(j) *A trade investment* is a long-term investment in another company whose business is connected with that of the investing company. If more than 50 per cent of the equity is held, it will count as a subsidiary, and if between 20 per cent and 50 per cent it will probably count as an associated company (unless there is no significant participation in the management).

7.2 Whale Limited (A): Simple consolidation

Whale Limited acquired all the shares of Minnow Limited for £20 000 cash on 1 January 1972. At 31 December 1971 (*before* the purchase price had been paid) the two companies' balance sheets were summarised as follows:

	Whale Limited £'000	Minnow Limited £'000
Share capital	50	8
Reserves	45	5
Shareholders' funds	95	13
Long-term debt	7	6
Capital employed	£102	£19
Fixed assets	79	15
Net current assets	23	4
Net assets	£102	£19

Draw up Whale Limited's consolidated balance sheet immediately after the acquisition.

The answer is shown overleaf.

Space for answer

7.2 Whale Limited (A)

Solution

WHALE LIMITED
Consolidated balance sheet
1 January 1972

	£'000
Share capital	50
Reserves	45
Shareholders' funds	95
Long-term debt	13
Capital employed	£108
Fixed assets	94
Goodwill	7 (1)
Net current assets	7 (2)
Net assets	£108

Notes

1 20 (price paid) — 13 (Minnow's shareholders' funds) = 7.

2 Whale 23 minus 20 cash price paid (to Minnow's *shareholders*, not to Minnow) = 3 + Minnow 4 = 7.

3 We assume that Whale has no other subsidiaries apart from Minnow.

4 We also assume that no inter-company balances need to be eliminated.

7.3 Whale Limited (B): Consolidation

In the year ended 31 December 1972 Whale Limited made a profit of £15 000 and Minnow Limited made a profit of £4000. No dividends were paid or proposed. Assume in each case that these profits were reflected entirely in additional net current assets and that long-term debt and the net book value of fixed assets remained unchanged from the figures shown in Whale Limited (A).

After referring back to the Whale Limited (A) problem draw up Whale Limited's consolidated balance sheet at 31 December 1972.

The answer is shown overleaf.

Space for answer

7.3 Whale Limited (B)

Solution

WHALE LIMITED
Consolidated balance sheet
31 December 1972

	£'000
Share capital	50
Reserves	64 (1)
Shareholders' funds	114
Long-term debt	13
Capital employed	£127
Fixed assets	94
Goodwill	7 (2)
Net current assets	26
Net assets	£127

Notes

1 Reserves 64 = Whale 60 + Minnow 9 − PAP 5.

2 As before

3 Note that Minnow's five reserves at 1 January 1972 represent "pre-acquisition profits", and are *not* added on to the consolidated reserves. Instead they are taken into account in calculating goodwill, which represents the excess of the purchase price over the (share of) equity purchased *at the date of acquisition.*

Answers to the following problems are shown at the end of the book.

7.4 Philip Limited: Inter-company trading

Philip Limited did a good deal of business with its wholly-owned subsidiary, Sidney Limited. In the year ending 31 March 1972, Sidney had sold to Philip for £80 000 goods which had cost £50 000. At 31 March 1972 Philip still held in stock goods which had been invoiced to it by Sidney for £20 000.

What, if any, consolidation adjustments are necessary?

7.5 Dexter Limited (A): Minority Interests

On the 1 April 1971, Dexter Limited acquired 75 per cent of its share capital of Close Limited for 50 000 £1 ordinary shares. At 31 March 1971 the two companies' summarised balance sheets were as follows:

	Dexter	Close
	£'000	£'000
Issued ordinary £1 shares	150	40
Reserves	87	24
Shareholders' funds	237	64
Long-term debt	78	20
Capital employed	£315	£84
Fixed assets	251	72
Net current assets	64	12
Net assets	£315	£84

Draw up Dexter's consolidated balance sheet immediately after the acquisition. At 31 March 1971, Dexter's £1 ordinary shares were quoted at 180p.

7.6 Dexter Limited (B)

At 31 March 1972 the balance sheets of Dexter Limited and Close Limited were as shown below.

Dexter had acquired 75 per cent of the share capital of Close on 31 March 1971, when Close's reserves amounted to £24 000.

In the year ended 31 March 1972 Dexter made a profit after tax of £40 000 and Close made a profit after tax of £12 000. Neither company paid a dividend in respect of the year.

Draw up Dexter's consolidated balance sheet at 31 March 1972 in the right-hand column below.

Balance sheets at 31 March 1972

	Dexter	Close	Dexter consolidated
£'000	£'000	£'000	£'000
Ordinary £1 shares	200	40	
Share premium	40		
Revenue reserves	127	36	
Shareholders' funds	367	76	
Long-term debt	90	26	
Capital employed	£457	£102	
Fixed assets	280	85	
Investment in Close	90	—	
Net current assets	87	17	
Net assets	£457	£102	
Profit after tax	£ 40	£ 12	

7.7 Barber Limited and Jenkins Limited: Non-consolidated subsidiaries

Barber Limited and Jenkins Limited are identical companies. At 31 December 1971 they each acquired 100 per cent of identical subsidiaries. The 1972 results are identical for the two holding companies and for the subsidiaries. But a difference between Barber and Jenkins arises in their proposed treatment of their subsidiaries, neither of which is to be consolidated. Barber proposes to use the "cost" method, Jenkins the "equity" method.

Summarised 1972 accounts for holding company and subsidiary are shown below, showing separately the £40 000 cash payment the holding company made at 31 December 1971 for the investment in the subsidiary.

Summarise the relevant parts of the final 1972 accounts of Barber Limited and Jenkins Limited.

	Holding company	Subsidiary
	£	£
Assets	360 000	28 000
Investment in subsidiary	40 000	
Profit after tax	50 000	10 000
Dividend paid	30 000	—
Retained profit	20 000	10 000

What difference would it make if the subsidiary paid a dividend of £7500?

7.8 Leach Limited and Dixon Limited: Mergers

Leach Limited and Dixon Limited agreed to combine their businesses at 1 April 1971. Their summarised balance sheets at 31 March 1971, are shown below.

The arrangement was that Leach Limited should exchange 20 million £1 shares in Leach Limited (valued at £2 each) for all Dixon Limited's shares.

Please show below how Leach's consolidated balance sheet would appear at 1 April 1971:

(a) If the combination were treated as an acquisition by Leach.

(b) If the combination were treated as a merger.

Summarised balance sheets: 31 March 1971

	Leach £m	Dixon £m
Share capital (£1 shares)	40	20
Retained profits	20	15
Net assets	£60	£35

Space for answer

	Acquisition £m	Merger £m
Share capital (£1 shares)		
Retained profits		
	—	—
	—	—
Net assets		
	—	—
	—	—

Section 8
Interpreting company accounts

THE NEED FOR CAUTION

We have now completed sections 3 to 7, which were introduced at the end of section 2 with the comment:

"It is crucially important that people who use accounting figures appreciate what accounts really mean. They need to understand how transactions are recorded and incorporated into accounting statements, and to be aware of the various possible ways in which profit can be measured and assets valued."

Now we know what is involved it is evident that in considering the meaning of company accounts the external analyst must exercise caution in drawing conclusions, whether he is a shareholder (actual or potential), an employee, a creditor, a professional financial analyst or a government official. The analyst must be aware of the normal margins of error which are inevitable in compiling accounts for large and complex organisations (even though the figures may be expressed to the nearest £1), and of the degree to which subjective judgements affect critical areas of asset valuation and hence profit determination.

We have looked at accounting statements from various angles, and it may be helpful in this final section to summarise the major points discussed under a number of headings:

1 Disclosure and accounting conventions
2 Comparisons over time and between companies
3 Accounting matters requiring special attention

DISCLOSURE AND ACCOUNTING CONVENTIONS

The major point to emphasise at the outset is that except where the results of a completed transaction are being measured accounting profit or loss is not a matter of certainty, but one involving judgement. The greater the number of incomplete transactions, the longer the time span between their beginning and completion and the greater their significance in relation to the total business during a period, the greater will be the range of possible profit figures.

The requirement for "consistency" of accounting treatment from year to year is aimed at minimising distortions due to changes in opinion. In a constantly changing business environment, however, it is not always easy to draw an exact parallel between the circumstances of this year and those of previous years, and changes in accounting treatment can legitimately occur from time to time. In judging performance measured in accounting terms, nevertheless, a trend in figures over time will generally be a much sounder measure than the figures for a single period.

Accounting conventions owe much to their historical roots and conservatism is a fundamental feature. This often leads to a tendency to understate the position. Intangible assets, such as goodwill, trade marks or the results of research and development effort, which provide no immediate physical security to creditors, are often incorporated at very small amounts or even omitted completely, although in terms of earning power they may be extremely valuable. Physical assets, with the growing exception of freehold and leasehold properties, are included in accounts at historical cost less accumulated depreciation although their current market value may be much higher.

In periods of continuous inflation the conventional accounting use of original money cost inadequately reflects the "real" position (the level of profit disclosed as well as the figures in the balance sheet), but no alternative treatment has yet found general acceptance. Unless companies retain sufficient reported profits, however, and thus increase their permanent capital in *money* terms, there is a very real danger that *purchasing power* capital may be distributed in the mistaken belief that it is "profit."

Company chairmen often say that their firm's most important asset is its workers. This asset, however, is not shown on company balance sheets. (Some wages may indirectly be capitalised, for example if connected with manufacturing stock, with research and development, or with making or installing fixed assets.)

No company *owns* its workers, though it may have contracted for their services over a certain future period. Nor is any capital sum usually paid directly in "acquiring" workers (football clubs are an exception), although many firms bear indirect costs such as removal expenses and training costs.

Even if it were desired to capitalise part of a man's pay, to match expenses better with future benefits, ("human resource accounting") it would be hard to tell what (probably fairly small) proportion to capitalise and how to amortise the asset.

Statutory regulations and accounting conventions require the basis used in arriving at disclosed figures to be stated—thus assets are shown "at cost" or "at valuation" or "after providing for depreciation"—but, as we have seen, great care is needed in examining company accounts to ensure that all the available information is allowed for. The analyst must study the notes to the accounts and the auditors' report as well as the balance sheet and profit and loss account. He must also read the directors' report and chairman's statement which are included with the published accounts. But even when all the available information is taken into account, there may still be areas of doubt as to the exact significance of the reported figures. Indeed, one result of the considerable increase in the last few years in the extent of published accounting information has been to emphasise how much is still not known.

A widespread feeling exists—among accountants and others—that accounting practices have not developed in recent years to reflect adequately the events which accounts seek to record. One far-reaching problem involves the role of companies in society. For whom are accounts prepared? Is it enough to think merely in terms of creditors, owners and managers? Is it sensible to think in terms of one set of requirements irrespective of the nature and size of companies, or should different rules apply to small private companies, large public companies and even larger international companies? How much detail should be required from each? Our studies in this book would suggest that more disclosure is required, but if a company has more than 300 subsidiaries in different industries in different countries, how many pages of detail should the accounts contain?

COMPARISONS OVER TIME AND BETWEEN COMPANIES

We have already seen that when figures have been prepared on a consistent basis, the trend in a company's results over a number of years provides a more useful means of appraising its performance and financial status than the results for a single year. The proviso of consistency is clearly important, and the analyst looking at published figures may well feel that some adjustments are necessary to disclose an acceptable trend. He must, of course, in presenting his conclusions, indicate the nature and extent of any such adjustments.

Comparisons between the published results of different companies, even between companies in the same industry, must be treated with much greater caution than comparisons made over time for a single company. Companies nominally in the same "industry" (which itself can be hard to define) may be carrying on very different activities: they may be of different size, and may have been established at different points in time. Thus in a stores comparison, one company may be a supermarket, another a department store and a third a small specialist grocer. All are in the "retail trade," but what does comparing their results show?

At a more technical accounting level, different companies may have adopted different approaches in compiling their accounts. In earlier sections of this book we have seen the differences in profit and asset levels which can arise from alternative approaches to stock valuation, depreciation methods, expenditure allocation and so on. In making a comparison between companies the effects of their using widely different approaches cannot sensibly be ignored.

The extent to which a different treatment of items in accounts can affect the disclosed results was dramatically illustrated in the take-over of AEI by GEC in late 1967. On the basis of ten months' actual figures and an annual budget the AEI board of directors forecast a pre-tax profit of £10 million in 1967. (This figure should be related to group sales of £260 million and gross assets at book value of £280 million, including stocks and work-in-progress of £100 million.)

Nine months later, after control of AEI had passed from its previous board to that of GEC, the 1967 accounts disclosed a £4½ million *loss*—that is £14½ million less than the forecast profit. An accounting investigation revealed that the difference was broadly due to cost of sales in excess of estimates (£3.4m), obsolescence of stocks (£4.3m), and provisions for losses on contracts in progress (£4.4m). No doubt this particular case is somewhat extreme, in that AEI was considering an ongoing business, while GEC was looking at a business which in some respects had effectively ceased to exist.

Nevertheless, in preparing company accounts considerable scope often exists for exercising judgement about the uncertain future, and analysts must try to allow for different opinions, and focus attention on those items in accounts which might be affected.

Financial information about major companies is given daily in the financial press, especially in the *Financial Times*, *The Times* and *Daily Telegraph*. Various investment services, such as Moodies Services and Exchange Telegraph, provide, on a longer-term basis, detailed information about the financial results of a whole range of public and private companies. Their analysis extends over the previous ten or fifteen years, and includes summaries of the latest information about the companies' businesses and prospects.

The figures shown for each company are generally based on information given in published accounts, but are usually adjusted to some extent in an attempt to make them as comparable as possible with other companies' figures. Adjustments may include standardising the tax charge, excluding "non-recurring" profits or losses, and adjusting the earnings per share figures on to a comparable basis over time when a scrip issue has been made during the period covered.

The results of industry-wide studies are also published from time to time, for example in the *Financial Times* and in *Trade and Industry*. These studies again are based on published accounting data, adjusted to exclude non-recurring items. The *Financial Times* industry analyses also adjust the "capital employed" figure to *include* bank overdrafts and to *exclude* intangible assets.

Detailed comparisons between the results of different companies within an industry are also made, for example by trade federations and by the Centre for Interfirm Comparison (set up in 1959 by the British Institute of Management and the British Productivity Council). Naturally the compilers of such comparative statistics are well aware of the difficulties inherent in comparisons based on published accounting information. The Centre for Interfirm Comparison, for example, makes extensive amendments to published accounting data by using a great deal of additional information supplied in confidence by subscribers to its service. Such adjustments are essential to obtain meaningful detailed comparisons.

Thus, where detailed figures are available, the analyst can adjust published results on to a more comparable basis. Considering how much reported figures can vary depending on the bases used in compiling them, it will be obvious that the conclusions which might be drawn from unadjusted figures could well be very different indeed from those which will result from an appraisal of properly adjusted figures. To the extent that the analyst is denied access to the required level of detail, he must move with considerable caution.

ACCOUNTING MATTERS REQUIRING SPECIAL ATTENTION

It may be useful to summarise here those items in accounts where the analyst must exercise special care. These are items where the required detail may not be readily available in the accounts and supporting notes and reports, or where alternative accounting treatments are permissible. Where adequate detail is not available, particular care will be needed in drawing conclusions from the figures.

Fixed assets

Where fixed assets are shown "at cost":
How old are they?
How would revaluation affect them (and depreciation charges)?

Where fixed assets are shown "at valuation":
When was the valuation made, and on what basis?
How have values changed since that date?
Might the assets be more valuable if used for other purposes?

What method of depreciation is used?
What asset lives are used?
Has adequate provision been made for technological obsolescence?

Are any assets leased? What is their value?
How much are the annual rental? How long is the commitment?

Is goodwill:
Shown as an asset?
Being amortised by charges against profit?
Or written off against reserves?

What is the difference between cost and market value of quoted investments?

Are investments in associated companies:
Shown by the "cost" method?
Or by the "equity" method?

Current assets

How is stock and work-in-progress valued?
How much overhead is being carried forward?
What provision has been made for slow-moving stock and losses?
How much profit has been taken on contracts in progress?

How much has been provided for bad debts?

How much "revenue" expenditure is being carried forward to future periods?
What does it represent? Advertising? Research? Development?
Is the amount deferred increasing from period to period?

Current liabilities

Have any bank overdrafts been outstanding for more than twelve months?

Is tax payable more than a year ahead included as a "current" liability?

Long-term liabilities

Is any long-term debt convertible into ordinary shares?
On what terms?

Is any long-term debt repayable within a short period?

Equity

What individual items have caused significant movements on reserves?
Do any of them really belong in the profit and loss account?

Has issued share capital changed?
If so, why? Take-over? Rights issue? Bonus issue?

Profit and loss account

Most balance sheet items above will also affect the profit and loss account.

How are sales and trading profit split among the major activities?
To what extent are changes due to price changes?
To what extent to volume changes?
Does inter-company transfer pricing policy distort the analysis?

Has the apparent proportion of profit taken in tax changed much?
Is there a tax equalisation account?

Has the share of profit (or loss) attributable to minority interest changed much?

Are profits and losses on sales of fixed assets:
Treated as adjustments of depreciation charges?
Treated as "below the line" items in the profit and loss account?
Transferred directly to reserves?

Are prior years' adjustments noted separately?

COMPARING THE RESULTS OF SUBSIDIARY COMPANIES OR DIVISIONS

In comparing the results of subsidiaries or divisions, special additional accounting problems arise, associated with the subordinate nature of the units being measured. Subsidiaries or divisions are generally subject to company-wide policies affecting prices at which goods or services are transferred within the group. This affects the profit or loss reported by each unit, as well as the sales figure. To make a meaningful comparison of the results of different divisions, adjustments will have to be made to record the transactions as far as possible on an arm's length basis—that is, as if they were transactions with parties outside the company. Failure to make such adjustments could lead management to draw conclusions which merely reflect the impact of policies external to the division without revealing the relative performance of the units concerned.

Another area in which company-wide policies are likely to affect comparisons is that of cash control. It is usual in a group of companies for surplus funds to be collected and managed at the centre. Operating subsidiaries or divisions will be allowed to draw money for current expenditure and for capital outlays, but will be expected to remit funds which are not being used immediately. Much of their financing will thus be through loans from the holding company or head office, and the subsidiary or division will clearly be altering its "capital employed" total as it draws or remits money. This has two major consequences.

First, the amount of a subsidiary's creditors will depend on how much money has been drawn from the centre to pay them. If the holding company current account (or loan account) is regarded as "capital employed," and if creditors are deducted from current assets, then subsidiaries will be able to *reduce* "capital employed" (and thus improve return on investment) by delaying payment to creditors. This may well be undesirable in the longer term, and it is quite usual, in measuring divisional performance, *not* to deduct creditors from current assets, but instead to include them in capital employed, thus relating profits to *total* assets.

Similarly, funds which represent the deduction from operating income for depreciation will be regularly withdrawn from a subsidiary, and re-injected only when new fixed assets are required. Therefore the "capital employed" total will decline as assets age and then rise sharply when new fixed assets are bought. Unless adjustments are made, this again may lead to distortions over time in the return on investment figures. One possible adjustment is to use *gross* rather than net book value for fixed assets—that is, bringing them into account at cost—for the purposes of appraising divisional performance. The profit used in making comparisons will still be that *after* charging depreciation, which is a proper charge against profit for using the asset.

In calculating a division's return on investment and related ratios, the basic formula is thus:

$$\frac{\text{Profit before interest and tax (but after depreciation)}}{\text{Fixed assets (gross of depreciation) + current assets}}$$

The adjustments are illustrated in the figures opposite, for two divisions of Hydra Limited.

Using the "return on total gross assets," both divisions appear to be earning a 20 per cent return.

If the "return on *net* assets" basis is used, the results would be:

Division *A*   48 per cent
Division *B*   25 per cent

Division *A*, with a heavily written-down investment in fixed assets and substantial creditors, shows a much higher return at 48 per cent.

Division *B*, with relatively new fixed assets and smaller creditors, shows a return of 25 per cent.

In the year in which division *A* replaces its fixed assets, on the net asset basis its return will fall very sharply. Using the total gross assets basis, however, on renewing fixed assets the fall in reported return will be much smaller.

HYDRA LIMITED

	Division A	Division B
	£	£
Share capital	40 000	20 000
Loans	10 000	60 000
Creditors	20 000	10 000
	£70 000	£90 000
Fixed assets, at cost	80 000	80 000
Less: Accumulated depreciation	50 000	10 000
	30 000	70 000
Current assets	40 000	20 000
	£70 000	£90 000
EBIT (after depreciation)	£24 000	£20 000
Return on total gross assets:	$\frac{24}{120} = 20\%$	$\frac{20}{100} = 20\%$
Return on net assets:	$\frac{24}{50} = 48\%$	$\frac{20}{80} = 25\%$

Profit and loss account

	1969	1970
	£m	
Sales	1355	1462
Trading profit	179[1]	151[1]
Investment income	19	18
	198	169
Less: Interest payable	31	35
Profit before tax	167	134
Taxation	74	52
Less: Investment grants	14	17
	60	35
Profit after tax	107	99
Minority interests	10	10
	97	89
Dividends paid and proposed:		
Preference	1	—
Ordinary	62	65
	63	65
Retained profit	£34	£24

	1969	1970
Depreciation charged	107	114
Loan interest payable	26	28

[1]After deducting £8 million employees' profit-sharing bonus (1969 £10 million)

Balance sheet

	1969	1970
	£m	
Fixed assets (net)	1016	1077
Goodwill	39	39
Interests in subsidiaries not consolidated	—	62
Interests in associated companies	118	112
	1173	1290
Current assets		
Stocks	309	321
Debtors	325	351
Cash	142	120
	776	792
Less: Current liabilities		
Creditors	325	330
Short-term borrowings	67	94
	392	424
	384	368
Net assets	£1557	£1658
Issued capital: ordinary	448	469
preference	8	8
Reserves	413	464
	869	941
Minority interests	113	117
Investment grants	68	81
Deferred and future taxation	95	77
Long-term loans	412	442
Capital employed	£1557	£1658

ANALYSIS OF ICI's 1970 ACCOUNTS

Having reminded ourselves of the problems of comparisons, especially between different companies, let us now consolidate the understanding gained from earlier sections by considering a further set of published company accounts.

The accounts for 1970 of Imperial Chemical Industries Limited are set out in summary form on the previous page. You are asked to analyse the accounts in a number of stages:

Investment measures
Measures of performance
Measures of financial status

The ratios for 1969 are calculated for you

After calculating each set of 1970 ratios, and comparing them with the same ratios for 1969, please check your answers with those shown on the following page. Please also read carefully the comments on the conclusions that can be drawn from the analysis.

Investment measures: ICI 1970 accounts

		1969	1970
Return on equity	$= \dfrac{\text{Profit for ordinary shareholders}}{\text{Ordinary capital + reserves}}$	$\dfrac{97 - 1^1}{448 + 413} = 10.0\%$ [1]Preference dividends	
Earnings per share	$= \dfrac{\text{Profit for ordinary shareholders}}{\text{Number of ordinary shares issued}}$	$\dfrac{96}{448} = 21.4\text{p}$	
Price/earnings ratio	$= \dfrac{\text{Market price per share}}{\text{Earnings per share}}$	$\dfrac{282^2}{21.4} = 13.2$ [2]Share price at year end	$\dfrac{240^2}{} =$
Dividend yield	$= \dfrac{\text{Dividend per share}}{\text{Market price per share}}$	$\dfrac{13.8}{282} = 4.9\%$	
Dividend cover	$= \dfrac{\text{Earnings per share}}{\text{Dividend per share}}$	$\dfrac{21.4}{13.8} = 1.6 \text{ times}$	

Investment measures

		1969	1970
Return on equity	$= \dfrac{\text{Profit for ordinary shareholders}}{\text{Ordinary capital} + \text{reserves}}$	$\dfrac{97 - 1}{448 + 413} = 10.0\%$	$\dfrac{89}{469 + 464} = 9.5\%$
Earnings per share	$= \dfrac{\text{Profit for ordinary shareholders}}{\text{Number of ordinary £1 shares issued}}$	$\dfrac{96}{448} = 21.4\text{p}$	$\dfrac{89}{469} = 19.0\text{p}$
Price/earnings ratio	$= \dfrac{\text{Market price per share}}{\text{Earnings per share}}$	$\dfrac{282}{21.4} = 13.2$	$\dfrac{240}{19.0} = 12.6$
Dividend yield	$= \dfrac{\text{Dividend per share}}{\text{Market price per share}}$	$\dfrac{13.8}{282} = 4.9\%$	$\dfrac{13.8}{240} = 5.7\%$
Dividend cover	$= \dfrac{\text{Earnings per share}}{\text{Dividend per share}}$	$\dfrac{21.4}{13.8} = 1.6$ times	$\dfrac{19.0}{13.8} = 1.4$ times

Comments:

The return on equity slightly worsened in 1970. At 9.5 per cent, it seems on the low side. Trading profits were 15 per cent down, but the tax charge (see Measures of Financial Status, p. 248) was 6½ percentage points less than in 1969, so profits after tax fell by only 7½ per cent.

Earnings per share fell by 11 per cent in 1970, while the dividend remained the same. Consequently the dividend cover fell slightly, to 1.4.

The market price per share fell by 15 per cent between the year-end dates, so the price/earnings ratio fell slightly, from 13.2 to 12.6, since earnings per share fell by 11 per cent. (By 31 December 1970, the ICI results for the three quarters ending 30 September would have been known in the market.)

To judge ICI's share price performance one needs to know how the rest of the market did in 1970. In fact the Financial Times Actuaries 500 Share Index fell by only 4 per cent, so ICI's shares did noticeably worse.

Since the dividend was maintained, the dividend yield rose from 4.9 per cent in 1969 to 5.7 per cent in 1970.

Note: In calculating return on equity, the base figure which we have used is ordinary capital + reserves. But what is the nature of the amount shown for investment grants? This represents amounts already received, which will be credited to the profit and loss account (by deduction from the tax charge) over the next few years. ICI credit the grants equally over ten years, the estimated average economic life of the relevant assets. It can be argued that this sum—£81 million at the end of 1970—should be added to the ordinary shareholders' equity (as is done by Moodies Services: see page 249). Obviously whether this adjustment is made or not, a consistent treatment must be applied from year to year.

Published share information

Information relating to ICI's share price has to be derived from a source other than the company's published accounts. Opposite is shown an extract from the *Financial Times* showing stock exchange and company information for 30 June 1971. This includes figures for ICI based on the accounts to 31 December 1970.

Reading from left to right, the first two columns show the "high" and "low" of the share price during 1971 so far (293p and 230p respectively for ICI). Then follows the name of the company (often abbreviated) and the nominal (par) value of the share quoted. (Where no amount is shown, the nominal value per share is 25p.) Then comes the closing market price per share on 30 June 1971—286p—and the change during the day, if any.

The dividend percentage of 13¾ relates to the *nominal* amount per share. Thus 13.75% × £1 = 13.75p, the same amount as that shown in our earlier analysis. The times covered (=dividend cover) is also the same, 1.4.

The final two columns relate to the closing market price each day. They differ from our earlier calculations because the market price per share has risen by 46p since 31 December, 1970. Gross yield per cent (=dividend yield) is obtained by dividing the dividend per share by the market price (13.8p/286p = 4.8 per cent). The P/E (price/earnings) ratio is obtained by dividing the market price by the earnings per share (286p/19.0p = 15.1).

Because the market price has *risen*, dividend yield (4.8 per cent) is now *less* than our calculated figure of 5.7 per cent; and the price/earnings ratio (15.1) is now *more* than our calculated figure of 12.6.

The *Financial Times* Thursday July 1 1971

F.T. SHARE INFORMATION SERVICE

1971 High	1971 Low	Stock	Closing Price	+ or −	Div. % or amount	Times covered	Gross yield pc	P/E Ratio
		CHEMICALS, PLASTICS, ETC.						
34	21	Albright Wils'n	25½	+½	2	U2.4	1.9	21.7
188	145	All'd Colloid 10p	158	—8	*h*25	3.1	1.6	20.5
86¼	65	Ancher Chem...	70	......	14.8	0.9	5.3	22.0
36	21¼	Ang.Am.Fbr10p	34	......	17½	1.8	5.2	10.7
56½	31	Ashe Chem. 5p.	52	+½	25	2·1	2.4	19.9
80	61	Ball (W. W.).....	73	—2	12	1.9	4.2	12.6
35½	16¼	Brent Chems10p	34	......	2½	5.3	0.7	26.5
107.	83½	Brit. Benzol 10p	99	+1	*b*30	2.7	3.0	12.4
30	20	Brit.TarPrd12½p	27½ xd	......	10	Φ	4.5	Φ
51	26¼	Broaley 10p....d	47	......	*h*22½	2.1	4.8	10.1
9¼	6¼	Burrell (5p)......	8¾	......	13½	1.7	7.7	7.5
117½	112½	Burt Boulton £1	117½	......	*t*4	—	3.4	—
95	55	Catalin	88	—2	22	2.0	6.2	8.0
81½	65	CoaliteChem10p	76	......	15	3.2	2.0	15.8
344	249⅜	Croda Int.........	336	......	32	2.3	2.4	18.5
21	11½	Crystalate 5p....	19½	+1¼	7½	2.1	1.9	24.7
55⅝	43	Enalon Plastics	47½	......	*d*22½	1.9	11.8	4.5
283	220	Fisons £1.........	270	......	10½	1.3	3.9	20.4
147½	110	Fordath	120	......	20	Φ	4.2	Φ
126	108	Glovers(Chems)	110	......	*h*18.2	1.9	4.1	12.9
332	251¼	HcksnWeich50p	332	......	17½	2.1	2.7	17.8
276¼	217½	Hoechst (Dm.5)	230	+5	20	1.4	♠	♠
46	33	HoltPr'ducts10p	34	......	20	1.5	5.9	11.4
293	**230**	**Imp. Chem. £1.**	**286**	....	**13¾**	**1.4**	**4.8**	**15.1**
54	50½	Do. 5pcPref.£1	50½	......	5	201.9	9.9	—
66	48¾	Kingsl'yKth10p	52	......	*u*32½	1.8	6.2	9.1
179⅜	142	Lankro Chem...	166 xd	......	20	Φ	3.0	Φ
148	91	LaportInds(50p)	94 xd	......	9.2	Φ	4.9	Φ
116¼	97	Philblack (50p).	110	—3	18	Φ	8.5	Φ
186	125	Plastic Coatings	184 xd	......	♦20	Φ	2.7	Φ
81½	51⅞	Plysu (10p).......	80	+2	*d*26	2.1	3.2	15.0
45	36	Ransom Wm.10p	43	......	24½	1.8	5.7	9.6
114	70	Rentokil (10p)...	113½	+1½	20	1.9	1.7	30.1
99	68	Revertex..........	95	—½	*b*22	1.2	5.8	14.2
73	56½	Stewart Plastics	66	......	*hd*15	1.8	5.7	9.7
41½	17½	Storey Bros......	37½	......	11	1.4	7.3	9.6
88	48	Sturge J. & E...	72	......	15	1.0	5.3	18.2
55	35	WillowsFrn (20p	50	......	—	—	—	—
174	110	Yorks. Dyeware	169 xd	+5	27	Φ	4.0	Φ
		CINEMAS, THEATRES AND TV						
,97	67½	Anglia TV 'A'...	92	......	30	1.2	8.2	9.9
180	126¼	Ass. Tele 'A'.....	156	......	28.5	*q*1.1	4.6	18.8
62	45	British Lion.....	47	......	17	1.0	9.0	10.8
36	17	Grampian'A'10p	31	+3	25	1.6	8.1	7.7
339	235	Granada 'A'......	327	......	40	1.4	3 0	23.1
44	27½	H'w'rdWy'd20p	42	—2	—	—	—	—
87	52½	Redifus'n Tv £1	73 xd	—1½	6½	3.7	8.7	—
40	25	Scott TV 'A' 10p	34	......	—	—	—	—
49	21⅞	TridentTV'A10p	43½	......	*b*15	2.2	3.1	14.4
43	25	Ulster TV 'A'—	41	......	12	1.2	7.3	11.4
21	15	W'stwardTV10p	20	......	*t*20	1.2	10.3	14.6
		DRAPERY AND STORES						
33	11⅞	AndreBern'd10p	33	......	10	Φ	3.0	Φ
30	25	Aquascutum 5p.	30	......	28	1.3	4.7	16.0
29½	20	Do. 'A' 5p......	29½	......	28	1.3	4.8	15.3
222½	177½	Army&Navy50p	207	......	13½	1.3	3.3	23.4
25	15	Baker's Strs. 10p	24	......	8	2.6	3.3	11.4
81¼	47½	Beattie (J.) 'A'..	79	+4	*h*13⅓	2.1	4.2	11.3
17	10	Benleys 10p ✠..	14	.....	‡*d*6	—	—	—
43	24	Benson'sHy.10p	33½	—½	18	2.2	5.4	8.5
80	64	Bentalls 10p.....	72	......	30	1.5	4.2	16.0

IMPERIAL CHEMICAL INDUSTRIES LIMITED

1970 Group Accounts

Profit and loss account

	1969	1970
	£m	
Sales	£1355	£1462
Trading profit	179[1]	151[1]
Investment income	19	18
	198	169
Less: Interest payable	31	35
Profit before tax	167	134
Taxation	74	52
Less: Investment grants	14	17
	60	35
Profit after tax	107	99
Minority interests	10	10
	97	89
Dividends paid and proposed:		
Preference	1	—
Ordinary	62	65
	63	65
Retained profit	£34	£24

	1969	1970
Depreciation charged	107	114
Loan interest payable	26	28

[1]After deducting £8 million employees' profit-sharing bonus (1969 £10 million)

Balance sheet

	1969	1970
	£m	
Fixed assets (net)	1016	1077
Goodwill	39	39
Interests in subsidiaries not consolidated	—	62
Interests in associated companies	118	112
	1173	1290
Current assets		
Stocks	309	321
Debtors	325	351
Cash	142	120
	776	792
Less: Current liabilities		
Creditors	325	330
Short-term borrowings	67	94
	392	424
	384	368
Net assets	£1557	£1658
Issued capital: ordinary	448	469
preference	8	8
Reserves	413	464
	869	941
Minority interests	113	117
Investment grants	68	81
Deferred and future taxation	95	77
Long-term loans	412	442
Capital employed	£1557	£1658

Please calculate the following ratios for 1970 on the same basis as those for 1969. Answers and comments are on the next page.

Measures of performance: ICI 1970 accounts		1969	1970
Return on net assets	$= \dfrac{\text{EBIT}}{\text{Net assets}}$	$\dfrac{167 + 26 + 14^{1}}{1557} = 13.3\%$	
Profit margin	$= \dfrac{\text{EBIT}}{\text{Net sales}}$	$\dfrac{167 + 26 + 14^{1}}{1355} = 15.3\%$	
Net asset turnover	$= \dfrac{\text{Sales}}{\text{Net assets}}$	$\dfrac{1355}{1557} = 0.87 \text{ times}$	
Fixed asset turnover	$= \dfrac{\text{Sales}}{\text{Fixed assets}}$	$\dfrac{1355}{1016} = 1.33 \text{ times}$	
Stock turnover	$= \dfrac{\text{Sales}}{\text{Stocks}}$	$\dfrac{1355}{309} = 4.39 \text{ times}$	
Debtor turnover	$= \dfrac{\text{Sales}}{\text{Debtors}}$	$\dfrac{1355}{325} = 4.17 \text{ times}$	

[1]ICI show the investment grants as reducing the tax charge. The alternative treatment would reduce the depreciation charge instead. So the investment grants have here been added back to the profit before tax figure (which is calculated *after* charging depreciation).

Measures of performance

		1969	1970
Return on net assets	$= \dfrac{\text{EBIT}}{\text{Net assets}}$	$\dfrac{167 + 26 + 14}{1557} = 13.3\%$	$\dfrac{134 + 28 + 17}{1658} = 10.8\%$
Profit margin	$= \dfrac{\text{EBIT}}{\text{Net sales}}$	$\dfrac{167 + 26 + 14}{1355} = 15.3\%$	$\dfrac{134 + 28 + 17}{1462} = 12.2\%$
Net asset turnover	$= \dfrac{\text{Sales}}{\text{Net assets}}$	$\dfrac{1355}{1557} = 0.87$ times	$\dfrac{1462}{1658} = 0.88$ times
Fixed asset turnover	$= \dfrac{\text{Sales}}{\text{Fixed assets}}$	$\dfrac{1355}{1016} = 1.33$ times	$\dfrac{1462}{1077} = 1.36$ times
Stock turnover	$= \dfrac{\text{Sales}}{\text{Stocks}}$	$\dfrac{1355}{309} = 4.39$ times	$\dfrac{1462}{321} = 4.55$ times
Debtor turnover	$= \dfrac{\text{Sales}}{\text{Debtors}}$	$\dfrac{1355}{325} = 4.17$ times	$\dfrac{1462}{351} = 4.17$ times

Comments:

The return on net assets is considerably lower in 1970 than in 1969. This is due to the group's profit margins falling with a similar level of asset turnover:

1969: $15.3\% \times 0.87 = 13.3\%$
1970: $12.2\% \times 0.88 = 10.8\%$

The fall of £28 million in profits before interest and tax (EBIT) is due to reduced profit margins on increased sales volume. The 15.3 per cent *old* profit margin on the *increase* in sales volume (£107 million) gives £16 million extra profit due to sales volume. But the 3.1 per cent *fall* in profit margin on the *old* sales volume (£1355 million) gives £42 million less profit due to profit margin worsening.

The balance of £2 million is due to the reduction in profit margin on the increase in sales volume (3.1% × £107 million), and cannot easily be apportioned between them. (We have "lost" £1 million on rounding.)

Note: In calculating the return on net assets we have treated the short-term borrowing as a current liability, following the balance sheet presentation. If the fairly large sums involved are considered to represent *medium-term* capital (an approach adopted by Moodies Services) they should then be treated as part of capital employed (as discussed in section 2). In that case, two adjustments would be required:

1 Increase net assets by reducing the deduction for current liabilities (1970 £94 million).
2 Increase EBIT by adding back interest on "short-term borrowing" (1970 £7 million).

In fact, both in 1969 and 1970 short-term borrowings of the group were more than matched by short-term deposits.

Analysis of sales and profit by classes of business

In addition to trends over time, another very important factor in analysing profit margins is changes in sales mix. Where a company is engaged in more than one kind of business, it is not unusual for there to be significant changes from year to year in the separate parts. Where the results of some are improving and others are declining, the total figure may inadequately reflect what is happening, and the analyst must seek to identify and analyse the more detailed results.

ICI carries on a variety of businesses, and sales and profit figures for the individual classes are included in the directors' report, and have been set out on the right. On the right-hand side the profit margin percentage for each class has been calculated. A study of the percentages shows that although overall profit margins have fallen by about one fifth, there are much sharper falls for fibres and dyes and for Imperial Metal Industries. Similarly, the overall sales volume increase of 8 per cent is made up of a 5 per cent increase in United Kingdom sales (less than the 1970 rise in the Retail Price Index) and a 12½ per cent increase in the sales of overseas subsidiaries.

Inside ICI, no doubt managers analyse these figures in much greater detail. For example, the £400 million sales and the £52 million trading profits for chemicals and plastics could be broken down, to give detailed profitability ratios right down to the level of individual product lines.

Another kind of detailed analysis, which would require information not available in the accounts or notes, would be to divide the capital employed over the types of business for which sales and profit figures have been given. This would permit the calculation of the return on net assets for each class of business.

Notice the deduction for inter-company (intra-group) sales. Clearly the transfer pricing policy could affect the split of profits between subsidiaries, and possibly disguise their real profitability.

Analysis of sales and profits between classes of business

	Sales 1969	Sales 1970	Trading profit 1969	Trading profit 1970	(calculated) Profit margin 1969	Profit margin 1970
	£m		£m		%	
United Kingdom						
Agricultural	145	157	8	10	6	6
Chemicals and plastics	371	400	62	52	17	13
Fibres and dyes	225	233	35	19	16	8
Paints	52	56	6	6	12	11
Pharmaceuticals	25	28	10	10	40	36
Imperial Metal Industries Ltd	188	208	18	11	10	5
Miscellaneous	27	—	—	1	—	—
	1033	1082	139	109	13	10
Overseas subsidiaries						
Australasia	152	164	16	17	11	10
Europe	123	139	12	10	10	7
North America	146	160	12	9	8	6
Other countries	112	137	11	14	10	10
	533	600	51	50	10	8
Less: Inter-class sales	(211)	(220)				
Total	1355	1462	190	159	14	11

IMPERIAL CHEMICAL INDUSTRIES LIMITED
1970 Group Accounts

Profit and loss account

	1969	1970
	£m	
Sales	1355	1462
Trading profit	179[1]	151[1]
Investment income	19	18
	198	169
Less: Interest payable	31	35
Profit before tax	167	134
Taxation	74	52
Less: Investment grants	14	17
	60	35
Profit after tax	107	99
Minority interests	10	10
	97	89
Dividends paid and proposed:		
Preference	1	—
Ordinary	62	65
	63	65
Retained profit	£ 34	£24

Depreciation charged	107	114
Loan interest payable	26	28

[1]After deducting £8m employees' profit-sharing bonus (1969 £10m)

Balance sheet

	1969	1970
	£m	
Fixed assets (net)	1016	1077
Goodwill	39	39
Interests in subsidiaries not consolidated	—	62
Interests in associated companies	118	112
	1173	1290
Current assets		
Stocks	309	321
Debtors	325	351
Cash	142	120
	776	792
Less: Current liabilities		
Creditors	325	330
Short-term borrowings	67	94
	392	424
	384	368
Net assets	£1557	£1658
Issued capital: ordinary	448	469
preference	8	8
Reserves	413	464
	869	941
Minority interests	113	117
Investment grants	68	81
Deferred and future taxation	95	77
Long-term loans	412	442
Capital employed	£1557	£1658

Please calculate the 1970 ratios and compare them with the 1969 ratios below. Then compare your answers and conclusions with those shown overleaf.

Measures of financial status: ICI 1970 accounts	1969	1970
Debt ratio $= \dfrac{\text{Long-term loans}}{\text{Capital employed}}$	$\dfrac{412}{1557} = 26.5\%$	
Interest cover $= \dfrac{\text{EBIT}}{\text{Long-term interest}}$	$\dfrac{167 + 26 + 14}{26} = 8.0 \text{ times}$	
Current ratio $= \dfrac{\text{Current assets}}{\text{Current liabilities}}$	$\dfrac{776}{392} = 1.98 \text{ times}$	
Acid test $= \dfrac{\text{Liquid assets}}{\text{Current liabilities}}$	$\dfrac{776 - 309}{392} = 1.19 \text{ times}$	
Tax ratio $= \dfrac{\text{Tax charged}}{\text{Profit before tax}}$	$\dfrac{74}{167 + 14^{1}} = 40.9\%$	

[1]Investment grants

Measures of financial status

		1969	1970
Debt ratio	$=\dfrac{\text{Long-term loans}}{\text{Capital employed}}$	$\dfrac{412}{1557} = 26.5\%$	$\dfrac{442}{1658} = 26.7\%$
Interest cover	$=\dfrac{\text{EBIT}}{\text{Long-term interest}}$	$\dfrac{167 + 26 + 14}{26} = 8.0$ times	$\dfrac{134 + 28 + 17}{28} = 6.4$ times
Current ratio	$=\dfrac{\text{Current assets}}{\text{Current liabilities}}$	$\dfrac{776}{392} = 1.98$ times	$\dfrac{792}{424} = 1.87$ times
Acid test	$=\dfrac{\text{Liquid assets}}{\text{Current liabilities}}$	$\dfrac{776 - 309}{392} = 1.19$ times	$\dfrac{792 - 321}{424} = 1.11$ times
Tax ratio	$=\dfrac{\text{Tax charged}}{\text{Profit before tax}}$	$\dfrac{74}{167 + 14^1} = 40.9\%$	$\dfrac{52}{134 + 17^1} = 34.4\%$

[1]Investment grants

Comments:

The debt ratio remained virtually the same as in 1969, but the fall in profits led to a decline in interest cover, from 8.0 times to 6.4 times.

The current ratio and acid test both declined slightly, but still indicate a reasonable cover for current liabilities. It should be noted that deferred tax of £77 million consists of £39 million tax equalisation and £38 million corporation tax payable on 1 January 1972 (a year and a day after the balance sheet date). If this latter figure had been included as a *current* liability, the acid test would decline to 1.02.

The investment grants have again been added back to profits before tax, in calculating the tax ratio; and the tax figure gross of investment grants has been used. Even though ICI uses a tax equalisation account (see section 5), there are several reasons why the tax ratio is not exactly equal to 42.5 per cent. Adjustments to previous years' figures (the corporation tax rate is announced retrospectively) may affect the charge in the current year, and overseas tax rates may differ from UK rates. The aim is to identify whether such factors are non-recurring or are likely to be a regular feature.

Trends

We have been comparing the results of only 2 years. Such a comparison minimises distortions due to varying accounting treatment of items, but is still narrowly based. The Moodies card for ICI, part of which is illustrated opposite, shows trends over 10 years.

The figures differ from our results, as we have already noted, in respect of investment grants and short-term borrowings, but the treatment is consistent throughout. The break which occurs in some of the equity trends in 1965 results from company tax changes in that year, and 1964 figures have been re-calculated on the new basis as well. Notice how Moodies show turnover and pre-tax profits as a percentage of "capital employed" both including and excluding goodwill.

The chart below shows the profit margin and return on net assets over the 10 years. It is of interest, in analysing ICI's 1970 accounts, to identify at what point in the rather regular 4-year cycle the company seems to be.

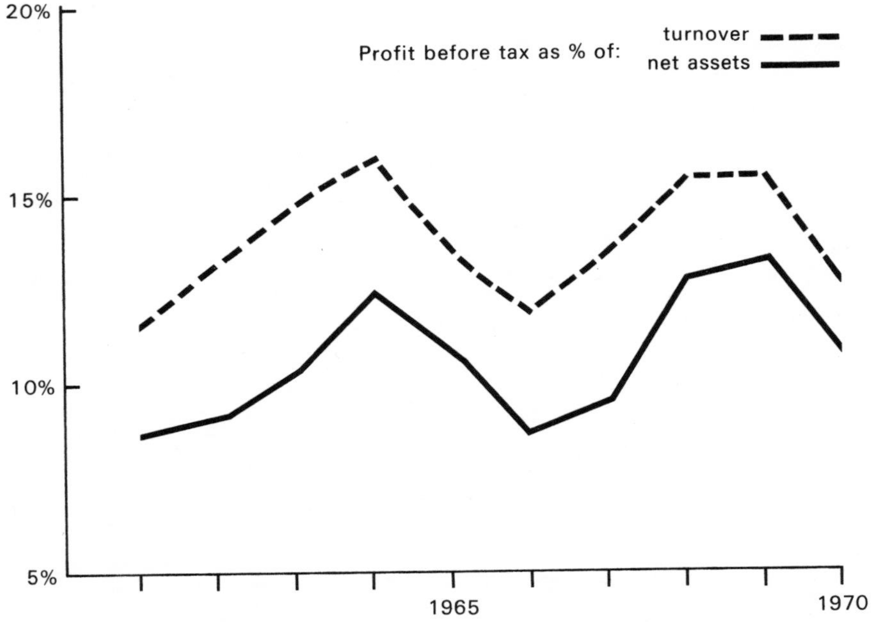

IMPERIAL CHEMICAL INDUSTRIES

IMPERIAL CHEMICAL INDUSTRIES LIMITED

HISTORICAL RECORD ADJUSTED - WHERE APPLICABLE - TO ALLOW FOR SHARE BONUSES AND RIGHTS ISSUES MADE DURING PERIOD COVERED

CAPITAL EMPLOYED - SOURCES AND GROWTH (£m's)

YEARS END 31st Dec.	GROUP LIABILITIES: LONG TERM DEBT: BANKERS	OTHER	TOTAL	%	OUTSIDE SHARE-HOLDERS	%	FUTURE TAX & OTHER PROVS.	%	PARENT COMPANY SHAREHOLDERS' INTEREST: ISSUED PREF. CAP.	%	ORD. HOLDERS' FUNDS: ISSUED CAP.	RESERVES CAP.	RESERVES REV.	*** TOTAL	%	TOTAL CAPITAL EMPLOYED
1966	54.2c	272.5c	326.7	25	73.6	6	71.8	6	34.7	3	441.5	184.2	148.7	774.4	60	1281.2c
1967	56.6c	350.7c	407.3	28	94.2	7	85.9	6	34.7	2	444.2	187.6	182.7	814.5	57	1436.6c
1968	57.2c	380.6c	437.8	28	105.1	7	106.5	7	34.7	2	446.1	---417.8---		863.9	56	1548.0c
1969	63.5c	414.7c	478.2	29	113.0	7	95.1	6	8.6	1	448.0	---482.7---		930.7	57	1625.6c
1970	76.4c	459.9	536.3	30	116.8	7	77.3	4	8.6	1	468.7	---544.5---		1013.2	58	1752.2c

CAPITAL EMPLOYED - HOW USED (£m's)

YEARS END 31st Dec.	FIXED ASSETS LESS DEPREC. & AMOUNTS W. O.: PROPERTY	PLANT ETC.	TRADE INV.	OTHER	TOTAL	CURRENT ASSETS: CASH & EQUIV.	STK. & W.I.P.	DEBTORS	TOTAL	CURRENT LIABILITIES: DUE BANKERS	DIVS. & TAX	CREDITORS	TOTAL	NET CURRENT ASSETS	RATIO CURRENT ASSETS / LIABS.	TOTAL ASSETS EXCL. G'WILL.	GOODWILL	TOTAL CAPITAL EMPLOYED
1966	194.7	684.0	118.9	1.5	991.1	50.0	195.8	197.7	443.5	54.2	59.0	160.4	273.6	169.9	1.6	1169.0	38.7	1207.7
1967	208.0	738.0	118.0	Nil	1064.0	109.2	226.4	234.4	570.0	56.6	75.5	166.7	298.8	271.2	1.9	133.5	38.7	1373.9
1968	215.3	757.2	110.8	Nil	1083.3	155.3	261.6	289.3	706.2	57.2	104.7	182.0	343.9	362.3	2.1	1445.6	38.7	1484.3
1969	217.0	799.1	117.8	Nil	1133.9	141.6	308.8	325.4	775.8	63.5	126.0	200.0	389.5	386.3	2.0	1520.2	38.7	1558.9
1970	231.3	845.2	174.3	Nil	1250.8	120.4	321.3	351.0	792.7	76.4	112.5	235.4	424.3	368.4	1.9	1619.2	38.7	1657.9

PROFITABILITY TREND - CASH FLOW - CAPITAL COMMITMENTS

YEARS END 31st Dec.	CAPITAL EMPLOYED (£m's	TURNOVER £m's	TURNOVER AS % CAP. EMPL. INCL. G'WILL.	EXCL. G'WILL.	PRE-TAX PROFITS BEFORE INTEREST £m's	AS % CAP. EMPL. INCL. G'WILL.	EXCL. G'WILL.	AS % OF TURNOVER	(£m's AFTER INTEREST	TAX RATIO TAX CHARGED £m's	AS % OF PROFIT AFTER INT.	CASH FLOW (£m's) RETAINED PROFIT	DEPREC.	TOTAL	CAPITAL COMMITMENTS £000's
1961	738.5	550.4	75		64.6	8.7		11.7	61.9	27.7	45	8.9	40.5	49.4	36.3
1962	842.9	578.9	69		76.9	9.1		13.3	70.4	32.0	45	12.3	44.5	56.8	30.9
1963	893.2	624.1	70		92.9	10.4		14.9	84.9	41.6	49	14.2	54.2	68.4	46.0
1964	966.0	720.2	75	78	115.8	12.0	12.5	16.1	108.4	47.2	44	24.5	61.3	85.8	103.0
1965	1041.7†	815.9	78	81	110.0	10.6	11.0	13.5	101.1	23.4	23	40.6	68.8	109.4	95.0
1966	1251.2†c	885.2	71	73	107.2	8.6	8.8	12.1	90.2	32.2	36	3.1	72.3j	79.9	74.0
1967	1436.6c	978.8	68	70	133.6	9.3	9.6	13.6	108.0	47.0	44	Dr. 1.1	80.6j	121.5a	53.0
1968	1548.0c	1237.3	80	82	193.1	12.5	12.8	15.6	163.5	72.1	44	23.9	94.5j	149.4a	63.0
1969	1625.6c	1355.1	83	85	212.7	13.1	13.4	15.7	181.2	69.2	38	38.7	92.6j	162.7a	61.0
1970	1752.2c	1462.4	83	85	186.5	10.6	10.9	12.8	151.8	55.0	36	21.9	96.5j	148.8a	82.0

DISTRIBUTION - EQUITY SHARE RECORDS ORD. STOCK (£1)

YEARS END 31st Dec.	DISTRIBUTION PRIORITY PER CENT: FXD. CHGS.	PREF. DIV.	ORD. DIV.	EARNED %	EARNED PER SH. Pence	DIVIDEND PAID %	PER SH. Pence	TIMES COVERED	ERNGS. AS % OF EQUITY ASSETS	NET ‡‡ ASSETS PER SH.	SHARE PRICES CALENDAR YEAR HIGH (Pence)	LOW (Pence)	PRICE/EARNINGS RATIO	YIELD RATIO ERNGS.	DIV.	NOTES
1961	2½	5½	73	12.8*	12.8	9.2	9.2	1.4	8.9	143	276	181	17.8		87	
1962	8	11	69	14.1*	14.1	9.2	9.2	1.5	9.6	147	207	157	12.9		89	
1963	9	11	68	15.6*	15.6	10.0	10.0	1.6	10.1	155	254	179	13.9		90	
1964	5½	7½	60	22.1*	22.1	12.5	12.5	1.8	13.6	162	248	205	10.2		92	
				16.5*	16.5			1.3	10.2				13.7			
1965	2½	5	77	16.3*	16.3	12.5	12.5	1.3	9.3	175	246	209	12.8e		104	
1966	7	10	106	11.6	11.6	12.5	12.5	0.9	6.6	175	226	165	14.8e		115	
1967	11	14	102	12.2	12.2	12.5	12.5	1.0	6.7	183	268	169	21.0e	74	99	
1968	8	10	74	18.3	18.3	12.9	12.9	1.4	9.4	194	373	234	16.4e	91	95	
1969	7	8	66	22.4	22.4	13.8	13.8	1.6	10.8	208	368	261	12.0e	106	97	
1970	8½	9	77	18.4	18.4	13.8	13.8	1.3	8.5	216	294	208	12.9e	87	94	

* After allowing for Profit sharing scheme only to extent of amt. charged in accounts. † Excls. "25.0" 7¼% Ln. Stk. in '65 & "30.0" 8% Unsec. Ln. Stk. in '66. ‡‡ Incls. G'will if any. (a) Incls. "42.0" in '67 & "31.0" in '68, "31.6" in '69. "30.4" in '70 Invest. Grants. (c) Incls. current Bank Debt (see current liabs.) & current Accept. Credits. (e) Based on prices at issue of A/cs (prev. yearly average). (j). After deducting years. proportion of Invest. Grants credited to P & L A/c

General comments

What other comments can be made about ICI's performance in 1970 and its position at the end of the year? A good deal of additional information is included in the notes to the published accounts and in the directors' report.

Fixed assets

ICI revalued the major part of its fixed assets in 1958, adding at that time £68 million to their net book value, and reducing the apparent return on net assets from about 9 per cent to about 8 per cent. What would be the result of a further revaluation in 1970? The figures are not available to make this calculation.

Goodwill

Goodwill has been charged against reserves, except that arising from the acquisition of British Nylon Spinners in 1964. If that amount, £39 million, were written off against reserves, it would reduce 1970 capital employed by about 2½ per cent. Writing the goodwill off against profit over 10 years would reduce profits after tax by about £4 million a year. (In fact the whole £39 million was written off against reserves in 1971.)

Interests in subsidiaries not consolidated

During 1970 the ICI Group acquired a 64 per cent holding in the equity capital of Carrington Viyella. ICI intends to reduce its holding to not more than 35 per cent as soon as practicable, but not to exercise more votes meanwhile than if the reduction had occurred. Therefore the accounts of this subsidiary have not been consolidated.

Net tangible assets attributable to ICI's shareholding were about £38 million at 31 December 1970, and the market value of the shares, based on the stock exchange quotation at the same date, was £24 million. No provision has been made for any loss in respect of this investment.

Current assets

Stocks have risen by only 4 per cent, compared with an increase of 8 per cent in sales, which accounts for the increase in the stock turnover ratio from 4.39 to 4.55. (It must be remembered, of course, that stock will provide *future* sales, so that a direct comparison with *past* sales may not always be helpful, even if the cost of past sales—rather than their selling price—were used.)

In valuing stocks, depreciation and certain other overhead expenses are excluded. If depreciation had been included, possibly a further £30 million (about 10 per cent) could have been added to the book value of stocks.

Investment grants

Investment grants are credited to a deferred revenue account in the balance sheet, and credited to profit and loss account (as a deduction from the tax charge) on the straight line basis over 10 years, the estimated average life of the relevant fixed assets. Grants are credited only when actually received, not when they become due, so it might be argued that there is a "hidden" asset of £33 million in respect of grants receivable at 31 December 1970.

These are some of the additional items of information which the analyst needs to bear in mind when interpreting the accounts. The amounts considered under each of the headings are significant in relation to both balance sheet and profit and loss account totals, and different accounting treatment could significantly affect the reported results.

FUNDS STATEMENTS

The two main conventional accounting statements are the profit and loss account for a period and the balance sheet at the end of the period. We mentioned earlier that businesses need to consider their liquidity position as well as their profitability, and in recent years there has been a growing use of funds statements which aim to show major changes in sources and uses of funds during an accounting period. Some people think that eventually the funds statement will be a regular third statement in the accounting "package."

The simplest form of funds statement, which we looked at in section 2, is prepared by merely listing the differences in a firm's balance sheet between two dates. In this section we are going to see what adjustments are necessary to such a statement of "balance sheet changes" in order to obtain a more informative idea of the actual sources and uses of funds during the period concerned.

It should be understood that only limited information is available in the published accounts, and companies preparing their own funds statements will have access to more details than an outside analyst. It is to be expected, therefore, that an internally prepared funds statement will usually not be identical with a funds statement prepared from published balance sheets, even after taking into account the adjustments to be discussed on the next few pages.

One further warning is in order. Terminology varies a good deal in this area, and it is often necessary to take some care to ensure that it is understood precisely what a particular "funds statement" is covering. In particular the expression "cash flow" is widely used without always being widely understood. It is usually meant to apply to a rather simple derivation from published profit and loss accounts, with two alternative definitions. "Cash flow" for a year generally means either:

(*a*) profits available for ordinary shareholders plus depreciation charged,

or

(*b*) retained earnings for the year plus depreciation charged.

It will be seen that the difference between these two definitions is the amount of ordinary dividends payable in respect of the period.

The funds statements we are about to examine contain more detail than the above rather crude single number representing "cash flow," and, we suggest, will as a rule be more useful. As usual with accounting statements, however, one needs to bear in mind the *purpose* for which the statement is being prepared.

Let us now turn to the preparation of a detailed funds statement for a company, Harris and Clark Limited, whose accounts are set out overleaf.

251

HARRIS AND CLARK LIMITED
Balance sheet, 31 December 1972

	£ m	
	1972	1971
Ordinary share capital	120	100
Reserves	155	135
Shareholders' funds	275	235
Loans	125	110
Capital employed	£400	£345
Fixed assets (net)	240	215
Investments	40	30
Working capital		
Stock	100	80
Debtors	85	75
Cash	45	40
	230	195
Less: Creditors*	110	95
	120	100
Net assets	£400	£345

*Including tax liability   25   15

HARRIS AND CLARK LIMITED
Profit and loss account, 1972

	£ m	
	1972	1971
Sales	510	460
Cost of goods sold*	440	415
Trading profit	70	45
Interest payable	15	10
Profit before tax	55	35
Taxation	25	15
Profit after tax	30	20
Ordinary dividends	20	15
Retained profits	£10	£ 5

*Including depreciation   35   30

Simple funds statement

The individual differences between the two balance sheets at 31 December 1971 and 1972 can easily be grouped in the form set out below, to give a simple funds statement for 1972:

HARRIS AND CLARK LIMITED

Simple funds statement, 1972   £m

Sources of funds

Ordinary capital issued	20
Reserves	20
Loans	15
	£55

Uses of funds

Fixed assets (net)	25
Investments	10
Working capital	20
	£55

Only the net changes have been shown, with the figures for current assets and current liabilities brought together in a single "working capital" figure. If it is thought desirable, the individual details can be shown:

		£m
Uses of funds:	Stocks	20
	Debtors	10
	Cash	5
		35
Less: Creditors	(Sources of funds)	15
Net use: Increase in working capital		£20

In several important areas the figures above represent "net balances", which cover larger sources and uses of funds. A more useful funds statement can be drawn up by expanding the net balances in the following areas:
1 Share capital and dividends
2 Depreciation of fixed assets
3 Disposal of fixed assets

1. Share capital and dividends

A note to the accounts will analyse the £20 million increase in reserves, let us say as follows. Share premium £10 million + retained profit £10 million.

(a) Share premiums

As we saw in section 6, share premiums represent amounts received in excess of the nominal value of share capital issued. So we must add the £10 million share premiums to the £20 million increase in nominal share capital shown in the simple funds statement, to record the total inflow of £30 million from issuing ordinary share capital in 1972.

(b) Dividend payments

The source of funds represented by the £10 million retained profit is only part of the movement in funds. The total movements were:

Profit £30 million less ordinary dividends £20 million.

We can incorporate the items dealt with above in the adjusted funds statement shown below:

HARRIS AND CLARK LIMITED

Adjusted funds statement, 1972—Stage 1

		£m
Sources of funds		
Ordinary capital issued (20 + 10)		30*
Funds from profit	30	
Less: Ordinary dividends paid	20	10*
Loans		15
		£55
Uses of funds		
Fixed assets (net)		25
Investments		10
Working capital		20
		£55

---

*Items that have changed

253

2. Depreciation of fixed assets

In our original simple funds statement, increased fixed assets showed as a £25 million use of funds. This figure is the net result of recording acquisitions at cost, deducting disposals in the year, and charging depreciation. Detailed figures in the notes to the accounts might show:

	1971	1972	Change
	£m	£m	£m
Gross fixed assets at cost	375	425	+ 50
Accumulated depreciation	160	185	+ 25
Net book value	215	240	+ 25

A more accurate figure for the increased investment in fixed assets is thus £50 million rather than the original £25 million. What is the source of the £25 million difference? Accumulated depreciation.

As explained in section 5, depreciation is not really a source of funds: it is a book-keeping entry allocating part of the historical cost of fixed assets as an expense in a particular accounting period. While a proper (and necessary) charge against profit, depreciation is not a drain on funds like most other expense items. (The use of funds occurs when the fixed assets are purchased.)

Thus the source of funds from operations is *understated* by taking only profit after charging depreciation. For funds statements, therefore, we "add back" the depreciation charge, treating it *as if* it were a source of funds. A similar amount (£25 million here) is added to the additions of fixed assets figure (a *use* of funds). Again the adjustments are incorporated below (left).

3 Disposal of fixed assets

In the previous column we added back £25 million to the net investment in fixed assets, representing the increase in accumulated depreciation. Why is this figure not the same as the £35 million depreciation charged in the profit and loss account? What has happened to the £10 million difference?

In the absence of more information one would normally assume the difference to be accumulated depreciation on fully written-down assets sold during the year (on disposal both the cost and accumulated depreciation figures would be reduced by the same amount). In the funds statement we would then add £10 million to both the depreciation and additions to fixed assets figures.

HARRIS AND CLARK LIMITED
Adjusted funds statement, 1972—Stage 2

		£ m
Sources of funds		
Ordinary capital issued		30
Funds from profit	30	
Add: Depreciation	25	
Funds from operations	55	
Less: Ordinary dividends paid	20	
		35*
Loans		15
		£80
Uses of funds		
Fixed asset additions (25 + 25)		50*
Investments		10
Working capital		20
		£80

*Items that have changed

HARRIS AND CLARK LIMITED
Adjusted funds statement, 1972—Stage 3

		£ m
Sources of funds		
Ordinary capital issued		30
Funds from profit	30	
Add: Depreciation (25 + 10)	35*	
Funds from operations	65*	
Less: Ordinary dividends paid	20	
		45*
Loans		15
		£90
Uses of funds		
Fixed asset additions (50 + 10)		60*
Investments		10
Working capital		20
		£90

*Items that have changed

Presentation of funds statements

There are several possible ways of presenting funds statements. The one chosen depends partly on personal preference and partly on the purpose for which the statement is required. In any presentation one would normally combine minor items where possible, in order to highlight the more significant items. It is a common mistake on all kinds of financial statements and reports to try to present too much information on a single sheet of paper, with the result that not even the important facts are properly communicated.

In a funds statement all the balance sheet figures are covered. The statement may list details of movements in working capital—that is, stocks, debtors, creditors, and so on—or it may deal with working capital as a single figure, as we have done earlier, showing in detail only the movements in the long-term, "permanent" capital and assets. It may, following the alternative presentation which we illustrated in looking at the Marks and Spencer accounts in section 2 (problem 3), be arranged to account for the change in the working capital figure between the beginning and end of the year.

On the next pages we show four possible styles of presentation, to give an idea of the variables:

Style A: follows balance sheet layout
Style B: distinguishes internal and external sources
Style C: highlights working capital change
Style D: highlights cash change

It is not possible to say definitely that one style is "better" than others. Funds statements in annual reports are still a fairly recent phenomenon, with only about one in five companies including a form of funds statement in 1970/71, and no particular style has yet won general acceptance.

Whichever form of presentation is used, matters revealed may include:

1 How much long-term capital is obtained from debt and how much from shareholders.

2 How new capital issued compares with funds retained from operations.

3 What proportion of profits available is paid out in dividends.

4 To what extent "depreciation funds" suffice to finance new acquisitions of fixed assets.

5 The relative importance of working capital and fixed assets as uses of funds.

It can also be very useful to prepare funds statements for longer periods than a year. Differences which may not appear very dramatic from year to year can make a significant cumulative change to a firm's balance sheet over a period of five or ten years. Further, funds flow analysis can be extended to cover *future* periods as well as those which are past. Such an analysis can greatly assist managers in their financial planning by highlighting the periods in which more long-term capital—equity or debt—will be required. If, for some reason, raising such capital seems likely to be difficult, planning ahead gives warning in good time that projected expenditure may need to be cut back.

FUNDS STATEMENT: STYLE A
—follows balance sheet layout

	£ m	
Sources of funds		
Equity: Ordinary capital issued	30	
Retained profits	10	40
Loans		15
		£55
Uses of funds		
Fixed assets	60	
Less: Depreciation	35	25
Investments		10
Working capital		
Stock	20	
Debtors	10	
Cash	5	
	35	
Less: Creditors	15	20
		£55

FUNDS STATEMENT: STYLE B
—distinguishes internal and external sources

	£ m	
Sources of funds		
External: Ordinary capital issued	30	
Loans	15	45
Internal: Profit	30	
Add: Depreciation	35	
Funds from operations	65	
Less: Ordinary dividends	20	45*
		£90
Uses of funds		
Fixed assets		60
Investments		10
Working capital		20
		£90

*This figure—retained profits (£10 million) plus depreciation (£35 million)—is sometimes called "cash flow:" it refers only to *internal* sources of funds, but can simply be calculated from the published profit and loss account.

FUNDS STATEMENT: STYLE C
—highlights working capital change

		£ m
Sources of funds		
Ordinary capital issued		30
Profit		30
Depreciation		35
Loans		15
		110
Less:		
Uses of funds		
Fixed assets	60	
Investments	10	
Dividends paid	20	
		90
Increase in working capital =		£20

FUNDS STATEMENT: STYLE D
—highlights cash change

		£ m
Sources of funds		
Sales		510
Less: Cash expenses*		445*
		65
Ordinary capital issued		30
Loans		15
Creditors		15
		125
Less:		
Uses of funds		
Dividends	20	
Fixed assets	60	
Investments	10	
Stocks	20	
Debtors	10	
		120
Increase in cash		£ 5

*Excluding depreciation: 440 + 15 + 25 − 35

SUMMARY

In this section we have reconsidered some of the problems of accrual account-ing, and listed some of the matters which need attention in trying to interpret accounts.

We then worked through an analysis of ICI's 1970 accounts. We calculated

Investment measures
Measures of performance
Measures of financial status

and compared the results for 1970 with those for 1969. We incorporated in our analysis information taken from the accounts, the notes, and the directors' report. We also used external "market" information taken from the financial press, and saw how analyses prepared by an investment service, indicating results over a number of years, can be used to provide additional details and trends of great interest. We then noted some items in respect of which possible different accounting treatment would have made a significant difference to ICI's reported figures.

Finally we prepared a detailed funds statement showing the major sources and uses of funds in the year. We started with simple balance sheet differences, and made a number of the most important common adjustments in order to provide more informative funds statements. We finished the section by showing four alternative styles of presentation for a funds statement.

From this section it should be evident that with an understanding of the structure and meaning of accounts, and the patience to pursue the analysis as far as possible, a great deal of information about a company's affairs can be obtained from a well-presented set of accounts such as those of ICI. It should also be clear that a funds statement may add to the information already disclosed by the profit and loss account and balance sheet, which every com-pany is required by statute to publish.

8.1 Corfield Limited

From the following information prepare a statement showing the sources and uses of funds of Corfield Limited, a large manufacturing company, over the 10 years between 1960 and 1970. What significant information does your statement reveal?

Profit after tax for the 10 years to 1970 totalled £62 million, dividends paid £43 million, and depreciation charged £76 million. Share premiums received during the period amounted to £14 million.

Space is left for you to enter balance sheet differences and adjustments, but you will need to use a separate sheet of paper to prepare the final funds statement, using the form of presentation you think most appropriate.

Balance sheet summaries

£ m	31 December 1960	31 December 1970	Difference	Adjustments	Figures for funds statement
Fixed assets: Gross	65	186			
Depreciation	13	78			
Net	52	108			
Investments	5	21			
Working capital: Stocks	14	32			
Debtors	9	35			
Cash	2	3			
(Creditors)	(15)	(37)			
	10	33			
	67	162			
Long-term loans	9	44			
Deferred liabilities	2	12			
Minority interests	4	12			
Shareholders' funds: Reserves	14	47			
Issued ordinary capital	38	47			
	52	94			
	67	162			

8.1 Corfield Limited

Solution

Balance sheet summaries

£ m	31 December 1960		1970		Difference Source	Use	Adjustments Source	Use	Figures for funds statement Source	Use
Fixed assets: Gross	65		186			121		+11a		132
Depreciation	13		78		65		+11a		76	
Net		52		108						
Investments		5		21	16					16
Working capital: Stocks	14		32			18				
Debtors	9		35			26				23
Cash	2		3			1				
(Creditors)	(15)		(37)		22					
		10		33						
		67		162						
Long-term loans		9		44	35				35	
Deferred liabilities		2		12	10				10	
Minority interests		4		12	8				8	
Shareholders' funds:										
Reserves	14		47		33		+43c −14b		62	
Issued ordinary capital	38	52	47	94	9		+14b		23	
Dividends paid								+43c		43
		67		162	182	182			214	214

a   11 = assumed fully written-off disposals of fixed assets

b   14 = share premiums

c   43 = dividends paid

8.1 Corfield Limited

Solution

CORFIELD LIMITED
Funds statement, 10 years to 31 December, 1970

		£ m
Sources of funds		
External: Ordinary capital issued	23	
Minority interests	8	
Deferred liabilities	10	
Long-term loans	35	
		76
Internal: Profit	62	
Add: Depreciation	76	
Funds from operations	138	
Less: Ordinary dividends	43	
		95
		£171
Uses of funds		
Fixed assets		132
Investments		16
Working capital		23
		£171

Comments:

1 The increase in working capital is made up as follows:

	£m
Stocks	18
Debtors	26
Cash	1
	45
Less: Creditors	22
	23

2 The dividend payout ratio averages 69 per cent.

3 Over half the funds come from internal sources.

4 Depreciation covers only 58 per cent of fixed assets acquired.

5 Fixed assets constitute by far the most important use of funds.

6 It would be of interest to have further details, for example the 1965 balance sheet so that two 5-year statements could be prepared to see if the pattern of sources and uses is changing.

8.2 Imperial Chemical Industries Limited 1971 accounts.

On the following pages are shown extracts from the published Annual Report and Accounts of Imperial Chemical Industries Limited. You will see that in addition to the Accounts themselves, and the Notes thereto and the Auditors' report, the Directors' Report is shown, which gives much additional information, and is particularly helpful in interpreting the accounts. The 1971 accounts show the comparative figures for 1970.

On subsequent pages are set out the major ratios, in a form suitable for working through, together with pages for a funds statement. In addition to working through the figures, please see what conclusions you are able to draw. Space has been left for you to *write down* significant comments that occur to you.

Suggested answers and some comments are given later.

Report of the Directors 1971

The Directors of Imperial Chemical Industries Limited submit their Forty-fifth Annual Report, together with the Accounts of the Company for the year 1971, which will be laid before the Stockholders at the Forty-fifth Annual General Meeting to be held on 29 March 1972.

ECONOMIC BACKGROUND

The continuing and powerful influence of inflation throughout the world, and the currency problems of the later months, provided an unfavourable background to the growth of world industrial production and trade in 1971. The increase in world industrial activity, at about 3 per cent, showed no improvement over the low rate recorded in 1970 and was below the average of recent years. A slow recovery in the USA was offset by a decline in the rate of growth of industrial production in both Western Europe and Japan.

The performance of the world's chemical industry was affected by these adverse economic conditions. World chemical production increased by under 4 per cent in 1971 compared with almost 5 per cent in 1970 and 8½ per cent per annum in the decade up to 1970. Output in Western Europe, after rising by over 8 per cent in 1970, increased by 5 per cent. The reduction in the growth rate aggravated the already difficult trading conditions resulting from world-wide excess capacity for many chemical products.

In the UK there was no improvement in the rate of economic growth in 1971, partly because of de-stocking by manufacturing industry. Industrial production increased by 1 per cent, about the same as in 1970 but substantially below the 3 per cent per annum rate of increase in the 1960's. The increase in the output of the chemical industry was only 2 per cent, compared with 6 per cent in 1970.

ICI's total sales in 1971 increased in value by a smaller percentage than in 1970 in the face of these difficult economic and market conditions. The expansion of sales volume was inhibited by the low demand for chemicals, especially in the UK. Inflation and low volume growth exerted strong pressures on all elements of cost; and, with the constraint on price increases imposed by world excess capacity, prices did not rise enough to cover the upward movement in total costs. 1971 was the third year running in which the Group was subjected to much higher costs for raw materials, wages and salaries not matched by proportionate increases in selling prices.

GROUP RESULTS

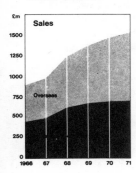

The following are the combined results of Imperial Chemical Industries Ltd and of all its subsidiary companies in the UK and overseas, except Carrington Viyella Ltd and its subsidiaries. The Carrington Viyella results have again not been consolidated in view of the Company's undertaking to HM Government on voting powers. Further reference to Carrington Viyella is made in Note 13 to the accounts. In 1971 for the first time the Group's full share of the profits of its principal associated companies, and not merely the proportion received as dividends, has been included in the profit and loss account.

Group sales in 1971 were £1,524m, an increase of about 4 per cent over the 1970 total. The percentage increase in sales volume was somewhat smaller since, on average, selling prices were slightly higher than last year. UK sales were £704m, compared with £693m in 1970, and sales overseas were £820m against £769m. Sales by associated companies have not been included in any of these figures.

Trading profit, after providing £129m for depreciation (£114m in 1970) was £145m, a reduction of £14m compared with the previous year. Cost increases, particularly in

the UK, were a continuing problem and were only partly offset by price increases which, in turn, were influenced by the Company's adherence to the Confederation of British Industry's undertaking on price restraint. Major items of cost increase were salaries and wages, raw materials and redundancy payments. Most of the increase in the provision for depreciation was in respect of new plants coming into use.

The Group's share of the profits of principal associated companies amounted to £22m before tax; the 1970 results have been adjusted for comparison and the corresponding figure was £16m. Dividends and interest received from other trade investments and income from the short-term investment of cash resources temporarily surplus to requirements, amounted to £13m (£12m in 1970).

Interest on total Group borrowings, both long and short-term, increased to £43m, compared with £35m in 1970. Employees' profit-sharing bonus was £7m against £8m in 1970.

Profit before taxation and investment grants was thus £130m (£144m in 1970). The table below summarises quarterly profit before taxation for the past two years; the figures published in the 1970 Report have been adjusted to include the profits of principal associated companies:—

Profit before taxation

——— Profit after taxation

	1970 £m	1971 £m
First quarter	41	**41**
Second quarter	41	**42**
Third quarter	31	**24**
Fourth quarter	31	**23**
	144	**130**

The charge for taxation on profit was £51m (£59m in 1970), comprising £43m for the Group (UK taxation £24m and overseas taxation £19m) and £8m in respect of associated companies. UK corporation tax has been provided at 40 per cent, but the 1971 charge has been reduced by £2m in respect of 1970, resulting from the reduction in rate which took effect on 1 April 1970. The credit to profits in respect of UK investment grants amounted to £19m (£17m in 1970).

Profit after taxation was £98m compared with £102m in 1970, of which £13m was applicable to minority shareholders in subsidiary companies and the remaining £85m was applicable to ICI Stockholders. A second interim dividend (which the Annual General Meeting will be asked to confirm as the final ordinary dividend for the year 1971) at the rate of 7·5p per £1 Ordinary Stock unit will be paid on 5 April 1972. This dividend, together with the interim dividend of 6·25p paid in November 1971 will make a gross distribution of 13·75p per Ordinary Stock unit for 1971 (the same rate as for 1970). Gross dividends, including those on the Preference Stock, require a total cash sum of £65m, of which £25m is payable to the Inland Revenue.

After payment of dividends, retained profits applicable to ICI Stockholders amount to £20m. Of this sum £5m is retained by the parent company and £8m by subsidiaries; the remaining £7m is retained in associated companies. Stockholders are reminded that the influence which the Group can exercise over the distribution of the profits of associated companies is necessarily limited.

The following table, which takes account of the changes in organization referred to below, shows the different classes of business carried on by the Group and the sales and trading profits attributed to each class:—

	Sales		Trading Profit	
	1970 £m	**1971 £m**	1970 £m	**1971 £m**
UK Divisions and Subsidiaries				
Agricultural	157	**158**	10	**18**
Fibres	150	**149**	14	**5**
General chemicals	261	**282**	37	**34**
Paints	56	**65**	6	**8**
Petrochemicals and plastics	262	**274**	19	**9**
Pharmaceuticals	28	**33**	10	**11**
Imperial Metal Industries Ltd Group	208	**180**	11	**15**
Miscellaneous	18	**20**	2	**—**
Overseas Subsidiaries				
Australasia	164	**172**	17	**16**
North America	160	**179**	9	**10**
Western Europe	139	**153**	10	**6**
Other countries	137	**145**	14	**13**
	1,740	**1,810**		
Less: Inter-class sales	278	**286**		
Totals as in profit and loss account	1,462	**1,524**	159	**145**

The sales and trading profits in the UK section of the above table relate to all sales in and exports from the UK. Those in the overseas section refer only to the manufacturing and trading activities of the overseas subsidiaries and thus exclude sales invoiced directly from the UK to external customers overseas.

UK trading operations

Early in 1971 some changes in organization were announced, as a result of which ICI Fibres Ltd has been reconstituted as a Division (but will trade under the business name of ICI Fibres), Dyestuffs Division has combined with part of Nobel Division to become Organics Division, Heavy Organic Chemicals Division has taken over fibres intermediates and has been renamed Petrochemicals Division, and a subsidiary company, Nobel's Explosives Company Ltd, has been formed to take over and operate the explosives assets of Nobel Division.

Agricultural
This sector consists of the fertilizer and crop protection businesses, with supporting chemical manufacture.

Profits from fertilizers improved as a result of better production and better sales realizations.

Sales of bipyridyl herbicides were again increased substantially, particularly overseas. 'Milstem', a new chemical for the control of cereal mildew, made good progress in the UK and is being introduced overseas.

Fibres
Sales of synthetic fibres were higher than in 1970. Poor trading conditions in the textile industry persisted, fibre prices declined further and profits were again very poor, reflecting low selling prices and increases in costs. Good progress was made in improving productivity and efficiency of all manufacturing units, and these efforts are continuing.

Recent improvements in the manufacture of bulked filament yarns require close integration of fibre production and texturising processes. To take advantage of these developments, Qualitex Ltd and the three texturising subsidiaries of Carrington Viyella Ltd were acquired during 1971 and are being merged into a wholly-owned subsidiary with the name Intex Yarns (Manufacturing) Ltd. This will help ICI Fibres to plan the progressive introduction of new processes, with cost and quality advantages whilst at the same time making full use of the equipment and marketing skills obtained through the acquisitions. These advantages will naturally take some time to materialise and meanwhile Qualitex has been operating at a loss. Provision has been made in the Group profit and loss account for the loss, estimated at £1m, incurred during the period 15 October (date of acquisition) to 31 December. The cost to ICI of acquiring Qualitex was £13m; at the date of acquisition the liabilities of Qualitex exceeded its tangible assets and it has been considered prudent to provide the sum of £18m against the investment by means of a charge against reserves.

The goodwill which arose on the acquisition by ICI of British Nylon Spinners Ltd in 1964, and which has been carried as an asset in the Company and Group balance sheets since that date, has now been written off against reserves in view of the changed circumstances of the market for nylon.

General chemicals
This sector includes alkalis, chlorine and its derivatives, dyes, rubber chemicals and other auxiliary chemicals.

Sales of chlor-alkali products were higher in 1971 than in 1970. Increased costs were partly offset by higher prices, but business was sluggish in some of the important industrial chemicals. Of increasing concern is the high price of electricity for the production of chlorine, compared with prices on the continent of Europe.

Sales of dyes, pigments and organic chemicals increased in home and export markets, particularly the latter. Many processes are labour intensive and the increased costs could not be recovered because of world-wide surplus capacity. Consequently profits were reduced despite some rationalization of production.

Paints
This includes paints, coated fabrics and wall coverings.

Sales of these products increased by 14 per cent over 1970. 'Dulux' Super 3, a thixotropic gloss paint containing silicone and polyurethane, was successfully launched early in 1971. The emulsion paint 'Dulux' Supercover remains a firm favourite with the "do-it-yourself" home-decorator.

The 'Vymura' range of vinyl wall coverings made steady progress, some 35 per cent being sold overseas.

Petrochemicals and plastics
This covers the Company's petrochemicals operations and manufacture of all fibres intermediates and plastics.

Lower than expected demand from the plastics and synthetic fibre industries affected petrochemicals sales which, although higher than in 1970, were well below plant capacity. Price increases were difficult to obtain in the home market, export prices continued to fall throughout the year and costs were substantially higher.

Although the tonnage of plastics sold in 1971 increased by 6 per cent, a substantially lower growth than in recent years, the value of sales was only 5 per cent above the 1970 figure. Trading conditions were generally depressed and there was severe competition from imports from Europe where there is large over-capacity in some of the major plastics.

Pharmaceuticals
Sales at home and overseas reached record levels with exports continuing to account for about two thirds of total sales. Progress with the heart drugs 'Atromid' S, 'Inderal' and 'Eraldin' was particularly encouraging. Increases in costs of wages and salaries and of most raw materials have again absorbed much of the increase in benefit arising from higher sales.

Imperial Metal Industries Ltd
Sales by the IMI Group were lower in value than in 1970, largely owing to the fall in the price of copper. The results for the year showed an improvement, however, having been helped by a substantial reduction in losses on metal stocks and by the release of part of a provision created in 1970 to meet expected losses arising from Rolls-Royce Ltd.

Exports from the UK

The f.o.b. value of Group exports from the UK in 1971 was £263m, an increase of £10m (4 per cent) over 1970.

The products contributing the largest increases in shipments were paraxylene, dyes, cardiovascular drugs and bipyridyl herbicides. Half the total improvement in 1971 was in exports to the European Economic Community, but this was offset in part by lower shipments to the rest of Western Europe. Other markets showing notable improvement were Africa, North America and Central and South America.

The following table shows exports from the UK to world markets for 1971 and the two previous years.

Exports

	1969 £m	1970 £m	**1971 £m**
Western Europe—			
European Economic Community	50	52	**57**
European Free Trade Area	41	47	**45**
Rest of Western Europe	20	19	**20**
	111	118	**122**
Africa	27	29	**32**
North America	23	19	**23**
Far East	17	18	**19**
Central and South America	16	16	**18**
Soviet Union and countries in Eastern Europe	14	17	**17**
Australasia	19	18	**16**
India, Pakistan, Ceylon	8	7	**6**
Rest of world	9	11	**10**
	244	253	**263**

Overseas trading operations

Manufacture and sales overseas continued to expand in 1971. The total value of Group sales overseas (including exports from the UK as well as goods manufactured by overseas subsidiary companies) was £820m in 1971, £51m more than the 1970 figure and £116m more than the total sales in the home market.

Australasia
Imperial Chemical Industries of Australia and New Zealand Ltd was renamed ICI Australia Ltd on 1 October 1971. Sales by the ICI Australia Group rose from £164m to £172m, but trading profit declined from £17m to £16m, owing largely to substantial cost increases in wages, raw materials and services, which were only partially offset by increased productivity. Prices and profits of synthetic fibres and yarns were seriously affected by the reduction in customs tariff in 1970, followed by a fall in world prices.

The continuing depressed state of agriculture and the low demand for fertilizers has led to a rationalization in the fertilizer industry resulting in some of the Group's assets being transferred to Consolidated Fertilisers Ltd in which ICI Australia holds 37·7 per cent of the equity, the other main shareholders being Dow Chemical Company and Swift & Company.

North America
Sales to customers in North America by ICI and its subsidiaries were £180m in 1971, an increase of 7 per cent over the comparable figure for 1970.

In the USA, Atlas Chemical Industries, Inc., an international manufacturer of pharmaceuticals, chemicals, explosives and aerospace components, was acquired during the year at a cost of £66m. This major acquisition not only broadened the base of the Group's US manufacture but also provided a valuable accretion of American marketing skills and management expertise, and will lead to a more rapid expansion of ICI's stake in the important American market. As a further step towards that objective, Atlas and the Company's existing US manufacturing subsidiary, ICI America Inc., have now been merged. During the nine months to 30 September 1971 Atlas achieved sales of £47m, but of these only £12m, being the sales since the date of acquisition, have been included above. As recently announced, ICI has agreed to the requirement of the US Federal Trade Commission that within a period of three years it will dispose of the explosives and aerospace components businesses acquired as part of Atlas.

The Canadian economy showed some sign of recovery in 1971. Sales by Canadian Industries Ltd and its subsidiaries were £10m above the comparable figure for 1970. The profit performance of most business areas was better in 1971 than in the previous year.

Canadian Industries is continuing its programme of expansion into products and services for Canada's resource industries, particularly mining and pulp and paper, and also into the pollution abatement field.

Western Europe
Total Group sales in Western Europe, including exports from the UK, increased by 5 per cent in 1971. There was an increase from £69m to £84m in sales of locally manufactured goods, the most important of which were fibres and plastics. Both of these suffered from difficult trading conditions and profits were low.

Other countries
In India, trading results were adversely affected by the severe textile recession and by industrial disputes. Sales by the ICI group of companies rose by 16 per cent to £54m, but profits were slightly lower than last year.

The newly-built pharmaceuticals factory at Dacca suffered only minor damage during the recent fighting in that area, and restricted production has already been resumed.

Sales throughout the Far East were slightly higher than last year, including a further increase in sales to Japan.

Group sales in Central and South America rose to £49m.

Sales by subsidiary companies in Africa rose to £25m, of which nearly half represented goods imported from ICI in the UK.

265

ICI's investments in its principal associated companies are referred to on page 36.

African Explosives and Chemical Industries Ltd
Sales by African Explosives and Chemical Industries Ltd were £81m compared with £76m in 1970. Profit after taxation was £11m (as in 1970) of which the Group's share was £5m. Sales in all the major spheres of activity were above the 1970 levels, but some profit margins were lower as a result of increased costs and also certain plant operational difficulties.

Fiber Industries, Inc.
Sales by Fiber Industries, Inc. were at a record level and profit after tax rose from £6m to £11m, of which the Group's share was £4m. This improvement results from a rapidly growing demand for jersey knitted polyester and from higher nylon sales. Plans for installing plant to produce textured polyester yarn, estimated to cost about £20m, are going ahead.

FINANCE

The following table summarises for the year 1971 and for the past ten years the sources from which the Group has derived the funds which it required for the development of its business:—

	Ten Years 1962/71 £m	1971 £m
Funds became available from:		
Trading operations		
Retained profit	198	20
Depreciation provisions	849	129
Investment grants received but not yet credited to profits	90	10
Temporary use of amounts set aside for taxation	23	(10)
Miscellaneous receipts	69	6
	1,229	155
Issues of Ordinary and Loan Stocks		
Issues of ICI Ordinary Stock for acquisitions and profit-sharing bonus	113	15
Issues of Loan Stocks		
United Kingdom	264	35
Overseas	247	99
Increased investments of minorities in subsidiaries	84	7
	1,937	311
Funds were used for:		
New fixed assets	1,373	183
New subsidiaries and trade investments	363	87
Additional working capital	184	29
Increased liquid resources	17	12
	1,937	311

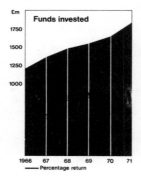

£m
Funds invested
1750
1500
1250
1000

1966 67 68 69 70 71
— Percentage return

During the year some £5m (nominal) new ICI Ordinary Stock has been issued, of which £3m was in connection with the acquisition of Qualitex Ltd and £2m was in respect of the Employees' Profit-Sharing Scheme. The share premiums arising, amounting in all to some £10m, have been credited to share premium account.

New borrowings by the Group during the year amounted to £103m; these were in addition to the £31m received as the second and third instalments on the 10¾ per cent Unsecured Loan Stock issued in December 1970. Loans raised in connection with the acquisition of Atlas Chemical Industries, Inc. amounted to the equivalent of £66m, of which £36m was borrowed in Euro-dollars and £30m in US Dollars. Other borrowings were £15m by means of a Sterling/Deutsche Mark bond issue and £12m in the form of Deutsche Mark bonds.

Total funds invested amounted to £1,774m at the end of the year, an increase of £116m over the amount reported at the end of 1970. Apart from £17m which arose as the result of a change in accounting practice, whereby the Group's share of retained profits of the principal associated companies is added to their book value, the main reasons for the increase were new issues of share and loan capital (£149m) and profits retained (£20m). These increases were partly offset by the special charges against reserves to which reference has been made on page 9.

The return on funds invested, reflecting the marked fall in profit, was 9·4 per cent in 1971 compared with the 1970 figure (adjusted to the new basis with regard to earnings and book value of principal associated companies) of 10·3 per cent.

CAPITAL PROGRAMME AND INVESTMENT

The value of new capital projects sanctioned in 1971 (£111m) was substantially lower than in the previous year, but expenditure (£183m) was somewhat higher than in the last two years. The following table summarises the Group position for the past three years:—

Fixed assets		1969 £m	1970 £m	1971 £m
Sanctioned	UK	125	128	72
	Overseas	84	64	39
	Total:	209	192	111
Spent	UK	111	118	118
	Overseas	48	54	65
	Total:	159	172	183
Sanctioned but unspent at end of year	UK	125	135	89
	Overseas	76	86	60
	Total:	201	221	149

United Kingdom

During 1971 the Company pursued a policy of selective investment to improve the overall profitability of its UK operations. The major projects sanctioned during the year were for crop protection chemicals, a plant for the production of 250,000 tons per annum of sulphuric acid, additional capacity for the manufacture of dyestuffs intermediates, additional capacity for anhydrous hydrogen fluoride (a raw material for fluorocarbons, anaesthetics, fire-fighting chemicals and fluorinated solvents), two plants for the manufacture of textured polyester yarns and a project to safeguard and increase the output from the rock salt mine. These projects are estimated to cost about £21m; the remaining sanctions, £51m, represent a large number of smaller projects concerned with replacement, modernization and minor plant extensions designed to increase capacity.

1971 saw the successful commissioning of several large plants, including a nitric acid unit, a sulphuric acid plant, a second aromatic hydrocarbons complex and a unit for making 'Propathene', ICI's brand of polypropylene, for the plastics fabricating industry.

Overseas

Capital expenditure by the Group in 1971 on fixed assets overseas amounted to £65m, of which £13m was spent in Australasia, £25m in Western Europe and £21m in North America.

In Australia and Canada expenditure was spread over a considerable number of relatively small or medium sized projects for the replacement, modernization and extension of manufacturing plants. In the USA, the £20m 'Melinex' polyester film plant was substantially completed.

In Western Europe, a new factory for the processing of pharmaceuticals was opened at Rheims in France, and a plant for the manufacture of synthetic fibres was brought into production at Offenbach, near Landau in Western Germany.

In Japan, ICI and Teijin Ltd jointly sanctioned a £4m plant for the manufacture of ICI's bipyridyl herbicide. In Indonesia, construction started on paints and pharmaceutical factories and a crop protection formulation plant was sanctioned.

WORKING CAPITAL

Considerable effort has again been directed to the control of the level of working capital. Although the Group balance sheet shows that stocks and debtors between them increased by some £40m during the year to a total of £711m, new subsidiaries accounted for additions of £45m so that effectively a small reduction was achieved elsewhere.

After adjusting for the effects of new subsidiaries, the value of raw material stocks was reduced by about 4 per cent despite higher average prices. Finished product stocks were some 4 per cent higher but this increase was proportionate to the growth in sales. Debtors, after similar adjustment for new subsidiaries, were reduced by 3 per cent despite the increased turnover.

RESEARCH AND DEVELOPMENT

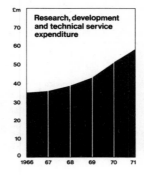

Research, development and technical service expenditure

Revenue expenditure by the Group in 1971 on research, development and technical service was £58m (compared with £51m in 1970), of which £46m (£42m 1970) was spent in the UK. The receipts in 1971 from licences granted by ICI were £13m, and £3m was paid for licences purchased from others.

Agricultural

Overseas activities are being strengthened by establishing field testing stations for plant protection products in several parts of the world. A research centre in North Carolina was announced in December and similar arrangements are in hand in Australia, Spain and the Far East.

Among new products either launched or in a late development stage are 'Promacyl', a new product for tick control, and 'Pirimor', a fast-acting and selective aphicide.

Pilot scale testing of the process to convert hydrocarbons to protein as a food for non-ruminant animals will start in 1972. It will include a novel system for large scale fermentation.

Chemicals

Joint work with British Leyland Motor Corporation Ltd has shown that catalysts recently developed by ICI can be used, without extensive engine modifications, to reduce the toxic constituents of automobile exhaust gas to well below the levels that will be permitted in the USA by 1976. Long term testing is now being carried out on the durability of the system.

The fire-fighting chemicals, 'BCF', a vaporising liquid, and 'Monnex', the most effective dry powder agent known, are both well established, and now a third chemical to improve the performances of foams for fire-fighting has been introduced.

Reactive dyes have been strengthened by the addition of the new 'Procion' H E series to give maximum efficiency in exhaust dyeing. A special range of dyes has been developed for the production of transfer papers to be used in a new method of textile printing.

Canadian Industries Ltd has made notable advances in the use of oxygen in pulp bleaching, and has developed a new process for making stable xanthates in a convenient form for the separation of minerals by froth flotation.

Fibres

A new technique for 'Crimplene' texturised polyester yarns gives an even dyeing product of a high standard. New staple fibres have been introduced to the knitting industry and a new 'Bri-Nylon' staple fibre is being used by many manufacturers of Axminster and Wilton carpets. Melded fabrics from 'Cambrelle' fibres are now used as loose covers, interlinings and carpet underlays.

Plastics

Research is being increasingly devoted to fabricated products. A polyurethane shoe-soling system has been developed, initially for boys' and men's shoes, which wears better than any competitive material, has improved comfort and slip resistance and is as

267

light as cork. The ICI sandwich moulding system, announced last year, has been licensed to a number of companies.

Pharmaceuticals

'Atromid' S, which has been available since 1962, reduces high levels of fat in the blood; results of long term tests by the medical profession confirm that it is a major advance in prolonging the life of patients with angina. 'Nolvadex', a drug which will help in the treatment of cancer of the breast, and has the advantage over existing hormonal treatments of being freer from unpleasant side effects, will be made available in 1972.

'Grofas', a growth-promoting drug for use in meat production, was added to the UK product range in 1971 and will become available elsewhere in Europe in 1972; it is not an antibiotic and is not used in human medicine.

The range of retail products based upon 'Hibitane' and 'Cetavlon' has been extended by the marketing of 'Savlon' Babycare preparations, and for hospitals 'Hibitane' has been formulated into a pre-operative skin preparation 'Hibiscrub'.

'Melcel' disposable fabrics, initially used for surgical drapes, were introduced on to the selling range in 1971, together with disposable forceps; a novel suturing device is intended for commercial introduction in Spring 1972.

PERSONNEL

The average number of persons employed by the Group in the UK in 1971 was 137,000 and their aggregate remuneration for the year was £262m. The corresponding number employed by the Group overseas was 53,000.

Employment costs in the UK

Wages and salaries were again increased in 1971. The proportion of employees on Weekly Staff Agreement conditions rose from 75 per cent at the beginning of 1971 to 92 per cent by the end of the year. These factors combined to increase the 1971 wages and salary bill by £21m compared with 1970 despite a reduction of 5,000 in the numbers employed.

The accompanying chart shows how increases in wage and salary costs over the past five years have outstripped raw material and selling price increases. This underlines the importance of achieving further improvements in the utilization of manpower.

Remuneration, raw material prices and selling prices ICI Group UK

Wages and salaries per employee
Average prices of raw materials
Average selling prices

(Index: 1966 equals 100)

Re-organization

Declining profitability in some business areas necessitated the re-organization of the Nobel, Dyestuffs and Heavy Organic Chemicals Divisions and ICI Fibres Ltd referred to on page 8. As a result a number of employees unfortunately became redundant, but special steps were taken to ensure that the situation was handled as sympathetically and efficiently as possible and that the maximum possible assistance was given to those declared redundant.

Accounts for the year 1971

Accounting Policies

The following paragraphs describe some of the main accounting policies of the Group. Legislation or local usage preclude some subsidiaries, mainly overseas, from conforming with certain of these policies and therefore, where appropriate, adjustments are made on consolidation in order that the Group accounts are presented on a consistent basis.

Depreciation
The Group's policy is to write off the book value of each fixed asset evenly over its estimated remaining life; annual reviews are made of the residual lives of all productive assets, taking account of commercial and technical obsolescence as well as normal wear and tear. Depreciation on assets qualifying for investment grants is calculated on their full cost.

Deferred taxation
The UK tax charge is adjusted each year to the figure which would have applied had there been no accelerated capital allowances. No account is taken of the difference between tax depreciation allowances, adjusted in this way, and the depreciation charged in the accounts. Adjustments of a similar nature are made in the accounts of certain overseas subsidiaries.
The Company balance sheet shows the sum of the UK adjustments made each year at the tax rates applicable to those years; the amount in the Group balance sheet includes the sum of the overseas adjustments.

Investment grants
The grants in respect of each year's capital expenditure are being credited to profit and loss account over a period of 10 years, the estimated average life of the relevant fixed assets. The investment grants shown in the balance sheets represent the total grants received to date less the amounts so far credited to profits.

Stock valuation
In general, finished goods are stated at the lower of cost or net realisable value, raw materials and other stocks at the lower of cost or replacement price. In determining cost for stock valuation purposes, depreciation, selling expenses and certain overhead expenses (principally central administration costs) are excluded.

Foreign currencies
Assets and liabilities in foreign currencies are converted into sterling at the rates of exchange ruling at the dates of the respective balance sheets, except in the cases of subsidiaries in South America where special rates to take account of inflation are used. Profit and loss accounts are converted into sterling at the same rates as are used for balance sheet purposes. Differences arising from changes in exchange rates are taken to reserve where they arise on capital items, and to profits in the case of items of a trading nature. The differences which arose as the result of the general re-alignment of currencies in December 1971 were not sufficiently material to warrant any departure from this normal practice.

Research and development
Research and development expenditure is charged to profits in the year in which it is incurred except for a small proportion which is capitalised as part of the cost of new plant.

Associated companies and other trade investments
An associated company is defined as a company, not being a subsidiary, in which the Group has a substantial interest and in whose commercial and financial policy decisions the Group participates. The Group's share of the profits of the principal associated companies is for the first time included in the 1971 Group profit and loss account and the 1970 figures have been adjusted for comparison. Since audited accounts for the calendar year are not available for any of these companies, accounts made up to dates not earlier than 30 June are used; these accounts are mainly unaudited. The profits of other companies in which the Group has trade investments, including the smaller associated companies, are included only to the extent of dividends received.
The Group's share of the post-acquisition retained profits and reserves of the principal associated companies is included in the book values of the investments in the Group balance sheet. The retained profits of other companies in which the Group has trade investments are included in the book values only to the extent of the nominal value of any scrip issues capitalised since acquisition.

Group profit and loss account
For the year ended 31 December 1971

(For composition of Group see Note 1)

	Notes	1970 £m	1971 £m
Sales to external customers		1,462·4	**1,524·4**
Trading profit	(2)	159·3	**145·5**
Investment income	(3)	12·2	**12·8**
		171·5	**158·3**
Interest payable	(4)	34·7	**43·3**
		136·8	**115·0**
Employees' profit-sharing bonus		8·0	**7·0**
		128·8	**108·0**
Share of profits of principal associated companies		15·6	**22·1**
Profit before taxation and investment grants		144·4	**130·1**
Taxation			
ICI Group	(5)	52·6	**42·9**
Associated companies		6·8	**7·8**
		59·4	**50·7**
Less: Investment grants	(6)	17·3	**18·4**
		42·1	**32·3**
Profit after taxation		102·3	**97·8**
Applicable to minorities		10·2	**12·5**
Applicable to parent company		92·1	**85·3**
Net dividends	(7)	38·1	**40·2**
Income tax on dividends		26·8	**25·4**
		64·9	**65·6**
Profit retained	(8)	27·2	**19·7**

Group balance sheet
At 31 December 1971

(For composition of Group see Note 1)

		Notes	1970 £m	1971 £m
Assets employed	Fixed assets	(10)	1,076·5	**1,157·1**
	Goodwill	(11)	38·7	**15·4**
	Interests in subsidiaries not consolidated	(13)	62·0	**57·1**
	Trade investments	(14)	129·7	**145·2**
	Net current assets	(15)		
	Stocks		321·3	**344·8**
	Debtors		351·0	**366·4**
	Liquid resources		120·4	**151·5**
			792·7	**862·7**
	Creditors		330·0	**350·1**
	Short-term borrowings		94·3	**113·5**
			424·3	**463·6**
			368·4	**399·1**
			1,675·3	**1,773·9**
Financed by	Capital and reserves			
	Applicable to parent company:			
	Issued capital	(16)	477·3	**482·6**
	Reserves	(9)	482·0	**448·6**
			959·3	**931·2**
	Applicable to minorities		116·2	**114·3**
			1,075·5	**1,045·5**
	Investment grants	(6)	80·5	**90·7**
	Deferred taxation			
	UK Corporation tax payable 1 January 1973		38·4	**11·1**
	Deferments due to accelerated capital allowances		38·9	**51·1**
			77·3	**62·2**
	Loans	(17)	442·0	**575·5**
			1,675·3	**1,773·9**

F. J. K. HILLEBRANDT, Treasurer

E. J. CALLARD Directors
A. E. FROST

Company balance sheet

At 31 December 1971

		Notes	1970 £m	1971 £m
Assets employed	**Fixed assets**	(10)	685·5	**709·6**
	Goodwill	(11)	38·7	—
	Interests in subsidiaries	(12)	313·4	**375·5**
	Trade investments	(14)	54·8	**49·6**
	Net current assets	(15)		
	Stocks		136·4	**143·1**
	Debtors		159·1	**144·6**
	Liquid resources		63·1	**55·0**
			358·6	**342·7**
	Creditors		187·2	**173·5**
	Short-term borrowings		25·8	**31·5**
			213·0	**205·0**
			145·6	137·7
			1,238·0	**1,272·4**
Financed by	**Capital and reserves**			
	Issued capital	(16)	477·3	**482·6**
	Reserves	(9)	368·1	**326·2**
			845·4	**808·8**
	Investment grants	(6)	76·8	**85·8**
	Deferred taxation			
	UK Corporation tax payable 1 January 1973		30·3	**2·7**
	Deferments due to accelerated capital allowances		32·9	**47·6**
			63·2	50·3
	Loans	(17)	252·6	**327·5**
			1,238·0	**1,272·4**

F. J. K. HILLEBRANDT, Treasurer

E. J. CALLARD }
A. E. FROST } Directors

Notes relating to the accounts

(Figures in italics represent deductions)

1 Composition of the Group

The Group accounts consolidate the accounts of the Company and 415 subsidiaries. Owing to seasonal trade or local conditions and to avoid undue delay in the presentation of the Group accounts, 247 subsidiaries make up their accounts to dates varying from 30 June to 31 October; 241 of them are made up to 30 September or later.

With the exception of Qualitex Ltd the accounts of subsidiaries acquired during the year have been included in Group figures from the effective dates of acquisition to the appropriate accounting dates. In the case of Qualitex, the Balance Sheet at 31 October 1971 has been consolidated and provision has been made in the Group profit and loss account for losses, estimated at £1m, incurred between the date of acquisition (15 October) and 31 December.

The accounts of Carrington Viyella Ltd and its subsidiaries have not been consolidated in the Group accounts (see Note 13).

		1970 £m	1971 £m
2 Trading profit	The following amounts have been charged in arriving at trading profit:		
	Depreciation	113·8	**129·4**
	Pension fund contributions, pensions and gratuities (including redundancy payments)	20·8	**30·4**
	Hire of plant	16·8	**18·3**
	Audit fees and expenses	·5	**·6**
3 Investment income	Dividends and interest from:		
	Subsidiaries not consolidated	·5	**1·2**
	Trade investments – quoted	1·6	**1·5**
	– unquoted	6·6	**8·3**
	Other quoted investments	·9	**1·4**
	Short-term deposits and sundry loans	8·3	**7·3**
		17·9	**19·7**
	Less: dividends from principal associated companies	5·7	**6·9**
		12·2	**12·8**
4 Interest payable	Loans – repayable within 5 years	4·2	**4·2**
	– not repayable within 5 years	23·5	**31·3**
	Bank overdrafts	4·8	**5·5**
	Other	2·2	**2·3**
		34·7	**43·3**

5 Taxation

	1970 £m	1971 £m
United Kingdom		
Corporation tax	45·1	17·7
Double taxation relief	10·5	10·3
	34·6	7·4
Adjustment of amount deferred due to accelerated capital allowances	·9	16·4
	33·7	23·8
Overseas		
Overseas taxes	18·1	17·1
Adjustment of amount deferred due to accelerated capital allowances	·8	2·0
	52·6	42·9

UK and overseas taxation has been provided on the profits earned for the periods covered by the Group accounts. UK corporation tax has been provided at the rate of 40 per cent for the year 1971; the 1971 charge has been reduced by an overprovision of £1·7m in respect of 1970 corporation tax consequent upon the reduction in rate from 42·5 per cent to 40 per cent with effect from 1 April 1970. The 1970 charge included an overprovision of £2·4m in respect of the previous year.

6 Investment grants

Investment grants on UK capital expenditure in 1971 (under contracts made on or before 26 October 1970) are expected to amount to £9m in the Group (1970 £31m) and £8m (£30m) in the Company. Grants not yet received at 31 December 1971 are estimated to amount to £13m in the Group (£33m) and £12m in the Company (£32m).

7 Net dividends

	1970 £m	1971 £m
5 per cent Cumulative Preference Stock	·2	·3
Ordinary Stock: Interim 6·25p per £1 unit – paid	17·2	18·1
Second interim 7·5p (1970 7·5p) per £1 unit – payable 5 April 1972 and to be confirmed as Final	20·7	21·8
	38·1	40·2

8 Profit retained

	1970 £m	1971 £m
By parent company	11·9	5·0
By subsidiaries	12·4	7·8
In associated companies	2·9	6·9
	27·2	19·7

9 Reserves

Details of movements in Group reserves applicable to the Company and in Company reserves are as follows:

	Group £m	Company £m
At beginning of year	482·0	368·1
Retained profit for the year – ICI	12·8	5·0
– associated companies	6·9	—
Share premiums received	9·7	9·7
Amounts provided against investments – Qualitex Ltd	18·0	18·0
– others	2·3	·8
	38·7	38·7
Goodwill written off – British Nylon Spinners Ltd	38·7	38·7
– new subsidiaries	5·0	—
Exchange differences	1·8	1·8
Other movements	·6	·9
At end of year	448·6	326·2

Reserves at end of year include share premiums amounting to £90·7m (1970 £81·0m). Group reserves include attributable retained profits and reserves of principal associated companies since acquisition amounting to £39·0m (£30·7m).

10 Fixed assets

	Land and buildings			Plant and equipment			Total
	Cost or as revalued £m	Depreciation £m	Net book value £m	Cost or as revalued £m	Depreciation £m	Net book value £m	Net book value £m
Group							
At beginning of year	349·3	118·0	231·3	1,512·1	666·9	845·2	1,076·5
New Subsidiaries	27·3	·2	27·1	39·5	9·6	29·9	57·0
Capital expenditure	27·5		27·5	155·7		155·7	183·2
Disposals and other movements	11·8	7·6	4·2	78·0	52·0	26·0	30·2
Depreciation for year	—	14·4	14·4	—	115·0	115·0	129·4
At end of year	392·3	125·0	267·3	1,629·3	739·5	889·8	1,157·1
Company							
At beginning of year	166·0	66·0	100·0	1,046·5	461·0	585·5	685·5
Capital expenditure	9·4	—	9·4	99·4	—	99·4	108·8
Disposals and transfers	1·2	1·6	·4	21·1	21·1	·4	·4
Depreciation for year	—	7·9	7·9	—	77·2	77·2	85·1
At end of year	174·2	72·3	101·9	1,124·8	517·1	607·7	709·6

The Company revalued the major part of its assets in 1958 and there have also been revaluations by various subsidiaries. At the end of the year the amounts (comprising original cost and revaluation adjustments) relating to such assets included in the 'cost or as revalued' columns of the above table were as follows:

	Year of revaluation	Land and buildings £m	Plant and equipment £m
Company	1958	63·5	175·8
Subsidiaries in:			
UK	1958	8·3	9·2
	1962	4·7	5·4
Australia	1960	15·7	15·2
Argentina	1964	3·2	8·9
Others	various	6·1	4·4
		101·5	218·9

Land and buildings comprise the following:

	Group 1970 £m	Group 1971 £m	Company 1970 £m	Company 1971 £m
Freeholds	321·7	362·0	160·4	168·0
Long leases (over 50 years unexpired)	21·4	24·1	4·9	5·7
Short leases	6·2	6·2	·7	·5
	349·3	392·3	166·0	174·2

11 Goodwill

On the acquisition of a business fair values are attributed to the net assets taken over. Goodwill arises where the price paid for the business exceeds the values attributable to the assets. Except for that which arose on the acquisition of Atlas Chemical Industries Inc. in 1971 all goodwill arising in the Company accounts and on consolidation has been charged against reserves. The goodwill which arose on the acquisition of British Nylon Spinners Ltd in 1964 has been charged against reserves in 1971.

12 Interests in subsidiaries

	1970 £m	1971 £m
Shares at cost less amounts provided	166·7	173·6
Scrip issues capitalised	14·2	14·0
Book value of shares*	180·9	187·6
Amounts owed by subsidiaries	175·2	255·4
Amounts owed to subsidiaries*	42·7	67·5
	313·4	375·5

*The amounts owed to dormant subsidiaries (£87·2m) have been set off against the book value of the corresponding investments.

Information relating to the principal subsidiaries is given on pages 34 and 35.

13 Subsidiaries not consolidated— Carrington Viyella Ltd group

In view of the undertaking given by ICI to the Government that its 64 per cent shareholding in Carrington Viyella Ltd, acquired in October 1970, would be reduced to not more than 35 per cent as soon as practicable and that if this had not been completed within 12 months, no more votes would be exercised than if it had, the accounts of Carrington Viyella Ltd and its subsidiaries have not been consolidated in the Group accounts of ICI.

The Group's interest in Carrington Viyella Ltd at 31 December 1971 amounted to £57·1m (1970 £62m), comprising book value of shares £55·5m and net indebtedness £1·6m. The net tangible assets attributable to the ICI shareholding amounted to approximately £29m at 31 December 1971 (£28m) and the market value of the shares based on Stock Exchange quotation at the same date was £43m (£24m).

The results of Carrington Viyella Ltd and its subsidiaries for the year ended 31 December 1971 are set out below. The 1970 figures, shown for comparison, comprised one year's profits of the former Viyella group and nine months' losses of the former Carrington & Dewhurst group.

	1970 £m		1971 £m
Sales	131·3		153·3
Profit before taxation and special items	1·0		5·8
Taxation	·6	2·2	
Special items (net of tax)	1·9	2·5	— 2·2
Profit (loss) after taxation and special items	1·5		3·6

After excluding preference and minority interests, the profit after taxation and special items attributable to ICI was £1·9m (£1·0m). The income from the Carrington Viyella group included in the ICI Group Profit and Loss Account amounted to £1·2m (£·5m) comprising dividends £1·1m (£·4m) and loan interest £·1m (£·1m).

ICI Group sales in 1971 included approximately £22m (£13m) to the Carrington Viyella group.

14 Trade investments

	Group		Company	
	1970 £m	1971 £m	1970 £m	1971 £m
Principal associated companies				
Shares and advances at cost less amounts provided	55·0	54·4	19·9	17·5
Group share of post-acquisition retained profits and reserves (excluding amounts capitalised)	17·4	25·6	—	—
Scrip issues capitalised	12·7	12·8	4·2	4·2
	85·1	92·8	24·1	21·7

Information relating to the principal associated companies is given on page 36.

	Group		Company	
Other trade investments				
Shares and advances at cost less amounts provided	43·2	51·0	29·3	26·5
Scrip issues capitalised	1·4	1·4	1·4	1·4
	44·6	52·4	30·7	27·9
Total	129·7	145·2	54·8	49·6

The division of the above as between quoted and unquoted investments is as follows:

	Group		Company	
Quoted shares	26·6	26·4	9·3	5·8
(market value)	(27·9)	(28·4)	(6·3)	(7·8)
Unquoted equity shares	88·9	101·9	34·7	31·7
Advances	14·2	16·9	10·8	12·1
	129·7	145·2	54·8	49·6

The following information is given in respect of the investments in unquoted equity shares:

	Group		Company	
	1970 £m	1971 £m	1970 £m	1971 £m
Amount included in ICI profit before taxation	6·1	8·0	2·2	3·4
ICI share of aggregate profits less losses per latest audited accounts received				
Before taxation	16·6	18·6	11·3	9·7
After taxation	10·0	13·0	6·3	5·8
ICI share of aggregate undistributed profits less losses since acquisition (including amounts capitalised)	14·9	20·8	13·8	17·3
Aggregate amounts provided by ICI in respect of losses	7·4	10·2	4·0	2·9

15 Net current assets

	Group		Company	
	1970 £m	1971 £m	1970 £m	1971 £m
Stocks				
Finished goods	184·5	205·5	82·5	88·5
Raw materials and other stocks	136·8	139·3	53·9	54·6
	321·3	344·8	136·4	143·1
Liquid resources				
Quoted investments	10·8	4·8	9·4	·2
Short-term deposits	90·2	121·6	52·0	54·6
Cash	19·4	25·1	1·7	·2
	120·4	151·5	63·1	55·0

The market value of the quoted investments at balance sheet dates was £4·8m in the Group (1970 £11·3m) and £·2m in the Company (£9·6m).

	Group		Company	
Creditors				
Trade and other creditors	217·5	248·9	101·1	103·4
Gross dividends	35·4	35·8	35·4	35·8
Current taxation	77·1	65·4	50·7	34·3
	330·0	350·1	187·2	173·5
Short-term borrowings				
Bank overdrafts — secured	15·6	18·6	—	—
— unsecured	60·8	74·7	15·5	17·8
Other short-term borrowings	17·9	20·2	10·3	13·7
	94·3	113·5	25·8	31·5

16 Capital of parent company

	Authorized £m	Issued 1970 £m	Issued 1971 £m
5 per cent Cumulative Preference stock (£1 units)	8·6	8·6	8·6
Ordinary stock (£1 units)	474·2	468·7	474·0
Unclassified shares (£1 each)	39·2	—	—
	522·0	477·3	482·6

17 Loans

		Group 1970 £m	Group 1971 £m	Company 1970 £m	Company 1971 £m
Secured loans					
United Kingdom		·7	**2·2**	—	—
Overseas					
Australia		38·2	**32·4**	—	—
Others		14·6	**15·1**	—	—
		53·5	**49·7**	—	—
Unsecured loans					
United Kingdom					
4¾ per cent stock	1972/74	30·0	**30·0**	30·0	**30·0**
6¾ per cent stock	1972/77	18·9	**18·9**	18·9	**18·9**
7¼ per cent stock	1986/91	71·1	**71·1**	59·2	**59·2**
7¾ per cent stock	1988/93	10·0	**10·0**	—	—
8 per cent stock	1988/93	60·0	**60·0**	60·0	**60·0**
10¾ per cent stock	1991/96	8·8	**42·7**	8·8	**42·7**
5½ per cent stock	1994/2004	26·1	**26·1**	26·1	**26·1**
Others		15·5	**20·5**	3·8	**8·8**
Overseas					
8⅛ per cent bank loan	1973/74	11·4	**11·7**	11·4	**11·7**
6½ per cent Euro-dollar bonds	1978/82	12·5	**11·5**	12·5	**11·5**
Euro-dollar bank loan	1976/78	—	**35·7**	—	**35·7**
8% Sterling/Deutsche Mark Bonds	1978/86	—	**14·7**	—	—
Australia		12·1	**10·8**	—	—
Canada		28·4	**25·9**	—	—
Germany		13·5	**26·9**	—	—
Holland		18·5	**19·2**	—	—
Switzerland		23·2	**24·2**	21·9	**22·9**
USA		22·5	**59·3**	—	—
Others		6·0	**6·6**	—	—
		388·5	**525·8**	252·6	**327·5**
Total		442·0	**575·5**	252·6	**327·5**
Repayable within 5 years		70·0	**65·6**	43·9	**44·2**
Not repayable within 5 years		372·0	**509·9**	208·7	**283·3**

18 Commitments and contingent liabilities

	Group 1970 £m	Group 1971 £m	Company 1970 £m	Company 1971 £m
Contracts placed for future capital expenditure on fixed assets	82	**60**	59	**42**
Expenditure sanctioned but not yet contracted	139	**89**	65	**41**
	221	**149**	124	**83**
Commitments to acquire share and loan capital in subsidiary and other companies	7	**3**	14	**4**

The Company is committed to pay to the Workers' Pension Fund five future annual instalments of £740,000 and to the Staff Pension Fund four future annual instalments of £130,000; these relate to initial liabilities for past service and improvements in benefits.

Contingent liabilities existed at 31 December 1971 in connection with (a) guarantees and uncalled capital relating to subsidiary and other companies, the maximum liability in respect of which would be £44m (1970 £53m) for the Group and £184m (£126m) for the Company, (b) guarantees relating to Pension Funds and (c) other guarantees and contingencies arising in the ordinary course of business.

19 Emoluments of directors and senior employees

The total emoluments of the directors of the Company for the year comprised fees £20,000 (1970 £19,000) and other emoluments £647,000 (£572,000). Pensions, commutations of pensions and gratuities in respect of executive service of former directors amounted to £639,000 (£576,000).

Two directors served as Chairman during the year, their emoluments whilst serving in that capacity being as follows:

	1970	1971
Sir Peter Allen	£62,670	**£15,560**
Mr E. J. Callard	—	**£48,330**

The table which follows shows the numbers of directors and senior employees of the Company whose emoluments during the year were within the bands stated. The table also shows the total amount of income tax and surtax at 1971/72 rates applicable at the higher end of each band over £10,000 and the corresponding take-home pay; it has been assumed that the recipient is a married man without children and with no other source of income.

Emoluments £	Tax £	Take-home pay £	1970	1971
Directors				
Up to 2,500			3	—
2,501 – 5,000			1	—
5,001 – 7,500			4	**5**
7,501 – 10,000			1	**1**
12,501 – 15,000	7,000	8,000	2	—
15,001 – 17,500	8,700	8,800	—	**1**
22,501 – 25,000	14,300	10,700	1	—
25,001 – 27,500	16,200	11,300	2	—
30,001 – 32,500	20,000	12,500	2	—
32,501 – 35,000	21,900	13,100	1	**4**
35,001 – 37,500	23,700	13,800	3	**1**
37,501 – 40,000	25,600	14,400	1	**5**
42,501 – 45,000	29,400	15,600	1	**1**
45,001 – 47,500	31,300	16,200	1	—
47,501 – 50,000	33,200	16,800	1	**1**
50,001 – 52,500	35,100	17,400	—	**1**
60,001 – 62,500	42,600	19,900	—	**1**
62,501 – 65,000	44,500	20,500	1	—
Employees				
10,001 – 12,500	5,300	7,200	78	**58**
12,501 – 15,000	7,000	8,000	28	**54**
15,001 – 17,500	8,700	8,800	19	**15**
17,501 – 20,000	10,600	9,400	10	**13**
20,001 – 22,500	12,400	10,100	2	**8**
22,501 – 25,000	14,300	10,700	1	**2**
25,001 – 27,500	16,200	11,300	—	**1**

Auditors' report

To the Members of Imperial Chemical Industries Limited

We have examined the accounts set out on pages 21 to 31 and 34 to 36. The accounts of one operating division and certain subsidiaries have been audited by other firms.

In our opinion the accounts comply with the Companies Acts, 1948 and 1967 and give a true and fair view of the state of affairs of the company and, so far as concerns the members, of the state of affairs and profit of the group.

London 24 February 1972

THOMSON McLINTOCK & CO
PRICE WATERHOUSE & CO

Group financial record

For the years ended 31 December

		1962 £m	1963 £m	1964 £m	1965 £m	1966 £m	1967 £m	1968 £m	1969 £m	1970 £m	1971 £m
Assets employed	Fixed assets	559	570	646	760	880	946	972	1,016	1,076	1,157
	Goodwill	—	—	39	39	39	39	39	39	39	16
	Interests in subsidiaries not consolidated	—	—	—	—	—	—	—	—	62	57
	Trade Investments	130	147	92	108	119	118	111	118	130	145
	Net current assets	154	176	189	160	170	271	365	384	368	399
	Total assets employed	**843**	**893**	**966**	**1,067**	**1,208**	**1,374**	**1,487**	**1,557**	**1,675**	**1,774**
Financed by	Ordinary capital of ICI	269	416	419	438	441	444	446	448	469	474
	Group reserves applicable to ICI Ordinary stockholders	325	227	262	326	333	342	372	413	482	449
	Capital and reserves applicable to ICI Ordinary stockholders	**594**	**643**	**681**	**764**	**774**	**786**	**818**	**861**	**951**	**923**
	Preference capital of ICI	35	35	35	35	35	35	35	9	9	9
	Minority interests	41	42	43	61	74	94	105	113	116	114
	Investment grants	—	—	—	—	—	28	48	67	80	91
	Deferred taxation	33	41	56	49	72	86	107	95	77	62
	Loans	140	132	151	158	253	345	374	412	442	575
	Total funds invested	**843**	**893**	**966**	**1,067**	**1,208**	**1,374**	**1,487**	**1,557**	**1,675**	**1,774**
Sales and profits	**Sales** (external) – U.K.	308	325	374	423	443	486	616	652	693	704
	– Overseas	271	299	346	393	442	493	621	703	769	820
	– Total	**579**	**624**	**720**	**816**	**885**	**979**	**1,237**	**1,355**	**1,462**	**1,524**
	Trading profit (after depreciation)	**73**	**85**	**113**	**113**	**99**	**122**	**175**	**190**	**159**	**145**
	Depreciation	44	54	61	69	77	88	105	107	114	129
	Share of profits of principal associated companies	—	—	—	—	—	—	—	—	16	22
	Profit before loan interest, taxation and investment grants	77	93	116	110	98	121	177	193	172	166
	Profit before taxation and investment grants	**70**	**85**	**108**	**101**	**86**	**101**	**153**	**167**	**144**	**130**
	Taxation	32	42	47	22	33	47	70	74	59	51
	Investment grants	—	—	—	—	4	9	11	14	17	19
	Profit after taxation	**38**	**43**	**61**	**79**	**57**	**63**	**94**	**107**	**102**	**98**
	Applicable to ICI	36	40	58	74	52	58	86	96	92	85
	Net dividends	24	26	33	33	33	33	35	37	38	40
	Income tax on dividends	—	—	—	—	17	24	25	26	27	25
	Profit retained	12	14	25	41	2	1	26	33	27	20
	Rate of gross Ordinary dividend per £1 stock (in pence)	9·2*	10·0	12·5	12·5	12·5	12·5	12·9	13·8	13·8	13·8
	Group profit before charging loan interest and before taxation and investment grants, as a percentage of total funds invested	9·1	10·4	12·0	10·3	8·1	8·8	11·9	12·4	10·3	9·4

*Adjusted for scrip issue in 1963.   The figures for 1970 and 1971 include the Group's share of profits of principal associated companies.

This time the information to be used for analysis comes from real published accounts, not from a simplified summary. We suggest you use figures only to the nearest £1 million.

In addition to working through ICI's 1971 investment measures, measures of performance, and measures of financial status, as set out on this and the next few pages, please see what conclusions you can draw, and write them down in the space left under "Comments". There is no point working through all the arithmetic if you are not prepared to *interpret* the resulting ratios.

Investment measures: ICI 1971 Accounts

	1970*	1971
Return on equity	9.7%	
Earnings per share	19.6p	
Price/earnings ratio	12.2	
Market price at year end:		
1970 = 240p		
1971 = 278p		
Dividend yield	5.7%	
Dividend cover	1.4 times	

*Note that the 1970 figures (and therefore ratios) are slightly different in the 1971 accounts from those in the 1970 accounts, due to a change in certain accounting practices.

Comments:

Investment measures: ICI 1971 Accounts

		1970	1971

Return on equity $= \dfrac{\text{Profit for ordinary shareholders}}{\text{Ordinary capital + reserves}}$ $\qquad \dfrac{92}{469 + 482} = 9.7\%$ $\qquad \dfrac{85}{474 + 449} = 9.2\%$

Earnings per share $= \dfrac{\text{Profit for ordinary shareholders}}{\text{Number of ordinary £1 shares issued}}$ $\qquad \dfrac{92}{469} = 19.6\text{p}$ $\qquad \dfrac{85}{474} = 17.9\text{p}$

Price/earnings ratio $= \dfrac{\text{Market price per share}}{\text{Earnings per share}}$ $\qquad \dfrac{240}{19.6} = 12.2$ $\qquad \dfrac{278}{17.9} = 15.5$

Dividend yield $= \dfrac{\text{Dividend per share}}{\text{Market price per share}}$ $\qquad \dfrac{13.75}{240} = 5.7\%$ $\qquad \dfrac{13.75}{278} = 4.9\%$

Dividend cover $= \dfrac{\text{Earnings per share}}{\text{Dividend per share}}$ $\qquad \dfrac{19.6}{13.75} = 1.4\text{ times}$ $\qquad \dfrac{17.9}{13.75} = 1.3\text{ times}^*$

*NB.   The comment on p. 1 of the directors' report (p. 263) about ICI's limited control over associated companies' dividend policies.

Comments:

Return on equity fell slightly in 1971 from its already rather low 1970 level, despite the writing-off of £39 million goodwill against reserves. Trading profit was 9 per cent down, but the tax charge was a lower proportion of profits in 1971. Earnings per share fell by 9 per cent, following the 11 per cent fall in 1970, the dividend was again maintained, so retained earnings and dividend cover fell for the second year running. The market price rose by 16 per cent, compared with a 39 per cent rise in the FT-Actuaries 500 Share Index, so again ICI's share price performed noticeably worse than average. The combination of higher market price and lower earnings per share produced a rise in the price/earnings ratio.

Measures of performance: ICI 1971 Accounts

	1970	1971
Return on net assets	11.3%	
Profit margin	12.9%	
Net asset turnover	0.87 times	
Fixed asset turnover	1.36 times	
Stock turnover	4.55 times	
Debtor turnover	4.17 times	

Comments:

Measures of performance: ICI 1971 Accounts

		1970	1971
Return on net assets	$= \dfrac{\text{EBIT}}{\text{Net assets}}$	$\dfrac{144 + 17 + 28}{1675} = 11.3\%$	$\dfrac{130 + 18 + 36}{1774} = 10.4\%$
Profit margin	$= \dfrac{\text{EBIT}}{\text{Sales}}$	$\dfrac{189}{1462} = 12.9\%$	$\dfrac{184}{1524} = 12.1\%$
Net asset turnover	$= \dfrac{\text{Sales}}{\text{Net assets}}$	$\dfrac{1462}{1675} = 0.87$ times	$\dfrac{1524}{1774} = 0.86$ times
Fixed asset turnover	$= \dfrac{\text{Sales}}{\text{Fixed assets}}$	$\dfrac{1462}{1077} = 1.36$ times	$\dfrac{1524}{1157} = 1.32$ times
Stock turnover	$= \dfrac{\text{Sales}}{\text{Stock}}$	$\dfrac{1462}{321} = 4.55$ times	$\dfrac{1524}{345} = 4.42$ times
Debtor turnover	$= \dfrac{\text{Sales}}{\text{Debtors}}$	$\dfrac{1462}{351} = 4.17$ times	$\dfrac{1524}{366} = 4.16$ times

Comments:

With an almost unchanged net asset turnover, the fall in return on net assets was mainly due to the lower profit margin. Depreciation rose by 14 per cent although gross fixed assets rose by only 9 per cent. Stock rose by $7\frac{1}{2}$ per cent, compared with a 4 per cent increase in sales. (Notice that the value of money—as measured by the Retail Price Index reciprocal—fell by 9 per cent in 1971.) £34 million was borrowed at $10\frac{3}{4}$ per cent, which compared with an *average* before-tax return of 10.4 per cent.

Measures of financial status: ICI 1971 Accounts

	1970	1971
Debt ratio	26.4%	
Interest cover	6.8 times	
Current ratio	1.87 times	
Acid test	1.11 times	
Tax ratio	36.6%	

Comments:

Measures of financial status: ICI 1971 Accounts

		1970	1971
Debt ratio	$= \dfrac{\text{Long-term debt}}{\text{Capital employed}}$	$\dfrac{442}{1675} = 26.4\%$	$\dfrac{576}{1774} = 32.5\%$
Interest cover	$= \dfrac{\text{EBIT}}{\text{Long-term interest}}$	$\dfrac{189}{28} = 6.8$ times	$\dfrac{184}{36} = 5.1$ times
Current ratio	$= \dfrac{\text{Current assets}}{\text{Current liabilities}}$	$\dfrac{793}{424} = 1.87$ times	$\dfrac{863}{464} = 1.86$ times
Acid test	$= \dfrac{\text{Liquid assets}}{\text{Current liabilities}}$	$\dfrac{471}{424} = 1.11$ times	$\dfrac{518}{464} = 1.12$ times
Tax ratio	$= \dfrac{\text{Tax}}{\text{Profit before tax}}$	$\dfrac{59}{144 + 17} = 36.6\%$	$\dfrac{51}{130 + 18} = 34.5\%$

Comments:

Long-term debt rose by £134 million, compared with an increase of £99 million in capital employed (which would have been £162 million before the £63 million goodwill write-off). As a result the debt ratio rose sharply and interest cover fell. The rate of interest on new borrowing (much of it in foreign currencies) is hard to discover. The £34 million unsecured loan stock 1991/96 carries a coupon rate of $10\frac{3}{4}$ per cent, compared with the average return on capital employed of only 10.4 per cent. £66 million was borrowed to pay for the acquisition of Atlas Chemicals Inc. The liquidity ratios remain acceptable; but the solvency ratios seem to have little immediate room for further borrowing, especially if retained earnings continue to fall.

ICI: 1971 Funds statement

Summarised ICI group balance sheets are shown below. Please complete the "difference" column, and make sure that the two totals balance.

Then go on to prepare a simple funds statement on the right.

Using the figures from your balance sheet "difference" column, please now prepare a simple funds statement. We suggest that you list all capital and liability items under "Sources" and all asset items under "Uses," and show *negative* figures where appropriate.

Use a **single** *figure for working capital.*

When you have completed your funds statement, please compare your answer with that shown on the next page.

Balance sheet differences

	1970	1971 £m	Difference £m
Fixed assets (net)	1077	1157	
Goodwill	39	16	
Trade and other investments	192	202	
Current assets			
Stocks	321	345	
Debtors	351	366	
Cash	120	152	
	792	863	
Less: Current liabilities			
Creditors	330	350	
Short-term borrowings	94	114	
	424	464	
Working capital	368	399	
Net assets	£1676	£1774	£
Issued capital: Ordinary	469	474	
Preference	8	8	
Reserves	483	449	
Shareholders' funds	960	931	
Minority interests	116	114	
Investment grants and deferred taxation	158	153	
Long-term loans	442	576	
Capital employed	£1676	£1774	£

SIMPLE FUNDS STATEMENT 1971   £m

SOURCES OF FUNDS

_____

_____

USES OF FUNDS

_____

_____

ICI: 1971 Funds statement

When you have checked your own answers on the previous page with those shown opposite in the left-hand column, please adjust the simple 1971 funds statement shown opposite to allow for the following:

(a) Share premiums of £10 million were received in respect of ordinary shares issued.

(b) Dividends of £66 million were paid.

(c) Depreciation of £129 million was charged.

(d) Goodwill of £63 million was written off against reserves.

The share premium adjustment has been made for you. Please now complete the others. Your final adjusted "reserves" figure should amount to £85 million (= profits after tax available for ordinary shareholders).

When you have finished, check that sources and uses balance. What conclusions can you draw? Please compare your answer with the adjustments and final 1971 funds statement shown on the next page but one.

ADJUSTMENTS TO SIMPLE 1971 FUNDS STATEMENT

	Simple 1971 funds statement	Adjustments Sources	Uses	Adjusted 1971 funds statement
	£m	£m	£m	£m
Sources of funds				
Ordinary capital issued	5	+10a		15
Reserves	(34)	−10a		
Depreciation				
Dividends paid				
Minority interests	(2)			
Deferred tax and grants	(5)			
Loans	134			
	£98			£
Uses of funds				
Fixed assets	80			
Goodwill	(23)			
Trade and other investments	10			
Working capital	31			
	£98			£

ICI 1971 accounts: General comments

Adjustments to the 1971 funds statement are shown on the next page.

1. Change in accounting policy

In 1971 for the first time ICI used the "equity" method instead of the "cost" method in accounting for interests in associated companies. (See section 7.)

The 1970 comparative figures have been adjusted on to the same basis in the 1971 accounts, which necessitated the following changes to the 1970 figures as originally published:

Profit and loss account	£m
Share of associated companies' profits	+16
Investment income	− 6
Profit before tax	+10
Taxation	+ 7
Retained profit	+ 3

Balance sheet	
Trade investments	+17
Reserves	+18
Minority interests	− 1

These changes account for the small changes in some of the ratios calculated earlier for 1970.

2. Investment grants

Even though investment grants ceased in respect of capital expenditure after October 1970, there were still grants receivable by ICI at December 1971 of £13 million. Since the grants are credited against the tax charge over a 10 year period, the credit will taper down to zero from the present level of £18 million over the next 10 years.

3. Qualitex Limited

£18 million has been written off against the reserves in respect of this investment during the year which cost £13 million.

4. Carrington Viyella Limited

This non-consolidated subsidiary is shown in the balance sheet at £57 million. Net tangible assets attributable are £29 million, and the market value of the shares £43 million. No provision for any possible loss has been made.

5. Goodwill

The £39 million goodwill attributable to the purchase of British Nylon Spinners Limited in 1964 was written off against reserves in the year, as were other amounts totalling £24 million. The balance of £15 million shown on the 1971 balance sheet is attributable to the acquisition of Atlas Chemical Industries Inc. in 1971. It is not entirely clear what accounting policy is being followed in respect of goodwill.

6. Fixed assets

The last major revaluation was in 1958. Notice the unusual depreciation policy (straight line over annually revised lives) outlined in the list of accounting policies.

ICI: 1971 Funds statement

ADJUSTMENTS TO SIMPLE 1971 FUNDS STATEMENT

	Simple 1971 funds statement	Adjustments		Adjusted 1971 funds statement
		Sources	Uses	
Sources of funds	£m	£m	£m	£m
Ordinary capital issued	5	+ 10a		15
Reserves	(34)	− 10a		85
		+ 66b		
		+ 63d		
Depreciation		+129c		129
Dividends paid		− 66b		(66)
Minority interests	(2)			(2)
Deferred tax and grants	(5)			(5)
Loans	134			134
	£98			£290
Uses of funds				
Fixed assets	80		+129c	209
Goodwill	(23)		+ 63d	40
Trade & other investments	10			10
Working capital	31			31
	£98			£290
		+192	+192	

ICI FUNDS STATEMENT 1971
A final version

	£m	
Sources of funds		
External:		
Issued ordinary capital	15	
Loans	134	
		149
Internal:		
Funds from profit	85	
Add: Depreciation	129	
Funds from operations	214	
Less: Dividends paid	66	
		148
		£297
Uses of funds		
Fixed assets		209
Goodwill		40
Working capital		31
Miscellaneous		17
		£297

8.3 The General Electric Company Limited

From the summarised accounts shown overleaf for the year ending 31 March 1971 you are asked:

(a) to prepare a funds statement for the year ending 31 March 1971, and to comment on it;

(b) to calculate investment measures, measures of performance, and measures of financial status, and to comment on them.

Your analysis and comments should explicitly deal with the three following features:

(1) the inclusion of bank overdrafts in current liabilities. What difference would it make if they were instead shown as medium-term loans?

(2) the potential conversion into ordinary shares at $112\frac{1}{2}$p of the $7\frac{1}{4}$% Convertible Stock 1987/92. What effect would conversion have on the investment measures and on the measures of financial status?

(3) the treatment of goodwill. What alternative accounting treatments are possible, and what effect would they have on the measures calculated?

Note. Market price per ordinary share:

31–3–71	113p
31–3–70	114p

THE GENERAL ELECTRIC COMPANY LIMITED
Balance sheet, 31 March 1971

	£m	
	1971	1970
Current assets (a)	646	643
Less: Current liabilities (b)	349	371
Net working capital	297	272
Investments	74	75
Fixed assets (net)	162	173
Goodwill	171	171
Net assets	£704	£691
Ordinary 25p shares	117	117
Preference shares	6	6
Share premium account	266	266
Reserves	88	66
Shareholders' interests	477	455
Minority interests	22	20
Long-term loans (c)	205	216
Capital employed	£704	£691

(a)	Stock	308	300
	Debtors	331	335
	Cash	7	8
(b)	Including bank overdrafts	48	63
(c)	Including $7\frac{1}{4}$% Convertible Stock 1987/92	78	80

THE GENERAL ELECTRIC COMPANY LIMITED
Profit and loss account,
for the year ending 31 March 1971

	£m	
	1971	1970
Sales	924	891
Trading profit before interest (d)	84	82
Interest payable (e)	21	24
Profit before tax	63	58
Taxation	26	27
Profit after tax	37	31
Minority interests	1	1
	36	30
Exceptional items	3	5
Profit available for ordinary shareholders	39	35
Ordinary dividends 15% ($14\frac{1}{2}$%)	18	17
Retained profits for the year	£21	£18

(d)	After depreciation	25	25
(e)	Interest on $7\frac{1}{4}$% Convertible Loan Stock 1987/92	6	6
	Other loan interest	8	9
	Bank overdraft interest	7	9

Appendix

ADJUSTING ACCOUNTS TO ALLOW FOR INFLATION

In this Appendix we consider in detail the adjustments necessary in order to convert conventional accounts into terms of currency of a constant purchasing power. These are the adjustments contained in Exposure Draft No. 8 of the Accounting Standards Steering Committee, issued in January 1973.

We also include details of the Retail Price Index month by month since June 1947, annual averages for the years ending 31st March and 31st December 1948–1972, and annual figures from 1948 to 1972 showing the fall in the value of the pound for the years ending 31st March and 31st December. The ASSC Exposure Draft recommends using the Consumer Price Index, but monthly figures are not available for this index, and the annual figures for the Consumer Price Index show relatively small differences since 1948 from the Retail Price Index annual averages.

We do not consider in this Appendix the arguments for and against making the adjustments discussed here. The Institute of Chartered Accountants in England and Wales has published two booklets entitled "Accounting for Inflation" giving more detailed working guides to the necessary adjustments; and there are several articles in the accounting journals discussing the general issues.

ILLUSTRATION OF INFLATION ADJUSTMENTS

C. D. Hawkins Limited was a merchandizing firm that had been in business for two years. During this period, the index of the general price level changed as follows:

Opening of business	150
First year, average	160
End of first year	175
Second year, average	190
End of second year	200

All of the company's revenues and expenses were earned or incurred fairly evenly throughout the year. The only exceptions were depreciation and that part of goods sold represented by opening stocks. Stocks were valued on a first-in first-out basis. Dividends were declared and paid at the end of each year.

The company's fixed assets were acquired on the first day of business and at the end of the first year. They were all depreciated on a straight-line basis over a ten year life.

At the start of the second year, the company paid off in cash £50,000 of the company's £350,000 long-term liabilities. The remaining £300,000 was converted into issued share capital.

The company's profit and loss accounts on a conventional historical cost basis for the first two years of operations are shown opposite (above). The balance sheets at the start of business, and at the end of each of the first two years, are shown opposite (below).

The requirement is to restate these accounts in pounds of the same purchasing power, in order to determine, inter alia, the company's real profit (or loss) in each of the first two years of business.

Detailed restatements, together with notes on the procedures, are shown on the next few pages.

Profit and loss accounts

	Year 1 £'000	Year 2 £'000
Sales	800	1000
Cost of goods sold	470	600
Depreciation	30	40
Other expenses (including tax)	280	300
	780	940
Net profit	20	60
Dividends paid	5	10
Retained profit for year	15	50
Add: Retained profit brought forward	–	15
Retained profit carried forward	15	65

Balance Sheets

	Start of Year 1 £'000	End of Year 1 £'000	End of Year 2 £'000
Fixed assets, cost	300	400	400
Less: depreciation	—	(30)	(70)
Fixed assets, net	300	370	330
Stocks	250	300	200
Cash, debtors, and monetary assets	200	195	235
	750	865	765
Current liabilities	100	200	100
Long-term liabilities	350	350	—
	450	550	100
Shareholders' funds:			
Issued capital	300	300	600
Retained profits	—	15	65
	750	865	765

C. D. HAWKINS LTD, YEAR 1 ACCOUNTS

Profit and loss account, year 1		Current-reported	Adjustment factor		End-of-year 1 money	End-of-year 2 money
Sales		800	175/160		875	1000
	250		175/150	292		
Cost of goods sold	220	470	175/160	241	533	609
Depreciation		30	(175/150)		35	40
Other expenses		280	175/160		306	350
(Monetary gain)		—			(42)	(48)
		780			832	951
Net profit		20			43	49
Dividend paid		5	175/175		5	6
Retained profits		15			38	43

Balance sheet, end of year 1		Current-reported	Adjustment factor		End-of-year 1 money	End-of-year 2 money
Fixed assets	300		175/150	350		
Cost	100	400	175/175	100	450	514
Depreciation		30			35	40
Net		370			415	474
Stocks		300	175/160		328	375
Cash, debtors, etc.		195	175/175		195	223
		865			938	1072
Current liabilities		200	175/175		200	229
Long-term liabilities		350	175/175		350	400
		550			550	629
Shareholders' funds:						
Issued capital		300	175/150		350	400
Retained profits		15			38	43
		865			938	1072

C. D. HAWKINS LTD, YEAR 2 ACCOUNTS

Profits and loss account, year 2

		Current-reported	Adjustment factor		End-of-year 2 money
Sales		1000	200/190		1053
	300		200/160	375	
Cost of goods sold	300	600	200/190	316	691
Depreciation		40			51
Other expenses		300	200/190		316
Monetary loss		—			2
		940			106
Net profit		60		loss	(7)
Dividend paid		10	200/200		10
Retained profits		50			(17)

Balance sheet, end of year 2

		Current-reported	Adjustment factor		End-of-year 2 money
Fixed assets Cost		400			514
	30			40	
Depreciation	40	70		51	91
Net		330			423
Stocks		200	200/190		211
Cash, debtors, etc.		235	200/200		235
		765			869
Current liabilities		100	200/200		100
Shareholders' funds:					
	300			400	
Issued capital	300	600	200/175	343	743
	15			43	
Retained profits	50	65		(17)	26
		765			869

NOTES ON THE ADJUSTMENTS

1 For year 1's results, adjusted figures have been shown both in terms of end-of-year 1 pounds and in terms of end-of-year 2 pounds. In practice, one would expect adjustments to be made year by year, i.e. year 1's accounts to be expressed in end-of-year 1 pounds, and year 2's accounts in end-of-year 2 pounds. To convert end-of-year 1 pounds into end-of-year 2 pounds, it is simply necessary to multiply *all* the figures in the end-of-year 1 accounts by 200/175.

2 Calculation of net monetary gains and losses is shown below.

3 Cost of goods sold could be calculated differently by using a different adjustment factor for (a) purchases in the year and (b) end-of-year stocks.

4 Because *different* adjustment factors are applied to the various profit and loss account (and balance sheet) items, it is *not* possible to obtain an adjusted profit or loss figure merely by applying a *single* adjustment factor to the reported profit or loss.

5 In practice, monthly indices would probably be used to adjust sales, etc., rather than average figures for a whole year.

6 In practice the adjusted figures are only approximate, for three reasons:

(a) Certain assumptions are made in choosing which index to apply
(b) The indices themselves are only approximate
(c) The accounting figures to which the indices are applied are also only approximate.

Beware of imputing too much accuracy to the adjusted figures!

C. D. HAWKINS LTD
Monetary gains and losses

Year 1	Current reported	Adjustment factor	End-of-year 1 money	End-of-year 2 money
IN				
Opening balance	100	175/150	117	134
Sales	800	175/160	875	1000
	900		992	1134
OUT				
Purchases	520	175/160	569	650
Other expenses	280	175/160	306	350
Dividends	5	175/175	5	6
Fixed assets	100	175/175	100	114
	905		980	1120
			12	14
Closing balance	(5)	175/175	(5)	(6)
Loss			(17)*	(20)*
Long-term liabilities				
Opening balance	350	175/150	409	468
Closing balance	350	175/175	350	400
Gain	—		59*	68*
Net gain			42	48

Year 2	Current reported	Adjustment factor	End-of-year 2 money
IN			
Opening balance	(5)	200/175	(6)
Sales	1000	200/190	1053
	995		1047
OUT			
Debt retirement	50	200/175	57
Purchases	500	200/190	527
Other expenses	300	200/190	316
Dividends	10	200/200	10
	860		910
Closing balance	135	200/200	137
			135
Loss			2

RETAIL PRICE INDEX
June 1947 to June 1973. (January 1962 = 100.0)

	1947	1949	1951	1953	1955	1957	1959	1961	1963	1965	1967	1969	1971	1973
January		60.5	64.9	76.6	81.2	88.5	93.6	95.3	102.7	109.5	118.5	129.1	147.0	171.3
February		60.5	65.5	77.2	81.2	88.5	93.6	95.3	103.6	109.5	118.6	129.8	147.8	172.4
March		60.5	66.1	77.8	81.2	88.5	93.6	96.2	103.7	109.9	118.6	130.3	149.0	173.4
April		60.5	67.2	78.3	81.7	88.5	93.6	96.2	104.0	112.0	119.5	131.7	152.2	176.7
May		61.6	68.8	77.8	81.7	89.4	92.8	97.0	103.9	112.4	119.4	131.5	153.2	178.0
June	55.5	61.6	69.4	78.3	83.4	90.2	92.8	97.9	103.9	112.7	119.9	132.1	154.3	178.9
July	56.0	61.6	69.9	78.3	83.4	91.1	92.8	97.9	103.3	112.7	119.2	132.1	155.2	
August	55.5	61.6	70.5	77.8	82.8	90.2	92.8	98.7	103.0	112.9	118.9	131.8	155.3	
September	56.0	62.2	71.0	77.8	83.4	90.2	92.8	97.9	103.3	113.0	118.8	132.2	155.5	
October	56.0	62.2	71.6	77.8	84.5	91.1	92.8	98.7	103.7	113.1	119.7	133.2	156.4	
November	57.1	62.2	71.6	77.8	85.6	91.9	93.6	99.6	104.0	113.6	120.4	133.5	157.3	
December	57.7	62.7	72.2	77.8	85.6	91.9	93.6	99.6	104.2	114.1	121.2	134.4	158.1	

	1948	1950	1952	1954	1956	1958	1960	1962	1964	1966	1968	1970	1972
January	57.7	62.7	73.3	77.8	85.1	91.9	93.6	100.0	104.7	114.3	121.6	135.5	159.0
February	58.8	62.7	73.8	77.8	85.1	91.9	93.6	100.1	104.8	114.4	122.2	136.2	159.8
March	58.8	62.7	73.8	78.3	86.0	91.9	93.6	100.5	105.2	114.6	122.6	137.0	160.3
April	59.9	63.3	74.9	78.9	87.7	93.6	93.6	101.9	106.1	116.0	124.8	139.1	161.8
May	59.9	63.3	74.9	78.3	87.7	92.8	93.6	102.2	107.0	116.8	124.9	139.5	162.6
June	61.0	63.3	76.6	78.9	86.8	93.6	94.5	102.9	107.4	117.1	125.4	139.9	163.7
July	59.9	63.3	76.6	80.5	86.8	92.8	94.5	102.5	107.4	116.6	125.5	140.9	164.2
August	59.9	62.7	76.1	80.0	86.8	91.9	93.6	101.6	107.8	117.3	125.7	140.8	165.5
September	59.9	63.3	75.5	79.5	86.8	91.9	93.6	T01.5	107.8	117.1	125.8	141.5	166.4
October	59.9	63.8	76.6	80.0	87.7	92.8	94.5	101.4	107.9	117.4	126.4	143.0	168.7
November	60.5	64.4	76.6	80.5	87.7	93.6	95.3	101.8	108.8	118.1	126.7	144.0	169.3
December	60.5	64.4	76.6	80.5	87.7	93.6	95.3	102.3	109.2	118.3	128.4	145.0	170.2

RETAIL PRICE INDEX
Annual averages of monthly index figures (January 1962 = 100.0)

| | Years ending 31st March | | Years ending 31st December | |
	Index	To convert to January 1962	Index	To convert to January 1962
1948	(56.7)	(176.4)	59.7	167.5
1949	60.2	166.1	61.5	162.6
1950	62.0	161.3	63.3	158.0
1951	64.0	156.2	69.1	144.7
1952	71.1	140.6	75.4	132.6
1953	76.3	131.1	77.8	128.5
1954	78.0	128.2	79.2	126.3
1955	80.1	124.8	83.0	120.5
1956	84.0	119.0	86.8	115.2
1957	87.6	114.2	90.0	111.1
1958	90.9	110.0	92.7	107.9
1959	93.1	107.4	93.2	107.3
1960	93.2	107.3	94.1	106.3
1961	94.6	105.7	97.5	102.6
1962	98.7	101.3	101.6	98.4
1963	102.4	97.7	103.6	96.5
1964	104.0	96.2	107.0	93.5
1965	108.2	92.4	112.1	89.2
1966	113.3	88.3	116.5	85.8
1967	117.5	85.1	119.4	83.8
1968	120.3	83.1	125.0	80.0
1969	126.9	78.8	131.8	75.9
1970	133.4	75.0	140.2	71.3
1971	143.1	69.9	153.4	65.2
1972	156.4	63.9	164.3	60.9
1973	167.5	59.7		

RETAIL PRICE INDEX
Fall in the value of money

| | Years to 31st March | | Years to 31st December | |
	Index	% fall	Index	% fall
			57.7	
1948	58.8	5.6	60.5	4.6
1949	60.5	2.8	62.7	3.5
1950	62.7	3.5	64.4	2.6
1951	66.1	5.1	72.2	10.8
1952	73.8	10.4	76.6	5.7
1953	77.8	5.1	77.8	1.5
1954	78.3	0.6	80.5	3.4
1955	81.2	3.6	85.6	6.0
1956	86.0	5.6	87.7	2.4
1957	88.5	2.8	91.9	4.6
1958	91.9	3.7	93.6	1.8
1959	93.6	1.8	93.6	—
1960	93.6	—	95.3	1.8
1961	96.2	2.7	99.6	4.3
1962	100.5	4.3	102.3	2.6
1963	103.7	3.1	104.2	1.8
1964	105.2	1.4	109.2	4.6
1965	109.9	4.3	114.1	4.3
1966	114.6	4.1	118.3	3.6
1967	118.6	3.4	121.2	2.4
1968	122.6	3.3	128.4	5.6
1969	130.3	5.9	134.4	4.5
1970	137.0	4.9	145.0	7.3
1971	149.0	8.1	158.1	8.3
1972	160.3	7.0	170.2	7.1
1973	173.4	7.6		

Bibliography

THE BACKGROUND TO COMPANY ACCOUNTS

Report of the Company Law Committee (The "Jenkins Report"): HMSO, Cmnd 1749, June 1962

The Principles of Modern Company Law: L C B Gower, Stevens, 3rd ed, 1969

Disclosure in Company Accounts: H B Rose, Institute of Economic Affairs, Eaton Paper 1, rev ed, 1965

Accounting Requirements of the Companies Acts: A G Touche, Butterworths, 1970

THE STRUCTURE OF COMPANY ACCOUNTS

ICA N18*: *Presentation of Balance Sheet and Profit and Loss Account*, 1958

Accounting Trends and Techniques: American Institute of Certified Public Accountants, 1972

Survey of Published Accounts 1971/72: General and Educational Trust of the Institute of Chartered Accountants in England and Wales, 1973

Introduction to Accounting: Harold C Edey, Hutchinsons University Library, 1963

ANALYSING COMPANY ACCOUNTS

Published Accounts: Your Yardsticks of Performance?: Centre for Interfirm Comparison, 1968

Security Analysis: Graham, Dodd and Cottle, McGraw-Hill, 4th ed, 1962

Techniques of Financial Analysis: Erich A Helfert, Irwin, 3rd ed, 1971

RECORDING BUSINESS TRANSACTIONS

Carter's Advanced Accounts: D Garbutt, Pitman, 6th ed, 1970

Spicer and Pegler's Book-keeping and Accounts: W W Bigg, H A R J Wilson and A E Langton, H F L (Publishers), 17th ed, 1971

Guide to Company Balance Sheets and Profit and Loss Accounts: Frank H Jones, Heffer & Sons, 7th ed, 1970

MEASURING PROFIT OR LOSS

ICA N23*: *Hire Purchase, Credit Sale and Rental Transactions*, 1964

Valuation of Stock and Work in Progress: Research and Publications Committee of the Institute of Chartered Accountants of Scotland

FIXED ASSETS AND DEPRECIATION

ICA N9*. *Depreciation of Fixed Assets*, 1945

ICA N15*. *Accounting in Relation to Changes in the Purchasing Power of Money*, 1952

Accounting for Stewardship in a Period of Inflation: Research Foundation of the Institute of Chartered Accountants in England and Wales, 1968

Reporting the Financial Effects of Price-level Changes: American Institute of Certified Public Accountants, Research Study No 6, 1963

CAPITAL STRUCTURE AND GEARING

Basic Business Finance: Pearson Hunt, Charles Williams and Gordon Donaldson, Irwin, 4th ed, 1972

The Theory of Financial Management: Ezra Solomon, Columbia University, 1963

Financial Management and Policy: James C. Van Horne, Prentice-Hall, 2nd ed, 1971.

CONSOLIDATED ACCOUNTS

Consolidated and Other Group Accounts: Sir Thomas B Robson and S M Duncan, Gee, 4th ed, 1969

International Accounting: Gerhard G Mueller, Collier-Macmillan, 1967

Consolidation of Financial Statements: H S Villiers, S Ross and A G Touche, Butterworths, 1969

INTERPRETING COMPANY ACCOUNTS

Accounting Flows: Income, Funds and Cash: R K Jaedicke and R T Sprouse, Prentice-Hall, 1965

Accounting for the Financial Analyst: J A Mavriello, Certified Financial Analysts, Monograph Series No 1, Irwin, 1967

Divisional Performance: Measurement and Control: D Solomons, Research Foundation of the Financial Executives Institute, 1965

*Recommendations of the Institute of Chartered Accountants in England and Wales.

GENERAL

Companies Acts 1948 and 1967

Management Accounting: Text and Cases: Robert N Anthony, Irwin, 4th ed, 1970

Studies in Accounting Theory: W T Baxter and S Davidson, Sweet and Maxwell, 1962

Readings in Accounting Theory: Paul Berger and Kenneth B Berg, Houghton Miflin, 1966

Accounting Finance and Management: R J Chambers, Butterworths, 1969

The Financial Manager: J B Cohen and S M Robbins, Harper, 1966

An Income Approach to Accounting Theory: Sidney Davidson, David Green, Jr, Charles T Horngren and George H Sorter, Prentice-Hall, 1964

The Theory and Measurement of Business Income: Edgar O Edwards and Philip W Bell, University of California, 1964

Accounting: A Management Approach: Myron J Gordon and Gordon Shillinglaw, Irwin, 4th ed, 1969

An Inventory of Generally Accepted Accounting Principles: Paul Grady, American Institute of Certified Public Accountants, Research Study number 7, 1965

Corporate Financial Reporting: David F. Hawkins, Irwin, 1971

Accounting: An Analysis of its Problems: M Moonitz and C H Jordan, Holt Rinehart and Winston, rev ed, 1964

On the Accuracy of Economic Observations: Oskar Morgenstern, Princeton University, 2nd ed, 1963

Contemporary Accounting Problems: Leonard E Morrissey, Prentice-Hall, 1963

A Theory of Accounting to Investors: George J Staubus, University of California, 1960

Financial Accounting Theory: S A Zeff and T F Keller, McGraw-Hill, 1964

STATEMENTS OF STANDARD ACCOUNTING PRACTICE
(issued by the Accounting Standards Steering Committee)

M 1. Accounting for the results of associated companies (Jan. 1971)

M 2. Disclosure of accounting policies (Nov. 1971)

M 3. Earnings per share (Feb. 1972)

(Proposed)

ED 3. Accounting for acquisitions and mergers

ED 6. Stocks and work in progress

ED 7. Accounting for extraordinary items

ED 8. Accounting for changes in the purchasing power of money

ED 9. The accounting treatment of grants under the Industry Act 1972

ED 10. Accounting for value added tax

ED 11. Accounting for deferred taxation

Glossary

AMERICAN TERMINOLOGY

Accounts payable	=	creditors
Accounts receivable	=	debtors
Capital stock	=	share capital
Common stock	=	ordinary shares
Corporation	=	company
Earned surplus	=	accumulated retained earnings
Income statement	=	profit and loss account
Inventories	=	stocks
Leverage	=	gearing
Net income	=	profit after tax
Notes payable	=	Loans (often from banks) fixed both in amount and in period
Paid in surplus	=	share premium
Pooling of interests	=	merger
Stock dividend	=	bonus issue of less than 25 per cent (1 for 4)
Treasury stock	=	a company's own common stock which the company itself has purchased but not cancelled. (Not allowed in the U.K.)

Solutions

1.4 The Acme Company Limited

Solution

Notes

1 Note the order of the items shown in current liabilities and current assets.

2 Note the grouping of items and sub-totals on each side of the balance sheet.

THE ACME COMPANY LIMITED
Balance sheet, 30 June 1972

		£			£
Share capital			**Fixed assets**		
£1 ordinary shares		20 000	Freehold shop		15 000
			Fixtures and fittings		3 000
					18 000
Revenue reserve					
Profit and loss account		5 000			
Shareholders' funds		25 000	**Current assets**		
			Stock	6000	
Current liabilities			Debtors	4000	
Current tax payable	2000		Cash	2000	
Creditors	3000				12 000
		5 000			
		£30 000			£30 000

1.5 General Contractors Limited

Solution

Notes

1 The heading for the profit and loss account includes the name of the company and indicates that the account is "for the year ending 31 December 1972."

2 Sales have to be disclosed, but it is common not to deduct a total "cost of sales" figure (in this case £105 000) to arrive at the trading profit.

3 Tax is not deducted with depreciation and interest, but separate sub-totals are shown for "profit before tax" and "profit for the year after tax."

4 The balance carried forward to the next account is arrived at by adding the unappropriated balance brought forward from last year to the amount retained from the current year's profit after tax.

1.6 The Marvel Trading Company Limited.

Solution

Notes

1 The whole account is normally presented as one. Strictly speaking, a separate appropriation account could be shown beginning with profit for the year after tax £57 000.

2 The sub-total £17 000, representing the amount retained in respect of the year (that is not paid or proposed to be paid out to shareholders as dividends) is not labelled as such in the above account. It is probably best to identify sub-totals where there is a convenient name for them, but some published accounts in practice do not always do so.

GENERAL CONTRACTORS LIMITED
Profit and loss account
for the year ending 31 December 1972

		£
Sales		125 000
Trading profit		20 000
Less: Depreciation	5000	
Interest	1000	
		6 000
Profit before tax		14 000
Tax		7 000
Profit for the year after tax		7 000
Proposed dividend		5 000
Retained out of the year's profit		2 000
Add: Unappropriated balance brought forward		3 000
Balance carried forward		£5 000

MARVEL TRADING COMPANY LIMITED
Profit and loss account
for the year ending 30 June 1972

	£
Trading profit after depreciation	100 000
Income from investments	10 000
	110 000
Deduct: Interest payable	8 000
Profit before tax	102 000
Tax	45 000
Profit for the year after tax	57 000
Proposed dividends	40 000
	17 000
Add: Unappropriated balance brought forward	8 000
Balance carried forward to next account	£25 000

1.7 The Fine Fare Catering Company Limited

Solution

Notes

1 The estimated tax liability features in both the profit and loss account and balance sheet. Under tax law the amount will not be payable for some months so that this "future tax" figure is correctly shown as the most distantly payable current liability.

2 The proposed dividend also appears in both the profit and loss account and the balance sheet. The dividend is immediately payable and is included in the appropriate position under current liabilities.

THE FINE FARE CATERING COMPANY LIMITED
Balance sheet, 31 March 1973

	£			£
Share capital		**Fixed assets**		
£1 ordinary shares	6 000	Leasehold restaurant		7 000
		Fixtures and fittings		1 000
Reserves				8 000
Profit and loss account	1 000			
Shareholders' funds	7 000			
Current liabilities				
Tax	1000			
Creditors	2000	**Current assets**		
Dividend	1000 4 000	Stock	2000	
		Cash	1000	
				3 000
	£11 000			£11 000

Profit and loss account, for the year ending 31 March 1973

	£
Sales	15 000
Trading profit after depreciation	3 000
Tax	1 000
Net profit after tax	2 000
Proposed dividend	1 000
Balance carried to balance sheet	£1 000

1.8 Andrew Hunt Limited

Solution

Notes

1 Ordinary shares need not be denominated as £1 shares. Andrew Hunt Limited has issued 15 000 ordinary shares of 50p each.

2 A profit and loss account may cover any period, not necessarily one year.

3 Rather than use the "account format" shown here, you may prefer to use the "net asset format" deducting current liabilities from current assets.

ANDREW HUNT LIMITED
Balance sheet, 30 September 1972

	£		£
Share capital		**Fixed assets**	
Ordinary 50p shares	7 500	Leasehold factory	6 000
		Plant and machinery	4 500
			10 500
Reserves			
Profit and loss account	1 600		
Shareholders' funds	9 100	**Current assets**	
		Stock	3300
Long-term loan		Debtors	4700
10% Debenture 1987	4 000	Cash	2000
Current liabilities			10 000
Tax	2700		
Creditors	3200		
Dividend	1500		
	7 400		
	£20 500		£20 500

ANDREW HUNT LIMITED
Profit and loss account
for the nine months ended 30 September 1972

	£	
Sales	34 000	
Trading profit before depreciation and interest	6 600	
Less: Depreciation	500	
Debenture interest	300	
	800	
Profit before tax	5 800	
Taxation	2 700	
Profit after tax	3 100	
Proposed ordinary dividend	1 500	
Retained profit for the period	£1 600	

2.4 King Limited and Fisher Limited

Solution

			King Limited		Fisher Limited	
(a)	Debt ratio	$= \dfrac{\text{Long-term debt}}{\text{Capital employed}}$	$\dfrac{5000}{25\,000}$	$= 20.0\%$	$\dfrac{20\,000}{60\,000}$	$= 33.3\%$
(b)	Interest cover	$= \dfrac{\text{EBIT}}{\text{Interest}}$	$\dfrac{5500}{500}$	$= 11.0$	$\dfrac{9000}{2000}$	$= 4.5$
(c)	Current ratio	$= \dfrac{\text{Current assets}}{\text{Current liabilities}}$	$\dfrac{25\,000}{15\,000}$	$= 1.67$	$\dfrac{35\,000}{20\,000}$	$= 1.75$
(d)	Acid test	$= \dfrac{\text{Liquid assets}}{\text{Current liabilities}}$	$\dfrac{10\,000}{15\,000}$	$= 0.67$	$\dfrac{20\,000}{20\,000}$	$= 1.00$

Comment: Although King's solvency ratios are much stronger than Fisher's, the acid test ratio shows that in terms of current liquidity King is in a worse position than Fisher.

2.5 Russell Enterprises Limited

Solution

			1970	1971	1972	Comment
(a)	Return on net assets	$= \dfrac{\text{Profit before tax and interest (EBIT)}}{\text{Capital employed}}$	$\dfrac{69.5}{300} = 23.2\%$	$\dfrac{85}{400} = 21.3\%$	$\dfrac{89}{410} = 21.7\%$	(a) *Return on net assets.* A small recovery is shown in 1972 following the fall between 1970 and 1971.
(b)	Profit margin	$= \dfrac{\text{Profit before tax and interest (EBIT)}}{\text{Sales}}$	$\dfrac{69.5}{480} = 14.5\%$	$\dfrac{85}{560} = 15.2\%$	$\dfrac{89}{690} = 12.9\%$	(b) *Profit margin.* The level of sales in 1972 was 23 per cent higher than in 1971 but margins were significantly lower. This followed a slight improvement in margin between 1970 and 1971.
(c)	Asset turnover	$= \dfrac{\text{Sales}}{\text{Net assets}}$	$\dfrac{480}{300} = 1.60$ times	$\dfrac{560}{400} = 1.40$ times	$\dfrac{690}{410} = 1.68$ times	(c) *Asset turnover.* The drop in 1971 may be accounted for by the large amount of additional capital not being productive for the full year. The improved capital utilisation in 1972 prevented the lower margins being reflected directly in the return on the net assets figure.
(d)	Return on equity	$= \dfrac{\text{Profit after tax}}{\text{Shareholders' funds}}$	$\dfrac{40}{235} = 17.0\%$	$\dfrac{45}{250} = 18.0\%$	$\dfrac{46}{260} = 17.7\%$	(d) *Return on equity.* The slight decline in 1972 compared with 1971 reflects an increased level of tax charge.
(e)	Earnings per share	$= \dfrac{\text{Profit after tax}}{\text{Number of shares issued}}$	$\dfrac{\pounds40}{600} = 6.7\text{p}$	$\dfrac{\pounds45}{600} = 7.5\text{p}$	$\dfrac{\pounds46}{600} = 7.7\text{p}$	(e) *Earnings per share.* After a significant increase in the previous year, the 1972 figure is only a little higher than 1971.
(f)	Price/earnings ratio	$= \dfrac{\text{Market price per share}}{\text{Earnings per share}}$	$\dfrac{100\text{p}}{6.7} = 15$	$\dfrac{150\text{p}}{7.5} = 20$	$\dfrac{125\text{p}}{7.7} = 16.2$	(f) *Price/earnings ratio.* A fall in 1972, possibly due to the market anticipating a decline in profit margins.
(g)	Dividend per share	$= \dfrac{\text{Dividends paid}}{\text{Number of shares issued}}$	$\dfrac{\pounds30}{600} = 5\text{p}$	$\dfrac{\pounds30}{600} = 5\text{p}$	$\dfrac{\pounds36}{600} = 6\text{p}$	(g) *Dividend per share.* Notice how the increase in the 1972 dividend cuts retained profits.
(h)	Dividend yield	$= \dfrac{\text{Dividend per share}}{\text{Market price per share}}$	$\dfrac{5}{100} = 5.0\%$	$\dfrac{5}{150} = 3.3\%$	$\dfrac{6}{125} = 4.8\%$	(h) *Dividend yield.* The fall in price and increase in dividend lead to a significant increase in the yield between 1971 and 1972.
(i)	Dividend cover	$= \dfrac{\text{Earnings per share}}{\text{Dividend per share}}$	$\dfrac{6.7}{5} = 1.34$	$\dfrac{7.5}{5} = 1.50$	$\dfrac{7.7}{6} = 1.28$	(i) *Dividend cover.* Relatively low now.

Final solution

ABACUS BOOK SHOP LIMITED
Balance sheet, 28 February 1972

	£		£
Share capital		**Fixed asset**	
Ordinary shares	3 000	Leasehold shop	6 000
Revenue reserve		**Current assets**	
Profit and loss account	6 500	Stock	5000
	9 500	Debtors	3000
		Cash	1500
			9 500
Long-term liability			
10% Loan (secured)	3 000		
Current liabilities			
Creditors	3 000		
	£15 500		£15 500

ABACUS BOOK SHOP LIMITED
Balance sheet, ~~31 January~~ 1972
28 February

	£			£
Share capital		**Fixed asset**		
Ordinary shares	3 000	Leasehold shop		6000 [b]
Revenue reserve	6500	**Current assets**		
Profit and loss account	~~5000~~	Stock	~~4000~~	5000
+1 000 [c]		−2000 [c] +2500 [e]		
+500 [d]	~~8000~~	−1500 [d] +2000 [f]		
10% Loan [a]	9,500			
	3000	Debtors	~~1000~~	3000
Current liabilities	~~3,800~~	+2000 [d]		
Creditors	~~1000~~	Cash	~~4000~~	1500
+2,000 [f]				
		+3000 [a]		
		−6000 [b]		
		+3000 [c]		9500
	~~15,500~~	−2500 [e]		~~9000~~
	9000			£~~9000~~
				15,500

Note

1 Notice the two new balance sheet categories:
  Fixed asset: Leasehold shop
  Long-term liability: 10% loan.

3.4 Chemical Engineering Company Limited

Solution

Final Solution

CHEMICAL ENGINEERING COMPANY LIMITED
Balance sheet, 31 August 1972

	£			£
Share capital		**Fixed assets**		
Ordinary shares	50 000	Plant at cost		40 000
Revenue reserve		**Current assets**		
Profit and loss account	17 000	Stock	7 000	
	67 000	Debtors	25 000	
		Cash	2 000	
				34 000
Current liabilities				
Creditors	7 000			
	£74 000			£74 000

CHEMICAL ENGINEERING COMPANY LIMITED
Balance sheet, 31 ~~July~~ August 1972

	£			£
Share capital		**Fixed assets**		
Ordinary shares	50 000	Plant at cost	~~30 000~~	
		+10,000 [a]		40,000
Revenue reserve		**Current assets**		
Profit and loss account	17,000 ~~20 000~~	Stock	7,000 ~~25 000~~	
	+15,000 [c]		−18,000 [d]	25,000
	−18,000 [d]	Debtors	~~15 000~~	
	~~70 000~~ 67,000		+15,000 [c]	
Current liabilities			− 5,000 [e]	2,000
Creditors	~~12 000~~	Cash	~~12 000~~	
	7,000		−10,000 [a]	
−5,000 [b]			− 5,000 [b]	34,000
			+ 5000 [e]	~~52,000~~
	~~£74,000~~			~~£82 000~~
	£82 000			£74,000

Notes

1 Notice that there was a *loss* on the sale of goods. Sales proceeds were £15 000 while the goods had cost £18 000. The loss of £3 000 (being a negative profit) is *deducted* from the £20 000 balance on profit and loss account.

3.5 Whitewash Laundry Limited

Solution

Final solution

WHITEWASH LAUNDRY LIMITED
Balance sheet, 31 March 1973

	£		£
Share capital		**Fixed asset**	
Ordinary shares	75 000	Laundry and equipment	50 000
Revenue reserve		**Current assets**	
Profit and loss account	24 000	Debtors	35 000
		Cash	14 000
			49 000
	£99 000		£99 000

Profit and loss account
for the quarter ending 31 March 1973

		£
Sales		60 000
Less: Supplies	6 000	
Operating expenses	30 000	
		36 000
Gross profit		24 000
Selling and administrative expenses		15 000
Net profit		9 000
Balance brought forward		15 000
Balance carried forward		£24 000

Working paper

WHITEWASH LAUNDRY LIMITED
Balance sheet, ~~1 January~~ 1973
    31 March

	£		£
Share capital		**Fixed asset**	
Ordinary shares	75 000	Laundry and equipment	50 000
Revenue reserve		**Current assets**	
Profit and loss account	24,000 / ~~15 000~~	Debtors	~~30 000~~ 35,000
See below		+60,000ᵃ	
		−55,000ᶜ	
		Cash	14,000 / ~~10 000~~
		− 6,000ᵇ	49,000
		+55,000ᶜ	~~40 000~~
		−30,000ᵈ	
		+15,000ᵉ	
	£99,000 / ~~£90 000~~		~~£90 000~~ £99,000

Profit and loss account

As shown on left.

3.10 A Green Limited

Solution

Cash book

1 April	Balance	3 000	(d)	Operating expenses	2 000
(b)	Sales	15 000	(e)	Creditors (suppliers)	14 000
(f)	Debtors	3 000		Balance c/d	5 000
		£21 000			£21 000
	Balance b/d	5 000			

Ledger

Share Capital

	1 April Balance	3 000

Profit and Loss Account

	1 April Balance	2 000

Creditors

(e)	Cash	14 000	1 April	Balance	3 000
	Balance c/d	5 000	(a)	Stock	16 000
		£19 000			£19 000
				Balance b/d	5 000

Vans

1 April Balance	4 000	

Stock

(a)	Creditors	16 000	(b)	Cost of sales	12 000
			(c)	Cost of sales	4 000
		£16 000			£16 000

Debtors

1 April	Balance	1 000	(f)	Cash	3 000
(c)	Sales	5 000		Balance c/d	3 000
		£6 000			£6 000
	Balance b/d	3 000			

Sales

			(b)	Cash	15 000
			(c)	Debtors	5 000
					20 000

Cost of Sales

(b)	Stock	12 000
(c)	Stock	4 000
		16 000

Operating Expenses

(d)	Cash	2 000

A GREEN LIMITED

Trial balance, 30 June 1973

	Total Dr	Total Cr	Profit and loss account Dr	Profit and loss account Cr	Balance sheet Dr	Balance sheet Cr
Share capital		3 000				3 000
Profit and loss account		2 000				2 000
Creditors		5 000				5 000
Vans	4 000				4 000	
Stock	—					
Debtors	3 000				3 000	
Sales		20 000		20 000		
Cost of sales	16 000		16 000			
Operating expenses	2 000		2 000			
Cash	5 000				5 000	
Profit for quarter			2 000			2 000
	£30 000	£30 000	£20 000	£20 000	£12 000	£12 000

A GREEN LIMITED
Balance sheet, 30 June 1973

	£			£
Share capital		**Fixed asset**		
Ordinary shares	3 000	Vans		4 000
Revenue reserve				
Profit and loss account	4 000			
	7 000			
Current liability		**Current assets**		
Creditors	5 000	Debtors	3000	
		Cash	5000	8 000
	£12 000			£12 000

A GREEN LIMITED
Profit and loss account
for the three months ending 30 June 1973

	£
Sales	20 000
Cost of sales	16 000
Gross profit	4 000
Operating expenses	2 000
Net profit	2 000

Did you remember to note the period covered by the profit and loss account?

3.11 Precision Engineering Limited

Solution

Cash book

1 July	Balance	4 000	(c)	Stock	25 000
(a)	Sales	35 000	(e)	Expenses	10 000
(g)	Debtors	13 000	(f)	Creditors	9 000
			Dec	Balance c/d	8 000
		£52 000			£52 000
1 Jan	Balance b/d	8 000			

Ledger

Share capital

			1 July Balance	30 000

Profit and loss account

			1 Jan Balance	13 000

Creditors

(f)	Cash	9 000	1 July Balance	10 000
	Balance c/d	9 000	(d) Stock	8 000
		£18 000		£18 000
			1 Jan Balance b/d	9 000

Factory and machinery

1 July	Balance	25 000	

Stock

1 July	Balance	20 000	(a)	Cost of Sales	25 000
(c)	Cash	25 000	(c)	Cost of Sales	11 000
(d)	Creditors	8 000		Balance c/d	17 000
		£53 000			£53 000
1 Jan	Balance b/d	17 000			

Debtors

1 July	Balance	6 000	(a)	Cash	13 000
(b)	Sales	15 000		Balance c/d	8 000
		£21 000			£21 000
1 Jan	Balance b/d	8 000			

Sales

		July	Balance	40 000
		(a)	Cash	35 000
		(b)	Debtors	15 000
				90 000

Cost of sales

1 July	Balance	30 000	
(a)	Stock	25 000	
(b)	Stock	11 000	
		66 000	

Expenses

1 July	Balance	7 000	
(a)	Cash	10 000	
		17 000	

Tax

1 July	Balance	1 000	

Trial balance, 31 December 1972

	Total Dr	Total Cr	Profit and loss account Dr	Profit and loss account Cr	Balance sheet Dr	Balance sheet Cr
Share capital		30 000				30 000
Profit and loss account		13 000				13 000
Creditors		9 000				9 000
Factory and machinery	25 000				25 000	
Stock	17 000				17 000	
Debtors	8 000				8 000	
Sales		90 000		90 000		
Cost of sales	66 000		66 000			
Expenses	17 000		17 000			
Tax	1 000		1 000			
Cash	8 000				8 000	
Profit for year			6 000			6 000
	£142 000	142 000	90 000	90 000	58 000	58 000

Note
The balance shown on the profit and loss account in the ledger at 30 June when the transactions for 1972 appear in separate ledger accounts is the balance as at 1 January 1972 not that appearing in the balance sheet at 30 June.

PRECISION ENGINEERING LIMITED
Balance sheet, 31 December 1972

	£		£
Share capital		**Fixed assets**	
Ordinary shares	30 000	Factory and machinery	25 000
Revenue reserve		**Current assets**	
Profit and loss account	19 000	Stock 17 000	
	49 000	Debtors 8 000	
		Cash 8 000	
			33 000
Current liabilities			
Creditors	9 000		
	£58 000		£58 000

Profit and loss account
for the year ending 31 December 1972

	£
Sales	90 000
Cost of sales	66 000
Gross profit	24 000
Expenses	17 000
Profit before tax	7 000
Tax	1 000
Profit after tax	6 000
Balance brought forward	13 000
Balance carried forward	£19 000

WHEELER LIMITED

	Trial balance Dr £	Cr £	Adjustments Dr £	Cr £	Profit and loss Dr £	Cr £	Balance sheet Dr £	Cr £
Cash book	20 100						20 100	
Ordinary share capital		20 000						20 000
Profit and loss account b/f		28 300						28 300
12% Loan		30 000						30 000
Fixed assets: cost	94 200						94 200	
Fixed assets: accumulated depreciation		34 700						34 700
Sales ledger control	18 300						18 300	
Stock	14 100			1 200			12 900	
Purchase ledger control		3 900						3 900
Accrued charges				500⎫ 900⎭				1 400
Tax liability				12 500				12 500
Dividend payable				8 000				8 000
Sales		144 200				144 200		
Cost of goods sold	81 800		1 200		83 000			
Selling and administrative expenses	29 900		500		30 400			
Loan interest	2 700		900		3 600			
Tax expense			12 500		12 500			
Ordinary dividend			8 000		8 000			
					137 500			
Profit for year retained					6 700			6 700*
	£261 100	261 100	23 100	23 100	144 200	144 200	145 500	145 500

*See note on next page.

WHEELER LIMITED

Notes on trial balance schedule solution

1 Notice that the names of accounts were included in the trial balance schedule even though there was no balance in the "trial balance" column itself, for instance for accrued charges, tax liability, dividend payable, tax expense and ordinary dividend. In practice, of course, one would have to be prepared to write in the names of accounts if necessary.

2 Three categories of accounts sometimes give difficulty: those connected with tax, dividends and depreciation. Perhaps tax is the easiest to use as an example.

In the Wheeler case notice that *two* accounts have been opened for tax: one for "tax expense," which is a debit (and appears in the profit and loss account as an expense), and the other for "tax liability," which is a credit (and appears in the balance sheet as a liability).

In practice it is not uncommon for only a single "tax" account to be opened. It would appear thus:

TAX

Balance c/d	12 500	Profit and loss a/c	12 500
		Balance b/d	12 500

Although an experienced accountant would have no difficulty in dealing with the necessary entries on a single account, it is probably simpler for anyone else to deliberately set up *two* accounts, one for the expense and the other for the liability.

In the same way it may be best to have *separate* accounts for "depreciation expense" and "accumulated depreciation," and for "dividend payable" (the liability) and "ordinary dividend" (the debit in the appropriation account).

3 Notice how the profit for the year in the trial balance schedule (£6 700) is the *excess* of the credits in the profit and loss account columns over the debits. It is therefore added to the debits, to "balance" the columns, and the *credit* balance is extended into the balance sheet columns. The new accumulated balance on the profit and loss account is now £35 000 (= £28 300 + £6 700).

4 The dividend is 40 per cent of the ordinary share capital, that is 40% × £20 000 = £8 000.

WHEELER LIMITED
Profit and loss account
for the year ended 31 March 1971

	£
Sales	144 200
Cost of goods sold	83 000
Gross profit	61 200
Selling and administrative expenses	30 400
	30 800
Loan interest payable	3 600
Profit before tax	27 200
Tax	12 500
Profit after tax	14 700
Ordinary dividend	8 000
Retained from the year's profit	£6 700

WHEELER LIMITED
Balance sheet, 31 March 1971

Share capital and reserve	£	Fixed assets	£
Ordinary share capital	20 000	at cost	94 200
Profit and loss account	35 000	*Less:* Accumulated	
		depreciation	34 700
	55 000		59 500
Loan			
12% Loan	30 000	**Current assets**	
		Stock	12 900
		Debtors	18 300
		Cash	20 100
			51 300
		Less: **Current liabilities**	
		Tax	12 500
		Creditors	3 900
		Accrued charges	1 400
		Dividend	8 000
			25 800
		Net current assets	25 500
	£85 000		£85 000

4.5 Canning and Sons Limited

Solution

CANNING AND SONS LIMITED
Balance sheet, 31 December 1970

	£			£
Share capital	40 000	Fixed assets, net		33 000
Profit and loss account	*23,100* ~~24 300~~	Current assets	*19,300*	
	~~64 300~~	Stock	~~21 300~~	
	63,100	Debtors	25 400	
		Cash	2 600	*47,300* ~~49 300~~

Current liabilities

Creditors	13 200			
Tax	~~4 800~~ *14,000*	*17,200* ~~18 000~~		*80,300*
		~~£82 300~~ *80,300*		~~£82 300~~

Profit and loss account for 1970

			£
Sales			112 700
Cost of sales: Opening stock		14 600	
Purchases		93 800	
		108 400	
Less: Closing stock	*19,300*	~~21 300~~	
		89,100	~~87 100~~
Gross profit		*23,600*	~~25 600~~
Selling and administrative expenses			11 300
Profit before tax		*12,300*	~~14 300~~
Tax		*4,000*	~~4 800~~
Profit after tax		*8,300*	~~£9 500~~

4.6 Anderson Tiles Limited

Solution

Closing stock valuation		
3000 cases at £5.00	=	£15 000
2000 cases at £4.75	=	£ 9 500
1000 cases at £4.25	=	£ 4 250
		£28 750

Cost of sales	
Opening stock	£12 000
Purchases	£41 500
	£53 500
Less: Closing stock	£28 750
	£24 750

Cost of sales identified		
3000 cases at £4.00	=	£12 000
3000 cases at £4.25	=	£12 750
		£24 750

4.7 Berwick Paper Limited

Solution

BERWICK PAPER LIMITED

Date 1970	Stock	Hundred-weights	Average cost £	Amount £	Value of Issues £
Jan	Opening	1200	21.0	25 200	
March	Issues	900	21.0	18 900	18 900
		300	21.0	6 300	
March	Purchases	1800	18.0	32 400	
		2100	18.4	38 700	
June	Issues	1700	18.4	31 300	31 300
		400	18.4	7 400	
June	Purchases	2400	15.0	36 000	
		2800	15.5	43 400	
Sept	Issues	1400	15.5	21 700	21 700
		1400	15.5	21 700	
Sept	Purchases	1200	25.0	30 000	
		2600	19.9	51 700	
Dec	Issues	1900	19.9	37 800	37 800
		700	19.9	13 900	
Dec	Purchases	1800	20.0	36 000	
	Closing	2500	£20.0	£49 900	£109 700

Opening stock		£ 25 200
Purchases		134 400
		159 600
Less: Closing stock		49 900
Cost of issues		£109 700

4.8 Newport Machines Limted

Solution

The overhead percentage is:

$$\frac{540\ 000}{300\ 000} = 180 \text{ per cent on direct labour}$$

The stock will therefore be valued as follows:

Direct materials	30 000
Direct labour	20 000
Overheads (180% × 20 000)	36 000
	£86 000

Note

The absorption cost method defers some *period* expenses by relating them to the *products* in stock. (Not all overheads, of course, are necessarily period costs)

4.9 Wingate Hardware Limited

Solution

Stock valuation, 31 August 1970

		£
Total per stock sheets		21 600
Less: Complete write-off of kitchen utensils (included at £200 at 31 August 1969)	200	
Write-down of dustbins from £1600 to £900	700	
		900
Stock value at 31 August 1970		£20 700

Cost of sales
for the year ending 31 August 1970

	£
Opening stock at 1 September 1969	17 400
Add: Purchases during year	52 700
	70 100
Less: Closing stock at 31 August 1970	20 700
Cost of sales for year	£49 400

4.10 Tiptop Office Supplies

Solution

Provision for bad debts

Sept 70 Balance c/d	2130	Oct 69	Balance b/f	1000
		Sept 70	Bad debts	1130
	£2130			£2130
		Oct 70	Balance b/d	2130

Bad debts expense

Sept 70 Debtors	1700	Sept 70	Profit and loss	
Sept 70 Provision for			account	2830
bad debts	1130			
	£2830			£2830

Provision for bad debts at 30 September 1970 is 5% × £42 600 = £2130.
(This, as the ledger account shows, is a *credit* balance, and is deducted on the balance sheet from the amount of the debtors. Thus "debtors" on the balance sheet will simply appear as £40 470 at 30 September 1970.)

Bad debt expense is the amount of bad debts written off, £1700, plus the *increase* in the provision for bad debts, £1130—a total of £2830.

5.5 Lawson Limited (A)

Solution

			(c)
(c)	Fixed asset, at cost		£7200
	Less: Accumulated depreciation		3300
	Net book value		£3900

Notes

1 Notice again how in each case the total amount written off over the asset's life is its total net cost:
   (a) £7200 − £3500 = £3700 = (4 × £1100) − £700.
   (b) £7200 − £1400 = £5800 = (5 × £1100) + £300.
2 Notice that where a residual value is taken into account in calculating depreciation the straight line method does *not* charge simply one sixth of cost (= £1200) each year. Instead the charge is one-sixth of the *expected net* cost (that is, one-sixth × £6600).

		(a) £	(b) £
	Cost	7200	7200
Year 1	Depreciation	1100	1100
	Net book value	6100	6100
Year 2	Depreciation	1100	1100
	Net book value	5000	5000
Year 3	Depreciation	1100	1100
	Net book value	3900	3900
Year 4	Depreciation	1100	1100
	Net book value	2800	2800
	Sales proceeds	3500	
	Profit on sale	£ 700	
Year 5	Depreciation		1100
	Net book value		1700
	Sales proceeds		1400
	Loss on sale		£(300)

5.6 Lawson Limited (B)

Solution

	Dr £	Cr £
Year 4 Cash	3500	
Realisation account		3500

To record cash proceeds on sale of asset.

	Dr £	Cr £
Year 4 Realisation account	700	
Profit and loss account		700

To transfer profit on sale of asset.

Note
The annual depreciation expense in each of years 1 to 4 would be transferred to the profit and loss account by crediting "depreciation expense" and debiting "profit and loss account."

		Dr £	Cr £
Year 1	Depreciation expense	1100	
	Accumulated depreciation		1100

To record the annual depreciation charge.

		Dr £	Cr £
Year 2	Depreciation expense	1100	
	Accumulated depreciation		1100

To record the annual depreciation charge.

		Dr £	Cr £
Year 3	Depreciation expense	1100	
	Accumulated depreciation		1100

To record the annual depreciation charge.

		Dr £	Cr £
Year 4	Depreciation expense	1100	
	Accumulated depreciation		1100

To record the annual depreciation charge.

		Dr £	Cr £
Year 4	Realisation account	2800	
	Accumulated depreciation	4400	
	Cost of fixed asset		7200

To transfer the net book value to realisation account.

Solution

Depreciation expense

		£			£
Year 1	Journal	1100	Year 1	P&L a/c	1100
Year 2	Journal	1100	Year 2	P&L a/c	1100
Year 3	Journal	1100	Year 3	P&L a/c	1100
Year 4	Journal	1100	Year 4	P&L a/c	1100

Realisation account

		£			£
Year 4	Journal (cost)	7200	Year 4	Journal (Depreciation to date)	4400
Year 4	P&L a/c (Profit on sale)	700	Year 4	Cash	3500
		£7900			£7900

Cash

		£			£
Year 4	Realisation	3500	Year 1	Asset	7200

Fixed asset: Cost

		£			£
Year 1	Cash	7200	Year 4	Journal (Realisation)	7200

Accumulated depreciation

		£			£
			Year 1	Journal (Expense)	1100
Year 2	Balance c/d	2200	Year 2	Journal (Expense)	1100
		£2200			£2200
			Year 3	Balance b/d	2200
Year 3	Balance c/d	3300	Year 3	Journal (Expense)	1100
		£3300			£3300
Year 4	Journal (Realisation)	4400	Year 4	Balance b/d	3300
			Year 4	Journal (Expense)	1100
		£4400			£4400

Note

It is not unusual to expect some profit or loss on sale in advance. With declining balance it is not always easy to find a rate that will conveniently write the asset down to its expected residual value over its expected life. With straight line depreciation residual value is often ignored, even though some proceeds are expected.

Note

An alternative approach would be not to write off any "ordinary" depreciation in year 6, and to treat the difference between the net book value at the end of year 5 (£250) and the sales proceeds (£600) as a "profit on sale" in year 6.

5.8 James Hillier Limited (A)

Solution

		£
	Cost	8000
Year 1	Depreciation (50%)	4000
	Net book value	4000
Year 2	Depreciation (50% of opening net book value)	2000
	Net book value	2000
Year 3	Depreciation	1000
	Net book value	1000
Year 4	Depreciation	500
	Net book value	500
	Expected proceeds	750
	Expected profit on sale	£250

5.9 James Hillier Limited (B)

Solution

(a)		£
Year 4	Net book value	500
Year 5	Depreciation (50%)	250
	Net book value	250
Year 6	Depreciation	125
	Net book value	125
	Sales proceeds	600
	Profit on sale	£475

Note

Entries (ii), (iii) and (iv) opposite could be combined in a *single* journal entry, as follows:

	Dr £	Cr £
Cash	600	
Accumulated depreciation	7875	
Cost of fixed asset		8000
Profit and loss account		475

In complicated cases (and perhaps even in simple cases) it may be desirable to go through three stages in dealing with disposals of fixed assets:

1 Transfer net book value to realisation account, clearing the cost and accumulated depreciation balances in the ledger accounts.
2 Enter proceeds in the realisation account.
3 Transfer the balance on the realisation account (the profit or loss on sale) to the profit and loss account.

Note

Notice how Sullivan has charged as much depreciation in the first year as Gilbert has charged in the first four years, due to an accelerated method and a 6-year estimated life, instead of a 10-year estimated life and the straight line method.

It is hard to suppose that these two companies, showing different profits, different total assets and different trends, would be rated in the same way by external analysts—even though they are identical except for their depreciation policies.

It is worth emphasising that the depreciation is *necessarily* only an estimate in most cases, since an asset's life is rarely known in advance. Any error in estimating a fixed asset's useful life involves a "misal-location" of depreciation between years, which affects the balance sheet as well as the profit and loss account.

There is no way of avoiding this problem.

(b) Journal entries for year 6

	Dr £	Cr £
(i) Depreciation expense	125	
Accumulated depreciation		125
Annual depreciation charge in year 6.		
(ii) Accumulated depreciation	7875	
Realisation of fixed assets	125	
Cost of fixed asset		8000
Transferring asset's net book value to a realisation account.		
(iii) Cash	600	
Realisation of fixed assets		600
Entering the sales proceeds in the realisation account.		
(iv) Realisation of fixed assets	475	
Profit and loss account		475
Transferring the profit on sale to the profit and loss account.		

5.10 Gilbert Limited and Sullivan Limited

Solution

		Gilbert Limited £	Sullivan Limited £
	Cost	7200	7200
Year 1	Depreciation	600	2400
	Net book value	6600	4800
Year 2	Depreciation	600	1600
	Net book value	6000	3200
Year 3	Depreciation	600	1067
	Net book value	5400	2133
Year 4	Depreciation	600	711
	Net book value	4800	1422
	Sales proceeds	200	200
	Loss on disposal	£4600	£1222

320

5.11 Hobson Limited

Solution

		£
	Cost	20 000
Year 1	Writing-down allowance 60%	12 000
	Written down value	8 000
Year 2	Writing-down allowance 25%	2 000
	Written down value	6 000
Year 3	Writing-down allowance 25%	1 500
	Written down value	4 500
Year 4	Writing-down allowance	1 125
	Written down value	3 375
Year 5	Writing-down allowance	844
	Written down value	2 531
Year 6	Writing-down allowance	633
	Written down value	1 898
Year 7	Sales proceeds	2 000
	Profit on sale*	£ 102

*Called a "balancing charge" for tax purposes, and subject to corporation tax at ordinary rates.

5.12 Adam Limited and Bede Limited (A)

Solution

(a) *Tax writing-down allowances* (same for both companies)

		£
	Cost	40 000
Year 1	Allowance 60%	24 000
	Written down value	16 000
Year 2	Allowance 25%	4 000
	Written down value	12 000
Year 3	Allowance 25%	3 000
	Written down value	9 000
Year 4	Allowance 25%	2 250
	Written down value	6 750
Year 5	Allowance 25%	1 687
	Written down value	5 063
	Sales proceeds	—
	Loss on sale ("Balancing allowance")	£5 063

(b) *Actual tax liability* (same for both companies)
Year 1   40% × £ 4 000 (£28 000 − £24 000) = £ 1 600
Year 2   40% × £24 000 (£28 000 − £ 4 000) = £ 9 600
Year 3   40% × £25 000 (£28 000 − £ 3 000) = £10 000
Year 4   40% × £25 750 (£28 000 − £ 2 250) = £10 300
Year 5   40% × £21 250 (£28 000 − £ 6 750) = £ 8 500

5.13 Adam Limited and Bede Limited (B)

Solution

(a) Reported profits

	Adam Limited			Bede Limited		
	Profit before tax	Tax	Profit after tax	Profit before tax	Tax	Profit after tax
	£	£	£	£	£	£
Year 1	20 000	1 600	18 400	20 000	8 000	12 000
Year 2	20 000	9 600	10 400	20 000	8 000	12 000
Year 3	20 000	10 000	10 000	20 000	8 000	12 000
Year 4	20 000	10 300	9 700	20 000	8 000	12 000
Year 5	20 000	8 500	11 500	20 000	8 000	12 000

Notes

1 Profit before tax is the annual profit before depreciation and tax (£28 000) less the reported depreciation charge (£8000), which is the cost of £40 000 divided by the expected life five years.

2 The reported tax charge is, of course, the *actual* tax liability for Adam (which ignores deferred tax). This is taken from the (A) problem. Bede charges 40 per cent of profit before tax each year.

(b) Deferred tax reserve account (Bede Limited only)

		Dr £	Cr £
Year 1	40% × £16 000 (£24 000$_t$ − £8 000$_r$)		6400
Year 2	40% × £ 4 000 (£ 8 000$_r$ − £4 000$_t$)	1600	
Year 3	40% × £ 5 000 (£ 8 000$_r$ − £3 000$_t$)	2000	
Year 4	40% × £ 5 750 (£ 8 000$_r$ − £2 250$_t$)	2300	
Year 5	40% × £ 1 250 (£ 8 000$_r$ − £6 750$_t$)	500	
		£6400	£6400

Notes

r = reported depreciation charge.

t = tax depreciation allowance.

Notice how the account is cleared over the life of the asset—necessarily, since total tax depreciation = total reported depreciation (= total net cost of the asset).

Notes

1 A 1 for 4 rights issue involves issuing a quarter of the shares now in issue. In this case the price per share is 200p so the proceeds from the issue will be:

$\frac{1}{4} \times 100 = 25\,000$ shares at 200p $=$ £50 000

2 The proceeds from the rights issue must be added to the cash balance.

3 On the capital side of the balance sheet, the proceeds from the new issue of shares are split between:

(a) Nominal share capital,
25 000 shares at 50p $=$ £12 500

(b) Share premium account,
25 000 shares at 200p $-$ 50p
at 150p $=$ £37 500

4 Notice that both assets and shareholders' funds have increased by £50 000—the cash received from the issue by the company.

6.5 Kent Traders Limited

Solution

KENT TRADERS LIMITED
Balance sheet, 30 April 1970

	£		£
125	*62,500* ~~50 000~~	Fixed assets at cost	93 000
~~100~~ 000 ordinary 50p shares		*Less:* accumulated depreciation	18 000
Share premium account	*37,500*		75 000
		Current assets	
Profit and loss account	26 000	Cash	*5*7 000
		Stock	26 000
		Debtors	19 000
	~~76~~ 000 *126*		~~52~~ 000 *102*
Long-term loans	27 000	*Less:*	
		Current tax	11 000
		Creditors	13 000
			24 000
	[153	Net current assets	*78* ~~28~~ 000
	£~~103~~,000		£~~103~~ 000 *[153*

323

Notes

1 Notice the £90 000 increase in reserves after conversion of the loan stock. The conversion rate—forty ordinary £1 shares for every £100 of loan stock—implies a price per share of £2.50p, which gives a *premium* of £1.50p per share above the *nominal* price of £1.00.

   If all the £150 000 loan stock is converted, 60 000 new £1 ordinary shares will be issued. Therefore £60 000 will be added to the share capital account, and £90 000 (= 60 000 shares at 150p premium) to the share premium account.

2 Total capital employed has not changed. No new capital has been raised, but one form of capital has been converted into another form.

3 Notice the significant reduction in the debt ratio. (Interest cover has also increased—from 6.2 to 17.8.) An analyst would want to be well aware of this *potential* change in the company's capital structure when analysing the accounts, even before conversion actually took place.

4 Finally, conversion reduces earnings per share by 10 per cent, although profit after tax increases.

6.6 Antrobus Lathes Limited

Solution

ANTROBUS LATHES LIMITED
Balance sheet, 1970

	Actual	With loan converted
	£'000	£'000
Ordinary £1 shares	240	300
Reserves	110	200
Shareholders' funds	350	500
10% Convertible loan stock	150	—
8% Loan stock	100	100
Capital employed	**£600**	**£600**
Debt ratio	$\frac{250}{600} = 42\%$	$\frac{100}{600} = 17\%$

Profit and loss account, 1970

	Actual		With loan converted
EBIT		143	143
Interest: 10% Loan	15		
8% Loan	8		8
		23	8
Profit before tax		120	135
Tax (40%)		48	54
Profit after tax		£ 72	£ 81
Earnings per share		$\frac{72}{240} = 30p$	$\frac{81}{300} = 27p$

Notes

1 The bonus issue in (*c*) involves capitalising reserves. Normal practice is to use up the most "permanent" reserves first—that is, share premium account, then other capital reserves, then the revenue reserves.

2 The cash dividend of £27 000 in (*d*) (= 12 per cent of £225 000) is deducted from the £38 000 profit for ordinary, leaving £11 000 retained profits for the year to be added to the accumulated balance on profit and loss account—and, by assumption, to working capital.

3 The 1 for 15 bonus issue (on issued capital of £225 000) capitalises more of the reserves; and since there is now no balance on either share premium account, or capital reserves, the amount to be capitalised, £15 000, must come from profit and loss account.

   But the bonus issue is a *capital* issue, and bears no relationship to the profit for the year.

4 Did you remember to change the description of land and buildings from "cost" to "valuation"?

Solution

WESTERN ENTERPRISES LIMITED
Balance sheet ~~1 January~~ *31 December* 1970

£'000

Fixed assets:		
Land and buildings, at ~~Cost~~ *Valuation*	150	70 $+80^b$
Plant, net book value	170	170
	320	240
Working capital	106	80 $+15^d + 11^d$
Net assets	426	£320
~~70~~ *240* 000 Ordinary £1 shares	240	70 $+5^a +150^c +15^d$
Share premium account	—	35 $+10^a -45^c$
Capital Reserve	—	$+80^b -80^c$
Profit and loss account	66	95 $+11^d -25^c -15^d$
Shareholders' funds	306	200
20 000 8% £1 Preference shares	20	20
10% Loan stock	100	100
Capital employed	426	£320

Notes

1 Converting preference capital into loan stock does affect the company's legal "capital" (which consists of ordinary plus preference share capital), though it does not change total capital employed.

2 The 5 for 1 share split does not affect the £300 000 ordinary share capital in total, but it changes 300 000 £1 shares into 1 500 000 20p shares.

3 Retained profits for the year in (d) are £3000 after a cash dividend of £45 000 (=15 per cent on £300 000) has been paid from profits for ordinary of £48 000.

Solution

WESTERN ENTERPRISES LIMITED
Balance sheet ~~1 January~~ 1971
                 31 December

	£'000			
Fixed assets:				
Land and buildings, at valuation	150	150		
Plant, net book value	170	170		
	320	320		
Working capital	179	106	$+70^a$	$+3^d$
	499	£426		
Net assets				
~~240 000~~ 1,650,000 Ordinary ~~£1~~ 20p shares	330	240	$+60^a$	$+30^d$
Share premium account	—		$+10^a$	-10^d
Profit and loss account	49	66		-20^d
				$+3^d$
Shareholders' funds	379	306		
20 000 8% £1 Preference shares	5	20	-15^b	
10% Loan stock	115	100	$+15^b$	
Capital employed	499	£426		

Notes

1 The layout has been changed, by subtotalling shareholders' funds and by deducting current liabilities from current assets.

2 A possible alternative "debt ratio" is to compare *total* liabilities with *total* assets, that is, long-term debt plus current liabilities with fixed assets plus current assets.

In this case the ratios would be:

(A) 80/160 = 50 per cent
(B) 110/250 = 44 per cent
(C) 400/750 = 53.3 per cent (450/750 = 60 per cent with preference capital).

But it is more usual (and generally more useful) to consider only the structure of *long-term* capital.

3 A 6 per cent after-tax preference dividend requires profits of 10 per cent before a 40 per cent tax. Thus including the preference dividend increases C's burden by £5000 (= £3000 × 100/100 − 40), and reduces the cover to 5.7 times.

6.9 Debt ratios

Solution

Debt ratios

	A £'000	B £'000	C £'000	
Ordinary share capital	30	60	100	
Reserves	50	80	200	
Shareholders' funds	80	140	300	
6% Preference share capital	—	—	50	
Long-term 10% loans	20	40	150	
Capital employed	£100	£180	£500	
Fixed assets, net	90	160	400	
Current assets	70	90	350	
Less: Current liabilities	60	70	250	
Net current assets	10	20	100	
Net assets	£100	£180	£500	
Debt	20	40	150	(200*)
Capital employed	100	180	500	(500*)
Debt/capital employed ratio	20%	22%	30%	(40%*)
Profit before interest and tax	32	44	115	(115*)
Interest	2	4	15	(20*)
Interest cover	16.0	11.0	7.7	(5.7*)

*Including preference share capital.

Notes

1 The ordinary dividend of 8 per cent is calculated on the *nominal* ordinary share capital of £200 000 (200 000 shares of £1 each), *not* on the ordinary shareholders' funds of £260 000.

2 Notice how the preference dividend of £3000 (= 5 per cent on 60 000 £1 shares) is "grossed up" to calculate the "before-tax" equivalent to be added to the loan interest. It would not make sense to add together a before-tax amount and an after-tax amount.

    To convert an after-tax amount £x into its before-tax equivalent, where the tax rate is *t*, the formula is:

$$\left(\frac{x}{100 - t}\right)100$$

3 Notice that "profit for ordinary" is often *not* shown as a separate sub-total where there are both preference dividends and ordinary dividends. The normal practice is for the two different kinds of dividend to be added together, and then deducted from profit after tax to give retained profits.

6.10 Sadler Limited (A)

Solution

		£'000
Earnings before interest and tax		48
10% Debenture interest		8
Profit before tax		40
Tax (at 40%)		16
Profit after tax		24
Dividends: 5% Preference	3	
8% Ordinary	16	
		19
Retained profits		£ 5

(*a*) Interest cover = 48/8 = 6.0 times.

(*b*) Interest payable (before tax)　　　　　　　　8
　　　Preference dividend (before tax*)　　　　　5
　　　Cover for interest and preference dividend = 48/13 = 3.7 times.
　* = £3000 after 40% tax.

(*c*) Profit for ordinary shareholders　　　21 (=24 − 3)
　　　8% ordinary dividend (on £200 000)　　16
　　　Dividend cover = 21/16 = 1.3 times.

Notes

1 In this case net assets realise enough to pay creditors (both short-term and long-term) in full. If there were not enough to do that, and assuming that all creditors were "unsecured," every creditor would be paid *pro rata* (except for certain debts, such as amounts due for wages, and taxes, which have statutory priority). There is *no* priority for current as opposed to longer-term creditors.

2 As you know, balance sheets are prepared on a going-concern basis, and do not purport to show the *realisable value* of *all* the company's assets. Balance sheets show the *unexpired costs* of those assets which have cost something. (Some valuable assets, for instance goodwill, may have cost nothing.)

3 Despite the above, some analysts refer to a calculation of "book value per share" from time to time. This simply assumes that net assets could be realised for their book value; and divides the ordinary shareholders' funds by the number of ordinary shares in issue.

For Sadler Limited, then, the "book value per share" is 130p (260/200).

6.11 Sadler Limited (B)

Solution

	£'000
Ordinary share capital	200
Profit and loss account	60
Ordinary shareholders' funds	260
5% Preference share capital	60
8% Debentures	80
Capital employed	**£400**

(a) Debt ratio = 80/400 = 20%.
(140/400 = 35% if preference share capital is counted as "debt".)

(b)

	£'000
If net assets realise	125
debentures amount to	80
leaving for preference and ordinary shareholders	45
but preference share capital is	60

Therefore preference shareholders will get only 75 per cent of the nominal amount of their shares, that is, 75p per share. Ordinary shareholders will get *nothing*.

(c)

	£'000
If net assets realise	190
debentures and preference capital	140
leave for ordinary shareholders	50 (=25p per share)

6.12 Bell Limited, Book Limited, and Candle Limited.

Solution

	Bell Limited £	Book Limited £	Candle Limited £
(a) 1970			
EBIT	18 000	18 000	18 000
Interest	6 000	2 000	—
Profit before tax	12 000	16 000	18 000
Tax at 40%	4 800	6 400	7 200
Profit after tax	£7 200	£9 600	£10 800
(i) Return on net assets	18%	18%	18%
(ii) Return on equity	18.0%	12.0%	10.8%
(iii) Interest cover	3.0	9.0	—
(iv) Earnings per share	48p	32p	27p
(b) 1971			
EBIT	5 000	5 000	5 000
Interest	6 000	2 000	—
Profit (loss) before tax	(1 000)	3 000	5 000
Tax at 40%	—*	1 200	2 000
Profit (loss) after tax	£(1 000)	£1 800	£3 000

*Tax refund of £400 might be available in respect of the loss.

(i) Return on net assets	5%	5%	5%
(ii) Return on equity	(2.5%)	2.25%	3.0%
(iii) Interest cover	0.83	2.5	—
(iv) Earnings per share	7p	6p	7.5p

7.4 Philip Limited

Solution

No profit for sales between companies within a group should be included in consolidated accounts until the goods have been sold to a customer *outside* the group. Only then is the profit "realised" from the group's point of view.

Arising from sales to Philip Limited in the year ending 31 March 1972, Sidney Limited will have incorporated the following transactions in its accounts.

Sales	£80 000
Cost of sales	£50 000
Profit	£30 000

Sidney has thus included in its accounts a profit of £30 000 in respect of inter-company sales, a quarter of which are still unrealised (from the group's point of view) at 31 March 1972, since at that date Philip still held in stock a quarter of the goods purchased from Sidney.

Consolidated profit should, therefore, be reduced by a quarter of £30 000 (= by £7500). (Group sales should be reduced by £20 000 and cost of sales by £12 500) and stock should also be reduced by £7500.

Any amount still owing by Philip to Sidney at 31 March 1972, in respect of the purchases will be cancelled out against the amount shown as "debtors" in Sidney's books.

7.5 Dexter Limited (A)

Solution

DEXTER LIMITED
Consolidated balance sheet, 1 April 1971

	£
Issued ordinary shares	200 000
Share premium[1]	40 000
Reserves	87 000
	327 000
Minority interests[2]	16 000
	343 000
Long-term debt	98 000
	£441 000
Fixed assets	323 000
Goodwill[3]	42 000
Net current assets	76 000
	£441 000

[1]50 000 new £1 shares issued at 180p (market price) = £90 000. £50 000 is "nominal" capital; therefore £40 000 excess is share premium.

[2]25% × Close's shareholders' funds of £64 000 = £16 000.

[3]Price paid = 50 000 shares at 180p = £90 000. Book value of assets acquired = 75% × £64 000 = £48 000. The difference, £42 000, is goodwill.

Notes

1 The goodwill figure of £42 000 was given in the
(*A*) problem solution, but can be calculated if
necessary from the information in the (*B*) problem.

Price paid: £90 000.

Close's net assets minus long-term debt at date
of acquisition = £76 000 less profit in 1972 (all
retained) of £12 000, that is, £64 000.

Dexter's 75 per cent share = £48 000
Goodwill = £90 000 − £48 000 = £42 000

2 Only the £12 000 profit earned by Close *since*
acquisition counts as revenue reserves in Dexter's
consolidated balance sheet; and 25 per cent of that
£12 000 relates to minority interests.

Thus, £127 000 + £9000 = £136 000

3 Minority interests = £16 000 at 31 March 1971
(25 per cent of £64 000) + £3000 (25 per cent of
1972 profit of £12 000) = £19 000.

7.6 Dexter Limited (B)

Solution

DEXTER LIMITED (B)
Balance sheets, 31 March 1972

	Dexter	Close	Dexter consolidated
	£'000	£'000	£'000
Ordinary £1 shares	200	40	200
Share premium	40	—	40
Revenue reserves	127	36	136
Shareholders' funds	367	76	376
Minority interests			19
Long-term debt	90	26	116
Capital employed	£457	£102	£511
Fixed assets	280	85	365
Goodwill			42
Investment in Close	90		
Net current assets	87	17	104
Net assets	£457	£102	£511
Profit after tax	£40	£12	£52
Less: Minority interest			3
			£49

7.7 Barber Limited and Jenkins Limited

Solution

	Barber Limited (cost) £	Jenkins Limited (equity) £
Assets	360 000	360 000
Investment in subsidiary	40 000	50 000[1]
	£400 000	£410 000
Profit after tax	50 000	60 000[1]
Dividend	30 000	30 000
Retained profit	£ 20 000	£ 30 000[1]

[1]That is including the holding company's 100 per cent share of the subsidiary's retained profits.

If the subsidiary paid a dividend of £7500 (all to the holding company) Barber ("cost" method) would include it in profit and add £7500 to cash. The two holding companies would treat differently only the subsidiaries' undistributed (retained) profit. Jenkins in that case would add £2500 to investment in subsidiary and to profit while Barber would ignore the subsidiary's £2500 retained profit.

Note that under the "equity" method Jenkins has already included all the subsidiary's profit whether or not any dividend is paid. The only effect of Jenkins subsidiary paying a £7500 dividend would be to increase assets (cash) by £7500 and *reduce* investment in subsidiary by the same amount.

7.8 Leach Limited and Dixon Limited

Solution

LEACH LIMITED AND DIXON LIMITED

	Acquisition £m	Merger £m
Share capital (£1 shares)	60	60
Share premium	20	—
Retained profits	20	35
Capital employed	£100	£ 95
Goodwill	5	
Net assets (other)	95	95
Net assets	£100	£ 95

Notes

1 Goodwill = £40 million purchase price − £35 million net assets acquired = £5 million.

2 Notice how retained profits are higher under the merger treatment than under the acquisition treatment.

8.3 The General Electric Company Limited

Solution

(a) Funds statement

Working schedule	Differences £m Sources	Uses	Adjustments £m Sources	Uses	Final £m Sources	Uses
Current assets		3				3
Current liabilities		22		−15c		7
Investments	1		− 1d			
Fixed assets	11			+25a		14
Reserves	22		− 1d +18b		39	
Minority interests	2		− 2d			
Loans		11				11
Depreciation			+25a		25	
Dividends				+18b		18
Bank overdrafts				+15c		15
Miscellaneous			+ 4d		4	
	£36	£36	+£43	+£43	£68	£68

Adjustments:
(a) Depreciation 25
(b) Dividends 18
(c) Bank overdrafts reduced 15
(d) Miscellaneous:

Investments	1
Minority interests	2
Reserves	1
	4

Funds statement
Year ending 31 March 1971

		£m
Sources of funds		
Profits	39	
Add: Depreciation	25	
Funds from operations	64	
Less: Dividends paid	18	
		46
Miscellaneous		4
		£50
Use of funds		
Reductions of borrowing:		
Bank overdrafts	15	
Long-term loans	11	
		26
Fixed assets		14
Working capital (excluding bank overdrafts)		10
		£50

Comments:
1. Half the uses of funds went to reduce borrowing.
2. Depreciation was nearly twice the net additions to fixed assets.

(b) Financial ratios

Investment measures	1971	1970
Return on equity	$\frac{36}{471} = 7.6\%$	$\frac{30}{449} = 6.7\%$
Earnings per share	$\frac{36}{468} = 7.7p$	$\frac{30}{468} = 6.4p$
Price/earnings ratio	$\frac{113}{7.7} = 14.7$	$\frac{114}{6.4} = 17.8$
Dividend yield	$\frac{3.75}{113} = 3.3\%$	$\frac{3.63}{114} = 3.2\%$
Dividend cover	$\frac{7.7}{3.75} = 2.1$	$\frac{6.4}{3.63} = 1.8$

Measures of performance	1971	1970
Return on net assets	$\frac{77}{704} = 10.9\%$	$\frac{73}{691} = 10.6\%$
Profit margin	$\frac{77}{924} = 8.3\%$	$\frac{73}{891} = 8.2\%$
Asset turnover	$\frac{924}{704} = 1.31$	$\frac{891}{691} = 1.29$
Fixed asset turnover	$\frac{924}{162} = 5.70$	$\frac{891}{173} = 5.15$
Stock turnover	$\frac{924}{308} = 3.00$	$\frac{891}{300} = 2.97$
Debtor turnover	$\frac{924}{331} = 2.79$	$\frac{891}{335} = 2.66$

Measures of financial status	1971	1970
Debt ratio	$\frac{205}{704} = 29.1\%$	$\frac{216}{691} = 31.3\%$
Interst cover	$\frac{77}{14} = 5.5$	$\frac{73}{15} = 4.9$
Current ratio	$\frac{646}{349} = 1.85$	$\frac{643}{371} = 1.73$
Acid test	$\frac{338}{349} = 0.97$	$\frac{343}{371} = 0.92$
Tax ratio	$\frac{26}{63} = 41.3\%$	$\frac{27}{58} = 46.6\%$

Comments:
1. Improvement in return on equity and in return on net assets, both of which are still low.
2. Dividend cover is fairly high now, at 2.1 times.
3. Fixed asset turnover seems high, at 5.7 times.
4. Financial status ratios show fairly high gearing, and acid test just below 1.00.
5. Lower tax charge contributed to improvement in return on equity.
6. Sales revenue up less than 4 per cent on 1970.

(b) Financial ratios (continued)

(1) If bank overdrafts were included as medium-term loans instead of as current liabilities, the following ratios would be affected:

	1971	1970
(i) Return on net assets	$\dfrac{84}{752} = 11.2\%$	$\dfrac{82}{754} = 10.9\%$
(ii) Profit margin	$\dfrac{84}{924} = 9.1\%$	$\dfrac{82}{891} = 9.2\%$
(iii) Asset turnover	$\dfrac{924}{752} = 1.23$	$\dfrac{891}{754} = 1.18$
(iv) Debt ratio	$\dfrac{253}{752} = 33.6\%$	$\dfrac{279}{754} = 37.0\%$
(v) Interest cover	$\dfrac{84}{21} = 4.0$	$\dfrac{82}{24} = 3.4$
(vi) Current ratio	$\dfrac{646}{301} = 2.15$	$\dfrac{643}{308} = 2.09$
(vii) Acid test	$\dfrac{338}{301} = 1.12$	$\dfrac{343}{308} = 1.11$

Comments:

The main effect is to worsen the solvency ratios (iv) and (v) and to improve the liquidity ratios (vi) and (vii). Compared with 1970 there is rather more improvement in the solvency ratios and rather less in the liquidity ratios than the earlier figures showed.

(2) Conversion of the $7\frac{1}{4}\%$. Loan Stock 1987/92 into ordinary 25p shares would change the following ratios:

	1971	1970
(i) Return on equity	$\dfrac{39\frac{1}{2}}{549} = 7.2\%$	$\dfrac{33\frac{1}{2}}{529} = 6.3\%$
(ii) Earnings per share	$\dfrac{39\frac{1}{2}}{537} = 7.4\text{p.}$	$\dfrac{33\frac{1}{2}}{539} = 6.2\text{p.}$
(iii) Price/earnings ratio	$\dfrac{113}{7.4} = 15.3$	$\dfrac{114}{6.2} = 18.4$
(iv) Dividend cover	$\dfrac{7.4}{3.75} = 2.0$	$\dfrac{6.2}{3.63} = 1.7$
(v) Debt ratio	$\dfrac{127}{704} = 18.0\%$	$\dfrac{136}{691} = 19.7\%$
(vi) Interest cover	$\dfrac{71}{8} = 8.9$	$\dfrac{67}{9} = 7.4$

(a) Assuming tax of £$2\frac{1}{2}$ million on convertible loan stock interest of £6 million (about 40 per cent)

(b) At $112\frac{1}{2}$ £78 million loan stock converts into 69 million shares, and £80 million loan stock converts into 71 million shares.

Comments:

Conversion reduces ("dilutes") earnings per share. But notice the significant reduction in the debt ratio and the increase in interest cover. Since the loan stock conversion price ($112\frac{1}{2}$p) is almost the same as the end-of-year market price per share, conversion of the loan stock would probably not much change the market price per ordinary share, and the price/earnings ratio would increase.

(b) Financial ratios (*continued*)

(3) There are two main alternative treatments for the £171 million goodwill:

(A) Writing goodwill off against reserves would affect the following ratios:

		1971	*1970*
(i)	Return on equity	$\dfrac{36}{300} = 12.0\%$	$\dfrac{30}{278} = 10.8\%$
(ii)	Return on net assets	$\dfrac{77}{533} = 14.4\%$	$\dfrac{73}{520} = 14.0\%$
(iii)	Asset turnover	$\dfrac{924}{533} = 1.73$	$\dfrac{891}{520} = 1.71$
(iv)	Debt ratio	$\dfrac{205}{533} = 38.5\%$	$\dfrac{216}{520} = 41.5\%$

Comments:
Reducing the equity or net asset base naturally increases the return ratios. Similarly the debt ratio increases. The changes are large because the £171 million goodwill is such a large proportion—24%—of the net assets.

(B) Writing goodwill off against profit over a number of years (say 10 years) would change the following ratios (after 1 year):

		1971	*1970*
(i)	Return on equity	$\dfrac{19}{454} = 4.2\%$	$\dfrac{13}{432} = 3.0\%$
(ii)	Earnings per share	$\dfrac{19}{468} = 4.1\text{p.}$	$\dfrac{13}{468} = 2.8\text{p.}$
(iii)	Price/earnings ratio	$\dfrac{113}{4.1} = 27.6$	$\dfrac{114}{2.8} = 40.7$
(iv)	Dividend cover	$\dfrac{4.1}{3.75} = 1.1$	$\dfrac{2.8}{3.63} = 0.8$
(v)	Return on net assets	$\dfrac{60}{687} = 8.7\%$	$\dfrac{56}{674} = 8.3\%$
(vi)	Profit margin	$\dfrac{60}{924} = 6.5\%$	$\dfrac{56}{891} = 6.3\%$
(vii)	Interest cover	$\dfrac{60}{14} = 4.3$	$\dfrac{56}{15} = 3.7$
(viii)	Tax ratio	$\dfrac{26}{46} = 56.5\%$	$\dfrac{27}{41} = 65.9\%$

Comments:
£17 million a year (not allowable for tax) is nearly half 1971 after-tax profits, and therefore significantly affects the profit measures. Notice too the effect on the tax ratio. Because the adverse effects on profit are so significant it might be thought unrealistic to suggest writing off goodwill against profit if there is any alternative acceptable accounting treatment.

Index